TOURISM AND SOCIAL MARKETING

Social marketing is the utilisation of marketing principles and methods to encourage individual and organisational behaviour change for the public good. Traditionally the domain of government, it is increasingly also utilised by non-government and non-profit organisations and other institutions of civil society as a non-regulatory means to achieve policy and public good goals. At a time when concerns over tourism's contribution to undesirable environmental, economic and social change is greater than ever, social marketing strategies are important for encouraging more appropriate and desirable behaviours by tourists and the tourism industry.

Tourism and Social Marketing is the first book to comprehensively detail the relevance of social marketing principles and practice to tourism, destination management and marketing. By considering this relationship and application of social marketing approaches to key issues facing contemporary tourism development, such as the environment, this book provides significant insights into how the behaviours of visitors and businesses may be changed so as to develop more sustainable forms of tourism and improve the quality of life of destination communities. It further provides a powerful impetus to the development of tourism-related forms of sustainable consumption and the promotion of ethical tourism and marketing. This innovative book is comprehensive in scope by considering a variety of fields relevant to tourism and social marketing practice including, health, non-profit organisations, governance, the politics of marketing and consumption, consumer advocacy and environmental and sustainable marketing. It integrates selected international case studies to help tourism students engage with the broader debates in social marketing, governance and the politics of behaviour change and shows the relationship of theory to practice.

Written by a leading authority in the field, topical and integrative, this book will be valuable reading for students, scholars and researchers in tourism.

C. Michael Hall is a Professor of Marketing at the University of Canterbury, New Zealand. He has longstanding teaching, publication and research interests in tourism, regional development and social/green marketing with particular emphasis on issues of place branding and marketing as well as conservation and environmental change, event management and marketing, and the use of tourism as an economic development and conservation mechanism. He is the author and editor of over 65 books as well as over 450 journal articles and book chapters, and has been active in a number of international research and business associations.

Routledge Critical Studies in Tourism, Business and Management

Series editors: Tim Coles, University of Exeter, UK and C. Michael Hall, University of Canterbury, New Zealand

This ground-breaking monograph series deals directly with theoretical and conceptual issues at the interface between business, management and tourism studies. It incorporates research-generated, highly specialised cutting-edge studies of new and emergent themes, such as knowledge management and innovation, that affect the future business and management of tourism. The books in this series are conceptually challenging, empirically rigorous, creative, and, above all, capable of driving current thinking and unfolding debate in the business and management of tourism. This monograph series will appeal to researchers, academics and practitioners in the fields of tourism, business and management, and the social sciences.

Published titles:

Commercial Homes in Tourism (2009)
Paul Lynch, Alison J. McIntosh and Hazel Tucker (eds)

Sustainable Marketing of Cultural and Heritage Tourism (2010)
Deepak Chhabra

Economics of Sustainable Tourism (2010)
Fabio Cerina, Anil Markyanda and Michael McAleer

Tourism and Crisis (2013)
Gustav Visser and Sanette Ferreira

Managing Ethical Consumption in Tourism (2013)
Edited by Clare Weeden and Karla Boluk

The *Routledge Critical Studies in Tourism, Business and Management* monograph series builds on core concepts explored in the corresponding *Routledge International Studies of Tourism, Business and Management* book series. Series editors: Tim Coles, University of Exeter, UK and C. Michael Hall, University of Canterbury, New Zealand.

Books in the series offer upper-level undergraduates and Masters students comprehensive, thought-provoking yet accessible books that combine essential theory and international best practice on issues in the business and management of tourism such as HRM, entrepreneurship, service quality management, leadership, CSR, strategy, operations, branding and marketing.

Published titles:

International Business and Tourism (2008)
Edited by Tim Coles and C. Michael Hall

Carbon Management in Tourism (2010)
Stefan Gössling

Tourism and Social Marketing
C. Michael Hall

TOURISM AND SOCIAL MARKETING

C. Michael Hall

LONDON AND NEW YORK

First published 2014
by Routledge
2 Park Square, Milton Park, Abingdon, Oxon OX14 4RN

and by Routledge
711 Third Avenue, New York, NY 10017

Routledge is an imprint of the Taylor & Francis Group, an informa business

© 2014 C. Michael Hall

British Library Cataloguing in Publication Data
A catalogue record for this book is available from the British Library

Library of Congress Cataloguing in Publication Data
Hall, Colin Michael, 1961-
Tourism and social marketing / C. Michael Hall.
pages cm. -- (Routledge international series in tourism, business and management)
Includes bibliographical references and index.
1. Tourism. 2. Social marketing. I. Title.
G155.A1.H3476 2014
910.68'8--dc23
2013030556

ISBN: 978-0-415-57665-9 (hbk)
ISBN: 978-0-415-57666-6 (pbk)
ISBN: 978-0-203-85425-9 (ebk)

Typeset in Bembo
by GreenGate Publishing Services, Tonbridge, Kent

Printed and bound by CPI Group (UK) Ltd, Croydon, CR0 4YY

CONTENTS

PLATES

FIGURES

TABLES

BOXES

FOREWORD AND ACKNOWLEDGEMENTS

Social marketing is the utilisation of marketing principles and methods to change behaviours for the benefit of individuals and communities. This is not a book about how your fourth generation phone and the Internet can promote your destination or tourism product. If you think that this is a book about tourism and social media marketing then put it down and slowly walk away. On second thoughts don't, you might even learn something! First, about the 'original' social marketing. Second, there actually is discussion on guerrilla and viral marketing and e-promotional channels (which are often overrated depending on your target audience, but you need to read on to learn about that). Third, because it may make you rethink about what tourism marketing can actually be about. And, finally, because my publishers, editors and I could actually do with the income, don't photocopy or scan it, *buy it*. Marketing is in great part about exchange, you pay for the book (or the library does), you get ideas and knowledge, we get to keep our jobs. It is, as Monty Python once said, 'a fair cop'.

The book arose in great part because I am someone who has tourism as a major research interest who got to teach a course on social marketing and it was extremely interesting to be able to combine a focus on behavioural change with a tourism context. More seriously perhaps, climate and environmental change, as well as the way that tourism sometimes overwhelms culture and places, provides a major challenge for trying to encourage behavioural change for more sustainable forms of tourism. As you will see if you read through the book I do not necessarily think that social marketing is going to solve all of the world's or tourism's problems for that matter, but it certainly does have a part to play.

Several colleagues in my department in New Zealand have provided very direct influence on the development of this book. Ekant Veer, Paul Ballantine, Lucie Ozanne and the annoyingly departed Tony Garry (splitter!) have all inputted positively into this book in various ways, while the department's incredible administrative staff of Irene, Irene and Donna have also helped create the space in which I can work. Similar thanks are also due to the Department of Service Management, Lund Helsingborg and the Freiburg Institute of Advanced Studies. The interests of various students in social marketing and tourism must also be acknowledged. Dao Truong's work on social marketing and pro-poor tourism has been outstanding while Tim Baird has helped develop some of the cases and examples used in this book. Elizabeth Raymond's work on volunteer tourism provided a valuable basis to assess the social marketing success of sending organisations. The insights of social marketing students

Angela McDonnell, Rebecca McNaughton, Michelle Moore and Sandra Wilson is gratefully noted; as are those of advanced marketing research students Alice Blair, Hayley Gargiulo, Caroline Gunn and Meaghan Parker; and tourism marketing and management students Jacqui Drake and Sacha Madden have also been extremely helpful. The generous assistance of René Baretje-Keller in providing tourism references is also very gratefully acknowledged.

A number of colleagues with whom I have undertaken research or discussed social marketing and tourism related issues over the years have also contributed to the development of this book in various ways. In particular, thanks to Nicole Aigner, Tim Baird, Dorothee Bohn, Bill Bramwell, Scott Cohen, Tim Coles, Hervé Corvellec, David Duval, Stefan Gössling, Anna Grundén, James Higham, Johan Hultman, John Jenkins, Bernard Lane, Harvey Lemelin, Simon McArthur, Ghazali Musa, Dieter Müller, Paul Peeters, Jarkko Saarinen, Anna Dóra Sæþórsdóttir, Sara Sbai, Daniel Scott, Liz Sharples, Dallen Timothy, Dao Truong, Sandra Wall and Maria José Zapata Campos for their thoughts, as well as for the sanity and stimulation of Beirut, Nick Cave, Bruce Cockburn, Elvis Costello, Stephen Cummings, Chris Difford and Glenn Tilbrook, Dimmer, Ebba Fosberg, Hoodoo Gurus, Frida Hyvönen, The Jackson Code, The Kills, Ed Kuepper, Laura Marling, Vinnie Reilly, David Sylvian, Twinemen, Jennifer Warnes, Chris Wilson, World's Tallest Man and *the Guardian* and BBC – without whom the four walls of a hotel room would be much more confining. A warm acknowledgement is also provided to Grüner Baum Merzhausen, Granville Island Market, AGRO Café, C4 Coffee, and the Nordic Choice hotel network, especially in Helsingborg and Kalmar for their contributions and spaces. Finally, Michael would like to thank the many people who have supported his work over the years, and especially the Js and the Cs who stay at home with the almonds, walnuts and Lucy and Wellington.

Finally, thanks and support is given to my Routledge muses Emma Travis and Pippa Mullins as well as the rest of the Taylor & Francis team that has supported this book and other work, particularly given the delays and tribulations caused by the Christchurch earthquakes.

C. Michael Hall
Riverstones
July 2013

ABBREVIATIONS

AMA	American Marketing Association
BITC	Business in the Community (UK)
CDC	Centers for Disease Control and Prevention (USA)
CERs	Certified Emission Reductions
LDCs	least developed countries
MERs	Mandatory Emission Reductions
NIMBY	Not In My Back Yard
NPM	new public management
NSMC	National Social Marketing Centre (UK)
PPT	pro-poor tourism
QOL	quality of life
SCR	Sustainable Consumption Roundtable
SWB	subjective well-being
UNCTAD	United Nations Conference on Trade and Development
UNEP	United Nations Environmental Programme
UNWTO	United Nations World Tourism Organization
VERs	Verified Emission Reductions or Voluntary Emission Reductions
WEF	World Economic Forum
WOM	word of mouth
WTO	World Tourism Organization
WTTC	World Travel and Tourism Council
YIMBY	Yes In My Back Yard

1

INTRODUCTION TO THE FIELD OF SOCIAL MARKETING

Creating social change?

Chapter 1 outlines the intellectual foundations of social marketing and the historical development of the field since the early 1970s. Key debates discussed include the extent to which marketing methods developed for commercial marketing practice can be applied to non-profit organisations and behavioural change (which in turn lead to a discussion as to whether marketing is inherently a field that encourages consumptive practices); differences between social marketing and education; and the ideological and political dimension of social marketing. This last point also allows a discussion on the connection between marketing ethics and the application of marketing principles and practice. A number of the issues and debates within social marketing also have a strong resonance with the tourism field as this provides a means of introducing the reader to the significance of social marketing for students of tourism. In particular the development of sub-fields of social marketing such as environmental marketing, health marketing and sustainable marketing is also reflected in some of the sub-fields of tourism. The chapter also provides an overall framework for the book. The first three chapters provide an overall context and introduction to social marketing principles, methods and issues before examining their application within specific problem areas and scales of analysis.

Introduction to social marketing and tourism

Social marketing is the use of commercial marketing concepts and tools to create behavioural change. The term 'social marketing' was first used in 1971 (Kotler and Zaltman 1971) in a special issue of the *Journal of Marketing* on marketing's changing social/environmental role (Box 1.1). The associated pictures on the journal contents page show traffic congested, rubbish on a street of what appears to be poor-quality housing and smog in a smokestack-filled industrial landscape. In many ways the pictures highlight the enormous range of fields, including health, well-being and quality of life, the environment, welfare and sustainability to which the notion of social marketing has since been applied. Yet 'despite widespread attention being given to the importance of changing the behaviors of both tourists and tourism businesses' (Truong and Hall 2013: 1), especially in the context of sustainable tourism (Gössling *et al.* 2008; Gössling, Hall and Weaver 2009), there is surprisingly little attention given to the potential of social marketing in the field of tourism (Dinan and Sargeant 2000; Kaczynski 2008; Shang *et al.* 2010). For example, although Lane (2009: 23) identifies social marketing as being a critical element in the development of more sustainable forms of tourism it is also significant that he argues: 'The concept of social marketing, of using marketing techniques to encourage behavioural change, rather than increased consumption of existing products, is in its infancy—and little understood by tourism marketing agencies, or the media'.

Social marketing – 'the use of marketing principles and techniques to influence a target audience to voluntarily accept, reject, modify or abandon a behaviour for the benefit of individuals, groups or society as a whole' (Kotler *et al.* 2002: 5) – is an area of marketing that is continuing to grow in significance, particularly as governments seek to use non-regulatory mechanisms to change individual and group behaviours to achieve policy goals. Such marketing strategies have recently been recognised as being potentially extremely important for tourism by encouraging appropriate visitor, host and business behaviours (Lane 2009); creating a better balance between tourism and the host community or attraction (e.g. Beeton and Benfield 2002); conserving cultural heritage and natural attractions; improving visitor experiences; as well as assisting in the development of new tourism opportunities (Truong 2013). Social marketing therefore has the potential to influence personal, community and business behaviours throughout the tourism system. However, as the chapter outlines, the field of social marketing is marked by considerable debate and controversy over its objectives as well as the ethical and political dimensions of behaviour change – themes that will be returned to throughout the book.

**BOX 1.1 ARTICLES IN THE 1971 SPECIAL ISSUE OF THE
JOURNAL OF MARKETING ON MARKETING'S CHANGING
SOCIAL/ENVIRONMENTAL ROLE**

- Social marketing: An approach to planned social change
- Marketing's application to fund raising
- Health service marketing: A suggested model
- Marketing and population problems
- Recycling solid wastes: A channels-of-distribution problem
- Comparing the cost of food to blacks and to whites
- Consumer protection via self-regulation
- Societal adaptation: A new challenge for marketing
- Incorporating ecology into marketing strategy: The case of air pollution
- Marketing science in the age of Aquarius

Source: *Journal of Marketing*, 35(3), contents page

Framing tourism

Tourism is a *fuzzy* (Markusen 1999) and *slippery* concept (Wincott 2003), that is seemingly easy to visualise yet difficult to define with precision because it changes meaning depending on the context of its analysis, purpose and use (Hall and Lew 2009). In distinguishing tourism from other types of human movement several factors are significant (Hall 2005a, 2005b).

- Tourism is voluntary and does not include the forced movement of people for political or environmental reasons, that is tourists are not refugees.
- Tourism can be distinguished from migration because a tourist is making a return trip from their home environment while the migrant is moving permanently away from what was their home environment.
- The distinction between tourism and migration sometimes becomes blurred because some people engage in return travel away from their usual home environment for an extended period, i.e. a 'gap year' or 'working holiday' in another country. In these types of situations, time (how long they are away from their normal or permanent place of residence) and distance (how far they have travelled or whether they have crossed jurisdictional borders) become determining factors in defining tourism statistically and distinguishing between migration and tourism.

Using the above approach there are a number of forms of voluntary travel that serve to constitute tourism both conceptually and statistically in addition to the leisure and pleasure travel that is usually conceived of by many people as being tourism:

- visiting friends and relations (VFR)
- business travel
- travel to second homes
- health- and medical-related travel
- education-related travel
- religious travel and pilgrimage
- travel for shopping and retail
- volunteer tourism.

Confusion over defining tourism does not end here. The word tourism is also used to describe *tourists* (the people who engage in voluntary return mobility), the notion of a *tourism industry* (which is the term used to describe those firms, organisations and individuals that enable tourists to travel) and the whole social and economic phenomenon of tourism, including tourists, the tourism industry, the people and places that comprise tourism destinations, as well as the effects of tourism on generating areas, transit zones and destinations; what is usually termed the tourism system (Hall and Lew 2009).

Based on generally accepted international agreements for collecting and comparing tourism and travel statistics, the term *tourism trip* refers to a trip of not more than 12 months and for a main purpose other than being employed at the destination (UN and UNWTO 2007). However, despite UN and UNWTO recommendations there are substantial differences between countries with respect to the length of time that they use to define a tourist, as well as how employment is defined (Lennon 2003; Hall and Page 2006). Three types of tourism are usually recognised:

1 *domestic tourism*, which includes the activities of resident visitors within their home country or economy of reference, either as part of a domestic or an international trip;
2 *inbound tourism*, which includes the activities of non-resident visitors within the destination country or economy of reference, either as part of a domestic or an international trip (from the perspective of the traveller's country of residence); and

3   *outbound tourism*, which includes the activities of resident visitors outside their home country or economy of reference, as part of either a domestic or an international trip.

In order to improve statistical collection and improve understanding of tourism, the UN and the UNWTO have long recommended differentiating between visitors, tourists and excursionists (Hall and Lew 2009). An international tourist can be defined as: 'a visitor who travels to a country other than that in which he or she has his or her usual residence for at least one night but not more than one year, and whose main purpose of visit is other than the exercise of an activity remunerated from within the country visited'; and an international excursionist (also referred to as a day-tripper; for example, a cruise-ship visitor) can be defined as: 'a visitor residing in a country who travels the same day to a different country for less than 24 hours without spending the night in the country visited, and whose main purpose of visit is other than the exercise of an activity remunerated from within the country visited'. Domestic day-tripping is often considered a form of recreation, rather than tourism – though this too confuses the definition of who is a tourist and who is not, especially as some government authorities include day-trippers in their tourism data (Hall and Lew 2009).

The term visit refers to the stay (stop) (overnight or same-day) in a place away from home during a trip. Entering a geographical area, such as a county or town, without stopping usually does not qualify as a visit to that place (UN and UNWTO 2007). Such definitional issues are of major importance with respect to estimating the economic and other impacts of tourism, as well as assessing tourist markets, distribution and flows. Unfortunately, despite the recommendations of international agencies individual countries often collect tourist data inconsistently, with information of excursionists and domestic tourism being the most poorly served at a global level (Lennon 2003).

Growth in tourism arrivals

One of the few publicly available estimates of total global tourism volume was made by the UNWTO in 2008 (UNWTO, UNEP and WMO 2008). This suggested that for 2005 total tourism demand (overnight and same-day, international and domestic) was estimated to have accounted for about 9.8 billion arrivals. Of these, five billion arrivals were estimated to be from same-day visitors (four billion domestic and one billion international) and 4.8 billion from arrivals of visitors staying overnight (tourists) (four billion domestic and 800 million international). Given that an international trip can generate arrivals in more than one destination country, the number of trips is somewhat lower than the number of arrivals. For 2005 the global number of international tourist trips (i.e., trips by overnight visitors) was estimated at 750 million (Scott *et al.* 2008: 122). This corresponds to approximately 16 per cent of the total number of tourist trips, while domestic trips represent the large majority (84 per cent or four billion). The UNWTO estimates highlight the potential economic significance of domestic tourism for many destinations, even though the major research, policy and marketing focus tends to be on international tourism.

In 2012, international tourist arrivals are expected to reach one billion for the first time, up from 25 million in 1950, 278 million in 1980 and 540 million in 1995 (UNWTO 2012) (Table 1.1). Although international tourism is usually the primary policy focus because of its international business and trade dimensions, and its role as a source of foreign exchange (Coles and Hall 2008), the vast majority of tourism is domestic in nature. For example, Cooper and Hall (2013) suggested that domestic tourism, excluding same-day visitors, accounted for an estimated 4.7 billion arrivals in 2010, and predicted that sometime between 2014 and 2017 the total number of visitor arrivals combined (domestic and international) would exceed the world's population for the first time. Nevertheless, although there are reasonable aggregate data sets available on international visitor arrivals at the national level, data for domestic tourism is often poor or non-existent in many jurisdictions. Thereby potentially affecting our understanding of tourism flows and patterns and its impacts but also the capacity for effective policy making and interventions.

In 2011 international tourist arrivals (overnight visitors) grew by 4.6 per cent worldwide to 983 million, up from 940 million in 2010 when arrivals increased by 6.4 per cent. These rapid rates of growth represent a rebound from the international financial crisis of 2008–10. Contrary to long-term trends, advanced economies (4.9 per cent) experienced higher visitor growth than emerging economies (4.3 per cent), reflecting the relative impacts of the financial crisis as well as the effects of political instability in the Middle East and North Africa, which experienced declines of 8.0 per cent and 9.1 per cent respectively (UNWTO 2012).

The UNWTO predicts the number of international tourist arrivals will increase by 3.3 per cent per year on average between 2010 and 2030 (an increase of 43 million arrivals a year on average), reaching an estimated 1.8 billion arrivals by 2030 (UNWTO 2011, 2012). UNWTO upper and lower forecasts for global tourism are between approximately two billion arrivals (under the 'real transport costs continue to fall' scenario) and 1.4 billion arrivals (under the 'slower than expected economic recovery and future growth' scenario) respectively (UNWTO 2011). Most of this growth is forecast to come from the emerging economies and the Asia-Pacific region, and by 2030 it is estimated that 57 per cent of international arrivals will be in what are currently classified as emerging economies (UNWTO 2011, 2012).

TABLE 1.1 International tourism arrivals and forecasts 1950–2030

Year	World	Africa	Americas	Asia and Pacific	Europe	Middle East
1950	25.3	0.5	7.5	0.2	16.8	0.2
1960	69.3	0.8	16.7	0.9	50.4	0.6
1965	112.9	1.4	23.2	2.1	83.7	2.4
1970	165.8	2.4	42.3	6.2	113.0	1.9
1975	222.3	4.7	50.0	10.2	153.9	3.5
1980	278.1	7.2	62.3	23.0	178.5	7.1
1985	320.1	9.7	65.1	32.9	204.3	8.1
1990	439.5	15.2	92.8	56.2	265.8	9.6
1995	540.6	20.4	109.0	82.4	315.0	13.7
2000	687.0	28.3	128.1	110.5	395.9	24.2
2005	806.8	37.3	133.5	155.4	441.5	39.0
2010	940	49.7	150.7	204.4	474.8	60.3
Forecast						
2020	1,360	85	199	355	620	101
2030	1,809	134	248	535	744	149

Source: World Tourism Organization 1997; UN WTO 2006a, 2012

Economic significance

Given the substantial growth rates for international tourism it should be no surprise that substantial emphasis is placed on its potential economic benefits. Tourism ranks as the fourth largest economic sector after fuels, chemicals and food, generates an estimated 5 per cent of world gross domestic product (GDP), and contributes an estimated 6–7 per cent of employment (direct and indirect) (UNWTO 2012). In contrast the World Travel and Tourism Council (WTTC), an umbrella lobby group comprising the major tourism corporations in the world, estimate that 'travel and tourism … accounts for US$6 trillion, or 9 per cent, of global gross domestic product (GDP) and it supports 260 million jobs worldwide, either directly or indirectly. That's almost 1 in 12 of all jobs on the planet' (World Travel and Tourism Council 2012: 3). Such disparities in estimates are reflective of some of the difficulties in assessing the sector's economic significance.

International tourism's export value, including international passenger transport, was US$1.2 trillion in 2011, accounting for 30 per cent of the world's exports of commercial services or six per cent of total exports (UNWTO 2012). Even though the relative proportion of tourism's contribution to international trade in services has declined as the contribution from ICT in particular has increased (Hall and Coles 2008), tourism remains an extremely significant contributor to the global economy, although its economic contribution, as with the flow of travellers, is uneven (Hall and Lew 2009). Nevertheless, tourism is one of the five top export earners in over 150 countries, while in 60 countries it is the number one export sector (UNCTAD 2010). It is also the main source of foreign exchange for one-third of developing countries and one-half of least-developed countries (LDCs) (UNWTO and UNEP 2011). The UNWTO (2006b) estimated that tourism was the primary source of foreign exchange earnings in 46 out of 50 of the world's LDCs. Considering the continued growth in international tourism it is not surprising that it is strongly promoted by some members of the international development community as an important element in poverty reduction strategies and development financing (World Travel and Tourism Council 2004; World Economic Forum 2009a, 2009b; UNCTAD 2010) (Box 1.2).

In 2011, international tourism receipts reached US$1,030 billion (€740 billion), up from US$927 billion (€699 billion) in 2010. This represented a 3.9 per cent growth in receipts in real terms. The export value of international passenger transport was estimated at US$196 billion (€141 billion) in 2011, up from US$170 billion (€131 billion) in 2010 (UNWTO 2012). According to the UNWTO (2012) receipts from international tourism were over US$1 billion for 85 countries in 2011. Although there is a strong correlation between international tourism arrivals and receipts, it is noticeable that growth in receipts from international tourism tends to lag behind growth in tourist numbers. This relative drop in the per capita value of international arrivals can be explained in part by the high level of competitiveness in the tourism industry, especially at a price-sensitive period when emerging from economic downturn, but is also because the length of stay per visit has been slowly declining in many mature country destinations as consumers purchase more 'short-break' holidays.

BOX 1.2 UNWTO: WHY TOURISM IS A SUITABLE ECONOMIC DEVELOPMENT SECTOR FOR LEAST-DEVELOPED COUNTRIES

The UNWTO (2006b: 1) outlines several reasons why tourism makes an 'especially suitable economic development sector for LDCs':

1   Tourism is consumed at the point of production; the tourist has to go to the destination and spend his/her money there, opening an opportunity for local businesses of all sorts, and allowing local communities to benefit through the informal economy, by selling goods and services directly to visitors.
2   Most LDCs have a comparative advantage in tourism over developed countries.
3   Tourism is a more diverse industry than many others. It has the potential to support other economic activities, both through providing flexible, part-time jobs that can complement other livelihood options, and through creating income throughout a complex supply chain of goods and services.
4   Tourism is labour intensive, which is particularly important in tackling poverty. It also provides a wide range of different employment opportunities especially for women and young people – from the highly skilled to the unskilled – and generally it requires relatively little training.
5   It creates opportunities for many small and micro entrepreneurs, either in the formal or informal economy; it is an industry in which start-up costs and barriers to entry are generally low or can easily be lowered.
6   Tourism provides not only material benefits for the poor but also cultural pride. It creates greater awareness of the natural environment and its economic value, a sense of ownership and reduced vulnerability through diversification of income sources.
7   The infrastructure required by tourism, such as transport and communications, water supply and sanitation, public security and health services, can also benefit poor communities.

So why does tourism need social marketing?

Given the size and growth rate of the tourism industry why does tourism need social marketing? Answer: it is exactly because of those growth rates that social marketing is being seen as potentially significant. In some cases social marketing may be used to promote more positive attitudes by a community towards tourists in order to make the tourist experience more welcoming. Such interventions are usually linked with a concern to maximise the economic benefits of tourism at a destination and to create positive visitor experiences and word-of-mouth. Social marketing has been recognised as one of the influences on place branding and marketing strategies because of the recognition that place promotion can also improve a community's self-perception (McDivitt 2003; Kavaratzis and Ashworth 2008; Warnaby 2009). In other cases social marketing may be used to promote codes of conduct to visitors or industry so as to ensure appropriate behaviours. However, the greatest attention is given to tourism's social and environmental impacts. Like any industry or form of development tourism has its negative aspects. Despite the significance attached to sustainability both inside and outside of the tourism industry, tourism is less sustainable than ever (Hall 2011a).

Although tourism has been promoted by some in the development community for over 40 years, the mid- to long-term relative contribution of tourism projects to development strategies remains poorly evaluated (Hawkins and Mann 2007; Zapata *et al.* 2011). For example, a study of tourism in Kenya, Tanzania and Uganda indicated that hotels and restaurants, and in particular the transport industry, provide below-average shares of income to poor households compared to other export sectors, leading to the conclusion that 'these results paint a fairly poor picture of the ability of tourism to alleviate poverty' (Blake 2008: 511), particularly because tourism tends to be disproportionally beneficial to the already wealthy (Schilcher 2007; Blake *et al.* 2008) and can reinforce existing inequalities (Chok *et al.* 2007; Hall 2007b; Scheyvens and Momsen 2008; Zapata *et al.* 2011). Indeed, the often highly gendered nature of employment in tourism together with poor pay and substantial levels of casualisation and short-term employment has also been criticised in destinations in developed countries (Campos-Soria *et al.* 2011; Cuccia and Rizzo 2011; Zampoukos and Ioannides, 2011), casting question marks over its relative contribution to regional development.

Tourism has also long been implicated in negative impacts on culture and communities (Billson 1988; Holden 2010; Nunkoo and Ramkissoon 2010), including senses of well-being (Kim *et al.* 2013), as well as damage to cultural artefacts and heritage sites (Yu 2008; Ashworth 2009). In the case of environmental impacts, notwithstanding its role in justifying national park establishment and maintenance, tourism is associated with increases in the rate of invasive species and disease introductions and increased risk to biodiversity (Gössling 2002; Mozumder *et al.* 2006; Hall 2010b, 2010c; Hall and James 2011), as well as landscape change (Gössling and Hall 2006a; Tzanopoulos and Vogiatzakis 2011). Of long-term concern is also the growing contribution of tourism to climate change, especially given that the absolute growth in tourism mobility is greater than any efficiencies being made with respect to emissions reduction. Tourism transport, accommodation and activities combined were estimated by UNWTO-commissioned study to contribute an estimated 5 per cent to global anthropogenic emissions of CO_2 in 2005 (Scott *et al.* 2008), of which approximately 40 per cent come from air transport, 32 per cent from car transport and 21 per cent from accommodation, with growth continuing to occur in all areas (Gössling *et al.* 2010). Based on a business-as-usual (BAU) scenario for 2035, Scott *et al.* (2008) suggest that CO_2 emissions from tourism will grow by about 135 per cent to 2035 compared with 2005, with much of this growth associated with air travel (see also World Economic Forum 2009a). According to Hall (2010a: 137) 'much tourism growth, as with much economic growth in general, is already uneconomic at the present margin as we currently measure it given that it is leading to a clear running down of natural capital'. Given this situation it is therefore perhaps not surprising that there is a growing interest in the potential role of social marketing to influence tourism-related behaviours and to potentially make it more sustainable (Lane 2009; Peeters *et al.* 2009).

Social marketing in tourism

Although there was prior interest in the concept of social marketing in tourism (Cowell 1979; Foxall 1984; Gilbert 1989; Bramwell 1991; Paddison 1993; Blamey and Braithwaite 1997; Walle 1997), including with respect to its role in city marketing and place branding (Ashworth and Voogd 1988; Stubbs *et al.* 2002), it was not until 2002 with the publication of two articles (Bright 2000) that social marketing became an explicit focus in tourism research.

Bright (2000) focused on the potential role of social marketing in recreation and leisure delivery by local and regional government agencies, noting a range of areas in which social marketing techniques could be used, including: participation of at-risk youth; support for and participation in recreation programmes designed to benefit persons with disabilities; appropriate management of private open space to preserve biodiversity or protect wildlife habitat; support for controversial land and wildlife management policies such as endangered species restoration or hunting techniques; physical activity of seniors with health conditions; health-related behaviours, through recreation, in cooperation with public health organisations; and vandalism and other destructive behaviours. Given the social or public welfare perspective of many local government recreation departments, Bright (2000) suggested that this constitutes a strong fit with the philosophical orientation of social marketing.

In contrast, Dinan and Sargeant's (2000) article adopted a much stronger focus on the potential role of the tools and techniques of social marketing for tourism organisations seeking a more sustainable approach to their market by focusing on not only attracting appropriate market segments but by also encouraging visitors to behave in an appropriate manner. The potential of social marketing to encourage more sustainable and ethical tourist behaviours has become a significant research theme (Weeden 2002; Chhabra 2010; Pomering *et al.* 2011; Lebel and Shamsub 2012) (Box 1.3), with Jamrozy (2007) even claiming that it was part of a paradigm shift in tourism marketing towards sustainability. Notwithstanding such optimism, it is apparent that social marketing has become recognised as a potential tool to encourage more sustainable visitor and business behaviour. For example, demarketing – 'that aspect of marketing that deals with discouraging customers in general or a certain class of customers in particular on either a temporary or permanent basis' (Kotler and Levy 1971: 76) – has been advocated as a means to reduce visitor pressure on sites in environmentally sensitive areas and national parks (Groff 1998; Beeton and Benfield 2002; Wearing *et al.* 2007), as well as on a larger scale (Clements 1989) (see Chapter 6), although perhaps the most recognisable exercise of social marketing practices within the tourism industry is the accommodation sector's encouragement of customers to reuse towels and linen so as to help reduce water and electricity use (while also lowering operating costs and improving their image) (Shang *et al.* 2010). In addition, social marketing strategies have been seen as a means to encourage behavioural change in tourism businesses with respect to sustainability (George and Frey 2010; Gössling 2010).

BOX 1.3 ENCOURAGING RESPONSIBLE AND ETHICAL TOURISM: THE CASE OF TEARFUND

Weeden (2002) writes that ethical tourism provides a platform for companies to compete on more than just price alone. The rise of this form of tourism and its impact as an added dimension to the decision-making process, which forms part of consumers' holiday purchasing decisions, was the subject of research by Goodwin and Francis (2003) who chose Tearfund, a United Kingdom-based responsible tourism initiative, as the focus of their case study research. In 1999 Tearfund commissioned a survey of consumer attitudes regarding ethical issues in tourism amongst residents in the United Kingdom, and targeted a nationally and regionally representative sample of adults aged 15 years and over as their sample population (Tearfund 2000b). Goodwin and Francis (2003) wanted to demonstrate exactly how the work of Tearfund had proved that there was a market demand for tourism that was grounded in responsible practices, and that this was an area that social marketers could potentially tap into in order to capitalise on this new form of consumer demand.

The findings of this survey revealed that tour operators (54 per cent) and travel agents (52 per cent) were regarded as being the main sources of information amongst participants in terms of providing details of what destinations were known for actively practising ethical tourism (Tearfund 2000b). Specific questions were also asked as to whether participants would be prepared to pay more for their holiday packages if these were based around the 'ethical characteristics' (Goodwin and Francis 2003: 274) that they themselves aspired to. Tearfund (2000b) found that 59 per cent of respondents would be willing to pay more if this extra revenue was either used to ensure an improvement in the quality of working conditions and wages in the regions that they were planning to visit, to help to preserve the quality of the local environment or be given directly to locally based charity organisations.

In response to the findings of their 1999 survey, Tearfund released *A Tearfund Guide to Tourism: Don't Forget Your Ethics* the following year (Tearfund 2000a). This publication was designed to highlight the ethical issues associated with tourism, and was distributed amongst tour operators in the United Kingdom. The contents of the publication focused on how the way in which visitors travelled from one country to another raised ethical issues around employment and working conditions, whilst simultaneously also bringing to the fore the environmental consequences that the mere act of travelling from one destination to another can present (Tearfund 2000a). Questions were also raised regarding the human rights records of some tourism destinations and whether democratic political processes were present within the destinations that tourists had chosen to visit. Tearfund also raised the question 'Do local people want tourists visiting them?' in this survey (Tearfund 2000a), which in itself was quite a radical suggestion. This was argued by Tearfund (2000a) as being based on the fact that holidays are a consumer purchase and that 'our choice of holiday, just like any other consumer choice, affects other people'. The key aim of publicising these issues for Tearfund was to try and attempt to move tour operators beyond merely focusing on the environmental effects of travel to include both social and economic dimensions as well (Tearfund 2000b). This was done by Tearfund suggesting that tour operators should try their upmost to ensure that work conditions in the countries where they conducted business were known to be good, and that local communities received a greater share of the revenue garnered from tourism in their area (Tearfund 2000a, 2000b; Goodwin and Francis 2003).

Weeden (2002) points out that existing research in the field of psychology shows that there is a dilemma that exists between the conscience of the consumer and their subsequent purchasing behaviours. Those who chose to find out more information regarding responsible tourism practices – labelled as 'rebellious consumers' (Goodwin and Francis 2003: 282) – take into account not only price when purchasing holiday packages, but are also increasingly being drawn to deals that decree to provide or practice levels of economic, social and environmental responsibility (Krippendorf 1987; King 2002). Goodwin and Francis (2003: 282) also suggest that while the choices on offer to consumers are constrained by both price and availability 'the responsible elements of a tourism product are only a part of the motivation to purchase, but for an increasing number of operators [are] a significant part'. Whether social marketing is able to utilise advertising appeals designed to educate and inform whilst still making holiday destinations appear appealing remains to be seen. There is one aspect of the intangibility offered by ethical holiday choices – as Goodwin and Francis (2003: 282) observe 'The responsible tourism product has one particular advantage over many other ethical products – the consumer will often experience the difference'.

Another dimension of social marketing that has been begun to be explored in tourism is in relation to tourism advertising and the potential adoption of more socially responsible practices. Drawing on early societal marketing literature (Lill *et al.* 1986), Sirakaya and Somez examined gender images in state tourism brochures and concluded:

> Not only is the manipulation of visual imagery of women's roles in society harmful from a sociological perspective, but representations of women in tourism promotions are in direct opposition to the fact that women are primary decision makers in vacation travel decisions. One can conclude that marketers either are unaware of their target market and message audience or do not properly use market research data.
>
> (Sirakaya and Somez 2000: 361)

Another perspective of course is that the representation of women, along with other groups in society, reflects broader social and political issues. Indeed, Sirakaya and Somez (2000) cite the work of Simondson (1995: 23) who argues that 'tourist brochures, and the imagery contained within them, are examples of the traces left by power, and can be considered the visual evidence of the points of contact between superior and inferior social groups who exist in a power relationship'. Indeed, what is perhaps more noticeable in this example is the extent to which, in many Western societies at least, the role of tourism- and leisure-related advertising in the representation of such things as gender, body, minority cultures and children remains a controversial and contested topic (Nelson and Paek 2005; Caton and Santos 2009; Alessio and Jóhannsdóttir 2011; Burton and Klemm 2011; Chhabra *et al.* 2011), therefore perhaps suggesting not only the potential of social marketing with respect to changing social attitudes and behaviours (Chhabra *et al.* 2011; Truong and Hall 2013) but also its limits.

Social marketing

Social marketing is not usually regarded as a theory in its own right but instead draws upon a range of other theoretical bases to explore behavioural change (Gordon *et al.* 2006). Only in the early 2000s has it 'entered its growth phase after approximately two decades of sustained introductory period' and has begun to be accepted by 'academics and practitioners alike, as influencing behaviour, rather than promoting ideas, as the means to effect social change for the benefit of wider society' (Andreasen 2003: 326). However, the symbiotic relationship between social, commercial and critical marketing thought can also be interpreted as being a meta-theoretical domain that potentially has the capacity to provide a critique of commercial marketing and its role in consumerism and its effects (Hastings and Saren 2003). Nevertheless, there is also significant disagreement over the academic terrain of social marketing as well as its relationship to cognate areas of marketing. Indeed, one of the difficulties in assessing social marketing is the extent to which its principles have also been utilised in areas such as environmental, sustainable and societal marketing as well as macro-marketing.

As this section discusses, the changing and contested nature of social marketing is also a reflection of shifts in thinking within the marketing community as well as being a response to changes in society (Figure 1.1). For example, Table 1.2 shows the changing definitions of marketing as used by the American Marketing Association (AMA). Along with the ongoing expansion of the domain of marketing, or as Kotler (2005) describes it 'the broadening of marketing movement', one of the most significant aspects of the 2007 definition is the way that it positions marketing as providing long-term value, including for society as a whole, rather than being primarily focused on an exchange of money (short-term) for the benefit of the shareholder/organisation. According to Nancy Costopulos, chief marketing officer of the AMA, 'Marketing is no longer a function – it is an educational process … Marketing and its various elements change with the times … American Marketing Association recognize that shifts in the marketing world warrant a change in the way we define our marketing practice' (quoted in American Marketing Association 2008: 1, 2).

Figure 1.1 also identifies some of the other core shifts in the nature of social marketing. These include not only the expansion of the fields to which marketing is applied as well as its definition but also an increasing focus on behavioural change. Importantly for understanding the change agency that seeks to implement behavioural change interventions, social marketing also needs to contextualise within shifts to understanding the role of government and governance as well the rights and responsibilities of business and individuals.

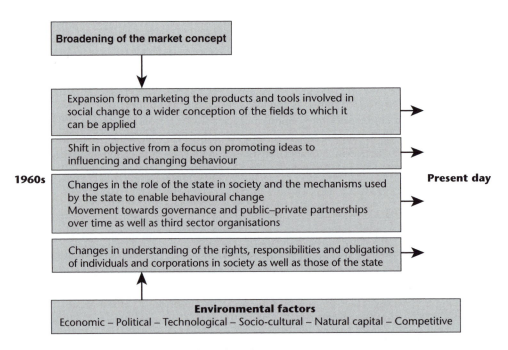

FIGURE 1.1 The changing dynamics of social marketing

TABLE 1.2 American Marketing Association (AMA) definitions of marketing

Date	Definition
1935	[Marketing is] the performance of business activities that direct the flow of goods and services from producers to consumers.*
1985	[Marketing is] the process of planning and executing the conception, pricing, promotion and distribution of ideas, goods and services to create exchanges that satisfy individual and organisational objectives.
2004	Marketing is an organisational function and a set of processes for creating, communicating and delivering value to customers and for managing customer relationships in ways that benefit the organisation and its stakeholders.
2007	Marketing is the activity, set of institutions and processes for creating, communicating, delivering and exchanging offerings that have value for customers, clients, partners and society at large.

* Definition adopted by the National Association of Marketing Teachers, an AMA predecessor organisation

Source: American Marketing Association 2008

The contested space of social marketing

Although it is generally recognised that social marketing as we would now understand it began in the late 1960s and early 1970s (Kotler and Zaltman 1971), there has long been argument over exactly what social marketing is and how it should be used. This has meant that social marketing has struggled at times to gain its own identity (Andreasen 2003). Today marketing and social marketing scholars can generally be placed into two main groups, both of which highlight what they perceive to be the true essence of social marketing. Glenane-Antoniadis *et al.* (2003) describes these as either 'traditionalists' or 'convergents'. 'Traditionalists' are those who advocate 'intentionally or unintentionally, the transfer of traditional marketing tools, the same ones that have tended to be employed in commercial settings, to the social marketing arena … employing a rational economic model of behaviour' (Glenane-Antoniadis *et al.* 2003: 326). In contrast, 'convergents' argue in favour of an 'interdisciplinary approach to the study of social marketing and use of other tools that go beyond traditional notions' (Glenane-Antoniadis *et al.* 2003: 329). Similarly, Peattie and Peattie (2003) suggest that social marketing should be defined outside commercial marketing techniques, and should develop its own set of definitions that will be further investigated later on in this essay.

However, to this we can arguably add an emerging third group that not only extends the interdisciplinary focus of the convergent school with respect to the engagement of social marketing in social and environmental change, but who are also using traditional marketing tools to provide a critique of marketing's embeddedness in consumer culture. Perhaps best exemplified by the Vancouver-based group the Adbusters Media Foundation and their project of 'culture jamming', this approach moves beyond notions of ethical consumption to question the very basis of consumption itself. Cox (2001: 67) sees culture jammers as 'people who are finding innovative and alternative ways to communicate using the very means the corporate sector itself uses, to different ends'. Perhaps slightly misleadingly described as 'anti-consumption', as after all consumption and exchange is necessary for the survival of communities and societies as well as individuals, this approach asks fundamental questions as to why we consume the way we do and the notion of consumer 'choice' in society as part of developing a path towards sustainable levels of consumption.

Wood (2008) also argues that there are conceptual and practical problems in understanding and applying concepts such as exchange, value and the 4Ps in social marketing situations (product, promotion, place, price) (see Kotler and Zaltman 1971 for their original use). Wood suggests that the use of behavioural change models (see Chapter 2) only adds further complexity to the setting and measurement of goals and it can be difficult to identify and sell the benefits of these changes in a similar way to commercial product marketing. Indeed, he also notes that commercial marketing is itself undergoing substantial change and reappraisal in light of greater appreciation of the role of relationships, networks and branding as well as ethical issues. Similarly, Desai (2009) suggests that the revised logic of marketing towards co-creation and relational approaches are more accommodative of social marketing, particularly as the result of the impact of the Internet and other new communications technology on networking behaviours (Lefebvre 2007).

In their seminal work Kotler and Zaltman (1971) argued that social marketing was a promising framework for planning and implementing social change and that the application of commercial marketing logic to promote social goals was a natural development for planned social change. However, if we consider the nature and development of marketing concepts over the past few decades, it is understandable how many theorists have been cautious to accept social marketing as a marketing focus. Yet to a great extent changes in the nature of marketing as both a craft and as a field of study also make sense when placed in their macro-environmental context. Indeed, Kotler (2006) argues that marketing is now operating within a dynamic global environment where rapid change can quickly make competitive strategies obsolete. He suggests there are new challenges and opportunities this century with the growth in non-profit marketing, increased global competition, a variable world economy and a call for greater social responsibility and social challenges. To be successful in the twenty-first century profit and non-profit organisations have to be strongly market oriented by being customer focused, competitor aware and sharing information across all functions within the organisation. This perspective would suggest that as well as addressing the dynamism of marketing over time we must also address changes in the concepts and application of marketing processes – and in particular social marketing processes – over time as well.

Kotler and Zaltman's (1971) viewpoint that the application of marketing logic to social goals as a natural development makes sense in the context of the evolution of commercial marketing. For Kotler and Zaltman:

> [T]he core idea of marketing lies in the *exchange process. Marketing does not occur unless there are two or more parties, each with something to exchange, and both able to carry out communications and distribution.* Typically the subject of marketing is the exchange of goods or services for other goods or services or for money.
>
> (1971: 4, emphasis in the original)

Marketing as an exchange process was first recognised as a business activity at the turn of the twentieth century and was 'essentially an adjunct of production and agriculture' (Assael 1990: 16). The shift from a production orientation to a sales orientation occurred during the Great Depression of the 1930s and a business mindset of 'hard-selling' what the company made rather than defining customer need. Assael (1990) asserts that this hard sell approach has created problems for marketing's image and may be why there was resistance and caution urged towards the overt marketing of social objectives. Indeed, Kotler and Zaltman (1971) asserted that charges could be made that social marketing was 'manipulative' and that it would just increase the amount of 'promotional noise'. Support for this implication was made by Laczniak *et al.* (1979) who found general agreement within their four respondent study groups with the statement that 'the application of marketing techniques to social issues and ideas is a step toward a society wherein the opinions held by the population can be manipulated' (Laczniak *et al.* 1979: 32). It is interesting to note that Laczniak *et al.* (1979) were wondering if social marketing would open a 'Pandora's box' with respect to the ethics of commercial marketing, and noted that 'to pursue the path of increased marketing of social programs and ideas without anticipating possible ethical consequences would seem rather naïve' (Laczniak *et al.* 1979: 29) (see also Abratt and Sacks 1988; Andreasen 2001; Brenkert 2002). Nevertheless, as Kotler and Zaltman (1971: 3) stated:

> The application of commercial ideas and methods to promote social goals will be seen by many as another example of business's lack of taste and self-restraint. Yet the application of the logic of marketing to social goals is a natural development and on the whole a promising one. The idea will not disappear by ignoring it or ralling [sic] against it.

There was a shift in the 1950s to the marketing concept and consumers became more selective in their purchases and companies became more customer rather than sales oriented. Assael (1990) suggested that meeting customer need should be viewed in a broader framework that included competition, the economy, technology, government regulation, demography and lifestyle and that those variables were likely to influence consumer purchases. Kotler and Zaltman (1971) depicted social marketing as a part of a planning system framework that recognised input variables from the macro-environment to a change agency (Figure 1.2). The process that social marketing uses is important to keep in mind as it is the impact of the macro-environmental inputs to the change agency and the subsequent implementation of a planned marketing mix that is significant in our analysis of the development and changes to social marketing concepts since its conception.

Shuptrine and Osmanski (1975) predicted that a shift from a consumer focus to a resource focus during the 1970s and 1980s would be radical and inevitably reshape marketing more dramatically than ever before in the evolution of marketing. In the same way that Kotler and Zaltman's (1971) suggestions for the role of social marketing in planned social change was a response to the social and political turmoil of the 1960s United States, which was marked by the increasing demands of civil rights, consumer, peace and environmental movements for radical change: 'It offers a useful framework for effective social planning at a time when social issues have become more relevant and critical' (Kotler and Zaltman 1971: 12). Shuptrine and Osmanski's (1975) suggesting that personal consumption stimulated by advertising is a spiritually unhealthy way of life was a response not only to the 1960s but also to the effects of the oil and natural resource crises of the early 1970s, and the exit of the United States from the Vietnam War. It is therefore almost with a sense of déjà vu that one reads their assertion that as a reaction to the then negative emphasis on mass consumption the three 'c's' had emerged and would continue to influence change in the 1970s. *Consumerism, clean-up* and *conservation* undoubtedly had a positive impact on commercial organisations at the time including General Electric and Union Carbide (Shuptrine and Osmanski 1975). *Consumerism* stood for truth in

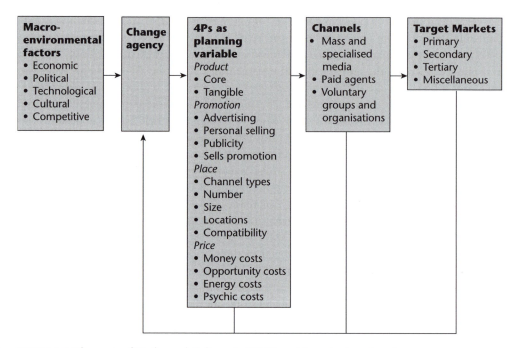

FIGURE 1.2 Elements of Kotler and Zaltman's (1971) social marketing planning system

advertising, safety and quality of ingredients and full labelling. *Clean-up* focused on waste disposal, ecological concern and recycling. The *conservation* of natural resources at the time was literally fuelled by the energy crisis of that decade as well as the limits to growth debate, i.e. that there were resource limits on economic growth (Meadows *et al.* 1972).

Similarly, Fisk (1973) called for the development of a theory of responsible consumption to assess the ecological implications of marketing decisions, which again reads as if it could be written in the present day, given concerns over the impacts of global environmental change and the financial crisis:

> Social indicators must be holistic, embracing the entire social system, rather than a single purpose as are measures of profit and market share. The economic viewpoint, so long dominated by cost reduction, is gradually yielding to the holistic view of ecological interdependence. The redefinition and measurement of consumption behavior in ecological systems terms thus provides a challenge to marketing theory and measurement that will extend far beyond our lifetimes, but the theory of responsible consumption gives managers a tool for starting this formidable task. The appalling alternatives to this effort are documented in alarming scientific reports.
>
> (Fisk 1973: 31)

Undoubtedly public and commercial interest in environmental issues and their implications did lead to an expansion in the scope of marketing to appropriate concerns over the sustainability of resources and consumption (Peattie 1992; Coddington 1993; Van Dam and Apeldoorn 1996; Crane 2000; Dolan 2002; Hunt 2012). However, even though we are now revisiting many of the same questions and issues, especially with respect to the impacts of tourism (Gössing and Hall 2006a, 2006b; Hall and Lew 2009), no redefinition of consumer behaviour as a result of ecological constraints occurred. Instead, a combination of a revival in the supply of cheap oil, a rolling back of regulatory assistance for the promotion of renewable energy as well as the environment and a push to withdraw government from certain areas of economic and social activity under Reagan in the US and Thatcher in the UK – what we would now term neoliberalism – led to an even greater expansion of consumerism as well as the market into people's lives. This did not mean of course that social marketing stopped developing, but it did mean that it developed in some directions and not others, and what could have been the development of a far more radical critique of consumption, economic growth and the role of business and marketing in society was delayed for almost four decades.

It is therefore no surprise that social marketing (Fox and Kotler 1980), as with all aspects of marketing (Zeithaml and Zeithaml 1984), is influenced by broad macro-environmental factors to produce and induce social change. These factors include technological development, legal and political forces, economic and informational factors. Indeed, Fox and Kotler (1980) suggest that social marketing originated in the informational approach of social advertising, which was adapted from commercial advertising, to induce behaviour change. Social advertising evolved into social communication after it was realised that the mass approach did not maximise the use of broader communication messages (Kotler and Zaltman 1971; Laczniak *et al.* 1979). Social marketing in turn replaced social advertising and communication, as it included elements of market research, product development, the use of incentives and facilitation, and was defined by Kotler and Zaltman (1971: 5) as:

> [T]he design, implementation, and control of programs calculated to influence the acceptability of social ideas and involving considerations of product planning, pricing, communications, distribution and market research.

Kotler and Zaltman's (1971) interpretation emphasised that it was the explicit use of marketing skills to translate social action into effective programmes that elicited the desired response. The marketing techniques deployed were the bridging mechanism between knowledge possessed of human behaviour and the socially useful implementation of what that knowledge allowed.

Kotler (1983: 602) later provided a more elaborate definition of social marketing as:

> The design, implementation, and control or programs seeking to increase the acceptability of a social idea, cause or practice in a target group(s). It utilizes market segmentation, consumer research, concept development, communications, facilitation, incentives, and exchange theory to maximize target group response.

Kotler's (1983) new definition of social marketing had an emphasis on target market selection. At the time, Kotler felt social marketing was too new to evaluate its effectiveness compared to other social change strategies and especially as it relied on voluntary response. Social marketing at that stage had only been applied to a limited subject matter including family planning, driver safety, public transportation, improved nutrition, environmental protection and energy conservation.

The area of voluntary response in social marketing was also an integral part of Andreasen's (1995: 7) influential definition of social marketing:

> Social Marketing is the application of commercial marketing technologies to the analysis, planning, execution, and evaluation of programs designed to influence the voluntary behaviour of target audiences in order to influence their personal welfare and that of their society.

Andreasen's (1995) agreed with Kotler and Zaltman that social marketing required the application of commercial marketing tactics and included that in his definition, however, his definition differed in that the ultimate goal of social marketing was to benefit the end target audience. In contrast, under the Kotler and Zaltman (1971) definition, the goal was to benefit the 'sponsoring organization and not – except as a means to an end the target audience or the broader society' (Andreasen 1995: 7). Kotler and Zaltman's (1971) perspective was that the social marketing process required mass and specialised communication media through agents and voluntary groups to reach target audiences. Whereas in Andreasen's (1995) view, having the end target audience as the focal goal distinguishes social marketing from commercial marketing and aligns it more closely with non-profit marketing. Andreasen cautions that although similar to non-profit marketing, social marketing is 'more precisely focused on directly improving welfare' rather than just lobbying or fundraising.

Donovan and Henley (2003) considered Andreasen's definition too restrictive in its emphasis on voluntary behaviour arguing that voluntary behaviour change may be made by producers and involuntary behaviour change by consumers. They cite as an example that a social marketing campaign initiated by a government health body – with an aim to reduce fat levels in food – may require a voluntary behaviour change by the food manufacturers, but the consequential consumer change in fat intake from the food manufacturer's product is involuntary and that consumers are forced to accept what manufacturers decide. Donovan and Henley (2003) therefore argued that social marketing includes not just the targeting of individual voluntary behaviour change but also changes to the environment and structures that facilitate change.

Donovan and Henley (2003) extend Andreasen's (1995) definition by adding two key points. First, recognition of the United Nations Universal Declaration of Human Rights as the 'baseline with respect to the common good' (Donovan and Henley 2003: 6). Second, Donovan and Henley (2003) believe most social marketing has focused on achieving individual behaviour change independent of individual social and economic circumstances. They therefore see a future for social marketing in achieving change by also tackling the social determinants of health and well-being. Donovan and Henley (2003) argue that social marketing is distinguishable from other areas of marketing in that campaigns to bring about social change that are directed towards lobbying manufacturers to change their practices can be regarded as a form of social marketing, while forming alliances with commercial partners in a campaign would not be social marketing.

Perhaps less controversially, Andreasen (2006) added to his previous work by suggesting three further principal features in social marketing:

1 An audience-centred approach rather than an organisation-centred or introspective mindset.

2   A process for implementing social marketing campaigns that is somewhat similar to the launching of a new product. The elements of Andreasen's (2006) process include listening, planning, pre-testing, implementing, monitoring and revising.

3   A set of concepts that make the process effective. These concepts include the 'stages of change' model used in health behaviour interventions (Luca and Suggs 2013) (see Chapter 2) that use tactics to move target audiences through various stages to achieve behaviour change.

Nevertheless, Andreasen (2006) has argued that a narrow view of social marketing underestimates its real potential and that target audiences encompass more than just 'problem people'. Andreasen referred to this sort of top-down process from institutions as a 'downstream focus', which he argued was 'to [sic] narrow and too limiting for social marketing's vast potential' (Andreasen 2006: 7). Focusing on the downstream behaviours of target audiences or 'victims' detracts from where the focus should lie – upstream. Andreasen therefore argues that society should aim to fix the structures and processes upstream that help create problems in the first place. Upstream social marketing practices therefore assist in enabling more information, policy focus and social pressure being placed on government. In the case of an area such as the regulation of cigarette smoking such measures may enjoy a degree of public support given their connection to health behaviours. However, in other areas, such as curbing tourism related greenhouse gas emissions via taxation and awareness campaigns, such upstream measures may have far less support. Indeed, upstream social marketing campaigns are often strongly related to the lobbying and public interest activities of pressure groups. Yet in many cases successful social marketing practices may require both upstream and downstream measures to be successful.

For example, the New Zealand Ministry for the Environment (2003) ran a successful pilot campaign together with regional councils, territorial local authorities and business partners on a national basis to promote environmental awareness and action in the community. The 'Reduce Your Rubbish' campaign was a partnership to raise awareness of New Zealand's growing waste problem and to encourage householders to take simple actions to reduce their rubbish. Specific voluntary household behaviours were targeted as a result of research findings including recycling, composting and environmental shopping. The campaign findings concluded that 'public education to promote voluntary behaviour change must be clearly integrated with other policy objectives and tools such as regulation and economic incentives'. Nevertheless, in addition, simple, positive messages to encourage behaviour change must be linked to 'local infrastructures and services … to improve the "vertical integration" of solutions to environmental problems, by informing policy development and providing a much better understanding of the barriers to changing individual behaviour' (Ministry for the Environment 2003).

As research on social marketing expanded so new centres of social marketing expertise and approaches started to develop in different countries. The influence of the work of both Andreasen and Donovan and Henley are perhaps seen in the definitions of social marketing used by the UK National Social Marketing Centre (NSMC), which defined social marketing as:

> The systematic application of marketing, alongside other concepts and techniques, to achieve specific behavioural goals, for a social good.
>
> (National Social Marketing Centre 2008)

This was updated more recently to:

> Social marketing is an approach used to develop activities aimed at changing or maintaining people's behaviour for their benefit.
> Whereas marketing in the commercial world ultimately seeks to influence consumer behaviour for profit, social marketing encourages behaviours that provide benefit for individuals and society as a whole.
>
> (National Social Marketing Centre 2010b)

Given the fluidity in definition over time and in different jurisdictions it is perhaps therefore no surprise that there have been attempts to develop 'consensus', 'common ground' or 'integrated' definitions of social marketing. Dann (2010) used text-mining techniques as well as drawing on recent changes in the definition of marketing to create a new definition of social marketing, which integrated the commercial definitions of the AMA and Chartered Institute of Marketing (CIM) with established social marketing definitions from the past 40 years of social marketing conceptual development. Following this approach Dann (2010: 151) defined social marketing as:

> the adaptation and adoption of commercial marketing activities, institutions and processes as a means to induce behavioral change in a targeted audience on a temporary or permanent basis to achieve a social goal.

Under Dann's approach:

- 'induce' is used rather than 'influence' in order to frame social marketing as a social leadership approach that involves the deliberate use of influence and persuasion to move a target market towards a specific course of action;
- 'benefit' is where the return on social investment through actual or perceived returns exceeds the financial and non-financial costs of the social marketing activity;
- 'targeted audience' reflects the use of the customer orientation by targeting social marketing activity on specific, identifiable and reachable market segmentation within a broader community population;
- 'social goal' represents the objective of the campaign to change or maintain society in accordance with the long-term objectives of the campaign's organisers (Dann 2010: 151, 152).

Lefebvre (2011) used a different approach to arrive at an integrated definition for social marketing. He argues that the field of social marketing has developed on two independent tracks over the past 40 years, which correspond to the contexts in which social marketing evolved: its earliest and primary use in developing countries to foster the use of various health-related products and services and its application in developed world contexts to reduce behavioural risk factors for diseases. Although seemingly ignoring much of the non-health social marketing research and practice that has been conducted, Lefebvre's (2011) analysis does recall Glenane-Antoniadis *et al.*'s (2003) description of social marketers as either 'traditionalists' or 'convergents' that was noted at the start of this discussion of the development of social marketing.

Lefebvre (2011) suggested that there are two distinguishing elements of an integrated social marketing approach:

1   Social marketing is focused on people, their wants and needs, aspirations, lifestyle, freedom of choice.
2   Social marketing aims for aggregated behavior change – priority segments of the population or markets, not individuals, are the focus of programs (Lefebvre 2011: 58).

While Lee *et al.* (2011: 1) in their *Declaration of Social Marketing's Unique Principles and Distinctions* (see also Box 1.4) claimed that:

> Social marketing is a process that uses marketing principles and techniques to influence target audience behaviors that will benefit society, as well as the individual. This strategically oriented discipline relies on creating, communicating, delivering, and exchanging offerings that have positive value for individuals, clients, partners, and society at large.

Clearly there is no consensus on exactly how to define social marketing. Definitions have changed over time in relation to a number of factors and will continue to change. What we can say is that social marketing is about the application of marketing concepts and tools to behavioural change. But differences will undoubtedly continue to remain with respect to targets, the focus of programmes, the degree to which behaviour change is voluntary, and the appropriate change agency.

BOX 1.4 SOCIAL MARKETING'S UNIQUE VALUE PROPOSITION

Social Marketing's unique position in the marketplace of behavior change ideas is to integrate [its] shared and unique characteristics described … into a program of behavior change. Social marketing is a process rooted in the belief that more than words and/or regulations are needed in order to succeed at influencing people's behavior. Social marketers understand and build upon the consumer's perception of:

- Self-interest
- Barriers to behaviour
- Competitive forces that create attractive choices.

These lead to interventions that

- Reduce barriers
- Increase benefits that matter to the audience and, in the end, move people to action.

Source: Lee *et al.* (2011)

PLATE 1.1 SARS campaign poster, Singapore

PLATE 1.2 EU/UK biosecurity campaign poster

Commercial organisations and social marketing

Even though social marketing can be characterised by 'a general model of intersector transfer of marketing concepts and tools from the commercial to the nonprofit sector ... There are many enterprises—commercial, governmental, and nonprofit—that design, implement, and monitor social change programs' (Andreasen 2002: 4, 6). Indeed, Andreasen goes on to conclude, 'Commercial marketing and its academic allies should not pass up what can be an important opportunity to reposition the entire field of marketing' (2002: 14). Similarly, Hastings noted:

> Commercial agencies and consultancies are also springing up claiming social marketing expertise. Not-for-profit *and* for-profit organizations are using some or all the sorts of practices discussed in [Hasting's] book to bring about social change ... this, at the very least, raises important ethical issues.
>
> (2007: 6, this author's emphasis)

The issue of the relationship between commercial and non-commercial dimensions of social marketing raises some fundamental issues in understanding what social marketing is seeking to achieve as well as perhaps some cynicism that may exist with respect to the validity of marketing's role in influencing behaviours for worse – as well as for good (Sheth and Sisodia 2006; Jahdi and Acikdilli 2009). Sheth and Sisodia (2005) reported a study that found that 62 per cent of consumer respondents had a negative attitude toward marketing, 28 per cent were neutral, and only 10 per cent had a positive attitude. Undoubtedly, much of the negative perception of marketing relates to issues of truth in advertising, its influence on people, especially those who are more economically and socially vulnerable, and its contribution to contemporary consumerism. For example, Hastings comments:

> [C]ommercial marketers are demonstrating ... an enviable capacity to influence behaviour. They are past masters at getting us to do things – buy their products, visit their shops, attend to their messages, deliver their messages, buy their products again. And, crucially – for the most part at least – we cooperate voluntarily.
>
> (Hastings 2007: 4)

Indeed, Hastings (2007) uses Lazer and Kelley's (1973: ix) definition of social marketing: 'Social marketing is concerned with the application of marketing knowledge, concepts and techniques to enhance social *as well as* economic ends. It is also concerned with analysis of the social consequence of marketing policies, decisions and activities' (this author's emphasis).

As Luck (1974) noted, the more philosophical viewpoint of Lazer and Kelley's definition is important, as it deals with the societal perspective of mainstream or 'managerial marketing'. However, if social marketing is also concerned with private economic ends then there would appear to be some potential for conflict between some of the different interpretations of social marketing discussed in this chapter. As noted above if social marketing is to be concerned with upstream as well as downstream affects on behaviour then it potentially calls for greater critique of the activities of corporations – who may use social marketing programmes to lay a foundation to increase their own sales. Of course it could be asked what is wrong with a company making a profit if it also does good for others. However, how far upstream should we go in trying to understand and influence behaviour? Is there a need for an even more fundamental critique of the social, economic and political systems within which individuals – as well as social marketing practitioners – are embedded?

This book does not take the position that social marketing should exist to enhance private economic ends but it does propose that it should enhance public economic, as well as social and environmental ends. In the sense that public economic ends, and issues such as equity, distribution of wealth, employment opportunities as well as access to health, education, welfare and leisure opportunities, are an extremely important economic component of the structures that affect individual behaviours. Instead, the employment of social marketing approaches to increase a company's profits is just commercial marketing by any other name. This does not mean that it is intrinsically bad. It is just not social marketing!

Nevertheless, these issues do highlight some of very complex situations that surround change agents and their *legitimacy* from a social marketing perspective as well as the systems within which they operate. This means understanding that the relative roles of the private sector in society are different between countries and has changed over time. Such a situation creates a substantial challenge for the understanding of social marketing, and marketing and tourism studies as a whole, because much of our understanding of these subjects, and especially many texts, have emerged from particular positions on the relationship between the state and the individual, and their relative rights and responsibilities, as well as notions of public good, the common wealth and the limits that should be applied to corporate interests. However, if we are to truly unbundle and change upstream as well as downstream systems' influences on behaviour then these are the difficult questions that need to be asked, not only of business and government but also of the fields of marketing and tourism studies.

Chapter summary and outline of book

The definitions of social marketing provided by various authors have a number of similarities. Nevertheless, there have been marked differences that have emerged as the field of social marketing has evolved. The influential works of Andreasen (1995) and Kotler and Zaltman (1971) suggest that social marketing could use commercial marketing concepts and tools to effectively bring about behaviour change. However, they disagree on whether the focus of social marketing goals is the change agency or the target audience, although over time there has generally been a greater focus on the latter.

Kotler (1983) argued that social marketing could pursue different objectives to product or services marketing, however, for social marketing to be effective, it still must resemble selling a product or service and go through a normal marketing planning process. Social marketing practices and subject matter also reflect the changeable nature of macro-environmental forces. Nevertheless, the limited though sometimes significant influence that a downstream focus has to effect change in a systematic way – like Kotler and Zaltman's (1971) social marketing planning process model – has highlighted the need in recent years for a shift in focus upstream of social marketing practices and the social–economic systems within which they are embedded (Andreasen 2006).

Kotler (2006) asserted that every decade demands that marketing managers to think in fresh ways about their marketing objectives and practices. Rapid changes could quickly make yesterday's winning strategies out of date. Kotler based this thinking on Peter Drucker's observation that an organisation's 'winning formula for the last decade would probably be its undoing in the next decade' (Kotler *et al.* 2001: 84). The need for appropriate innovation and response is clearly significant for tourism as it faces increased challenges with respect to sustainability and its contribution to society and destination economies. It is therefore in this context that social marketing may serve as a focal point not only for understanding ways in which behaviour may be influenced but also to pose some of the bigger, upstream questions regarding tourism and business and individual behaviour.

Book outline

Tourism and Social Marketing is divided into three main sections. The first five chapters introduce the reader to the history and development of the social marketing field and its relationship to tourism marketing and management issues, and provides the foundations of social marketing's relevance to tourism. This first chapter has outlined a broad overview of some of the main themes in the intellectual development of social marketing and its relationship to tourism. Given the importance of behavioural change to social marketing, Chapter 2 discusses some of the main theories with respect to behavioural change that are utilised in social marketing practice and highlights some of the advantages and disadvantages of each one together with identifying some of the main areas to which they have contributed. Chapter 3 examines the changing notion of governance and the role of the state and its relevance to social marketing given the significance of government as a major change agency (or *the* major change agency depending on political context) and the growth in public–private partnerships. Theories of behavioural change as well as the role of change agencies are then used to contextualise the process of social marketing, which is discussed in Chapter 4. Chapter 5 concludes the contextual chapters by returning to the theme of the relationship between commercial and social marketing, discussed above, in the context of the practice of social marketing and its behavioural change focus. This then leads to a discussion of the importance of a craft approach to social marketing, and how in its application argument and persuasion are inseparable from the choice of intervention.

The second section looks at the application of social marketing with respect to a number of fields including the environment, corporate social responsibility, green marketing, quality of life, social development, health and politically oriented marketing. The chapters in this section therefore cover not only a number of the key issues facing contemporary tourism development but also illustrate the importance of social marketing approaches to branding, communication, interpretation, marketing strategies, demarketing, consumer activism and visitor management. A broad tourism system approach is used to organise the chapters. Chapter 6 focuses on the use of demarketing as a specific application of social marketing by visitor attractions and destinations. Chapter 7 discusses the use of social marketing methods in changing tourist and visitor behaviour. Chapter 8 examines community-based tourism and social marketing approaches, which primarily aim to contribute to personal and community well-being.

The two chapters of the final section then bring together a number of themes of the book and address the way in which social marketing is related to the growth of broader forms of sustainable and alternative consumption as well as discussing the ethics of contemporary tourism and social marketing practice and the future of social marketing and tourism. Chapter 9 seeks to integrate a number of approaches and dimensions of the book by examining the role of social marketing and other interventions in sustainable tourism consumption. The chapter also identifies some of the potential limits of social marketing. Chapter 10 looks at the future of social marketing and tourism and revisits some of the strengths and weaknesses in the application of social marketing to behavioural change. It also notes the growing significance of alternative consumption approaches in tourism but suggests that there may be some paradoxes in their application. Finally, it throws some ethical curveballs with respect to the practice and learning of tourism as well as the 'right' of change agencies to change people's and business' behaviour in the first place.

Although the key social marketing concepts and definitions may have changed since the 1970s, the essence of social marketing, its focus on behavioural change and its relevance is as strong today as it was at its inception. Social marketing has been reshaped since the 1970s and will continue to be so in the future to meet current social need. The impetus of the changing macro-environment on the design and form of social marketing policies requires the application of an adaptable attitude and approach to social marketing as a field that uses commercial marketing activities and processes to reshape social marketing and tourism concepts in the future.

Further reading and websites

Some useful readings in the development of social marketing include:

Alves, H. (2010) 'The who, where, and when of social marketing', *Journal of Nonprofit and Public Sector Marketing*, 22(4): 288–311.

Andreasen, A. R. (2003) 'The life trajectory of social marketing some implications', *Marketing Theory*, 3(3): 293–303.

Hastings, G. and Saren, M. (2003) 'The critical contribution of social marketing theory and application', *Marketing Theory*, 3(3): 305–322.

Kotler, P. and Zaltman, G. (1971) 'Social marketing: An approach to planned social change', *Journal of Marketing*, 35(3): 3–12.

Luca, N. R. and Suggs, L. S. (2013) 'Theory and model use in social marketing health interventions', *Journal of Health Communication*, 18(1): 20–40.

Peattie, S. and Peattie, K. (2003) 'Ready to fly solo? Reducing social marketing's dependence on commercial marketing theory', *Marketing Theory*, 3(3): 365–385.

A number of social marketing research agencies and centres maintain a valuable online presence:

Centers for Disease Control and Prevention: Gateway to Health Communication & Social Marketing Practice: www.cdc.gov/healthcommunication

International Social Marketing Association: www.i-socialmarketing.org

National Social Marketing Centre: www.nsmcentre.org.uk

Social Marketing Institute: www.social-marketing.org/sm.html

BOX 1.5 PERSONAL ACTIVITY: WEEKLY PERSONAL BEHAVIOUR CHANGE DIARY/JOURNAL

Overview:

- Engage in a personal behaviour change project.
- For a ten-week period, you will record your actions and insights. The purpose of these entries is for you to understand the habituated nature of your behaviour and apply the concepts that we are studying to one's own behaviour.
- You need to set weekly goals to enable you to see how you are doing.
- Also, these diary entries will serve as the primary source in the development of later personal activities.

Journal format:

- You should make a total of ten weekly entries that are typed of about a page each.
- This should be an honest and open discussion. It is not being graded on your writing style or punctuation – so relax. The style and tone of your entries is entirely up to you. This will be your reflection about your successes and failures throughout the week. It is essential that you reflect deeply on the triggers, feelings, thoughts, settings and people that surround your target behaviour.
- This is your chance to change a behaviour that is important to you and it is also an opportunity for you to see the power of marketing concepts applied to a new domain.
- You might think about carrying a pocket diary to enable you to record your feelings and experiences when they happen.

Please note:

- This should be written up alone. However, it would be great to discuss your experiences with other people who are engaging in similar lifestyle changes. This is a great exercise to learn from one another. Collaboration can be very helpful so you might consider partnering up with someone to see if this helps you.
- If being done for any course what you submit needs to be typed up. The main focus of any marking of these diaries will be your ability to link what is being done in class and the reading of this book to your own personal change process.

2

INTERVENTION AND THEORIES OF BEHAVIOUR

This chapter examines a number of the major theories on behaviour change. A theory is an organised, heuristic, coherent and systematic articulation of a set of statements related to significant questions that are communicated in a meaningful whole for the purpose of providing a generalisable form of understanding. Six major macro-theoretical and mid-range theoretical approaches are discussed:

1 passive;
2 behavioural learning;
3 communication;
4 cognitive;
5 self-regulation; and
6 stage or transtheoretical perspectives.

The key components of each approach are identified and illustrated along with criticisms and their connection to social marketing interventions. The chapter concludes by highlighting the considerable issues that emerge in connecting theories of behavioural change to social marketing practice.

Social marketing and theories of behaviour

If social marketing is concerned with changing behaviours then most readers would likely assume that this is undertaken upon a clear understanding of what actually causes people to change their behaviour. Unfortunately, you would be wrong. While there is a reasonable partial understanding from a research standpoint, many campaigns and interventions are undertaken by governments, agencies and organisations on the basis of lay knowledge and assumptions, often without reference to theory or evidence-based methods of changing behaviour (Luca and Suggs 2013; Michie and West 2013). For example, in a study of Australian health promotion practitioners' awareness, understanding and utilisation of the major health promotion theories and models derived from research in the areas of psychology and communication, Jones and Donovan (2004) found that none of the 'standard' theories and models taught in health promotion courses, and included in the leading textbooks, were used by more than 50 per cent of practitioners in their work.

This situation does not necessarily mean that some of these campaigns will have no desired results. They might. But if interventions are based on intuition or personal belief and philosophies with respect to individual behaviour and responsibility then it makes it extremely difficult to identify common factors in effective intervention (Johnston and Dixon 2008). Furthermore, interventions are often characterised by a lack of a coherent language and sets of theoretical constructs to describe behaviour as well as what constitutes evidence of change (Van den Broucke 2012).

> Labelling phenomena such as exercise, coping, treatment, adherence and implementation as 'behaviour' taps into these theories for explanation. Failure to use the label results in apparently innovative theory, but more usually in 'rediscovering the wheel' or creating theoretical constructs which are only contextual variants of those that have already been well developed.
> (Johnston and Dixon 2008: 511–52)

This chapter therefore provides an overview of some of the major theories of behaviour change, it draws strongly on the psychological and health literatures, but a number of these theories are also widely referred to in other social science areas. However, it should be noted that in many of the cases and examples referred to in the following chapters explicit reference was usually not made to the underlying theory of behavioural change that was being used to frame the social marketing intervention. There are three main reasons for advocating the use of theory in designing social marketing and related interventions (Michie *et al.* 2008):

1   Interventions are likely to be more effective if they target causal determinants of behaviour and behaviour change; this requires understanding these causal determinants, i.e. theoretical mechanisms of change.
2   Theory can be developed and tested by evaluations of interventions only if those interventions and evaluations are themselves theoretically informed.
3   Theory-based interventions facilitate an understanding of what works and thus a basis for developing better theory across different behaviours, contexts, geographical regions, issues and populations.

Nevertheless, although the use of theory is important it must be stressed that there are many theories of behaviour. For example, Michie *et al.* (2005) identified at least 33 psychological theories of behaviour, with over 130 theoretical constructs, making it potentially extremely difficult to choose the most appropriate one when designing interventions (Munro *et al.* 2007). Leventhal and Cameron (1987) identified five main theoretical perspectives related to long-term adherence to behaviour change in a health context: (1) biomedical (here described as 'passive' in relation to the wider use of the perspective outside of health-related behaviours); (2) behavioural learning; (3) communication; (4) cognitive; and (5) self-regulatory perspectives. Using meta-analyses of research of sustained long-term change, such as adherence to medications or particular sets of behaviours, with respect to health Munro *et al.* (2007) identified 11 major behaviour models that fit within Leventhal and Cameron's categories together with a transtheoretical category. To this is also added norm activation theory, which is extremely significant for altruistic and prosocial and environmental behaviours. These are briefly described in the present chapter with respect to their primary focus and relationship to social marketing and behavioural interventions as well as criticisms. The chapter then concludes with a further assessment of some of the key issues that have been identified from research on behavioural change.

BOX 2.1 INSUFFICIENT UNDERSTANDING OF TOURIST ADAPTIVE BEHAVIOUR TO CLIMATE CHANGE

Within the tourism sector tourists are considered to have the greatest capacity to adapt to the risks and opportunities posed by climate change because of the tremendous flexibility leisure tourists have to substitute the place, timing and type of holiday – even at very short notice (Scott *et al.* 2012a, 2012b). However, the adaptive capacity of tourists is only now beginning to be explored. For example, tourists may learn to accept a 'green' winter environment in the absence of snow, to avoid hot periods of the day by staying in air-conditioned rooms or in areas with coastal breezes, to acclimatise physically over time with warmer average temperatures at home, to adjust their perception of acceptable or preferred environmental conditions (a reduced beach or a drastically diminished glacier becomes the norm) or to focus on a different set of activities supported by prevailing environmental conditions. There therefore remains much scope to understand adaptive capacity better by assessing climate change analogue events and utilising research techniques from fields such as acceptable limits to change (Scott *et al.* 2012a, 2012b).

Short-term versus longer-term changes in travel behaviour

The impact of many events, such as storms, drought and wildfires, on tourist perceptions of a destination is likely to be short-lived, but some impacts are likely to be more enduring in the minds of consumers and may over time widely alter the perceived attractiveness of a destination. The potential expansion of geographical areas susceptible to the transmission of vector-borne diseases such as malaria and dengue (Hall 2006a; Scott 2006) to popular tourism destinations where these diseases are not currently prevalent is one such example. How would travellers respond if required to take malaria medication or other preventive procedures in order to go to the Azores, South Africa, Cuba or Mexico in the future? Travellers' responses to media coverage of regional outbreaks and perceived changes in disease risk could also have important implications for travel patterns, and remains an important area for further research (Gössling *et al.* 2012).

Various short-term reactions to climate and climate-induced environmental conditions have been reported, including last-minute booking or spontaneous change of destinations (Scott and Lemieux 2009; Nilsson and Gössling 2013). However, many of the changes associated with climate change will occur in the medium- to long-term future. Consequently, the stated behavioural response to climate change impacts in the extant literature usually refers to unknown, hypothetical futures. Some exceptions, such as the study of Dawson and Scott (2010), utilise change scenarios based on recent historical events that tourists may have experienced or read about. Moreover, in longer-term scenarios, destinations, tour operators and activity providers may be able to adapt, possibly in many situations still offering viable and attractive experiences. It is thus questionable whether studies suggesting long-term changes in travel behaviour will prove to predict longer-term changes in travel patterns correctly (Gössling *et al.* 2012; Scott *et al.* 2012a, 2012b).

Theories of behaviour change

Passive

This theory, which Munro *et al.* (2007) also refers to as a 'biomedical perspective' in the context of the health behaviour literature, assumes individuals to be passive recipients of instructions (Figure 2.1). The approach is geared very much to the notion that individuals are rational beings who will make behavioural changes on the basis of advice from experts in their own self-interests. Non-adherence is understood as being caused by characteristics such as age and gender (Blackwell 1992). A major limitation of the approach is that it does not consider that the perceptions of a target individual or group may differ from those of the expert, nor does it adequately consider psycho-social influences and the impacts of the socio-economic environment on individual behaviours. Indeed, a fundamental tenet of most theories of behavioural change is that individuals tend to be active decision makers.

Behavioural learning

The behavioural learning approach focuses on the role of the environment and the teaching of skills to manage behaviour and is most associated with the work of Skinner (1953, 1989). It is characterised by use of the principles of operant conditioning in which learning is understood as the increased probability of a behaviour based on reinforcement, which has taken place in the past, so that the antecedents of the new behaviour include the consequences of previous behaviour, thereby creating a circular ABC model (Figure 2.2). However, the simple ABC model can be modified to illustrate that antecedents may be either internal to the individual or external from the environment (Figure 2.3). Depending on the circumstances the consequences of the behaviour change may include punishments or rewards for behaviour, i.e. with respect to the use of economic incentives to change behaviours, an improved personal sense of self, or improvements in health and well-being in the case of medical interventions.

The general awareness of the approach among policy communities, even if only in lay form, has meant that the approach has been hugely influential, especially with respect to economic psychology, behavioural economics and consumer behaviour (Foxall 1986, 1992, 1993, 2001; Earl 1990, 2005; Foxall *et al.* 2011) and the nature of state interventions in encouraging behavioural change (Marnet 2008; Bickel *et al.* 2010; Anand and Lea 2011).

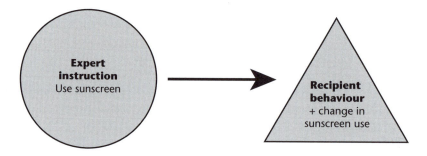

FIGURE 2.1 The passive model of behaviour

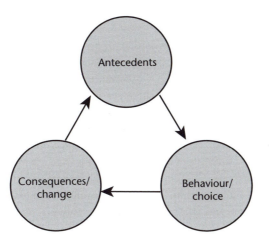

FIGURE 2.2 The ABC (antecedents, behaviour/choice, consequences/change) choice of behavioural learning

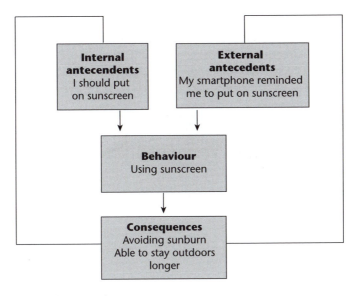

FIGURE 2.3 Behavioural learning theory

In the health field behavioural promoting strategies informed by this perspective with respect to the use of reminder systems have been found to be beneficial (Dunbar *et al.* 1979). However, more recent research has found either no change or even a negative result (Mannheimer *et al.* 2006; Simoni *et al.* 2006). Despite the approach's influence Munro *et al.* (2007: 104) found no meta-analysis that examined the perspective although they did note that the approach has been criticised 'for lacking an individualised approach and for not considering less conscious influences on behaviour not linked to immediate rewards'. These may include things such as habits, past behaviours and lack of acceptance of the reality facing an individual; this could range from a personal health issue to something leading to environmental change, such as climate change.

Communication and education

The communication perspective contends that improved communication from those trying to encourage behaviour change to the target individuals or market segment will increase the adoption of positive behaviours. That communication needs to be clear and comprehensible to the recipient of educational messages is clearly important. A communications approach also suggests that the timing of communication, and the nature of instruction, is also extremely important (Maibach and Parrott 1995; Hornik 2002; Dutta–Bergman 2005; Cox 2013). Communication, defined as the transmission or constitution of a message between two or more people, involves a number of factors: sender; message; channel; receiver; perception; and feedback (Longo 2007: 3). The key aspects of the communication process include purpose and scope of the communication, audience, framing, messages, messengers, modes and channels of communication, and assessing the outcomes and effectiveness of a communication (Figure 2.4).

Using an information search theory approach, Eichhorn *et al.* (2008) investigated accessibility schemes as communication sources and their potential to fulfil the informational needs of tourists with disabilities. Several interrelated need components were identified: information richness and reliability, appropriate sources, communication tools and customer-oriented services. The results of their research indicated that, despite complying with the reliability function at the regional and national level, existing schemes only partly comply with informational requirements. Eichhorn *et al.* (2008) concluded that to achieve information satisfaction and fully enable access to tourism for people with disabilities, a more sophisticated understanding of differential needs and appropriate sources is regarded as essential.

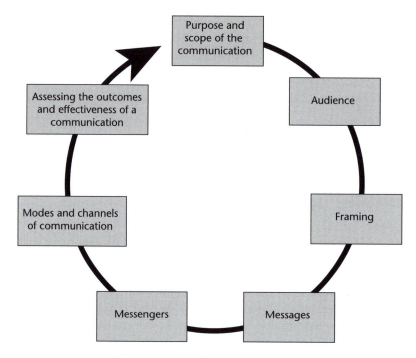

FIGURE 2.4 Purpose and scope of the communication

However, focusing on communication and education alone means that attitudinal, motivational and interpersonal factors that may interfere with the reception of the message and the translation of knowledge into behaviour change may be ignored (Blackwell 1992; Munro *et al.* 2007). Indeed, Moser (2010) stresses some of these issues in her historical overview of climate change communication when she identifies the challenges that communicators face in trying to convey the issue of climate change: invisibility of causes, distant impacts, lack of immediacy and direct experience of the impacts, lack of gratification for taking mitigative actions, disbelief in a humanity's global influence, complexity and uncertainty, inadequate signals indicating the need for change, perceptual limits and self-interest.

Furthermore, under a constitutive model rather than a transmission model of communication, the elements of communication 'are not fixed in advance, but instead are reflexively constituted by the act of communication itself. Communication thus becomes more than a technical question of efficiently achieving one's objective, but rather a social issue with complex moral and political dimensions' (Longo 2007: 3–4) – an observation that has substantial implications for how we might understand the political and ethical dimensions of social marketing. In addition, such an approach suggests that not only is the social psychological approach to communication relevant to social marketing but other communication traditions as well (Griffin 2011) (Table 2.1), even if they are more difficult theories to 'test' in a formal sense.

TABLE 2.1 Research traditions in communication process

Tradition	Explanation
Critical	The critical tradition views communication as a reflexive, dialectical discourse that places demands on the cultural and ideological aspects of power.
Cybernetics	Conceptualises communication in terms of information processing as a function of a system. Includes attention to issues of chaos, complexity, feedback, scale.
Phenomenology	The intentional analysis of everyday life from the standpoint of the person living it. The basis for communication lies in our common existence with others in a shared world that may be constituted differently in experience.
Rhetoric	Assumes a number of different postures: as a particular kind of communication (e.g., as persuasive communication); as a facet of the transmission model (e.g., as a manipulative technique for imposing one's view); or as a constitutive social process.
Semiotics	Views communication as a process that relies on signs (or words as symbols) to bridge the gaps between subjective viewpoints.
Social psychology	Focuses on social influence and interaction in communication; can take either a transmission model approach (a receiver is influenced by a source) or constitutive model approach (interaction reciprocally changes the participants and leads to collective outcomes that would not otherwise have occurred).
Socio–cultural	Views communication as a symbolic process that produces and reproduces shared meanings, rituals and social structures. Involves the coordination of activities among actors with communication problems being revealed in difficulties and breakdowns of coordination.

Source: After Longo (2007); Griffin (2011)

Cognitive perspective

The cognitive perspective includes theories such as the belief model, social–cognitive theory, the theories of reasoned action and planned behaviour, and protection motivation theory that focus on cognitive variables as part of behaviour change. The theories also share the assumption that attitudes and beliefs, as well as expectations of future events and outcomes, are major determinants of human behaviour (Gebhardt and Maes 2001; Conner and Norman 2005a; Munro *et al.* 2007). The latter is an extremely important factor in tourism and leisure behaviour because of the extent to which potential future events and outcomes are related to risk perceptions in the undertaking of travel or a leisure activity (Okun *et al.* 2003; Lee and Lemyre 2009), as well as in the potential consumption of more environmentally friendly tourism products (Kim and Han 2010; Lee *et al.* 2010).

A common element of all the theories in the cognitive perspective is that they suggest that individuals will choose the course of behavioural action that will lead most likely to positive outcomes. Each of these theories emphasises that human behaviours are rational. Therefore, the behaviours that are predicted as the result of a social marketing intervention from the cognitive perspective are considered to be the end result of a rational decision-making process based upon systematic and deliberative processing of information. As with the behavioural learning approach from which it evolved the cognitive perspective assumes that individuals generally aim to maximise utility and so select behaviours that are associated with the highest expected personal utility. This means that the overall utility of a behaviour is assumed to be based upon the sum of the probability (expectancy) and utility (value) of specific, salient outcomes or consequences (Conner and Norman 2005b).

This assumption of the expected utility of a behaviour can be expressed as:

$$SEU_j = \sum_{i=1}^{i=m} P_{ij} . U_{ij}$$

Where SEU_j is the subjective expected utility of behaviour j, P_{ij} is the perceived probability of outcome i of action j, U_{ij} is the subjective utility or value of outcome i of action j, and m is the number of salient outcomes. 'Each behaviour may have differing subjective expected utilities because of the value of different outcomes associated with each behaviour and the probability of each behaviour being associated with each outcome' (Conner and Norman 2005b: 7). Although such a model allows for subjective assessments of utility and probability it still assumes that such assessments are then combined in a rational way. The difficulty with such an approach of course is that while such a cognitive perspective may approximate the decision making attached to some behaviours it does not provide a complete description of the manner in which individuals make decisions. In particular it does not adequately address that:

1   non-voluntary factors can affect behaviour;
2   these theories do not adequately address the behavioural skills needed to ensure adherence, and they give little attention to the origin of beliefs and how these beliefs may influence other behaviours;
3   other factors that may impact on adherence behaviour, such as power, relationships and social reputations; and
4   the possibility that risk behaviour may involve more than one person.

(Munro *et al.* 2007)

Nevertheless, despite such criticisms and shortcomings the perspective has remained extremely influential in social marketing practice and behavioural change initiatives (Airhihenbuwa and Obregon 2000; Andreasen 2002). The rest of this section will now outline some of the key characteristics of the theories that contribute to the cognitive approach.

Belief model

The belief model, also referred to as the health belief model (Glanz *et al.* 2008), views behaviour change as being based on a rational appraisal of the balance between the barriers to and benefits of action. According to this model, the perceived seriousness of, and susceptibility to, an event will influence an individual's perceived threat posed by that event. This may be significant for example with respect to the perceived threat posed to tourists by criminal activity or by disease (Hanson and Benedict 2002). Perceived benefits and perceived barriers will also influence perceptions of the effectiveness of any change in behaviour. Demographic and socio-psychological variables therefore influence perceived susceptibility and seriousness, as well as the perceived benefits and perceived barriers to action. Perceived threat is also influenced by cues to action; in the case of traveller health for example these may be internal (e.g. symptom perception) or external (e.g. health communication and marketing campaign, word-of-mouth). High-perceived threat, low barriers and high perceived benefits to action would therefore increase the likelihood of engaging in recommended behaviours (Munro *et al.* 2007) (Figure 2.5).

All of the belief model's components are regarded as independent predictors of behaviour although perceived severity may not be as important as perceived susceptibility (Munro *et al.* 2007). Rosenstock *et al.* (1988) posited a revision of the health belief model that incorporated the notion of self-efficacy to the theory; this refers to the need of an individual to feel competent before effecting long-term behavioural change. Perceived self-efficacy is concerned with people's beliefs in their ability to influence events that affect their lives. According to Bandura (1977, 2010) this core belief is the foundation of human motivation, performance accomplishments and emotional well-being, and unless people believe they can produce desired effects by their actions, they have little incentive to undertake activities or to persevere in the face of difficulties.

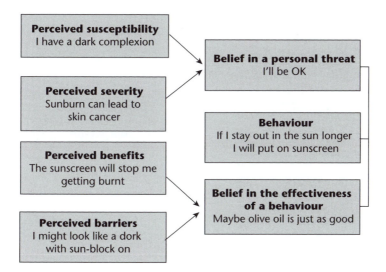

FIGURE 2.5 The belief model

The approach is subject to two major criticisms. First, the relationships between the variables have not been explicitly stated and it is assumed that the variables are not moderated by each other and have an additive effect. Second, important behavioural determinants such as the positive effects of negative behaviours, social influence, habit and culture are not included (Munro *et al.* 2007). Blackwell (1992: 165) notes that although the theory may predict behavioural change in some situations, it has not been found to do so for 'risk reduction behaviours that are more linked to socially determined or unconscious motivations'.

The protection motivation theory

According to the protection motivation theory behaviour change may be achieved by appealing to an individual's fears. Protection motivation theory was originally proposed by Rogers (1975) to provide greater understanding of fear appeals. The theory postulates that the three crucial components of a fear appeal are: (a) the magnitude of noxiousness of a depicted event; (b) the probability of that event's occurrence; and (c) the efficacy of a protective response (Figure 2.6). A 1983 revision of protection motivation theory (Rogers 1983) extended the theory to a more general theory of persuasive communication, which has been extremely influential in health and risk-related marketing (Tanner Jr. *et al.* 1989, 1991; Donovan and Henley 1997; Henley and Donovan 1999; Stroebe 2000; Keller and Lehmann 2008) (Figure 2.7), and has been used in relation to a range of different behavioural interventions including with respect to smoking (Pechmann *et al.* 2003; Gallopel-Morvan 2011), driving and driver safety (Lewis *et al.* 2007a, 2007b; Cismaru *et al.* 2009), and earthquake preparedness (Mulilis and Lippa 1990).

Protection motivation theory is the only theory within the broader cognitive perspective that explicitly uses the benefits and costs of existing and recommended behaviour to predict the likelihood of change (Trifiletti *et al.* 2005; Munro *et al.* 2007). Cismaru and Lavack (2007) suggest that perceived cost is the main driver of persuasion and propose that consumers use a combination of decision-making strategies, with an initial use of the elimination by aspects rule followed by the weighted additive rule. In their model of protection motivation

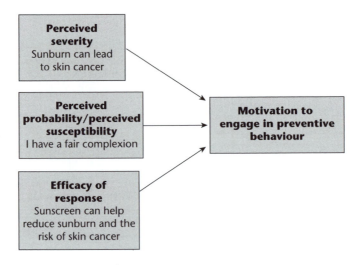

FIGURE 2.6 Protection motivation theory

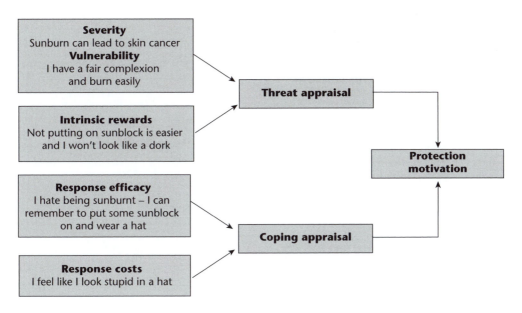

FIGURE 2.7 Revised protection motivation theory

theory variables, consumers rank the variables and set minimum cut-offs. A weighted additive relationship takes place only when and if the minimum cut-off levels for variables are met. However, an important limitation of this theory is that not all cognitive and environmental variables that could impact on attitude change (such as the pressure to conform to social norms) are identified (Munro *et al.* 2007).

Social cognitive theory

Social cognitive theory suggests that a multifaceted causal structure operated in the regulation of human motivation, action and well-being, and offers predictors of long-term behavioural change as well as guidelines as to how it may be promoted (Munro *et al.* 2007). The theory proposes that behavioural change will occur if individuals perceive that they have control over outcomes, that there are few external barriers and they have confidence in their ability to undertake the behaviour (Figure 2.8). The theory assumes that human action and motivation are based upon three types of expectancies (Conner and Norman 2005b):

1 Situation-outcome expectancies represent beliefs about which consequences will occur without interfering with personal action. Personal susceptibility to a particular threat is one example of situation-outcome expectancy.
2 Action-outcome expectancy is the belief that a particular behaviour will or will not lead to a given outcome. These may include social approval or disapproval of an action.
3 Perceived self-efficacy is the belief of an individual in their ability to influence events that affect their life and exerts its influence through cognitive, motivational, affective and selection processes (Bandura 2010).

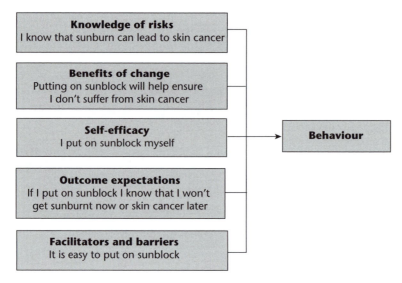

FIGURE 2.8 Social cognitive theory

Munro *et al.* (2007) conclude that the theory is difficult to operationalise and is often used only in part. Keller *et al.* (1999) reviewed 27 studies that examined the relationship between the construct of social cognitive theory, self-efficacy and physical activity. All of the descriptive studies found a statistically significant relationship between self-efficacy and exercise behaviour of between 4 per cent and 26 per cent of variance in behaviour. Even though the theory is regarded as difficult to operationalise it nevertheless has an important influence in social marketing campaigns, especially in the health field (Nutbeam 2000; Gregson *et al.* 2001; Evans 2006).

Theory of planned behaviour

The theory of planned behaviour is a model that is an extension of the social psychological theory of reasoned action (Fishbein and Ajzen 1975, 2010; Madden *et al.* 1992), which assumed that most behaviours are under an individual's control and that intention to undertake a behaviour is both a determinant and a predictor of the actual behaviour (Figure 2.9). Similarly, the theory of planned behaviour outlines the factors that determine an individual's decision to undertake a particular behaviour (Conner and Norman 2005b). It proposes that the most significant determinants of behaviour are an individual's intention to engage in a particular behaviour and their perception of control over that behaviour.

The notion of perceived behavioural control is similar to that of Bandura's (2010) concept of self-efficacy with it ranging on a continuum from easily executed behaviour at one end to hard to achieve at the other (for reasons of opportunities, resources or skills). However, there was insufficient attention to the impacts of past behaviour on current behaviour in the theory of reasoned action as well as the sometimes lack of volitional control (Stroebe 2000), which Fishbein and Ajzen recognised in their extension of the theory to include behavioural control in the theory of planned behaviour (Sutton 1997, 1998). Judgements of perceived behavioural control are influenced by perceptions as to whether an individual has access to the opportunities and resources necessary to undertake the behaviour as well as the internal and external control factors that facilitate or inhibit behaviours (Conner and Norman 2005b) (Figure 2.10).

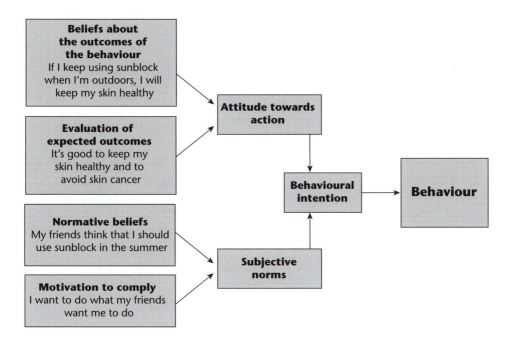

FIGURE 2.9 Theory of reasoned action

In a meta-analytic review of 185 independent studies that utilised the theory of planned behaviour Armitage and Conner (2001) found that the theory accounted for 27 per cent and 39 per cent of the variance in behaviour and intention, respectively. The perceived behavioural control construct was found to account for significant amounts of variance in intention and behaviour, independent of theory of reasoned action variables. Similar variation was identified in a later meta-analysis (Manning 2009). As well as being used in health interventions (Godin and Kok 1996; Ajzen 2012; Head and Noar 2013) and examinations of environmental behaviour (Clark *et al.* 2003; Swim *et al.* 2010; Whitmarsh 2009), the theory of planned behaviour has also been explicitly applied to leisure and tourism research (Ajzen and Driver 1992; Hrubes *et al.* 2001; Cunningham and Kwon 2003; Sirakaya and Woodside 2005; Lam and Hsu 2006).

Despite the theory's wide use substantial gaps remain in its utility for interventions as it still largely relies on notions of rational decision making (Munro *et al.* 2007). Godin *et al.*'s (2005) examination of whether intentions aligned with moral norms were a better predictor of behaviour compared with intentions aligned with attitudes is therefore of interest because of its implications for norm activation theory (see below). Their analysis indicated that participants whose intentions were more aligned with their moral norm were more likely to perform behaviours compared with participants whose intentions were more aligned with their attitudes. However, further analysis indicated that this moderation effect was only present when participants construed the behaviour in moral terms. Their findings suggest that the theory of planned behaviour should therefore provide greater recognition of the importance of internalised norms and self-expectations in the development of motivations to adopt a given behaviour.

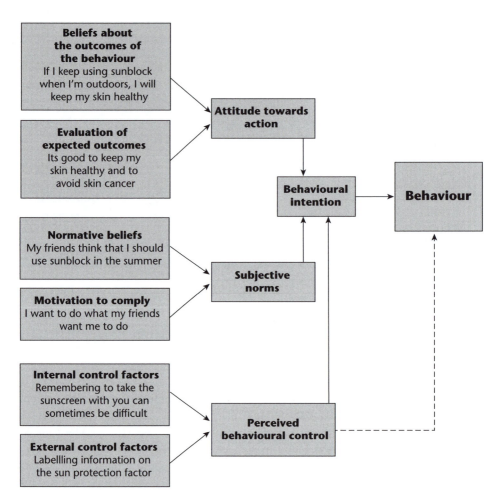

FIGURE 2.10 Theory of planned behaviour

Information–motivation–behavioural skills theory

The information–motivation–behavioural skills theory is a generalisable model for promoting and evaluating AIDS-risk behaviour change in a population of interest. The model states that AIDS-risk reduction is a function of people's information about AIDS transmission and prevention. Their motivation to reduce AIDS risk and their behavioural skills are fundamental determinants of adherence to the often complex and toxic highly active antiretroviral therapy (HAART) regimens required by HIV-positive persons (Fisher and Fisher 1992; Fisher *et al.* 2006) (Figure 2.11). The model is relevant to social marketing, and to health-related social marketing in particular where adherence to specific behavioural regimes is necessary, because adherence-related information provided via social marketing along with motivation are regarded as activating adherence-related behaviour (Fisher *et al.* 2006; Luca and Suggs 2010; Michielsen *et al.* 2012). Sabaté (2003) reports that the theory is moderately effective in promoting behaviour change, although Munro *et al.* (2007) note that no meta-analysis has been undertaken on the approach.

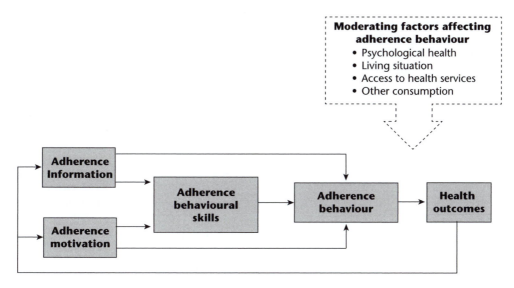

FIGURE 2.11 Information–motivation–behavioural skills model

Norm activation theory

A theoretical link between cognitive perspectives and self-determination/regulation theories (see below) is to be found in Schwartz's (1970, 1973, 1974, 1975, 1977) norm activation theory. However, unlike the other models discussed in this chapter that tend to focus on response to personal threats and are very much based within the health behaviour literature, the norm activation theory is grounded in seeking to understand pro-social behaviour. This has meant that in addition to seeking to understand acts of altruism, donations and volunteering it has become an extremely important theory in the understanding of pro-environmental behaviour (Van Liere and Dunlap 1978; Stern *et al.* 1986; Hopper and Nielsen 1991; Stern 2000; Joireman *et al.* 2001; Harland *et al.* 2007), including with respect to travel (Hunecke *et al.* 2001; Nordlund and Garvill 2003; Fujii 2010; Bamberg *et al.* 2011), climate change (Nilsson *et al.* 2004; Nolan 2010; Tikir and Lehmann 2011) and sustainable consumption (Zepeda and Deal 2009; Jansson *et al.* 2010, 2011). Pro-environmental behaviour is also believed to be a special case of pro-social behaviour because it also implies that people benefit others, whereas often no immediate direct individual benefits are received by those engaging in such behaviours (De Groot and Steg 2009).

Norm activation refers to a process in which individuals construct self-expectations regarding pro-social behaviour. The activation of personal norms involve 'situation-specific reflections of the cognitive and affective implications of a person's values for specific actions' (Schwartz and Howard 1981: 199). Although expectations and potential sanctions stemming from social norms are grounded in the social environment, expectations and sanctions from personal norms come from within an individual. Personal expectations are therefore experienced as feelings of moral obligation to engage in particular behaviours, i.e. a desire to helps others by volunteering. When an individual keeps to these expectations it may lead to enhanced self-appreciation and pride. However, as an individual acts against them it may result in feelings of guilt and self-depreciation (Schwartz 1977).

Norm activation theory includes three types of variables to predict pro-social intentions and behaviour. A set of personal norms, referred to as a feeling a 'moral obligation to perform or refrain from specific actions' (Schwartz and Howard 1981: 191). Central to the process of norm activation are four situational factors (*awareness of need, situational responsibility, efficacy* and *ability*) and two personality traits: *awareness of consequences* refers to a person's receptivity to situational cues of need (i.e. whether someone is aware of the negative consequences for others or for other things one values when not acting pro-socially) and *ascription of responsibility*, sometimes referred to as 'denial of responsibility', defined as feelings of responsibility for the negative consequences of not acting pro-socially (Harland *et al.* 2007).

Awareness of need refers to the extent to which a person's attention is focused on the existence of a person or a more abstract entity, such as the environment or democracy, which is in need. Situational responsibility refers to the extent to which a person feels responsible for the consequences of that need. For example, Schwartz (1977: 246) observed that when it is apparent to an individual that other people have caused the need, the likelihood that the individual feels some responsibility in that situation diminishes. Efficacy refers to the extent to which actions are identified that might alleviate the need, while ability refers to an individual's perception of the availability of the resources or capabilities that are required to perform the pro-social behaviour.

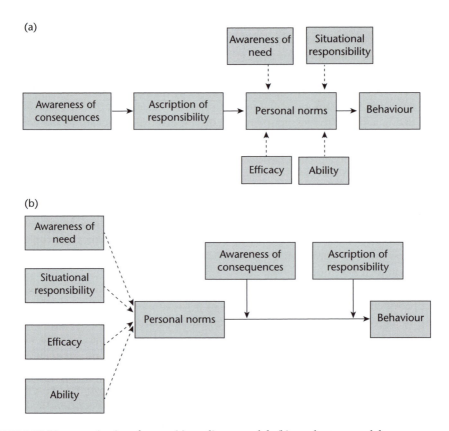

FIGURE 2.12 Norm-activation theory: (a) mediator model; (b) moderator model

Although, as noted above, there is substantial support for the norm activation model in the social and environmental behaviour literature, the relationships between the key variables of the model are not completely clear (De Ruyter and Wetzels 2000; De Groot and Steg 2009). De Groot and Steg (2009) suggest that two interpretations of the model have been postulated, with some scholars suggesting that awareness of consequences is an antecedent of ascription of responsibility, ascription of responsibility is an antecedent of personal norms, and personal norms affect behaviour (Figure 2.12a), whereas others assume that the effect of personal norms on pro-social behaviour is moderated by awareness of consequences and ascription of responsibility (Figure 2.12b). As DeGroot and Steg (2009) highlighted, knowing how the various variables are related to pro-social intentions is important for social marketing and policy interventions because such intentions may enhance efficient promotion of these behaviours. For example, when the mediator model is prevalent, social marketing interventions would be relatively more successful if they would first target awareness of the problem before focusing on responsibility or norms thereby strengthening moral obligations for taking pro-social actions. In contrast, the moderator model suggests that increasing responsibility may be sufficient when promoting pro-social behaviour.

De Groot and Steg's (2009) research found that the variables included in the norm activation theory were successful predictors of various kinds of pro-social intentions. Furthermore, their five studies, three in an environmental context and two in a social context, indicated that the NAM should best be interpreted as a mediator model. The result of such research has very clear implications for seeking to encourage pro-environmental behaviours (Steg 2008; Steg and Vlek 2009; Steg and Abrahamse 2010; De Groot and Schuitema 2012). Indeed, in a study of the relative importance of six policy outcomes related to different fairness principles for the perceived fairness and acceptability of pricing policies aimed at changing transport behaviour, Schuitema et al. (2011) found that the fairness and acceptability of the transport pricing policies was systematically higher if policy outcomes were related to environmental justice and equality. Transport policy outcomes related to distributions that focus on collective considerations therefore appear to be more important for the fairness and acceptability of pricing policies than those focusing on individual interests (Schuitema et al. 2011). Similarly, in a field experiment Bolderdijk et al. (2012) found that appealing to economic self-interest may not be advantageous as biospheric appeals in seeking to secure behaviour change. This is because people may care more about maintaining a favourable view of themselves, i.e. a positive self-concept, and seeing themselves as 'green' rather than 'greedy', than saving a relatively small amount of money. Such issues of the connection between behaviour and identity are also examined further in Chapter 9 in the context of sustainable consumption in tourism.

Self-regulation theory

Self-regulation theory, sometimes referred to as 'self-management' theory or the 'common sense' model of self-regulation (Hale et al. 2007; Boekaerts et al. 2005), argues that it is necessary to focus on the individuals' subjective experience of threat to understand the manner in which they respond to such threats. According to this theory, which was primarily developed in relation to health threats (Leventhal et al. 1998; Cameron and Leventhal 2003), individuals form cognitive representations of health threats (and related emotional responses) that guide the selection of coping strategies by combining new information with past experiences, and consequently influence related behaviours and outcomes (Munro et al. 2007;

Detweiler-Bedell *et al.* 2008). Five components are usually identified in cognitive representation (Hale *et al.* 2007):

1 *Identity*: the label or name given to the condition and the symptoms that are associated with it.
2 *Cause*: an individual's ideas about the perceived cause of the condition, which may not be scientifically accurate.
3 *Time-line*: the predictive belief about how long the condition might last.
4 *Consequences*: an individual's beliefs about the social and physical consequences of a condition. These are re-evaluated over time by the individual.
5 *Controllability/curability*: the belief as to whether a condition is controllable or curable and the individual's role in achieving this.

The approach provides a shift in perspective from one that regards individuals as relative passive respondents of health messages to one in which people are far more active. However, this relies on the assumption that individuals are motivated to avoid and treat illness threats and that people are active, self-regulating problem solvers. Maes and Karoly (2005) distinguish three stages in the goal-guidance process associated with self-regulation: (a) goal selection, setting and construal/representation; (b) active goal pursuit; and (c) goal attainment and maintenance or, when appropriate, goal disengagement. Leventhal *et al.* (1983) characterise this as a parallel response model, which describes how subjects process information and generate coping responses to solve problems posed by both an objective health threat and their subjective fear (Figure 2.13). This assessment matches well with how the properties of self-regulation theory has generally been assessed within the health literature (Cameron and Leventhal 2003). A first common dimension is the extent to which self-regulation is regarded as a dynamic motivational system with respect to goal setting and achievement. The second common characteristic is the extent to which the self-regulation perspective manages emotional responses as a crucial component of the motivational system that underlies behaviour. However, regardless of the primary focus it is therefore essentially a cyclical approach because the feedback from prior performance is used to make adjustments to current efforts to achieve goals (Ridder and de Wit 2006).

Although self-regulation theory is extremely influential in health management practices (Cameron and Levanthal 2003), Munro *et al.* (2007) argue that the theory offers little guidance with respect to the design of intervention: 'While the theory seems intuitively appropriate, specific suggestions are needed as to how these processes could promote adherence' (Munro *et al.* 2007: 112).

Stage perspectives

The transtheoretical model is the dominant stage model in health promotion and psychology (Armitage 2009; Luca and Suggs 2013). Developed in the 1980s the model was derived from the analysis of systems of psychotherapy and behaviour change and it was initially applied to the area of smoking cessation in which it was found that behaviour change can be regarded as unfolding through a series of stages (Prochaska and Velicer 1997). The notion of transtheoretical comes from its attempt to integrate an area that had fragmented into more than 300 theories of psychotherapy (Prochaska *et al.* 2008). Although often referred to as the 'stages of

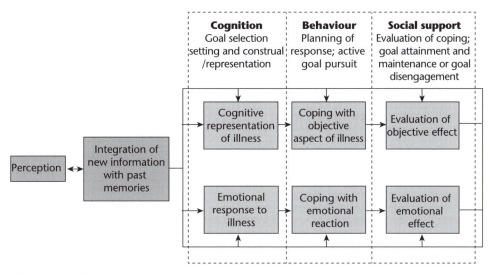

FIGURE 2.13 Self-regulation theory

change' model, it includes several different constructs: the stages of change, which highlights the temporal characteristics of behaviour; the decision balance (the pros and cons of changing behaviour); self-efficacy (confidence and temptation); and the processes of change (Prochaska *et al.* 2002) (Figure 2.14). The following assumptions drive research and practice with respect to the model:

- No single theory can account for all complexities of behaviour change. However, a more comprehensive model of behavioural change is likely to emerge from the integration of theoretical constructs and approaches.
- Behavioural change is a process that unfolds over time via a sequence of stages.
- Stages are both stable and open to change.
- The majority of at-risk populations are not prepared for action and will not be served effectively by traditional action-oriented behaviour change programmes.
- Specific processes and principles of change should be emphasised at specific stages to maximise the efficacy of interventions.

Research and interventions based on the model are regarded as integrated with or complementary to social marketing (Marcus *et al.* 1998; Thackeray and Neiger 2000; Diehr *et al.* 2011). For example, Kelly *et al.* (2003) developed a community readiness model designed to assess and build a community's capacity to take action on social issues that provides a framework for assessing the social contexts in which individual behaviour takes place and by measuring changes in readiness related to community-wide efforts (see also Slater *et al.* 2000). Most of the work based on the transtheoretical approach is health oriented although it has been subject to substantial criticism (Brug *et al.* 2005). Armitage (2009) notes that much of the criticism of the model has been with respect to the appropriateness of the named stages and suggests that the notion of a motivational phase followed by a volitional phase may better fit the results of empirical research. He also suggests that the processes of change components of the transtheoretical model may potentially prove to be the most useful contributions of

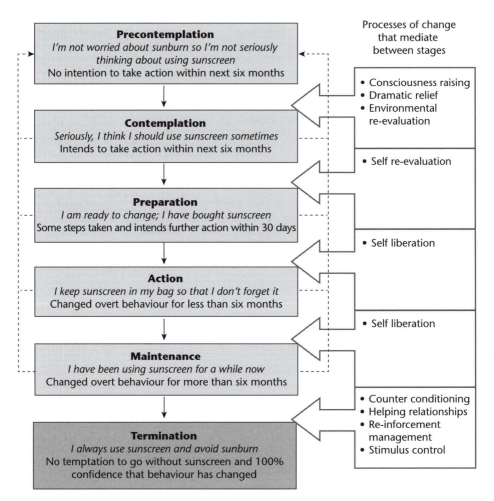

FIGURE 2.14 Transtheoretical model

the approach, yet these have been experimentally under-researched. Even given these limitations he nevertheless suggests that the stages of change concept currently has more to offer health behaviour change than dominant social marketing practice. Yet despite such criticisms the model is now increasingly beginning to be applied outside of the health sphere to complement social marketing activity with respect to environmental protection and sustainable behaviour and consumption (Carrigan *et al.* 2011; Cheng *et al.* 2011; Shaw *et al.* 2011).

Applying theories of behaviour in social marketing and tourism

Although the use of theory to develop social marketing interventions to promote behavioural change would appear to offer several advantages, it also has some substantial limitations. First, there is often little evidence that allows for the direct comparison of the different theories. Even combining studies based on a single theory – in order to perform a meta-analysis to assess its effectiveness in predicting behavioural change – is usually difficult due to various

PLATE 2.1 Sometimes despite their best efforts social marketing campaigns do not change behaviour: photo taken at English Bay Beach, Vancouver

methodological differences in the original studies (Munro *et al.* 2007). Furthermore, there are an enormous number of theories with respect to behavioural change, consumer behaviour and tourist behaviour that each have a particular focus. In addition to the broader concern of the manner of theory generation and 'testing' in the realm of human behaviour there are also issues with respect to role of socio-cultural factors in influencing behaviour. For example, in much of the literature relating to tourist and consumer behaviour fundamental questions over whether the results of a study undertaken in one culture can be applied in another remain not only unanswered but also unposed! In addition, in the case of seeking to change tourist behaviour there are substantial issues about where in the various stages of the travel process one should intervene. At the decision-making time when the tourist is still at home? When in transit? Or at the destination itself? Depending on the behavioural change sought in some cases intervention may even be required on the return stage or when the traveller returns to their home environment (see Chapter 4). Furthermore, how does behaviour change contribute overall towards feelings of happiness and subjective well-being in the individuals we are seeking to influence?

Second, although often developed in a specific context, behavioural change theories are then often applied to a much greater range of interventions, many of which are qualitatively different. As Munro *et al.* (2007: 115) noted in the case of health research: 'Particular theories may be more applicable than others to improving adherence to specific health behaviours. … It is difficult therefore to compare the effects of the theories across health categories or even within individual categories'.

Third, there is lack of long-term studies of behavioural change. Many social marketing and tourism studies do not track individuals over time to see the extent to which behaviours are maintained. The lack of such long-term research remains a substantial gap in our understanding of the value of social marketing as well as reasons for recidivism.

However, perhaps a devil's advocate position on these issues would be 'so what? So long as it works!' Indeed, this is an extremely valid position and one that many practitioners would no doubt take. Yet the problem is that what is regarded as 'working' in social marketing constitutes only relatively small levels of change. This, of course, may be acceptable in terms of public and organisational policies but it may not be sufficient to deal with some of the complex problems such as climate and environmental change, biodiversity conservation and disease mobility that face contemporary tourism. In many cases discussed in the social marketing and behavioural change literature we can note small positive changes as a result of an intervention, but what about the behaviours of those that remain unchanged? In seeking to illustrate why social marketing works we therefore come to a fundamental problem: that many studies of social marketing are not explicitly connected to theory in a useful way. Citing a theory or a study is not the same as explicitly testing it and its constructs.

Luca and Suggs (2013) highlight an ongoing lack of use or underreporting of the use of theory in social marketing campaigns and reinforce the call to action for applying and reporting theory to guide and evaluate interventions (see also Jones and Donovan 2004). Yet despite this situation there is probably more interest by governments in the role of social marketing to influence behaviours than ever before, while some behavioural economists and psychologists are actively advocating their capacities to assist governments in enabling behavioural change. For example, in 2010 the UK House of Lords' Science and Technology Select Committee ran an inquiry into behaviour change in which behavioural psychologists contributed current knowledge about what interventions can effectively influence behaviour, how behaviour change interventions can be used to achieve policy goals and what factors should be taken into account by government in determining whether a particular behaviour change intervention is appropriate (Michie and West 2013). This is not to suggest of course that behavioural psychologists should not be inputting into such policy making but, as this chapter has demonstrated, despite a number of theories with respect to behaviours huge gaps in our knowledge remain, including with respect to tourist behaviour (e.g. Cohen *et al.* 2011; Ong and Musa 2011; Antimova *et al.* 2012; Gössling *et al.* 2012; Gössling 2013).

The implications of our knowledge gaps with respect to behavioural change are profound. It may well mean for example that some interventions are being utilised that may have unforeseen and undesirable long-term effects within systems of consumption or even with individuals. By focusing on some approaches others may even be ignored. These are clearly important points to which we will return in the last two chapters of the book. However, for now we will deal with the problem pragmatically and focus in the next chapter on the processes of social marketing and in following chapters on their application. This does not mean that behavioural theory is absent in the approaches and interventions discussed in the following chapters, rather it means that it is in the 'background', usually implicitly informing some social marketing thinking rather than being at the forefront of campaigns, interventions and research. Instead, as the next chapter discusses, much social marketing is a craft grounded in experience of the application of the tools of marketing with its acceptability being judged by governmental and organisational stakeholders as well as the people it is meant to be assisting.

BOX 2.2 HAPPINESS AND SUBJECTIVE WELL-BEING

Behaviour change is often being conducted to contribute to individual and community well-being and happiness. But what does this mean? The term happiness can be used in a number of ways. A person can be happy about their childhood, about a funny story they were told, they can be a happy person, or they can have a happy relationship with their partner (Ahuvia and Friedman 1998). This shows the ambiguity that comes with the term happiness and is why researchers often use the term subjective well-being (SWB).

Ahuvia and Friedman (1998) refer to SWB as a general long-term condition or state of being. Compared to happiness, it is a more constant state. Cognitive judgments that a person makes, such as how well they are doing in life, and affective views such as positive and negative feelings felt, affects a person's overall SWB. This is similar to Diener's (2000) definition of SWB in that it refers to how people view and feel about their lives, and that it is cognitive and affective conclusions that help a person to reach these views and feelings.

Although there is ambiguity in regards to the term happiness, a lot of researchers still use this term either instead of, or interchangeably with, SWB. Easterlin (1973), who was one of the first researchers to start the debate over the extent to which income contributes to happiness, used the term happiness in his research rather than SWB. Indeed, Seligman and Csikszentmihalyi (2000: 9) suggested that subjective well-being was 'a more scientific sounding term for what people usually mean by happiness'. Diener and Buswas-Diener (2002) refers to SWB as a term used to illustrate many of the different evaluations people make in their life, the circumstances that they live in, their body and mind, and the events that happen in their life. This approach also takes into consideration short-term effects, for example an event such as a visit to a theme park may result in short-term happiness, however, the effects of this visit on happiness will not generally last. Regardless, it seems likely that the two terms will remain being used interchangeably.

The most common way to measure SWB is through self-report data. Through this, an individual's emotional state, life satisfaction, and sense of meaning is evaluated (Ahuvia 2008). In the earlier stages of measuring SWB, researchers tended to focus on the demographic characteristics of what makes a happy person, however, there has been a shift in focus towards the process of what are the factors in becoming a happy person (Diener *et al.* 1999).

Question framing is very important when measuring SWB. As SWB can be categorised into an affective component and a cognitive component (Diener *et al.* 1999), questions that measure these are often used. In order to measure affective components, researchers often look at how often individuals experience positive or negative affect (Graham 2011), for example laughing. When measuring the cognitive component, life satisfaction questions are asked that relate to several life domains, such as health and family, as well as overall general life questions (Graham 2011). A typical general life question is: 'Taken all together, would you say that you are very happy, pretty happy, or not too happy?' (Kahneman *et al.* 2006: 1908) with four to seven point scales generally being used for possible answers (Graham 2005). This is used to try and encourage respondents to focus on their life as a whole rather than specific life events that might cause temporary changes in happiness.

On top of measures that ask simple and general questions, more complex measures of SWB have also been created with Watson *et al.* (1988) developing the positive and negative affect schedule (PANAS). This measures both positive and negative effect on ten affect items. In regards to data collection, researchers have also used information provided by the World Values Survey (WVS), which provides cross-country data that looks at SWB, life satisfaction and happiness (Bjørnskov 2010). In 2006, a new set of data became available called the Gallup World Poll. It continually studies over 140 different countries in all areas of the world and is said to be the most accurate source of global behavioural data available in the world today (Gallup 2006). The Gallup poll asks two different types of questions known as global core questions and region specific questions. An example of a global core question used to measure well-being is 'All things considered, how satisfied are you with your life as a whole these days?' (Gallup 2006: 5), with a 0–10 scale used where 0 is dissatisfied and 10 is satisfied. Results from the Gallup poll have also been used in studies to help contribute to the income-happiness debate (see Tella and MacCulloch 2008; Diener *et al.* 2010; Sacks *et al.* 2010).

Questions for reflection:

- How would you best measure your own feeling of happiness?
- To what extent does travel contribute to your happiness? How does it rank when compared to such things as income, relationships with family, sexual relationships, sport, where you live and getting a job?
- What behaviour changes would contribute to an improved level of happiness for you and why?

Further reading and websites

Many of the behavioural theories and approaches used in the health field have been hugely influential on social marketing practice and theory. Useful reviews that cover the theories discussed in this chapter can be found in:

Conner, M. and Norman, P. (2005) *Predicting Health Behaviour*, second edition. Maidenhead: Open University Press and McGraw-Hill Education.
Glanz, K., Rimer, B. K. and Viswanath, K. (eds) (2008) *Health Behavior and Health Education: Theory, Research, and Practice*, fourth edition. San Francisco, CA: Jossey-Bass.
Munro, S., Lewin, S., Swart, T. and Volmink, J. (2007) 'A review of health behaviour theories: How useful are these for developing interventions to promote long-term medication adherence for TB and HIV/AIDS?' *BMC Public Health*, 7: 104.

An extremely useful review of norm-activation theory in the content of encouraging pro-social environmental behaviours is:

Steg, L. and Vlek, C. (2009) 'Encouraging pro-environmental behaviour: An integrative review and research agenda', *Journal of Environmental Psychology*, 29(3): 309–317.

A valuable overview from within a behavioral perspective is:

Foxall, G.R., Castro, J., James, V., Yani-de-Soriano, M. and Sigurdsson, V. (2006) 'Consumer behavior analysis and social marketing: The case of environmental conservation', *Behavior and Social Issues*, 15: 101–124.

Discussions of the gaps in understanding tourism behaviour in the context of climate change, and therefore in other areas where tourist behavioural change are sought, include:

Gössling, S. and Hall, C.M. (2006) 'Uncertainties in predicting tourist flows under scenarios of climate change', *Climatic Change*, 79(3–4): 163–173.
Gössling, S., Scott, D., Hall, C.M., Ceron, J-P. and Dubois, G. (2012) 'Consumer behaviour and demand response of tourists to climate change', *Annals of Tourism Research*, 39: 36–58.
Scott, D., Gössling, S. and Hall, C.M. (2012) *Tourism and Climate Change: Impacts, Adaptation and Mitigation*. London: Routledge.

An application of the theory of planned behaviour to green hotel choice can be found in:

Han, H., Hsu, L. T. and Sheu, C. (2010) 'Application of the theory of planned behavior to green hotel choice: Testing the effect of environmental friendly activities', *Tourism Management*, 31: 325–334.
Han, H. and Kim, Y. (2010) 'An investigation of green hotel customers' decision formation: Developing an extended model of the theory of planned behavior', *International Journal of Hospitality Management*, 29: 659–668.

With respect to undertaking field research in tourism with respect to behavioural change see:

Hall, C. M. (ed.) (2011) *Fieldwork in Tourism: Methods, Issues and Reflections*. London: Routledge.

3

THE CHANGING CONTEXT OF CHANGE AGENTS

Social marketing and governance

Chapter 3 discusses the concept of governance and its significance in social marketing. Different forms of tourism governance suggest potentially different forms of intervention in influencing behaviour. Such understandings are important because the nature of governance has changed substantially since the concept of social marketing first arose, especially with respect to the growth in non-government organisation use of social marketing as well as the increasing use by government of public–private partnerships to achieve social, economic and environmental goals, and subsequent social marketing campaigns.

Introduction

Chapter 1 noted the role of the change agency in social marketing. This is the organisation that integrates the social marketing planning process in 'an administrative process framework … Continuous information is collected from the environment by the change agency. Plans and messages are created and sent through channels to audiences, and the results are monitored by the change agency' (Kotler and Zaltman 1971: 10) (see Figure 1.2). However, Kotler and Zaltman (1971) never defined the organisational status of the change agency, although they did provide the example of the work of the US National Safety Council, which also referred to the work of state and local safety councils, a non-profit non-government organisation founded in 1913 and chartered by the US Congress in 1953,

> whose mission is to save lives by preventing injuries and deaths at work, in homes and communities and on the road through leadership, research, education and advocacy. NSC advances this mission by partnering with businesses, government agencies, elected officials and the public to make an impact where the most preventable injuries and deaths occur, in areas such as distracted driving, teen driving, workplace safety and beyond the workplace, particularly in and near our homes.
>
> (National Safety Council 2013)

Undoubtedly many of the organisations cited in the social marketing literature engaged in behavioural change are non-profit bodies, and there is also a strong theme with respect to social marketing not being used for commercial ends. Government is also clearly a major change agency. However, there remains substantial disagreement over the extent that commercial organisations can undertake social marketing campaigns and interventions. Nevertheless, as the chapter notes there has been a substantial change in the activities of government so that public–private partnerships have become more prevalent and private-for-private organisations may be employed to undertake the work of government. Furthermore, the growth of partnerships and networks that government seeks to influence to achieve policy goals only further blurs the public–private/commercial-non-commercial boundaries as well as the nature of social marketing interventions. Yet, as the chapter argues, the very nature of governance affects the type of interventions that governments apply.

The role of government in tourism and the influence of state policy on tourism development has long been of interest to scholars (Jenkins 1980; Jenkins and Henry 1982; Hall 1994a; Hall and Jenkins 1995; Bramwell and Lane 2000). However, since the 1990s there has been a gradual shift in approach in the tourism policy literature from the notion of government to that of governance (Greenwood 1993; Hall 1999; Trousdale 1999; Göymen 2000; Hall 2005b; Yüksel *et al.* 2005; Beaumont and Dredge 2010; Bramwell and Lane 2011). Interestingly, in the social marketing literature there is far more emphasis on the potential of social marketing to influence governance than there is on the ways in which governance affects social marketing practices and utilisation (Buurma 2001; McMahon 2002; Moor 2012). For example, Andreasen (2006: 152) suggests despite possible criticism for infringing into the area of legislative behaviour by political scientists, 'Social marketing is appropriate if the goal is to induce someone in power to create, lobby for, or vote for specific legislation to bring about a desirable social change'. Some of the reasons for state-based marketing interventions include:

- citizen/consumer education;
- citizen/consumer protection;
- curbing potential harm to people;
- meeting basic human needs;
- curbing potential externalities from human behaviours, such as harm to the environment or to communities.

This chapter identifies how the instruments of state intervention in tourism and social marketing are framed by different constructs of governance and provides a typology of the different conceptual frameworks of governance. Indeed, different forms of intervention are used by government to steer policy stakeholders in different directions. The chapter first discusses the definition of the concept of governance. The second section outlines the key issues involved in the development of typologies of governance with respect to tourism and identifies four main conceptualisations of governance. The chapter concludes by noting the importance of typologies as an analytical tool particularly in areas of policy and theoretical complexity such as governance.

BOX 3.1 EXAMINING POLICY CONSTRAINTS AND PROSPECTS FOR IMPROVEMENT: MARINE CONSERVATION POLICY IN SEYCHELLES

Income derived from both tourism and fishing is fundamental to the economy of the Seychelles. Clifton *et al.* (2012) sought to investigate the effectiveness of a number of policy initiatives and interventions that had been introduced at the Curieuse Marine National Park, which is one of the major areas of marine conservation in the Seychelles. Recent large-scale tourist developments had served to create problems for marine life in the area creating a situation where 'the resilience of these ecosystems to environmental stresses is again uncertain, but is highly likely to be compromised by poorly planned land-based development and will be subject to future increased disturbance associated to climate change' (Clifton *et al.* 2012: 830).

Resource management strategies designed to mitigate the effects on the local ecosystems were found by Clifton *et al.* (2012) to lack appropriate governance given the size of the problems that tourism development had created for the area. It was suggested that the development of strategies designed to specifically protect the marine assets of the area could potentially be transferred to other island jurisdictions where long-term behavioural changes by stakeholders are required.

Whilst these transitions towards collaborative and standardised management of marine protected areas in Seychelles would represent a major policy shift, it is argued that such an approach is better suited to the current and future economic conditions affecting the country and offers the prospect of improved conservation and marine resource management which could also serve as a model for other remote small island developing states.

(Clifton *et al.* 2012: 830)

Defining governance

Governance is an increasingly significant issue in the tourism public policy and planning literature (Bramwell and Rawding 1994; Göymen 2000; Dredge 2001, 2006a; Cornelissen 2005; Hall 2005b, 2007a, 2008a, 2008b; Yüksel *et al.* 2005; Dredge and Jenkins 2007; Beaumont and Dredge 2010). It has assumed importance as researchers as well as stakeholders have sought to understand how the state can best act to mediate contemporary tourism–related social, economic, political and environmental policy problems, such as global environmental change or the encouragement of economic and social development. Attention to governance issues in tourism mirrors the broader growth of interest in public policy studies (Rhodes 1997; Pierre 2000a; Kooiman 2003; Kersbergen and Waarden 2004; Jordan *et al.* 2005; Pierre and Peters 2005), while the growth of new supranational policy structures and multi–level scales of governance (Hooghe and Marks 2003; Bache and Flinders 2004) has also led to research with a more defined geo–political focus, for example especially with respect to the policies and actions of the EU (Hooghe 1996; Marks *et al.* 1996; Sutcliffe 1999; Hooghe and Marks 2001; Jordan 2001; Gualini 2004; Kern and Bulkeley 2009). However, while the influence of supranational organisations, such as the UNWTO, the UNEP or the World Bank/IMF, has been recognised as significant for tourism governance (Hall 2005b, 2007b; Hawkins and Mann 2007), there is a dearth of critical research on how governance processes relate to different public policy perspectives and the nature of interventions.

There is no single accepted definition of governance. This is reflected in Kooiman's (2003: 4) concept of governance as 'the totality of theoretical conceptions on governing'. Definitions tend to suggest recognition of a change in political practices involving, amongst other things, increasing globalisation, the rise of networks that cross the public–private divide, the marketisation and corporatisation of the state, and increasing institutional fragmentation (Pierre 2000a; Kjaer 2004; Pierre and Peters 2005).

Two broad meanings of governance can be recognised. First, it is used to describe contemporary state adaptation to its economic and political environment with respect to how it operates. This is often referred to as 'new governance'. Yee (2004: 487) provided a very basic definition of this approach by describing new modes of governance as 'new governing activities that do not occur solely through governments'. Similarly, in the European context Heritier (2002) focuses on new modes of governance that include private actors in policy formulation and/or while being based on public actors are only marginally based on regulative powers or not based on regulation at all. For Scott and Trubek (2002) the characteristics of these new models of governance are:

- *Participation and power-sharing*: Policy making is not regarded as the sole domain of regulators, but private and public stakeholders from different levels are meant to participate in the policy process as part of public–private partnership.
- *Multi-level integration*: Coordination between different levels of government needs to occur both horizontally and vertically and should involve private actors.
- *Diversity and decentralisation*: Rather than a standard legislative or regulatory approach a diverse range of coordinated approaches is instead encouraged.
- *Deliberation*: Greater deliberation is encouraged between public and private stakeholders so as to improve democratic legitimation of the policy-making processes.
- *Flexibility and revisability*: Soft law measures are often applied that rely on flexible guidelines and open-ended standards that are implemented voluntarily and may be revised as policy circumstances change.
- *Experimentation and knowledge creation*: Greater encouragement of local experimentation in governance measures as well as knowledge creation and sharing in connection with multilateral surveillance, benchmarking and the exchange of results and best practices.

The new modes of governance approach is closely related to new public management (NPM) strategies that re-focus the relationship between government and citizens to one of the citizen as consumer and the competitive interpretation of their needs and wants (Henneberg and O'Shaughnessy 2007). In a widely cited paper on the new public management Hood (1991) uses the term as a conceptual device to structure a discussion of contemporary changes in the organisation and management of executive government. In Hood's (1991) view, NPM is primarily an administrative argument, 'which is based upon public values that stress the efficient performance of tasks, rather than honesty and fairness, the robustness and adaptability of systems, or the logic of appropriateness' (Thompson 2008: 6). Such a reformulation of the rights and responsibilities of government and citizens also has substantial implications for social marketing, especially with respect to the adoption of more market-driven approaches (Collins *et al.* 2010).

The second broad meaning of governance is that it is used to denote a conceptual and theoretical representation of the role of the state in the coordination of socio-economic systems. However, it should be noted that the two approaches are not mutually exclusive as the use of the term 'governance' as a form of shorthand for new forms of governance in Western societies is itself predicated on particular conceptions of what the role of the state should be in contemporary society and how the state should intervene. This second meaning, which is the one that tends to be utilised in tourism planning and policy, can in turn be divided into two further categories (Peters 2000). The first focuses on state capacity to 'steer' the socio-economic system and therefore the relationships between the state and other policy actors (Pierre and Peters 2000). The second focuses on coordination and self-government, especially with respect to network relationships and public–private partnerships (Rhodes 1997).

Understanding how the institutional arrangements of governance are conceptualised is important as it determines the way in which the state intervenes in the tourism policy arena and therefore selects instruments that are used to achieve policy goals. The focus of most discussions on policy instruments in tourism is on their utilisation or their effects rather than on the understandings of governance that led such instruments to be selected (Pechlaner and Tschurtschenthaler 2003; Ayuso 2007; Hall 2008a, 2009b). Literature on the relationships between different concepts or images of tourism policy processes and instrument selection is limited. For example, Beaumont and Dredge (2010) investigated the advantages and disadvantages of three different governance approaches at the local level: council-led network governance structure, a participant-led community network governance structure and a local tourism organisation-led industry network governance structure. However, these comparisons, while useful at an operational level, did not then relate back to the conceptualisations of governance that underlie intervention and policy choice: why should the state intervene in one way and not another?

BOX 3.2 POLICY AND THEORY

Conceptual frameworks, such as images, models and theories, are fundamental to the development of understanding public and private institutions and the relationships between them. For example, in his extremely influential work Morgan (1986: 12) emphasised 'how many of our conventional ideas about organization and management build on a small number of taken-for-granted images, especially mechanical and biological ones'. Judge *et al.* (1995: 3) also noted that conceptual frameworks 'provide a language and frame of reference through which reality can be examined and lead theorists to ask questions that might not otherwise occur. The result, if successful, is new and fresh insights that other frameworks or perspectives might not have yielded'.

Typologies, an organised system of types, are an important means for looking at concept formation and measurement that are used widely through the social sciences, including in tourism studies and political science (Bailey 1994; George and Bennett 2005; Box-Steffensmeier *et al.* 2008; Coccossis and Constantoglou 2006, 2008). In policy terms typologies are used for both descriptive and explanatory purposes and can focus on variables related to causes, institutions and/or outcomes (Collier *et al.* 2008). Typologies play an important role as instruments in developing more general insights on the ways in which key concepts and ideas can be framed so as to facilitate comparative studies and map empirical and theoretical change, and, although usually associated with qualitative research, can also contribute to the quantitative analysis of categorical variables (Collier *et al.* 2008).

By exploring different conceptual frameworks and images it is possible to identify the ways in which empirical reality and theoretical models of that reality interact and how theory influences how the world is analysed, understood and acted upon. In public policy terms this notion is best illustrated by Pressman and Wildavsky's (1973: xv) insight that 'policies imply theories'. Majone (1980, 1981) understood policies as theories in terms of their development in a quasi-autonomous space of objective intellectual constructs, of thoughts-in-themselves, equivalent to Popper's (1978) third 'world' of reality (Lakatos 1971). For Majone (1981: 25) 'A policy, like a theory, is a cluster of conclusions in search of a premise; not the least important task of analysis is discovering the premises that make a set of conclusions internally consistent, and convincing to the widest possible audience'.

Similarly, the notion of governance as theory has also been extremely significant in studies of governance (Pierre 2000a; Kooiman 2003; Pierre and Peters 2005; Ansell and Gash 2008), with Stoker (1998) emphasising that the contribution of the concept of governance was neither with respect to the level of causal analysis nor as a new normative theory. Instead, 'the value of the governance perspective rests in its capacity to provide a framework for understanding changing processes of governing' (Stoker 1998: 18).

Core concepts in governance and behavioural intervention

The most common focus of most contributions to the governance debate in public policy terms is 'the role of the state in society' (Pierre 2000b: 4). Therefore, the core concept in governance in public policy terms, including with respect to behavioural change, is the relationship between state intervention/public authority and societal autonomy or self-regulation (Treib *et al.* 2007).

Figure 3.1 illustrates a continuum of intervention to support behaviour change that is widely referred to in the social marketing literature (Rothschild 1999; Social Marketing National Excellence Collaborative 2002; Grier and Bryant 2005; Pirani and Reizes 2005; Andreasen 2006). Drawing closely on the work of Lindblom (1977) on the relationships between politics, policy and markets, Rothschild (1999) contrasted social marketing with education and law as approaches in the management of behaviour change. From this perspective, education informs and persuades people to voluntarily adopt appropriate behaviours by creating awareness of the benefits of changing (see also Chapter 2 for a discussion on the communication and education approach to behavioural change). According to Grier and Bryant (2005) education is most effective when the goals of society are congruent with those of the target audience; the benefits of behaviour change are inherently attractive, immediate and obvious; the costs of changing are low; and the personal and collective skills and other resources needed to change are readily available.

Intervention	Education	Social marketing	Legislation and regulation
Behavioural state of target audience	Unaware/considering behavioural change/maintaining change behaviour	Aware of need to change/not considering change	Entrenched behaviours/no desire to change
Rights	Individual rights stronger		State/societal rights stronger
Externalities	Low	Moderate	High
Locus of power	Resides in individual	Relative balanced between change agency and individual	Resides in change agency
Community homogeneity	High	Moderate	Low
Lifestyle influences from government	Lessons	Hugs Nudges	Shoves Smacks

FIGURE 3.1 A continuum of behavioural interventions

By contrast, legislative and regulatory approaches use coercion or the threat of punishment to manage behaviour; for example, the use of fines or penalties for illegal behaviours. Legislation is regarded as the most effective tool for behavioural interventions when society is not willing to pay the costs associated with the continued practice of a behaviour that is an unhealthy or risky behaviour, e.g. drunk driving, or leads to negative externalities, e.g. the contributions of aviation to greenhouse gas emissions, yet citizens do not find it in their immediate self-interest to change (Grier and Bryant 2005).

Rothschild (1999) presents social marketing as an intermediate step between education and regulation as it influences behaviour by providing alternative choices that invite voluntary exchange. Marketing is regarded as the most effective strategy to be used for behavioural interventions when societal goals are not directly and immediately consistent with people's self-interest but citizens can be influenced to change by making the consequences more advantageous. As with education, marketing intervention offers the target audience freedom of choice; but unlike education, it changes the behavioural consequences of individual actions and decision making. Significantly, education and legislative and policy initiatives are often components of social marketing intervention and should be seen as complimentary rather than mutually exclusive strategies. However, 'marketing also creates an environment more conducive for change by enhancing the attractiveness of the benefits offered and minimizing the costs' (Grier and Bryant 2005: 326).

BOX 3.3 LESSONS, HUGS, SHOVES, NUDGES OR SMACKS?

These terms are used to describe a range of government mechanisms used to encourage behavioural change (Thaler and Sunstein 2008; Triggle 2013; see also Chapter 9):

- *Lesson* – The provision of information with respect to a certain behaviour and its externalities in the belief that individuals will change in their own self-interest.
- *Hug* – Covers a wide range of incentives – although these are not usually directly financial, but may include tax rebates, vouchers or discounts. For example, in encouraging the adoption of energy efficient technologies or participating in certain recreational and leisure activities.
- *Nudges* – Based on the idea that behaviour can be changed voluntarily without using compulsion. Can include enticing people to take up activities by using financial or time incentives or disincentives or the use of social marketing. For example, stressing social norms or desired social status may encourage people to change behaviour because they want to be perceived in a particular way or think of themselves in a certain way.
- *Shove* – More deliberate than a nudge; a mildly regulatory approach. For example, some planning departments may restrict certain businesses in some locations but not ban the activity altogether; this may be the use of zoning powers to ban fast food restaurants near schools or the deliberate location of casinos to minimise social impacts.
- *Smack* – The most coercive of all government regulatory measures by banning something outright. Often applied to alcohol and drugs as well as the sex industry.

Significantly, Rothschild recognised the interconnections between the selection of behavioural change interventions and public policy philosophy noting that:

> Democratic societies have an ongoing concern with the balance of free choice and externalities. Although the philosophy of marketing can provide a compromise position between the extremes of paternalism and libertarianism, the practice of marketing often is neglected in favor of education and law when such considerations are made. Marketing can offer a middle ground by allowing exchange through management of the environment (paternalism), as well as free choice and accommodation of self-interest (libertarianism). Trade-offs between individual and societal needs and rights create behavior management difficulties.
>
> (Rothschild 1999: 34)

Rothschild (1999) argued that the relationships between political philosophies and the selection of tools to achieve behavioural change would depend on:

- the externalities predicted to result from behaviour;
- the relative balance between the rights of the individual and those of the state;
- the relative locus of power of the various persons such as civil servants, non-profit administrators, legislators and/or private sector managers who attempt to direct the behaviour

of individuals for the good of society (as defined by the managers, the leaders and/or the constituents of the society); and

• the relative homogeneity of communities.

Knill and Lenschow's (2003) typology of modes of regulation in the EU, which built upon their previous work on the implementation of environmental policies in the EU (Knill and Lenschow 2000a, 2000b), has also proven influential in the development of European typologies of governance (Treib *et al.* 2007) and can be used to further extend our understanding of interventions. Knill and Lenschow (2003) utilise the dimensions of level of obligation and level of discretion with respect to the discretion EU member states have to implement EU rules. Their framework focuses more on the regulatory instruments that are utilised by implementing actors 'ranging from classical legal instruments to softer forms of steering the economy and society' (Knill and Lenschow 2003: 1), rather than providing general types of governance. These include new instruments (economic, communicative, framework regulation), regulatory standards, open methods of coordination (OMC) and self-regulation. Nevertheless, it is still useful in the current context as it illustrates some of the potential overlaps between social marketing and the 'steering mechanisms' employed by government to achieve policy goals. Table 3.1 illustrates the relationship between the three broad categories of intervention (education, social marketing and legislation) and the different types of regulatory instrument identified by Knill and Lenschow (2003).

As Knill and Lenschow (2003: 5) highlight 'each regulatory type implies a different mechanism of policy adaptation' and, hence, also a different model of governance. The European regulatory state, as with other jurisdictions, relied primarily on the hierarchal model of state governance with its implied powers of coercion. Such an approach makes no attempt to influence the awareness of the problem structure by the target segment by tackling either the strategic or cognitive foundations of behaviour. The new modes of regulatory governance depart from the hierarchical model to varying degrees. The least radical departure leads to the application of new instruments with the public delegation model relying on an authoritative state framework, but emphasises the creation of incentive structures. One of the reasons why this approach has been utilised in the EU context has been the inability or unwillingness of lower-level change agents to implement regulatory structures.

A more far-reaching departure from the hierarchical model of regulation is the private self-regulation or delegation model (Black 1996). This occurs when the state calls especially on economic actors to form a private network in order to solve particular problems collectively. This approach has been widely used in tourism to manage both business (Forsyth 1995; Williams and Montanari 1999; Haase *et al.* 2009) and visitor (Allen *et al.* 2007) behaviours. Under this approach the private network is responsible for setting regulatory standards and for ensuring members' compliance. The incentive to change behaviours come from compliance to self-regulatory frameworks that induces member organisations to comply with rules that have been formulated 'in their name' and in view of industry and/or sector needs and capacities (Knill and Lenschow 2003). However, lurking in the background as a form of encouragement to comply with such approaches is the possibility that the state may always intervene and regulate should policy objectives not be met. Nevertheless, one of the difficulties in applying this approach in tourism is the highly fractured nature of the tourism industry and the possibility that many 'target' organisations may not be members of formal tourism associations (Leiper *et al.* 2008).

TABLE 3.1 Intervention mechanisms and types of regulation

Intervention	Regulatory standards	New instruments	Self-regulation	Open method of coordination (OMC)
Legislation and regulation (coercion to comply)	Legally binding standards	Framework and procedural rules	Self-regulation is undertaken in the 'shadow' of the state, i.e. with the threat that the state could intervene and regulate if it wishes	Reporting and monitoring
Social marketing (the use of incentive structures to change behaviours)	–	Changes of procedural and/ or material opportunities	Regulatory standards influenced by private actors	Peer pressure
Education (redefinition of interests on the basis of new knowledge gathered due to the regulatory context and subsequent behavioural adaptation)	–	–	Communication in private networks	Best practice models
Policy model	Hierarchy model: power of coercion	Public delegation model: traditional subsidiarity	Private delegation model	Radical subsidiarity model: public learning approach

Source: Knill and Lenschow (2003); Hall (2011b, 2013)

According to Knill and Lenschow (2003) the greatest departure from state coercion is the OMC model where the potential use of hierarchical modes of regulation is not even considered as a fall-back position (Hodson and Maher 2001). There is no formal attempt by the state to control outcomes although they do assist in facilitation and participate in mutual learning following broad prior agreement on policy goals and principles. Instead, 'hierarchical elements in terms of reporting requirements and the reliance on incentive structures (peer pressure) [become] complementary steering mechanisms that stimulate learning and diffusion processes' (Knill and Lenschow 2003: 4).

In order to clarify the semantic field of governance it is therefore necessary to identify variables that serve to best clarify the core concept of governance. This can be done by reference to the relative use of hierarchical forms of regulation, i.e. legislation and the relative balance in the power relationship between the state and other policy actors as categorical variables (Figure 3.2). The use of these categories is well recognised in the governance literature. Frances *et al.* (1991) recognised three different models of coordination, also referred

---

BOX 3.4 PRIVATE SECTOR-LED MARINE CONSERVATION: A CASE STUDY OF TWO MARINE PROTECTED AREAS IN INDONESIA

Marine protected areas in Indonesia provided the focus of a case study by Bottema and Bush (2012) where entrepreneurial marine protected areas (EMPAs) were investigated in the context of the role that the private sector plays in marine ecotourism. A comparison between the Yayasan Karang Lestari coral reservation project on the Northwest coast of Bali and the marine tourism park on the island of Gili Trawangan off the West Coast of Lombok in Indonesia was undertaken (Bottema and Bush 2012). The reason for this comparison was to ascertain whether EMPAs provided an effective setting for private sector actors to pursue a long-term vision for marine conservation funding and management, and also investigated whether EMPAs gave these actors the scope to overcome implementation and enforcement failures of policies that had been a cause for concern in the past (Clemens and Cook 1999; Agrawal 2001).

Bottema and Bush (2012) discovered that the private sector was able to increase awareness of conservation amongst tourists and coastal communities, but needed state support to create long-lasting institutionalised arrangements. It was also noted that the private sector was also able to provide new income streams and the financial abilities to support marine conservation activities (Bottema and Bush 2012). As Bottema and Bush (2012: 41) point out 'the stock of social capital is equal to the level of associational involvement and participatory behaviour in a given network or community', which is also a valuable observation in terms of future community-level collaboration aimed at the conservation of protected areas.

---

to as meso-theoretical or intermediate theoretical categories, in Western liberal democratic countries: hierarchies, markets and networks. These categories were found to be useful not only in national political life but also in analysing the external relationships between states. According to Frances *et al.* (1991: 1), 'the three forms of social organization have a general applicability that transcends any particular geographical space or temporal order. They exemplify genuine "models" of coordination that can be characterized abstractly and then deployed in an analytical framework'. To these categories Pierre and Peters (2000) added a fourth common governance arrangement that they termed 'community'. Each of these conceptualisations of appropriate governance structures are also related to the use of particular sets of policy instruments or interventions. Critical to the value of the different modes of governance are the relationships that exist between public and private policy actors and steering modes that range from hierachical top-down steering to non-hierarchical approaches. The main elements of the four models or frameworks of governance are outlined in Table 3.2, which identifies their key characteristics, the policy instruments associated with each concept of governance and exemplars from the tourism literature that examine particular dimensions of the framework.

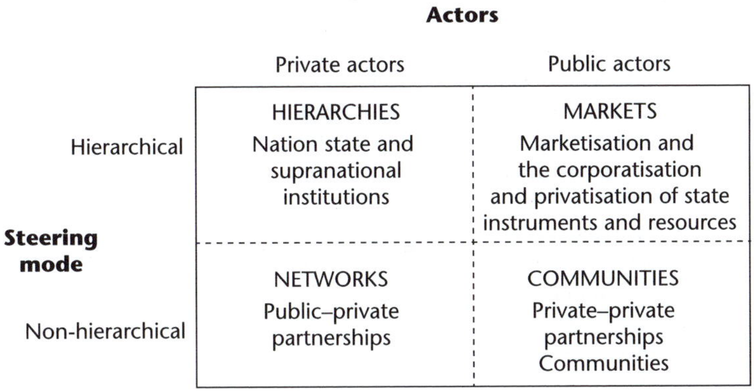

Actors

	Private actors	Public actors
Hierarchical	**HIERARCHIES** Nation state and supranational institutions	**MARKETS** Marketisation and the corporatisation and privatisation of state instruments and resources
Non-hierarchical	**NETWORKS** Public–private partnerships	**COMMUNITIES** Private–private partnerships Communities

Steering mode

FIGURE 3.2 Frameworks of governance typology

Source: After Hall (2011b)

TABLE 3.2 Frameworks of governance

Framework	Classificatory type characteristics	Policy instruments	Exemplars
Hierarchies	– Idealised model of democratic government and public administration – Distinguishes between public and private policy space – Focus on public or common good – Command and control (i.e. 'top-down' decision making) – Hierarchical relations between different levels of the state	– Law – Regulation – Clear allocation and transfers of power between different levels of the state – Development of clear set of institutional arrangements – Licensing, permits, consents and standards – Capacity to remove property rights	Scott 2001; Dredge and Jenkins, 2003; Hall 2008a, 2008b, 2009b; Plotkin and Hardiman 2009
Markets	– Belief in the market as the most efficient and just resource allocative mechanism – Belief in the empowerment of citizens via their role as consumers – Employment of monetary criteria to measure efficiency – Policy arena for economic actors where they cooperate to resolve common problems	– Corporatisation and/ or privatisation of state bodies – Use of pricing, subsidies and tax incentives to encourage desired behaviours – Use of regulatory and legal instruments to encourage market efficiencies – Voluntary instruments – Non–intervention as a deliberate policy measure	Jenkins 1982; Wanhill 1986; Hall and Jenkins 1995; Piga 2003; Gooroochurn and Sinclair 2005; Dredge and Jenkins 2007; Hall 2008a

Continued

Framework	Classificatory type characteristics	Policy instruments	Exemplars
Networks	– Facilitate coordination of public and private interests and resource allocation and therefore enhance efficiency of policy implementation – Range from coherent policy communities/ policy triangles through to single issue coalitions – Regulate and coordinate policy areas according to the preferences of network actors than public policy considerations – Mutual dependence between network and state	– Self–regulation – Accreditation schemes – Codes of practice – Industry associations – Partnership with non–government and private sector organisations to achieve policy goals	Hall 1999, 2008a, 2008b, 2009b; Pavlovich 2001; Tyler and Dinan 2001; Pforr 2002, 2006; Dredge 2006a, 2006b; Dredge and Jenkins, 2007; Anastasiadou 2008; Scott, Cooper and Baggio 2008; Beaumont and Dredge 2010
Communities	– Notion that communities should resolve their common problems with minimal state involvement – Builds on a consensual image of community and the positive involvement of its members in collective concerns – Governance without government – Fostering of civic spirit with developing large bureacracies	– Self–regulation – Public meetings/town hall meetings – Public participation – Non-intervention – Voluntary instruments – Information and education – Volunteer associations	Murphy 1983; Taylor 1995; Bramwell 2005; Nantongo *et al.* 2007; Okazaki 2008; Jamal and Watt 2011

Source: After Hall (2011b)

Hierarchical governance

In most of the tourism policy literature the ongoing legislative and regulatory role of the state remained unassessed. Although much contemporary governance in tourism stresses public–private relationships (Bramwell 2005; Dredge and Jenkins 2007), hierarchical governance remains significant because of the continued role of the state in international relations as well as the ongoing importance of legislation and regulation as part of the exercise of state control (Russell *et al.* 2008). There is very little direct discussion of hierarchical governance in tourism literature (Viken 2006 is an exception), rather it tends to be subsumed under a more general discussion about the roles of government in tourism (Hall 2008a). Nevertheless, there is a substantial body of literature that discusses hierarchical governance with respect to its effectiveness, particularly in relation to environmental management, in which its implications for tourism activities are noted (e.g. Jentoft 2007; Meadowcroft 2007; Korda *et al.* 2008; Kluvánková-Oravská *et al.* 2009).

Markets

Although the use of markets as a governance mechanism has been very much in political vogue since the mid-1980s (Pierre and Peters 2000), including with respect to the corporatisation and privatisation of tourism functions that had previously been the domain of the state (Hall and Jenkins 1995; Hall 1997, 1998; Jenkins 2000; Dredge and Jenkins 2003, 2007; Shone and Memon 2008), the decision by the state to allow the market to act as a form of governance does not mean that government ceases to influence the market. Rather, instead of using regulatory mechanisms, government will seek to use other forms of intervention, such as financial incentives, to encourage the tourism industry to move in the direction that it desires. Examples of this approach include public subsidies for certain kinds of tourism activity and the provision of tax incentives (Jenkins 1982; Wanhill 1986; Bradshaw and Blakely 1999; Hall and Williams 2008). Nevertheless, market failure and thereby the limits of the market as a form of governance has increasingly been recognised, especially with respect to the equity of policy outcomes and the effects of financial crisis on tourism (Schilcher 2007).

Networks

The concept of networks, and public–private partnerships in particular, has received considerable attention in tourism policy and planning (Pavlovich 2001; Bramwell 2005; Dredge 2006a; Hall 2008a; Scott, Cooper and Baggio 2008; Beaumont and Dredge 2010). Network governance is often regarded as a 'middle way' or 'third way' between hierarchical and market approaches to tourism governance (Scott, Cooper and Baggio 2008) and networks are also seen as a potential social marketing tool in their own right (Barrutia and Echebarria 2013).

The development of public–private partnerships is also regarded as a way of encouraging greater business philanthropy and involvement in cause-related marketing. For example, Business in the Community, which is a national not-for-profit organisation established with the backing of the then prime minister, Margaret Thatcher, by British business leaders in 1981 to encourage companies to invest more in the community (see Box 3.4) (Patten 1991; Hurd *et al.* 1998).

The nature of networks has also been proposed as a means to potentially integrate different policy and stakeholder perspectives, although integration capacity might depend on an open and inclusive planning process and on the importance of conditions influencing the actors' perceived payoffs from participation (Hovil and Stokke 2007). However, the extent to which networks may act to serve self-interest rather than a larger collective interest poses major challenges for their utility as a policy instrument (Hall 1999; Dredge 2006b). Erkuş-Öztürk and Eraydin (2010) for example, in a study of the contribution that networks may make to sustainable tourism in a Turkish destination, suggested that while there was an increase in local collaboration and self-help networking, their findings show that environmental motivations fall far behind economic considerations in networking practices. The shift from government towards governance has strengthened the position of policy networks (Pierre and Peters 2005). Nevertheless, some policy communities and sub-governments may become closed to the extent that policy alternatives are relatively closed with a policy arena (Hall 1999). Reflecting one of the dilemmas of the contemporary state in that while 'it needs networks to bring societal actors into joint projects, it tends to see its policies obstructed by those networks' (Pierre and Peters 2000: 20).

BOX 3.5 *PROFITABLE PARTNERSHIPS:* BUSINESS INVOLVEMENT IN CAUSE-RELATED CAMPAIGNS AND THE IMPACT ON CONSUMER HABITS

Cause-related marketing is any partnership between a business and charity, or business and a government agency, that markets an image, product or service for mutual benefit. Cause-related marketing campaigns operated by business and charitable partnerships can potentially have a significant impact on consumer habits and bring benefits to both businesses and the charities. One of the first detailed UK studies of the benefits of cause-related campaigns, which examined how people acted in response to such campaigns rather than how they think they would, found that there was very high public awareness of a number of such campaigns (Farquarson 2000). The study, *Profitable Partnerships*, commissioned by Business in the Community (BITC) in 2000, was based on a survey of 2,000 adults by the British Market Research Bureau. Almost 90 per cent of those surveyed had heard of at least one cause-related programme and almost half could spontaneously name a specific company or brand involved in a campaign. Two in three people believed more businesses should get involved. However, a small percentage did feel that such marketing was exploitative, or that it was inappropriate for business to become involved in social issues, an issue that is also raised in the academic literature (Hellsten and Mallin 2006).

Although previous research had established that a majority of people support the concept of cause-related marketing, and would probably express that support in their purchasing choices, the BITC (2000) research reported that this broad approval is affecting consumers' choices. The study found that more than 65 per cent of respondents stated they had participated in a cause-related marketing campaign. Of them, three-quarters had either switched brand, tried out a product or increased their usage; and four in five had felt more positive about certain purchases, more loyal to a company or brand, and more inclined to look out for further cause-related campaigns. Among a wide variety of factors cited by those surveyed were schemes that supported local community activity, a high level of donation or support for the project or charity and clearly communicated, unambiguous benefits.

According to Sue Adkins, BITC's director of marketing, 'This is not about corporate philanthropy … It's about commercial benefit for both cause and company. Any business which tries to project this sort of campaign as strings-free giving is heading for a fall; the public is not gullible' (quoted in Farquarson 2000). She also noted that unless campaigns are properly managed, and based on integrity and transparency, they can be counter-productive. Table 3.3 illustrates a continuum of business involvement in corporate philanthropy related to the nature of the philanthropy and its objectives. Indeed, there is also evidence that consumers are increasingly expecting businesses to be involved in cause-related marketing (Demetriou *et al.* 2009).

TABLE 3.3 Societal dimensions in sponsorship projects

Goals	Philanthropic ←				→ Marketing
Nature	Pure philanthropy	Targeted philanthropy	Hybrid corporate citizen	Exploratory sponsoring	Pragmatic sponsoring
Objectives	• Act as a good corporate citizen on the basis of a belief as to its appropriateness • Genuine community involvement without material considerations to business benefit	• Show community involvement • Contribute to quality of life of employees	• Marketing tool • Demonstrate capacity to act as a good corporate citizen by showing social and/or environmental responsibility • Improve brand / product image, and visibility	• Marketing tool • Encourage business-to-business relationships • Show community involvement	Marketing tool, especially for raising brand and product awareness

Polonsky *et al.* (2013) reports on the findings of community-based strategic philanthropy project the 'Respect for History', a project on Turkey's Gallipoli Peninsula sponsored by the Turkish oil company OPET. The project sought to enhance and protect the cultural and historical experiences of tourists visiting Gallipoli, and to bring direct and indirect benefits to local communities through enhancing tourism-related business opportunities and improving community infrastructure. The results of the project suggested that respondents generally believe that both their economic and social quality of life have improved as a result of the project. This has also positively influenced respondents' perspectives of the sponsoring organisation.

As Tim Mason, Tesco's marketing director, commenting on the BITC (2000) findings, stated: 'Successful marketing is all about meeting customer needs and most consumers expect companies to be socially responsible ... That's what is driving the rapid growth of cause related marketing and I am sure that growth will continue for the foreseeable future' (quoted in Farquarson 2000).

Communities

The fourth general model of governance is that of communities. Community governance in tourism planning was a significant theme in the tourism literature from the early 1980s on (Murphy 1983) before often becoming subsumed under general approaches towards sustainable tourism planning (Bramwell 2005; Hall 2008a). In some cases community-level governance developed because of the loss of local government authorities or powers as a result of political restructuring (O'Toole and Burdess 2005). Although the framework has been criticised as being overly idealistic and exaggerating the benefits of perceived consensus (Hall 2008a), community participation and even control over planning remains an important issue in tourism planning and policymaking (Bramwell and Sharman 1999; Dredge and Jenkins 2007), and has become fundamental to much thinking about local governance with respect to pro-poor tourism (Schilcher 2007), volunteer tourism (Raymond and Hall 2008) and the management of conservation initiatives (Nantongo *et al.* 2007) in less developed countries, as well as indigenous tourism research and development (Fennell 2008). Community-based approaches to tourism planning have a strong corollary in social marketing, where community-based interventions have been identified as successful in a range of settings ranging from sustainable consumption to active lifestyles and changes in travel behaviour (Slater *et al.* 2000; Haldeman and Turner 2009; McKenzie-Mohr 2011).

For example, community-based social marketing techniques were successfully used to affect people's transportation awareness and behaviour in Washington State's King County Metro Transit's In Motion programme (Cooper 2007). The In Motion approach focuses on neighbourhood-based outreach instead of a more typical employer-based trip reduction programme and addressed the potential to change any trip from drive alone to an alternative mode instead of focusing exclusively on commute trips. The In Motion intervention provided neighbourhood residents with incentives to drive less, raised individual awareness of alternative travel options and broke the 'automatic reflex' to drive for all trips. After implementation in four neighbourhoods programme participants reported increased transit ridership and use of other non-single-occupant vehicle modes, such as carpooling, biking and walking. The pre- and post-participant reported mode shares indicated a 24 per cent to greater than 50 per cent decrease in driving alone and a 20 per cent to almost 50 per cent increase in transit use. These self-reported numbers were supported by bus stop counts and analysis of overall transit ridership (Cooper 2007). The success of the programme has meant that the approach is seen as having potential to be applied to other situations where reductions in car use are sought (Graham-Rowe *et al.* 2011).

Chapter summary

This chapter has investigated the conceptualisation of the construct of governance, a concept that is frequently used but that demonstrates a variety of different approaches in its understanding and application in tourism-related behavioural change interventions. The study of concept formation in governance has been presented via the development of various typologies, a method that is widely utilised in the social sciences (Bailey 1994; George and Bennett 2005). Within the context of political science and public policy studies typologies are used for both descriptive and explanatory purposes with respect to the framing of key concepts and to contribute to the analysis of categorical variables (Box-Steffensmeier *et al.* 2008; Collier *et al.* 2008).

The overarching concept in governance in public policy and behavioural intervention terms is the relationship between state intervention/public authority and societal autonomy or self-regulation (Pierre 2000b). This is also reflected in the widespread understanding of social marketing being part of a continuum of intervention that ranges from education to legislation/state coercion (Rothschild 1999; Grier *et al.* 2007; Guion *et al.* 2007; Steg and Vlek 2009). The three approaches of education, social marketing and legislation were also related to different forms of regulation identified by Knill and Lenschow (2003) in the

European context. Significantly, three of the forms of regulation are part of the new modes of governance developed since the 1990s and which are closely connected to the growth in government interest in social marketing as a non-legislative form of intervention (Bode 2006; Bell *et al.* 2010).

The categorical variables that were selected that illustrate the concept of governance were the relative balance of the power relationships that exist between public and private policy actors and steering modes that range from hierarchical top-down steering to non-hierarchical approaches. The resultant matrix identified four frameworks or types of governance that are readily identified in the governance literature: hierarchies, markets, networks and communities as well as the range of policy instruments that is normally associated with them.

Typologies help conceptualise and describe empirical developments. They therefore serve as an appropriate analytic framework with which to structure analysis and comparison and can potentially be used for the development of quantitative as well as qualitative analysis. However, like all maps a typology of governance applies a simplifying lens to a complex reality. As Stoker (1998: 26) commented: 'The issue is not that it has simplified matters but whether that simplification has illuminated our understanding and enabled us to find an appropriate path or direction'. Nevertheless, as argued by Rhodes (2005: 5), some of 'the most fascinating puzzles may be found at the boundaries of governing modes, both old and new, where they overlap, merge into one another and develop hybrid forms'. Indeed, further comparative empirical research may likely assist the improved categorisation of governance types. In one sense, therefore, the provision of typologies of governance, as with the theories of behavioural change discussed in the previous chapter, provide only a partial understanding of the possibilities of intervention success and need to be understood within their particular political and socio-economic context.

Yet as with the need for greater clarity on concepts of behavioural change identified in Chapter 2, this chapter also highlights the importance of accuracy and consistency in addressing key concepts in tourism as well as ensuring that they are used in a manner that allows for comparison. The value of clear construction of categorical variables is that it also allows for an assessment of change over time at various scales of assessment. This includes the overall semantic domain of governance as well as the utilisation of specific policy instruments and behavioural interventions.

There has been a strong focus on various elements of network governance in tourism since the late 1990s (Scott, Cooper and Baggio 2008), but other dimensions of policy networks, such as policy communities and sub-governments, have not received the same level of attention as it does in environmental (Folke *et al.* 2005) or economic policy (Jessop 1998; Bradford 2003). Although there are some notable exceptions (Hall 1999, 2008a; Pforr 2005; Dredge 2006b; Beaumont and Dredge 2010), the general focus on instruments such as collaboration and partnership in tourism networks at the expense of critically understanding how governance is conceptualised or imagined, and therefore why a governance approach is used when alternatives are ignored, means that the capacity to understand tourism governance as well as contribute to broader debates on governance and intervention has been substantially limited. In addition, key issues in the promotion of the virtues of certain governance frames, such as market governance and public–private partnerships with respect to the application of democratic values, have also not been addressed. In many countries the public administration of tourism has been transformed from a hierarchical governance position that was intended to serve a public interest to market-like organisations of service delivery with very strong links to industry stakeholders. To paraphrase Pierre (2009), if tourism governance is being reinvented does democratic governance also require change? Indeed, a fundamental question of any intervention should be: whose interests is it designed to serve? As Rothschild (1999: 34) commented: 'All societies attempt to manage the behavior of their citizens at some level, the question now is not whether to manage public health and social issue behavior but rather how to do so appropriately'.

This chapter has stressed that behavioural interventions as instruments of governance need to be understood as occurring within particular frames or images of governance rather than in isolation. Such an approach emphasises the critical importance of understanding that policies imply theories and that, for improved understanding of behavioural intervention processes and outcomes, the empirical should not be divorced from the theoretical.

Further reading and websites

Some useful readings with respect to the growing role of social marketing as a component of governance include:

Bell, S., Hindmoor, A. and Mols, F. (2010) 'Persuasion as governance: A state-centric relational perspective', *Public Administration*, 88(3): 851–870.
Kaplan, A. M. and Haenlein, M. (2009) 'The increasing importance of public marketing: Explanations, applications and limits of marketing within public administration', *European Management Journal*, 27(3): 197–212.

With respect to tourism and governance see:

Bramwell, B. and Lane, B. (2011) 'Critical research on the governance of tourism and sustainability', *Journal of Sustainable Tourism*, 19(4-5): 411–421.
Hall, C. M. (2011) 'A typology of governance and its implications for tourism policy analysis', *Journal of Sustainable Tourism*, 19(4-5): 437–457 (this article also applies some of the frameworks used in this chapter to the specific case of the Convention of Biological Diversity).

For business perspectives on public–private partnerships and the role they can play in cause-related and social marketing see:

Business in the Community (UK): www.bitc.org.uk
Centre on Philanthropy (Bermuda): www.centreonphilanthropy.com
The Philanthropy Roundtable (USA): www.philanthropyroundtable.org

BOX 3.6 WHAT IS YOUR PERSPECTIVE ON THE RELATIVE RIGHTS OF THE INDIVIDUAL AND THE STATE?

As this chapter has highlighted one of the major implications of issues of governance in social marketing is the relative balance between the rights of the individual and the rights of the state with respect to behavioural interventions. Importantly, how you see those rights will not be consistent across all issues or types of interventions. Given the contestation and disagreement that can surround individual rights, reflect on your attitudes towards the following policy options and consider the factors that influence your response.

It is 2020 and continued growth in tourism has meant that it is now one of the largest contributors to greenhouse gas (GHG) emissions at a global and national scale. Scientific research has shown that a 20 per cent increase in the cost of flights would ensure that the aviation sector would become carbon neutral and begin to reduce its emissions. Without such a change it is expected that:

1   In order to reduce the effects of tourism's contribution to greenhouse gas emissions the government announce that they will establish a voluntary 20 per cent carbon surcharge on all flights to be paid by the customer at the time of ticket purchase and announce that all monies raised will go into general revenues.
2   In order to reduce the effects of tourism's contribution to greenhouse gas emissions the government announce that they will establish a voluntary 20 per cent carbon surcharge on all flights to be paid by the customer at the time of ticket purchase and announce that all monies raised will go into a separate fund that will be used for carbon savings and improved energy efficiencies in the aviation and tourism sector.
3   In order to reduce the effects of tourism's contribution to greenhouse gas emissions the government announce that they will impose a compulsory 20 per cent carbon surcharge on all flights to be paid by the customer at the time of ticket purchase and announce that all monies raised will go into general revenues.
4   In order to reduce the effects of tourism's contribution to greenhouse gas emissions the government announce that they will impose a compulsory 20 per cent carbon surcharge on all flights to be paid by the customer at the time of ticket purchase and announce that all monies raised will go into a separate fund that will be used for carbon savings and improved energy efficiencies in the aviation and tourism sector.

4

THE PROCESS OF
SOCIAL MARKETING

Chapter 4 develops an idealised social marketing process in relation to the five Ps of social marketing (in the social marketing literature politics is usually referred to as the fifth 'P'). In brief the stages of the process are:

- define problem;
- conduct marketing research;
- segment and target market;
- establish goals/objectives for intervention and/or programme;
- design appropriate marketing strategy that includes consideration of the five Ps: product (service), price, place, promotion and politics;
- implement and monitor intervention programme;
- evaluate the programme;
- start again! (re)define problem.

Each of these stages are discussed in detail using examples. It is stressed that this is the idealised process with the reality being that many stages or elements, particularly with respect to monitoring and evaluation, are often conflated or left out because of time, cost, politics or approach.

The social marketing process

As with commercial marketing social marketing is still substantially founded on concepts of exchange and competition (Henley *et al*. 2011; Andreasen 2012). However, 'nonprofit and social marketing comprise not minor applications of commercial concepts and tools but rather the most complex of cases; commercial marketing is the special, narrower application' (Andreasen 2012: 37).

Social marketing extends the exchange concept of commercial marketing by framing social marketing as the voluntary exchange of behavioural change in the target audience for direct and indirect benefits to that audience. The costs associated with behavioural change can therefore take a number of forms, not only monetary but also such things as forms of pleasure and status among peer groups. Ultimately, the perceived benefits of the new behaviour must outweigh the perceived costs in order for people to try it. In order to do that focus may be put on

- increasing and highlighting the benefits to the target audience;
- decreasing or de-emphasising the barriers to the adoption of new behaviours;
- changing the product, place, price or promotion to meet the exchange.

The competition concept in social marketing means that the new behaviour being offered to the target audience is competing with existing behaviours and/or other potential new behaviours that could be adopted.

> [B]ehavioral change is the process of altering, maintaining or encouraging the cessation of a specific activity undertaken by the *targeted audience*. Behavioral change is achieved through the creation, communication, delivery and exchange of a competitive *social marketing offer* that induces voluntary change in the targeted audience, and which results in *benefit* to the social change campaign's recipients, partners and the broader society at large.
>
> (Dann 2010: 151) (emphasis in original)

The offer to the target audience may therefore be used to make competing behaviours less attractive, for example in terms of economic or time cost, or with respect to their social acceptability or status. Other upstream approaches may also seek to make the behavioural opportunities less available.

Figure 4.1 illustrates some of the elements and stages of the social marketing process. The model draws substantially on the approach of the Turning Point Social Marketing National Excellence Collaborative (Turning Point) (2002, 2007), which was an initiative to improve public health practices in the United States (Padgett *et al.* 2005; Pirani and Reizes 2005; Newton-Ward 2007), but shares similarities with many authors' representations of the framing of the stages of the social marketing process (Table 4.1).

BOX 4.1 THE IMPORTANCE OF EXCHANGE

Social marketing aims to develop products, services and messages that provide people with an exchange they will value. This concept is extremely important in wanting to achieve sustainable behaviour change. Merritt *et al.* (2011) compared the success of two different behavioural change campaigns.

The UK government, in line with World Health Organization guidance, recommended an intake of at least five portions of fruit or vegetables per person per day under the Department of Health's five-a-day initiative. Hazel Blears, then minister for public health in 2003 when the campaign was launched, said: 'The evidence shows that eating at least five portions of fruit and vegetables each day could help prevent up to 20% of deaths from our nation's biggest killers such as heart disease and some cancers'. However, despite the investment in the five-a-day message, the campaign has failed to have a positive impact on people's actual behaviour. In 2008 UK consumers ate one per cent more fruit compared with the previous five-year average, but vegetable consumption had fallen by 11 per cent. According to Merritt *et al.* (2011):

So, what was the actual exchange being offered? If you want to achieve sustainable behaviour change, success lies in understanding your consumer and then using this understanding to offer them an exchange they will value. The exchange offered by the five-a-day campaign focused mainly on long-term benefits, as opposed to both short- and long-term benefits, which are more valued by the target audience.

They contrasted the five-a-day campaign with a social marketing programme that was launched in the USA at around the same time. Chesapeake Bay is the largest estuary in the USA but a rapidly growing population in the surrounding areas had contributed to increased pollution of the bay, often in the form of agricultural chemicals from sewage and lawn fertiliser run-off. Although regulation had meant a reduction in pollution levels by the local industry, environmental campaigning had failed to achieve any sustainable behaviour change from the residents of the bay and the wider area. A social marketing approach was taken to find a way to motivate them into action and a suitable exchange was needed in order to get around resident scepticism and inertia.

The focus of the exchange proposition became the blue crab, a seafood favourite, which was found to be under threat from the pollution because of habitat change. Local residents were therefore asked to change their behaviour by viewing fertiliser run-off as a culinary rather than an environmental problem. The focus was not to stop people from fertilising their lawns altogether but to persuade them to fertilise in the autumn instead of spring, when heavy rains washed fertiliser into the bay. A humorous, 'Save the crabs, then eat 'em!' campaign ran in the media that promoted how residents could go about looking after their lawns in a more effective way as well as look after the bay overall. This was run under the guidance of the Chesapeake Club and initiative of the Chesapeake Bay Program, a regional partnership of federal and state agencies, local governments, non-profit organisations and academic institutions. After the intervention, there was increased awareness of lawn-care behaviours that contribute to pollution, and a corresponding decrease in intent to fertilise in the spring. As Merritt *et al.* (2011) conclude:

> This is a great example of how social marketing was able to identify an exchange that changed the behaviour of people jaded by decades of message-based appeals.

Whether consciously or not, people analyse costs and benefits at some level before they decide to act. By taking a social marketing approach and developing an exchange, you can ensure that the benefits offered are ones your audience value.

- Chesapeake Bay Program: www.chesapeakebay.net/
- The Chesapeake Club: www.chesapeakeclub.org/index.shtml
- Merritt *et al.* (2011) Social marketing can help achieve sustainable behaviour change: www.guardian.co.uk/sustainable-business/blog/social-marketing-behaviour-change?

However, the model highlights that social marketing interventions do not occur in isolation and there are significant internal and external influences on social marketing *throughout* an intervention programme. This can include the ongoing pressures on change agencies from politicians and lobby groups as well as the role of theory, including some of the theories of behavioural change discussed in Chapter 2, together with the craft experiences of social marketing practitioners from previous interventions.

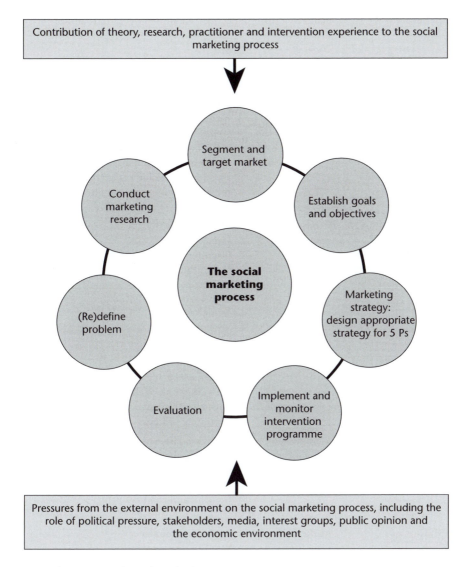

Contribution of theory, research, practitioner and intervention experience to the social marketing process

Segment and target market

Conduct marketing research

Establish goals and objectives

The social marketing process

Marketing strategy: design appropriate strategy for 5 Ps

(Re)define problem

Implement and monitor intervention programme

Evaluation

Pressures from the external environment on the social marketing process, including the role of political pressure, stakeholders, media, interest groups, public opinion and the economic environment

FIGURE 4.1 The process of social marketing

Defining the problem

One of the greatest problems in any behavioural intervention is in defining the problem! Problem definition is important because the process aims to develop goals and objectives for any intervention programme and develop initial understandings of the nature of the intervention that could reduce the problem and identify relevant target audiences. Problem definition is itself influenced by a number of significant factors and stakeholders including governmental priorities and policies, public and stakeholder interest and concerns, the emergence of new data and knowledge with respect to behavioural interventions and the externalities of behaviours, and the priorities of change agencies. Problem selection and agenda setting is not a fully

TABLE 4.1 Stages of the social marketing planning process identified by various authors

Author	Date published	Name of framework	Stages
CDC/ Roper	1993	CDC framework for health communication	1. Review background information 2. Set communication objectives 3. Analyse and segment target audiences 4. Identify message concepts and pre-test 5. Select communication channels 6. Create messages and materials and pre-test 7. Develop promotion plan 8. Implement communication strategies 9. Assess effect 10. Feedback (loop back to step 1)
Andreasen	1995	Strategic marketing stages	1. Listening 2. Planning 3. Structuring 4. Pre-testing 5. Implementing 6. Monitoring
Kassirer and McKenzie-Mohr	1998	Tools of change	1. Setting objectives 2. Developing partners 3. Getting informed 4. Targeting the audience 5. Choosing tools of change 6. Financing the programme 7. Measuring achievements
McKenzie-Mohr and Smith	1999	Community-based social marketing	1. Identifying barriers and benefits 2. Designing strategies and interventions (based on behavioural change tools) 3. Pilot-testing 4. Implementing and evaluating
Kotler, Roberto and Lee	2002	Strategic marketing planning process	1. Analyse the environment 2. Select target audiences 3. Set objectives and goals 4. Deepen understanding of the target audiences and competition 5. Develop strategies 6. Develop a plan for evaluation and monitoring 7. Establish budgets and find funding sources 8. Complete an implementation plan and sustain behaviour
Andreasen	2006	The social marketing process	1. Listening 2. Planning 3. Pre-testing 4. Implementing 5. Monitoring 6. Revising (Loop back to step 1 or 2)

Author	Date published	Name of framework	Stages
National Social Marketing Centre	2006	Total process planning model	1. Scope 2. Develop 3. Implement 4. Evaluate 5. Follow-up
Turning Point	2007	Six phases of social marketing	1. Describe the problem 2. Conduct the market research 3. Create the marketing strategy 4. Plan the intervention 5. Plan programme monitoring and evaluation 6. Implement interventions and evaluation
McKenzie-Mohr	2011	Community-based social marketing	1. Selecting behaviours 2. Identifying barriers and benefits 3. Developing strategies 4. Conducting a pilot 5. Broad scale implementation

rational process and is often affected by political considerations (Bernier and Clavier 2011) and the issue-attention cycle. As Shove (2010: 1283) observes, 'policy makers are highly selective in the models of change on which they draw, and ... their tastes in social theory are anything but random. An emphasis on individual choice has significant political advantage'. Nevertheless, in some cases there may also be positive advantages in involving the audiences or communities that are being asked to change to be actively involved in the problem definition process so that they have more ownership of the social marketing process (Pettibone *et al.* 2013).

Conduct marketing research

An intermediate step between problem definition and segmentation of the target market is a market research process that seeks to gain information on potential target audiences. In some cases this stage may not occur because a clear target audience has already been identified as part of the problem definition process. However, in many cases where there is a lack of specific existing knowledge there is a need to gain information about the behaviours of particular populations, sometimes including the population as a whole, before developing more focused strategies. For example, as part of the development of a sustainable consumption strategy for the UK, the Sustainable Consumption Roundtable (SCR) (2006a: 9) already recognised that

> Fewer than one in three people have heard of the term 'sustainable development'; and qualitative studies suggest that very few, even of these, can explain what it means ... So [in trying to encourage more sustainable behaviours] it makes sense to start from how people understand their own lives, and the connections to the world around them.

In order to do this the SCR

> used the research technique of a structured, deliberative Consumer Forum. We commissioned Opinion Leader Research (OLR) to run an event in which over a hundred people, from all walks of life, deliberated on their aspirations and how these fitted with ideas of policies to encourage more sustainable consumption. In designing this, and learning from it, we also drew on a previous pilot event run by Defra, as well as qualitative and quantitative work by Brook Lyndhurst, MORI and others on public attitudes on the environment
> (Sustainable Consumption Roundtable 2006a: 9)

The result of this more general research was extremely useful for later strategy development with one finding being: 'In a world of information overload, it is not more information campaigns or leaflets that are needed' (Sustainable Consumption Roundtable 2006a: 9).

In many cases this stage will also be based on existing research that seeks not to 'reinvent the wheel'. However, the direct applicability of existing research, especially from other countries and cultures, to the problems faced in a domestic context always needs to be carefully considered, although examples of interventions may provide insights into strategies that could be applied locally. An important component of this stage is the conduct of a situation analysis that should include not only an understanding of the behavioural change issue and what the organisation is capable of providing within a marketing context, e.g. an internal analysis, but should also include an external analysis that places changes in the external environment in marketing terms, especially with respect to key stakeholder groups, such as visitors in the case of tourism (Hall and McArthur 1998).

One of the most commonly used tools in a situation analysis is a SWOT analysis of internal strengths and weaknesses and the opportunities and threats that exist in the external environment (Turning Point 2002). However, while a SWOT analysis is a useful tool, it is often misapplied because part of its value is to identify and rank the critical factors and influences on an organisation following the conduct of relevant research and analysis.

The purpose of the internal analysis is to determine an organisation's capabilities and ability to respond to external threats and opportunities. The purpose of the external analysis is to determine the uncontrollable factors that impact an organisation but which need to be identified and understood.

According to Turning Point (2007: 8) some important questions that can be asked at this stage include:

- What most distinguishes between key audience segments?
- Which target audiences appear most ready to change? Why?
- What benefits and barriers do target audiences ascribe to the desired and competing behaviours?
- What appear to be attractive exchanges for the respective audience segments?

Such questions not only provide a framework for consideration of potential target segments and associated behaviours but also for the allocation of resources. Indeed, a key issue for any change agency with a finite budget will be how to maximise their expenditure in relation to behaviour change. Change agencies therefore have to weigh up whether to target those who are most likely to change behaviours (a low-hanging fruit approach) versus those who are engaging in the most serious behaviours, but who are the ones that most need to change.

Segment and target market

Market or audience segmentation aims to define homogeneous sub-groups of a population for (1) product and message design purposes and (2) identification of similar behaviours. As Tunbridge and Ashworth (1996: 23) observed with respect to the development of dissonance in heritage management: 'Tensions arise through a failure to appreciate the existence of a segmented market, failure to target its diverse segments, or more usually a failure of the targeting strategies themselves to penetrate their intended markets'.

The basic idea of segmentation is straightforward: divide a population into groups whose members are more like each other than members of other segments. For example, a tourist market segment could be identified by grouping together all those potential visitors with similar motivations and/or propensities towards particular types of attractions, products, visitor experiences or behaviours. Segments must be definable, mutually exclusive, measurable, accessible, relevant to an intervention's aims and objectives, reachable with communications in a cost-effective way, and large enough to satisfy the change agency's objectives (Walsh *et al.* 2010). Change agencies should define their market segments and consumer expectations by finding answers to three questions:

- Who is being satisfied (which stakeholder/visitor/consumer segments)?
- What is being satisfied (which stakeholder/visitor/consumer expectations)?
- How are stakeholder/visitor/consumer needs being satisfied (by what communication and media technologies)?

Segments may be identified along several lines including:

- *Geographical segmentation*: In the case of tourism change agencies should know how many people there are in the 'catchment region' of destinations and what distances people are away from sites in terms of different public and private modes of transport.
- *Demographic segmentation*: Markets may be segmented along the lines of such variables as age, sex, occupation, level of income, ethnic association, religion, level of education and class.
- *Psychographic segmentation*: Markets may be identified in terms of people's motivations and self-images.
- *Behavioural segmentation*: Markets may be based on criteria such as responsiveness/ease of behavioural change; the size and impact of the behavioural change; and/or the need to change.
- *Benefit segmentation*: Markets can be identified by the particular product characteristics they prefer, such as a particular type of visitor experience or activity.
- *Media segmentation*: For some programmes the media channel(s) that the target market utilise may be the most cost-effective segmentation method.

The behaviour of market segments can usually be best understood when inferred variables (e.g. motivations, expectations and attitudes) that are measured by questioning members of a population (e.g., visitors or potential visitors) directly are used rather than objective variables that can be measured from secondary sources (e.g. demographic, geographic and socio-economic factors and previous travel, visitation and purchase patterns). However, although inferred variables are more effective in segmentation, social marketing managers often use objective measures because they are more available, less expensive to gather and reduce the costs of media and interpersonal communication needed to reach the target segment (Bowes 1997; Lefebvre and Rochlin 1997; Kazbare *et al.* 2010; Pieniak *et al.* 2010; Cini *et al.* 2012).

Establish goals and objectives

The development of appropriate goals and objectives is critical in social marketing and provides the framework for the achievement of stakeholder satisfaction. To put it bluntly, to be effective, marketers most know what they have to accomplish. Most fundamentally, change agencies must set and use measurable and actionable goals and objectives to guide the intervention and its implementation and evaluation. Table 4.2 outlines the way in which marketing performance objectives can be directed in the context of national parks and natural heritage management (Hall and McArthur 1998). Goals and objectives should ideally be formulated through the involvement of all relevant staff with due consideration of the results of the situation analysis and, where appropriate, input from relevant stakeholder groups. Opportunities and issues arising from the situation analysis should be prioritised by the type of marketing action required, the decision level required to implement such actions, and the long and short-term effects of actions on the behaviours of the target audience(s), as well as associated physical and human resources of the change agency. This will enable managers to identify what can be achieved, within an appropriate time span, and the costs and benefits of specific marketing actions. This is something that is especially important at a time when there may be budget and funding restrictions put in place for social marketing activities (Box 4.2 indicates the conclusions of the Chartered Institute of Marketing's [2011] study into the implications of UK government cutbacks on governmental social marketing and how the marketing community should respond).

BOX 4.2 RESPONSES TO CUTBACKS IN FUNDING FOR MARKETING IN THE UK CENTRAL GOVERNMENT

Government marketing:

- Have a clear evidence base that there is a role for marketing.
- See situations from the point of view of the individual.
- Where appropriate, avoid making messages appear to come directly from a government or establishment source. Some campaigns have been successful because their messages do not seem to come directly or exclusively from government.
- A portal (via Facebook and equivalents) where citizens can access information about government marketing that gives evidence of its value.
- Communicate internally and externally the figures that show that cutting government marketing is a false economy.

- Where possible, logos and designs to be completed in-house to avoid media criticism of wasteful spending.
- Ensure clear objectives are put in place at the start of each campaign and that these objectives are achievable, relevant and desirable.
- Monitor the objectives during and after campaigns.

Behaviour change marketing:

- Identify key motivators and barriers to provide insight into the role of marketing.
- Positive messages can succeed more than negative ones – provide rewards or incentives where possible, instead of punishments, within the remit of the legislative background.
- Promote the benefits as well as the risks of certain behaviours.
- Personalisation where possible leads to the fullest understanding of motivators and barriers to behavioural change.
- Where personalisation is not possible, then use segmentation.
- Promote not making a change seem too much like hard work.
- Target the right audience by using messages they understand.
- Tell a story, and make it personal.

Marketing outside behavioural change:

- Market the marketers: where possible, give consistent and continual evidence that marketing generates savings or quantifiable benefits to society, not additional costs.

Source: adapted from the Chartered Institute of Marketing (2011): 43–44.
The Chartered Institute of Marketing: www.cim.co.uk/Home.aspx

TABLE 4.2 Direction of marketing performance objectives

Direction	Example
Market penetration • Existing products in existing markets	Maintaining or increasing the level of visitation to a national park without attracting new visitors or changing the experience through, for example, encouraging visitors to return and see the park again
New product development • New products in existing markets	Encourage repeat visitation within the existing set of visitors by developing new experiences through, for example, new interpretation, tours or special events
Market development • Existing products in new markets	Promoting the existing range of visitor experiences to appeal to new audiences by, for example, ensuring that promotional material is specifically prepared and targeted to the intended audience
Diversification • New products in new markets	Develop and promote new natural heritage interpretive experiences for a new audience, e.g., by developing a children's nature trail on a site where previously none existed

Source: After Hall and McArthur (1998)

Marketing strategy

Having established a set of social marketing objectives for the intervention it is essential to determine how these objectives can be achieved. This requires a review of the identified target audience and behaviour as well as the sought behavioural change. This helps ensure the soundness and feasibility of the goals as well as ensuring that there are sufficient resources to achieve them (Turning Point 2007). The identification of potential barriers to the successful development of an intervention is extremely important. As McKenzie-Mohr (2005: 20) commented:

> Significant pressures, such as time and staffing constraints, and increased project costs often result in this first step, the identification of barriers, being skipped. While these pressures are real and important, failure to identify barriers and benefits will often result in a program that either has a diminished impact or no impact at all.

Marketing strategies can broadly be categorised into two main types: marketing mix strategies and positioning strategies. Marketing mix strategies refer to strategic decisions concerned with products, prices, distribution and marketing communication. Positioning strategies refers to finding ways to effectively position the organisation, programme or intervention against its competitors to create and maintain a sustainable advantage.

Marketing mix strategies

The design of an appropriate social marketing mix strategy for interventions consists of analysing market opportunities, identifying and targeting market segments, and developing an appropriate market mix for each segment. The traditional 'four Ps' of the marketing mix are:

- *Product*/service characteristics: the product, image, packaging and the experience. In tourism the intangible and perishable nature of tourism services being especially important because of the centrality of the experience with respect to the visitor market.
- *Promotional* decisions concerning channels and messages: also referred to as the promotional mix or the marketing communication mix, this refers to such things as advertising, sales promotion and public and media relations.
- *Price* of the products/services: the value of the product, service and/or behaviour, which can also be understood in terms of the cost of behavioural change to the targets of some behavioural changes. This is not just financial cost, but also time, effort, lifestyle and psychological cost (Turning Point 2002).
- *Places* and methods of distribution of products/services: the availability of the product and services, including their image, location and accessibility. It also includes intermediaries, such as agents, wholesalers and retailers, who then sell to the consumer. Decisions have to be made with respect to not only how long the chain of distribution will be to the market but also the extent to which change agencies have control over distribution and their product. In social marketing a selective distribution strategy tends to be supported because of the degree of control it provides with respect to being able to influence consumption behaviours.

Although the '4Ps' approach to social marketing has been criticised for being outdated because of its supposed lack of attention to relationality and co-creation (Gordon 2012), it is still one of the most common ways of thinking about social marketing strategies. Gordon (2012), for example, proposes a social marketing mix consisting of:

- *Circumstance* – The social and structural environment within which the consumer is located, which is influenced by political agendas, social norms, the media and other external environmental factors.
- *Organisation and competition* – The structure of and relationships between the stakeholders delivering interventions as well as competing stakeholders. This element of the proposed mix also includes goals and objectives, behavioural competition and the policy agenda.
- *Costs* – These are the various costs, including financial costs, opportunity costs, time costs and social costs, associated with behavioural change as well as the cost of non-behavioural change.
- *Processes* – This element includes theory and design, relational thinking, consumer orientation, strategic and holistic dimensions, long-term processes, co-creation, value-drivers and stakeholder and community engagement.
- *Channels and strategies* – Including product, price, place, promotion, people, policy, advocacy, lobbying, public and media relations and information provision.

These five elements then all interact with the *consumer* through a process that is meant to be consumer oriented, community and/or participant owned, co-created, and research and evaluation driven (Gordon 2012). Undoubtedly many of these elements are present in the approach discussed in this chapter and issues of relationality and transformation are also discussed elsewhere in the social marketing literature (e.g. Waters *et al.* 2011; Lefebvre 2012).

In addition to the traditional four Ps of marketing, other Ps have been suggested. Given the contested terrain of much social marketing a fifth P is often recognised in the form of politics, including another P of public opinion (Jones 1982; Geller 1989; Andreasen 2006; Raftopoulou and Hogg 2010). Although the model used here explicitly recognises the role of political pressures throughout the social marketing process, it is nevertheless useful to highlight the role of politics in the definition of social marketing issues as well as the formulation, implementation and evaluation of interventions. This also reflects the role of governance issues and the extent to which different philosophies of governance are connected to preferences for different forms of intervention and not others (see Chapter 3).

Tourism researchers such as Feng and Morrison (2002) also suggest another four Ps that may be held as relevant to tourism marketing: people, programming, partnership and packaging.

- The *people* dimension refers primarily to the role of staff in providing experiences and assisting in the delivery of interventions. This personal dimension may be extremely important where personal contact influences behaviour change, for example via the role of interpretation in national parks and ecotourism (Atkinson and Mullins 1998; Kohl 2005; Smith *et al.* 2008). In the case of community-based tourism and social marketing the people dimension can also refer to the activities of communities in shaping the destination or attraction product (see also Chapter 8).

- *Programming* refers to the variation of service or product in order to change the behaviours of the target audience; this may include increasing consumer spending on particular services or influencing visitor behaviour in a heritage site so as to reduce impact. For example, many gallery or museum exhibitions will include a programme of events in order to vary the nature of the experience that a visitor will have at an exhibition. Interestingly, the potential significance of programming to social marketing was identified in the seminal Kotler and Zaltman (1971) article and has been frequently referred to in the social marketing literature (e.g. Glider *et al.* 2001; Marcel *et al.* 2004).

- *Partnership* refers to the cooperation that often develops between different organisations in the pursuit of behavioural interventions and the mutual or shared benefits that may result (Hastings 2003). Sponsorship may be seen as a form of partnership in which the change agency and the sponsors seek a range of benefits from the sponsorship arrangement (see Chapter 3 for a discussion on this in the context of changing notions of governance). Strategic alliances occur when two or more sometimes competing organisations collaborate to achieve common objectives (Mendleson and Polonsky 1995; Prakash 2002; Wymer and Samu 2003). For example, environmental organisations may engage in joint promotion with tourist firms in order to draw more visitors to nature-based tourism destinations in order raise funds for conservation purposes (Bhattacharya *et al.* 2009). The growth of partnerships becomes even more likely at times of economic constraint or changes in funding policy by government. Nevertheless, as the previous chapter indicated, the growth of public–private partnerships along with alliances between environmental and social change groups with corporations is often open to criticism in social marketing terms, for although it may allow interventions that deal with downstream behaviours in the short-term it may have little or no upstream effects. Furthermore, in the health policy arena Eagle *et al.* (2011) suggested that many government policy documents treat public–private partnerships aimed at addressing behaviours seen as contrary to individual or societal health and well-being as not only central to achieving government policy, but also as unproblematic. They examined alcohol moderation promotion, something of great significance to the hospitality industry, and argued that greater clarification is needed in terms of roles and responsibilities for all stakeholders involved in partnerships. Not only is there evidence to challenge the assumed effectiveness of communication and social strategies, but 'boomerang' effects suggest that this activity may even be counter-productive.

- *Packaging* is the combination of related and complimentary services within a single price offering and is widely used in social marketing offerings (Hastings 2007). For example, packaging strategies may be used in the reduction of consumption behaviours and reducing emissions by making public transport more attractive than private transport (Peattie and Peattie 2009).

In tourism the notion of place also takes on another dimension that is more important in tourism than in other areas of marketing. This is not just because place is an intrinsic part of tourism promotion but because tourists that may be the target of interventions are mobile. Therefore a key question in tourism-related behavioural change becomes whereabouts in the stages of a trip should intervention occur?

Figure 4.2 indicates the various geographical, psychological and industrial dimensions of a tourism system (Hall 2005b). Each of the stages has different psychological elements for travellers (although not explicitly stated this also includes the social dimensions of decision-making and travel that are undertaken in conjunction with friends and/or family), for members of destination, transit and return communities, as well as for the tourism workforce. In addition, the elements of the tourism industry that the traveller encounters will be different at each stage. Social marketing operates at each of these stages and with all these groups. Although tourists are often the target of behavioural change interventions, so too are destination communities (i.e. encouragement to be welcoming to tourists) and workers (i.e. service improvement campaigns). The industry is also the subject of social marketing campaigns that aim to improve a range of behaviours (i.e. adopting environmental measures). Therefore the complexity of the tourism system highlights the importance of not only ensuring that marketing mix strategies are appropriate but also that they are clearly targeted.

Target marketing

Target marketing is one of the most effective elements of social marketing as it increases programme effectiveness and efficiency by tailoring strategies to address the needs of distinct groups (Grier and Bryant 2005). Andreasen and Kotler (2007) contrasted 'target marketing' (in which an organisation develops products for specific market segments) with 'mass marketing' (in which an organisation develops one product and attempts to get every possible person to use it) and 'product-differentiated marketing' (in which products are designed not so much for different segments but simply to offer alternatives to everyone in the market). Target market identification typically involves three stages. First, a decision regarding how many market segments change agencies wish to target given objectives and the availability of resources, e.g., which market segment(s) will bring the most behavioural benefits? Second, the development of a market profile for each segment. Third, the development of a marketing strategy that is appropriate to the profile of the selected segments.

Some change agencies may select a 'concentrated' strategy by which they focus on a single segment. Indeed, this will be the likely strategy for many cultural heritage sites. However, some heritage attractions, such as national parks, will have a range of environments and, therefore, a range of experiences available to visitors. Therefore, park managers may be able to target a number of visitor segments (a differentiated strategy) each with their own set of expectations, motivations and desired experiences and activities. As Chhabra (2009: 306) notes: 'Regardless of the segmentation approach, the entire process of identifying target markers is aimed to inform and guide appropriate communication strategies so that effective messages can be designed and communicated'.

An influential contribution to the communication of behavioural change is from Kreuter *et al.* (2000) who focused on personal health communication and provided a framework to classify approaches to behavioural change communication by level of assessment and the nature of the content (Figure 4.3). According to Kreuter *et al.* (2000) traditional health education materials were *generic* and did not seek to tailor messages to target segments or individuals and instead assumed that people would sift through materials to find messages relevant to them. This approach reflects Andreasen and Kotler's (2007) attention given to mass marketing approaches. Similarly, *targeted* materials reflect targeted marketing that is focused towards a population subgroup. However, as Kreuter *et al.* (2000: 4) argue, 'targeted materials cannot address naturally occurring variations between individuals on important factors that are not demographic in nature'.

Another targeted approach is direct marketing (see below) that utilises *personalisation*, i.e. using a person's name to draw attention to otherwise generic messages. Something that many

Geographical elements	Psychological elements (Traveller/s)	Psychological elements (Community)	Psychological elements (Labour)	Formal industrial elements
Home/ Generating region →	• Decision to travel • Decision to purchase • Service encounters • Attitudes and behaviours before travel	• WOM effects • Cultural, social and economic distance	• Service encounters • Emotional labour	• Travel agencies/wholesalers • Destination marketing, promotion and imaging
Transit route →	• Travel to destination • Service encounters	• Demonstration effects • Cultural, social and economic distance • Interaction with tourists	• Service encounters • Emotional labour	Transport Transit route infrastructure: • Motels and other accommodation • Highway cafés and restaurants • Service stations • information services
Destination region →	• Behaviour and activities at destination • Interaction with destination community	• Demonstration effects • Cultural, social and economic distance • Interaction with tourists	• Service encounters • Emotional labour	• Tourist accommodation • Restaurants, • Visitor information services • Attractions, • Retailing • Events • Conventions and meetings • Tourism business districts, • Vacation and second homes • Souvenir shops

Transit route

Transport
Transit route infrastructure:
• Motels and other accommodation,
• Highway cafés and restaurants
• Service stations
Ongoing efforts by travel agencies, destination and business within destination to encourage return visits

• Demonstration effects
• Cultural, social and economic distance
• Interaction with tourists

• Service encounters
• Emotional labour

• Travel from destination
• Service encounter

Home/
Generating
region

• Recollection stage
• Attitudes and behaviours on return home
• Potential service encounter

• Reverse demonstration effects
• WOM effects
• Cultural, social and economic distance

• Service encounters
• Emotional labour

Tourism generating region

Travel to destination

Travel from destination

Destination region

Environment

FIGURE 4.2 Geographical, psychological and industrial elements of a tourism system

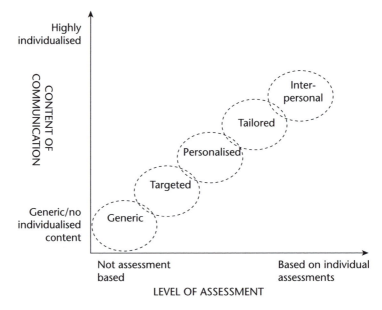

FIGURE 4.3 Approaches to social marketing communication by level of assessment and nature of content

Source: After Kreuter *et al.* (2000)

readers will be familiar with via their junk mail! However, although both targeted and personalised communications base their messages on segmenting characteristics,

> these factors alone provide little information about the health patterns that influence people's [lifestyle and consumption] decisions and actions. As a result, both approaches lack the depth of understanding that is often necessary in order to develop truly individualized strategies to address complex lifestyle behaviours.
>
> (Kreuter *et al.* 2000: 4)

Therefore, Kreuter *et al.* (2000) argued that tailored communication would be a more appropriate strategy. *Tailored* behavioural change materials 'are any combination of information and behavior change strategies intended to reach one specific person, based on characteristics that are unique to that person, related to the outcome of interest, and derived from an individual assessment' (Kreuter *et al.* 2000: 4). This definition highlights the assessment-based and individual focus of tailored communication (Kreuter and Wray 2003) (Figure 4.3). However, as well as assisting in health-related interventions, the approach has significant potential to contribute to wider social-marketing-related behavioural change because of its ability to utilise the Internet and Web 2.0 capacities, such as Twitter and email prompts and messaging, to individualise interventions (Noar *et al.* 2007; Krebs *et al.* 2010; Schneider *et al.* 2013). According to a systematic review and meta-analysis of using the Internet to promote health behaviour change by Webb *et al.* (2010) interventions had a statistically small but significant effect on health-related behaviours. Interestingly, in light of the discussion of theory in Chapter 2, more extensive use of theory was associated with increases in effect size while interventions based on the theory of planned behaviour tended to have substantial effects on behaviour. Interestingly, with respect to social marketing strategies, interventions that incorporated more behaviour change techniques also tended to have larger effects. Importantly, the effectiveness of Internet-based interventions was enhanced by the use of additional methods of communicating with participants, especially the use of short message service (SMS) or text messages (Webb *et al.* 2010).

An even more personalised form of behavioural change intervention is *interpersonal* communication, which refers to the interactive and immediate communication process that occurs between people (Kreuter *et al.* 2000). This approach is utilised within community-based social marketing as it can take advantage of volunteers to persuade and influence the behaviours of targeted individuals. However, such an approach may need to be integrated with other marketing channels and prompts in order to sustain behaviour change over the longer term. Haq *et al.* (2008) reported on the results of a project in York, UK, to foster voluntary travel behavioural change. Using face-to-face discussions, personalised information and incentives, a statistically significant reduction in car use and an increase in cycling and the use of public transport were achieved over a six-month period. However, the change had not been sustained 12 months later (Haq *et al.* 2008).

PLATE 4.1 Changi Airport recycling bins

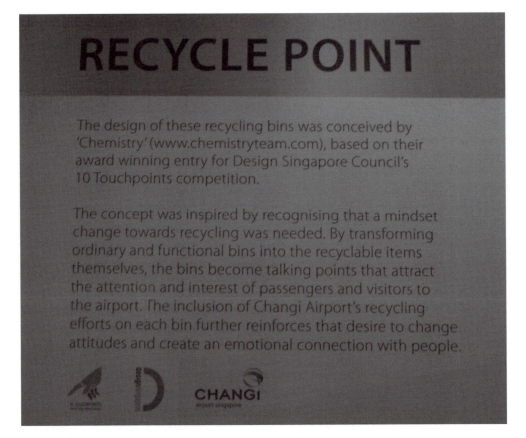

PLATE 4.2 Changi Airport recycling bins' design principles

Positioning strategies

Social marketing strategies also need to consider the positioning of interventions and product offerings in relation to competing experiences in the same target market(s) (Smith 2000). Positioning is the art of developing and communicating meaningful differences between a heritage product's offerings and those of competitors serving the same target market(s) (Andreasen and Kotler 2007). Positioning will therefore usually mean differentiating one product or experience from other potential experiences and products available to a target market in order to encourage behavioural adoptions. For example, in the case of an active leisure campaign Grier and Bryant (2005) report the value of the positioning of physical activity as fun and exciting rather than using a serious, factual description of the health benefits of physical activity in order to encourage uptake. However, in certain cases, it may involve emphasising similarity to a competitor. For example, in the case of natural heritage conservation, if a low-visitation site shares similar attributes to a high-visitation site, management authorities may promote the similarities of the low-visitation site to the more favoured site in the target market in order to shift the impacts of visitation, meet conservation goals and maintain visitor satisfaction levels (Hall and McArthur 1998).

The key to positioning is to identify the key attributes of the target market to select a specific exchange among competitive offerings (Andreasen and Kotler 2007). This requires a clear understanding of the market and what it seeks. A number of positioning alternatives for cultural heritage are outlined in Table 4.3. Ultimately, the goal of a marketing strategy should be to establish an integrated marketing programme, with each of the components of the strategy helping to position interventions in relation to the target market(s) that the change agency chooses to serve, or not, as the case may be.

TABLE 4.3 Positioning alternatives for heritage products

Positioning alternative	Example
Product attribute	
Associate the product with an attribute or feature that may be unique	Many heritage sites will have a degree of uniqueness that often provides one of the reasons for conservation in the first place
Benefit	
Relate the product to a benefit, need or want of a stakeholder or consumer	Positive community relations for a sponsor or educational or self-perception benefits for a visitor
Price/quality	
Value for money	Convey the impression that there will be a very high-quality visitor experience at low cost to the visitor
Use or application	
Uniqueness or significance of heritage products	May possibly apply to the ongoing use of old industrial heritage sites and/or connection to well known products
Type of user of the product	
Relate heritage to a particular lifestyle or desirable personal attribute	Associate visiting an urban gallery, museum or cultural precinct with a cosmopolitan lifestyle
Product class	
Relate heritage to a particular product category	International profile museums or collections
Competition	
Relate to a competitor, although not often used with respect to heritage	Compare a heritage site or a museum with a named well-known site or museum in order to convey a sense of prestige or significance to certain stakeholders

Source: After Hall and McArthur (1998); Chhabra (2009)

Marketing management

The development of marketing strategies with clearly identified target markets and product mix is not the end of the marketing process. Marketing management is the process that allocates the resources of the change agency toward marketing activities. Change agencies therefore have to ensure that marketing strategies can be implemented and the target market reached through the development of appropriate resourcing and communication strategies. Human and financial resources have to be available for the development and promotion of the social marketing product, while new relationships may have to be formed with stakeholder groups that may even include those who behaviour is suggested for change as well as other members of the community (McKenzie-Mohr 2000a, 2011). For every major management action or responsibility that is required to give effect to the marketing strategy, plans of action should be developed that identify the communication and marketing strategy that is to be adopted. The plan of action will outline the required action, tasks, responsibilities, timeline for implementation, cost estimates and relative priority. Therefore, the plan of action becomes a valuable mechanism for ensuring not only the effectiveness of the marketing strategy but also ensuring that it is undertaken in as efficient a manner as possible (Shrum *et al.* 1994; Hall and McArthur 1998; Swinburn *et al.* 2005; Yu and Waller 2010; Knight *et al.* 2011).

Promotional techniques

One of the most important aspects of marketing management is the selection of the appropriate promotional channel by which marketing will connect the product with the customer. There are a number of marketing communication strategies many of which will be familiar to readers, such as advertising, publicity and public relations. Table 4.4 outlines the major forms of marketing communication strategies and their various advantages and disadvantages. All of these techniques can be utilised by change agencies in various ways.

Advertising

Advertising is one of the most commonly used strategies of change agencies. However, while advertising may reach a wide audience, careful consideration may need to be given to the extent to which an advertising campaign will reach the desired market rather than many markets. There are four main decisions to be made with respect to the various media available, i.e. Internet and social networks, newspapers, magazines, television and radio.

- Select the media mix; e.g., what combination, if any, of media do you require?
- Determine the level of target audience reach and frequency; e.g., what proportion of your target audience do you want to receive your message and how often?
- Establish timing and scheduling of the advertising campaign; e.g. how often do you want to advertise over what period?
- Negotiate and purchase media; what's the best deal you can get in terms of the effectiveness you require?

In addition, there are a number of criteria that can be addressed when trying to ascertain the appropriateness and value of any advertisement (Table 4.5).

TABLE 4.4 The advantages and disadvantages of different social marketing communication strategies

Technique	Explanation	Strengths	Weaknesses
Advertising	Paid for advertisements or commercials in the media and on the Internet.	• Low cost per person reached • Ability to create images and perceptions	• Difficult to close sale/exchange • People can easily 'switch off' • Difficult to gauge effectiveness
Direct marketing	Communication to individuals at home or at business via the mail, Internet or personal delivery – a form of advertising.	• Provides quick feedback • Can target markets on a cost-efficient basis	• Direct mail marketing may be treated as junk mail • Direct Internet marketing may be treated as spam
Personal selling	Communication to a target market via personal representation or by telephone. May also utilise the assistance of volunteers, which can be extremely significant for community-based social marketing or online social marketing.	• Can close a sale/exchange • Easier to hold people's attention • Provides immediate feedback • Can establish and maintain customer loyalty	• High cost per person • Images not as strong as advertising
Sales promotion	Short-term incentives to encourage purchase or sale of a product or service. Widely used in non-profit social marketing by organisations such as museums, art galleries and heritage sites to attract visitors at non-peak times.	• Immediate sales response • Can offer low prices for a short period of time without changing longer term pricing strategies • Provides fast feedback on effectiveness • Low-cost wastage	• Extremely short term in regard to market development • Unless well managed may harm image • If used too often customers may shift their purchasing behaviour to accommodate sales promotion
Event marketing	A specialised form of sales promotion.	• Capacity for high profile	• Must be integrated with other strategies in order to ensure long-term effectiveness

Continued

Technique	Explanation	Strengths	Weaknesses
Publicity	Product information disseminated in the main and social media as part of editorial and programme content or blogs and newsgroups respectively (targeted and non-targeted).	• Low cost • Potentially large impact	• Lack of control
Public relations	Communication directed at 'publics' (often corporate or governmental), as well as influencing public opinion.	• Useful for building up stakeholder support	• Long term • Difficult to measure effectiveness • Receivers of message may not be interested in intervention or may respond negatively
Word of mouth	Communication to individuals from people who have either experienced or are in favour of the product. Becomes a directed marketing communication strategy through use of volunteer network. Viral marketing is a form of word of mouth.	• If positive may create substantial interest and stakeholder support • Low cost • Potentially large impact	• If negative may lead to loss of interest • Lack of control

TABLE 4.5 Questions to ask in advertisement evaluation for behavioural change

1	Does the advertisement match the positioning strategy? Is it single-minded?
2	Does the advertisement clearly address its intended target audience? Are the words appropriate?
3	Will the advertisement be strong enough to gain the attention of its target audience? Will the advertisement be distinctive?
4	Will the advertisement develop brand awareness recall, i.e. will they remember your heritage organisation or site?
5	Will the key point/positioning statement be comprehended, i.e. will your intended audience understand what you are trying to convey?
6	Is the emotional factor important? If so, will this advertisement capture the emotions? Is it likeable? Does the picture tell the story? Does it shock?
7	How credible will the advertisement be? That is, will it develop conviction – if this is intended?
8	Will the advertisement be persuasive and lead the target audience to action – that is, to change behaviour or intend to change behaviour?
9	Is the tone appropriate?
10	How will it be received by funders for the change agency, i.e. government or private sponsors?
11	How will it be received by stakeholders, including the wider public?
12	How does the advertisement fit in with the wider intervention strategy, i.e. is it complimentary to other elements of the communication strategy in the short and long term?
13	How does the advertisement 'fit in' with theories of behavioural change, i.e. is it supported by theories of change? (This is always the least-asked question.)

One of the greatest difficulties for social marketing interventions based on advertising is that social marketing campaigns may be ineffective when commercial marketing activities create an environment that encourages and maintains negative externalities such as unhealthy behaviours (Wymer 2010; Szmigin *et al.* 2011; Chandon and Wansink 2012). One response to the advertising congestion that surrounds many issues has been to try and make advertisements more provocative or shocking so as to have impact on the audience. However, the success of such measures has become a source of substantial debate (Hastings *et al.* 2004; Jäger and Eisend 2013). According to Hastings *et al.* (2004: 961), field research suggests that

> Ethical concerns about fear appeals include maladaptive responses such as chronic heightened anxiety among those most at risk and, paradoxically, complacency among those not directly targeted, and increased social inequity between those who respond to fear campaigns, who tend to be better off, and those who do not, who tend to be the less educated and poorer members of society. Alternatives to fear appeals are the use of positive reinforcement appeals aimed at the good behavior, the use of humor, and, for younger audiences, the use of postmodern irony.

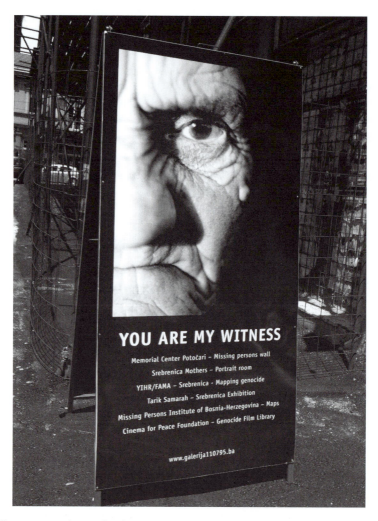

PLATE 4.3 You are my witness, Sarajevo

BOX 4.3 SHOCK ADVERTISING

Shock advertising is advertising that deliberately, rather than inadvertently, startles and offends its audience, and which attempts to surprise an audience by deliberately violating norms of societal values and personal ideals (Dahl *et al.* 2003). This may be done by transgressions of law, religion or custom, e.g. indecent sexual references, obscenity; breaches of a moral or social code, e.g. profanity, vulgarity; or things that offend moral or physical sensibilities, e.g. gratuitous violence. There are of course inherent difficulties in any advertising related to controversial products, services or behaviours (Waller 2005). Just advertising 'unmentionables', such as feminine hygiene products, contraceptives, alcohol and even underwear, can mean that an advertisement is deemed offensive or shocking by some. Indeed, Barnes and Dotson (1990) differentiate between 'offensive products' and 'offensive execution', with shock advertising usually referring to the latter.

There are a number of different types of shock appeals (Dahl *et al.* 2003):

- *Disgusting images* – references to human body parts and functions, as well as health dimensions, harm, death and decay.
- *Sexual references* – reference to full or part nudity, sexual acts.
- *Profanity* – swearing, racism and obscene gestures.
- *Vulgarity* – reference to crude or distasteful acts by humans or animals.
- *Impropriety* – violations of social conventions.
- *Moral offensiveness* – harming innocent people, gratuitous sex and violence, violating standards of fair behaviour, putting children in provocative situations, alluding to people or objects that may encourage violence.
- *Religious taboos* – inappropriate use of religious symbols or reference to rituals and taboos.

Fear appeals are often considered separate to shock advertising papers (Shanahan and Hopkins 2007; Cunningham *et al.* 2010), although it depends on the norms of particular jurisdictions. It is a very common form of advertising in public service campaigns, such as road safety, where messages graphically warn the public about the consequences of speeding (Lewis *et al.* 2007a).

There are significantly different viewpoints on whether shock advertising works. Dahl *et al.* (2003) found that shock advertising increased attention, increased recall and recognition of the advertisements and also found that participants were actually likely to engage in message-relevant behaviour. Vezina and Paul (1997) agree that it increases attention but may negatively impact attitude towards the brand. In contrast, if advertisers use negative images in their adverts it may actually cause consumers to develop a mental link between the negative images and the advertised product, leading consumers to avoid them (Parry *et al.* 2013). Interestingly, although this situation would be extremely negative for commercial organisations, it would actually be ideal for change agencies seeking to encourage voluntary behavioural change.

It is potentially more acceptable for charities to produce shock advertisements than commercial advertisers. The Barnardos charity is well recognised for using shock advertising to highlight their cause to care for vulnerable children and young people. The creative director John O'Keeffe at Bartle Bogle Hegarty, the agency behind some of the controversial Barnardos campaigns, stated: '[T]he things Barnardos deals with on a daily basis are more shocking than anything we could show in advertising. We're justified in at least talking about some of the things' (as cited in Brabbs 2000). Indeed, in Britain support for using 'shock tactics' is highest for charities working in domestic violence (82 per cent), child poverty (78 per cent) and animal cruelty (75 per cent), while there is less support for the use of shock tactic advertising for charities working in the environmental sector (62 per cent) or with physical disability (65 per cent) and mental illness (68 per cent) (Information Daily 2010). Furthermore, 40 per cent took action as a result of seeing a shocking advert, the overwhelming majority of which was positive, such as making a donation (13 per cent) or looking for more information (9 per cent). Furthermore,

20 per cent chatted about the advert to a friend or relative, or even sent the advert to them (2 per cent). Only 2 per cent did something negative, such as cancel donations or make a complaint. Commenting on the results of the research, Naomi Barber, senior research executive in YouGov's Public Sector Consulting team said: 'These results provide interesting reading for a sector which must negotiate ways to get a memorable message across to the public, while being wary of alienating them' (quoted in Information Daily 2010). In slight contrast, Davy (2009) reported that before a shocking marketing campaign on child poverty was undertaken by Barnardos, a third of its respondents were likely to donate in the next six months while 16 per cent were very unlikely to do so. After the shocking Barnardos advert was aired the proportion of respondents that probably would give to Barnardos increased to almost 50 per cent. However, the number of non-donors also increased to 21 per cent.

Response to a shock advertisement is also dependent on culture (Polegato and Bjerke 2009; Frith and Mueller 2010) and gender (Andersson *et al.* 2004). Waller (1999) found that females tended to be more offended than males by alcohol advertisements, while males were more offended by advertisements about male underwear. Waller also found that women are more offended by racist and sexist advertisements, as well as by those advertisements that contained anti-social behaviour and indecent language. Andersson *et al.* (2004) indicated that consumers can also interpret shock advertisement differently to what the advertiser intended. Often shock advertisements are perceived much more shocking and offensive than what they were intended to be and as a result can possibly damage an organisation's reputation or harm an intervention. Shock advertisements can al so cause confusion for consumers as to what the aim of the advertisement is and what the intended message is if the advertisement is not clear enough, while repeat exposure has the potential to reduce shock value (Rossiter and Thornton 2004). Thereby further suggesting that shock advertisements are a tool that need to be used very carefully and within the context of a wider strategic campaign.

Direct marketing

Direct marketing is a form of advertising that has become increasingly important. The most common forms of direct marketing utilised in social marketing are direct mail (postal and non-postal), telemarketing (telephone inbound and outbound), newspaper and magazine inserts, and Internet campaigns. Direct marketing provides an opportunity for an organisation to directly convey their message to an intended market and is therefore potentially more cost effective than general advertising (Dorsey 2010; Grier and Kumanyika 2010; Shaw *et al.* 2012), although there is potential for considerable clutter as the result of spam and junk mail. Nevertheless, the development of marketing databases together with new information technologies has provided a strong platform for more effective direct marketing for behavioural change purposes.

Personal selling

Personal selling is a selective form of communication, designed to be informative, persuasive or to foster a relationship, which permits the tailoring of a message to the specific needs of an individual buyer or buying influence. It has historically been one of the least used forms of marketing communication for behavioural change, although it has become increasingly important as a result of the growth of community-based social marketing and interventions (Keller *et al.* 2012), when one-on-one selling is included in the social marketing strategy to sell the idea of behavioural change through influential advocates (Bailey *et al.* 2010; Henley *et al.* 2011).

Sales promotion

Sales promotion is the function in marketing of providing inducements to purchase or exchange, offered for a limited time only, at the time and place the purchasing or exchange decision is made, which are supplementary to a product's normal value. In other words, sales promotion is a form of special offers. Examples of sales promotion include reduced prices for certain periods of time for a non-profit attraction in order to modify visitor behaviour, or a joint campaign between a museum and a sponsor to provide free entry to an exhibition following purchase of a sponsor's product. Indeed, both sales promotions and sponsorship are regarded as important dimensions of cause-related marketing (Bhattacharya *et al.* 2009; Westberg and Pope 2012).

By virtue of the fact that events are of limited duration, event marketing can be regarded as a special form of sales promotion. Examples of event marketing that have a social marketing or behavioural change component include: the hosting of festivals and fairs at a heritage site in order to boost visitation and awareness of the site (Hall and McArthur 1998); the use of music festivals and sports events to promote social marketing messages (Bell and Blakey 2010; Ferrand and Stotlar 2010); and the development of more sustainable events (Tinnish and Mangal 2012).

Publicity and public relations

Publicity and public relations are two related aspects of marketing communication that have long been a component of change agencies, although often their purpose within the wider strategic marketing context has not been fully appreciated (Buchthal *et al.* 2011; Evans-Lacko *et al.* 2013). Publicity can include such things as editorial information, entertainment, events and sponsorships, personal appearances by major figures or personalities, educational efforts, and the dissemination of information through controlled media, i.e. membership newsletters and magazines, as well as uncontrolled media. Public relations is the dissemination of information to audiences that may not be potential buyers or users of the product or service at all. Public relations is therefore used to create an overall climate of support from stakeholders and decision makers for organisational and behavioural change objectives, whereas publicity may create a much wider awareness (Athey *et al.* 2012).

In research on post-disaster public campaigns after Hurricane Katrina, Raggio and Folse (2011) suggested that it is not only appropriate, but also beneficial, in the wake of a major disaster, for governments to spend public funds to support official gratitude campaigns in response to outside assistance. Their evidence demonstrated increased consumer willingness to purchase products produced in the area and intentions to continue pro-social support through volunteerism and financial donations after receiving expressions of gratitude. In addition, they suggested that public expressions of gratitude encourage those that did not participate in prior relief/recovery activities to do so in the future.

Word of mouth

Word of mouth (WOM) marketing occurs by both traditional and non-traditional means, both of which are supportive to marketing practices (Moore 2012), and which greatly influence other consumers' exchange behaviour (product trial, adoption and switching) (Richins and Root-Shaffer 1988). Traditional WOM is akin to a more conventional means of communicating (e.g. face-to-face, volunteering, emailing, text messaging) and is primarily a one-to-one (consumer-to-consumer) relationship in information sharing. Non-traditional WOM is a one-to-many means of sharing information and is primarily geared to Internet-based WOM using, for example, online blogs, testimonials, social networking and other electronic media. Non-traditional WOM is also closely related to the concepts of viral marketing (Box 4.4) and guerrilla marketing (Box 4.5), also referred to as 'buzz marketing', which can be defined in social marketing terms as a form of consumer-to-consumer connected marketing that is controlled by the organisation, essentially in the form of campaigns (Carl 2006). With the adaption of Internet-based WOM, marketing becomes substantially cheaper, with customers becoming the predominant means for communicating the marketing message. It is therefore no surprise that both online and offline networks are increasingly being seen as an important social marketing tool (Barrutia and Echebarria 2013).

Another significant social marketing dimension of WOM is through the use of volunteers (Tan *et al.* 2010; Mui *et al.* 2013). Although there is a long history of volunteering in many countries it is only in recent years that there has been a shift in their role from one of providing free labour to achieve tasks to one that can be used within communities to change attitudes and behaviours as a result of their personal contact with other people. Volunteers are therefore essential to community-based approaches to social marketing (McKenzie-Mohr 2011). Hall and McArthur (1998), in discussing the use of volunteers in national parks and heritage sites, also noted that while the early use of volunteers by heritage managers was usually as a source of cheap labour for menial tasks, e.g., track building and replanting, volunteers are now perceived as offering much more. Many national parks, museums, art galleries and communities around the world now use volunteers as tour guides and interpreters. One of their major attributes is the ability to use volunteers as a promotional vehicle by virtue of their enthusiasm and commitment for the heritage site or organisation. Although volunteers, like visitors, need to have positive experiences in order to create favourable WOM, their capacity to share their experiences with friends, colleagues and the people they meet is a powerful communication tool.

BOX 4.4 VIRAL MARKETING AND SOCIAL MEDIA

The expression 'viral marketing' was established in the late 1990s as a method to describe the accelerated growth of WOM communication. Anderson (1998: 6) refers to WOM being the informal interaction among 'private parties' regarding 'positive, neutral or negative' goods and services evaluations, yet with the growth in the Internet the greater degree of access to information that others have shared through WOM makes it less private (Moore 2012).

Social media has become the major mechanism to communicate viral marketing campaigns to a target audience (Brown *et al.* 2007; Chu 2011). Social media can come in various forms, such as social networks (e.g. Facebook, MySpace), blogs (e.g. Twitter), forums/bulletins, content communities (e.g. YouTube, StumbleUpon), virtual social worlds (e.g. Second Life), virtual game worlds (e.g. World of Warcraft) and content aggregators (e.g. Wikipedia), all of which are avenues for viral marketing campaigns (Palmer and Koenig-Lewis 2009). Viral marketing can be adopted in discrete or more obvious ways and sometimes to the consumer's immediate direct benefit. Many organisations create customised emails, online newsletters or develop a dedicated page on their website for consumers to write testimonials on. This allows potential customers or clients to look at the page and determine whether it is of high self-relevance. If the individuals who are writing the testimonials are congruent with the viewer's own values, it then encourages purchase or use of the product or service on offer.

The formulation of *blogs* (online journals) has established a framework for organisations to network with customers as a means to expand brands and obtain feedback on products as well as the organisation. Blogs can also take the form of video blogs ('vlogs') that involve consumers uploading videos and/or audio material to the Internet. Twitter can be treated as a form of mini-blog.

Social networking is an essential component of viral marketing with many marketers relying on online social networks to promote products or services. The growth of online social networking is linked to the development of Web 2.0 and it allows for individuals to connect with others by explicitly exchanging personal information, perspectives and opinions (Palmer and Koenig-Lewis 2009; Chu 2011) either socially or professionally (Trusov *et al.* 2009). Veer (2011) suggests that many individuals communicate information (whether personal or non-personal) to a greater depth when online as opposed to offline circumstances. There are many competing social networking websites in the online world such as Friendster, MySpace, Bebo, with Facebook being one of the most known, although as Weaver and Morrison (2008: 98) highlight, 'Different social networks emphasize different aspects of human interaction'.

Facebook has a link in which users can click to directly share any piece of information and practitioners must take this into significant consideration when establishing a marketing plan. Several billion pieces of information are shared on social network sites on a weekly basis, emphasising their potential role in marketing campaigns. Palmer and Koenig-Lewis (2009) suggest that social networks are a very important source of information in developing and understanding target markets as they enable relatively easy access to personal information such as lifestyle and demographics, and perhaps preferences and requirements.

Pelling and White (2009) suggest that those individuals who are seeking a greater sense of belonging (nostalgia) tend to be higher users of social networking websites and identified self-identity as a key factor as to whether a person uses social networking websites and is involved in viral marketing campaigns.

Forums and bulletins are used predominantly for conversing about favourable hobbies and interests that are similar to every user (Palmer and Koenig-Lewis 2009). These are regarded as extremely useful for accessing interest-based target markets at a very low cost.

Kaplan and Haenlein (2010) suggest that *content communities* are websites in which individuals can share media content amongst one another. YouTube is a very effective example of a content community where videos are posted online in order to reach a wider audience. Its audience popularity as well as ease of use for uploading make it a very useful social marketing tool. For example, Stead *et al.* (2013) report on two innovative and creative community-led projects in Edinburgh, Scotland where community residents were integrally involved, not just as participants in research and as project beneficiaries, but as decision makers, creators and implementers. The project members developed a range of communication approaches including: a project newsletter, co-written by local people; logos and straplines developed by local school children; and a short viral video.

Although viral marketing campaigns are proficient in gauging consumer awareness of a brand or issues along with potential sales (Ferguson 2008), there are potential drawbacks to this method of marketing that can affect the way in which organisations and interventions are viewed and can also have negative effects on consumers. Due to the extent of web utilisation, it has become much easier to get viruses on computers and also to receive spam via email, social networks, content communities and other various types of social media. Phelps *et al.* (2004) concluded that spam can reduce the efficiency of marketing techniques, and it is consequently why WOM is a very good foundation when it comes from reliable sources but can also be inadequate.

Viral marketing can also go significantly wrong also when seemingly trustworthy sources convey favourable messages that are not genuine to a motivated audience. Research suggests that if a combination of information from both consumers and organisations is readily apparent in an online social network setting, confusion may result leading to consumer frustration in attempting to distinguish what comments are bona fide opinions of consumers and what are not (Palmer and Koenig-Lewis 2009).

BOX 4.5 GUERRILLA MARKETING

'Guerrilla marketing' was developed as an advertising concept by Levinson (1987) based on the ideals of the guerrilla soldier who ventured into warfare lightly armed with only his wit and his knowledge of nature. For Levinson (1987) guerrilla marketing was originally defined as any marketing activity that was developed and performed without the use of traditional marketing weapons such as television and print media and was developed for small to medium-sized enterprises that did not have a large financial advantage yet needed to advertise. For these businesses, Levinson (1987) simplified his new marketing concept into seven key concepts: assortment, commitment, investment, consistent, confident, patient and subsequent. For a guerrilla marketing campaign to be successful it must therefore use an assortment of marketing 'weapons', those involved must be committed to the marketing plan; they must recognise the cost as an investment not an expense, their message must be consistent, they must be confident in their strategy, which will reflect to their consumer, they must be patient and their efforts must not finish when they make the sale or exchange (Levinson 1987: 90).

While Levinson was the first to develop the term guerrilla marketing, the nature of marketing without the tools of traditional media has existed long beforehand. Countries with low literature rates have historically used industrial theatre as a marketing method to portray key messages to large groups of people with poor media access and/or literacy skills. For example, this was the case under apartheid rule in South Africa where government, product and industrial messages were delivered through song, dance and theatre (Foxton 2005).

As new marketing forms have grown and expanded, guerrilla marketing is now used as an umbrella term for many new marketing practices that all fall into a 'marketing without traditional forms' category, such as print, television and radio media, and, given that it is now a standard media form, the Internet. A key element of guerrilla marketing is the connection and relationship with brand and consumers at a personal level (Owen and Humphrey 2009; Galer-Unti 2009). Experimental marketing is another form of marketing that falls under the guerrilla marketing umbrella as it encompasses tactics that include giving out free product samples, free trials and organising events (Heitzler *et al.* 2008). Entrepreneurial marketing is often used as an element of guerrilla marketing as it can be broadly described as a function of marketing by taking into account 'innovativeness, risk taking, reactiveness and pursuit of opportunism without the regard for the resources currently controlled' (Kraus *et al.* 2009: 19). Hutter and Hoffmann (2011) also suggest that ambient marketing and sensation marketing are guerrilla marketing tactics used to surprise consumers with advertisements in unexpected places, along with 'buzz marketing' (Foxton 2005). The overall connection between all of these different dimensions of guerrilla marketing is their influence on consumers' WOM. Any marketing programme is said to be successful if it promotes a positive WOM effect. Guerrilla marketing has an extremely powerful force in comparison to traditional marketing tactics as people think they are discovering the message and the brand themselves, meaning the buzz spreads throughout their peers without over selling the message (Carter 2003).

Guerrilla marketing is regarded as a means to recruit hard-to-reach groups to behaviour change interventions (Luca and Suggs 2010; Sadler *et al.* 2010). Guerrilla marketing campaigns have been designed to attract or retain post-modern consumers who are cynical of marketing and who typically avoid commitment (Dawes and Brown 2000) and which reflects the change, complexity, chaos and contradiction of the contemporary marketing environment (Addis and Podesta 2005), including the 'blurring of the line' between commercial and non-commercial forms of expression (Katyal 2010: 796). In such an environment guerrilla marketing tactics aim to embed the marketing message beyond what consumers usually notice and into a deeper subconscious level (Rotfeld 2008).

As guerrilla marketing focuses on using alternative and spontaneous forms of media to spread a message, the process of planning and controlling diffusion is more difficult than other media forms (Hutter *et al.* 2011). Successful guerrilla campaigns use non-traditional advertising to create buzz and generate interest from their target market. Once a successful guerrilla marketing campaign has generated excitement and buzz it will be able to successfully diffuse widely throughout the target market with the aid of media, public relations and word of mouth (Kirby and Marsden 2005).

Popular energy drink company Red Bull used guerrilla marketing techniques to begin their brand's advertising efforts by sponsoring niche sporting events and capturing their own video footage of the events. They then offered their films to media outlets for free giving Red Bull free media presence on primetime and prestigious publicity to their target market (Baltes and Leibing 2007). Successful guerrilla campaigns can be used to successfully promote social issues also by connecting with markets on a personal level. This tactic is especially important for connecting with children, as they are prone to being cynical of traditional advertising. An American campaign targeted to getting 9–13 year olds (tweens) to engage in physical activity called VERB used guerrilla experiential marketing to connect with their target market by actively going to the target consumer and spontaneously interacting with them face to face (Heitzler *et al.* 2008). Heitzler *et al.* (2008) concluded that the campaign's success was a result of the varied advertising efforts, and while guerrilla marketing was a key element of the campaign it is not a substitute for broadcast marketing but can be a powerful partner. Heitzler *et al.* (2008) concludes that the key to the success of a guerrilla campaign for marketers is to reach their market at a time where the consumers are most receptive to new ideas that are widely spread throughout other successful guerrilla marketing campaigns (see also Wong *et al.* 2008).

A significant factor that contributes to the successes of a campaign is the involvement of the audience in the advertising process. Some guerrilla marketing campaigns are successful because the audience are not aware that they are the targets of a marketing campaign. An example of this a successful guerrilla campaign for London Transport that aimed to heighten awareness of motorcycle crashes. The disclosed live buzz campaign played out in cinemas across London before the feature film was showed. The campaign included a dramatic acting sequence between an actress and a fictitious manager who interrupted the show to inform the woman that her husband was in a motorcycle accident, which was followed by an advert on motorcycle safety on the cinema screen (Foxton 2005). The campaign was a huge success and was deemed the most widely discussed and debated live buzz marketing campaign in the UK, and was judged as one of the top three cinema commercials of all time in *Campaign* magazine (Foxton 2005).

A major debate surrounding guerrilla marketing is the ethical practices that marketers follow when implementing their campaigns (Zuo and Veil 2006). Guerrilla marketing is often categorised as an aggressive marketing tactic, which uses strategies that are offensive in nature to gain social attention (Ay *et al.* 2010). However, guerrilla marketing can be a successful marketing tool used to bring about social change (Galer-Unti, 2009) and compete against corporate marketing campaigns especially in the youth market, which 'is sceptical of advertising and brands in general and companies are recognising that and are trying to reach consumers in a way that is more targeted and understands the consumer mindset and lifestyle' (Todd 2004: 2). As guerrilla marketing is typically offline, innovative and surprising, it is therefore seen as a refreshing response away from being bombarded by deceiving messages (Foxton 2005).

Rather than using words and images like in print and television, guerrilla marketing offers consumers a 'feeling' sparked from their personal interactions, which adds to their relationship with the brand (Groot *et al.* 2011). The buzz created by a guerrilla marketing campaign allows a brand to connect with the consumers as interested members of the target market are drawn into the campaign, creating a connection with the brands and the spread of positive WOM.

A successful tactic that guerrilla marketers use to ensure that younger generations are responding to their campaigns is by using 'cool' young people to work on their promotional efforts to represent brand essence. This tactic is used throughout guerrilla campaigns and is found to be very successful as it draws the younger generation into further thinking the brand or behaviour is 'cool'. Outgoing students and young adults with high energy and great social and communication skills are used to promote a brand's sprit and feel, whilst making the brand cool (Smith and Reynolds 2007). Microsoft uses this tactic successfully by employing popular students with large social networks as brand ambassadors (Schweitzer 2005). Their roles include door-to-door selling, promoting the software to friends, securing sponsorship, persuading student newspapers to mention their brand, chalking footpaths and filling noticeboards with company posters. A managing partner of a New York based marketing firm that specialises in college marketing, Matt Britton, confirms the validity of using young brand ambassadors by explaining: '[T]he student ambassador tactic embraces all the elements that corporations find most effective: its peer-to-peer, its word of mouth, its flexible, and it breaks through the clutter of all other media. For all that, it's growing very quickly' (Schweitzer 2005: A1).

Sponsorship

Once considered a form of philanthropy, sponsorship is now recognised as a powerful promotional and marketing tool for social marketing. Indeed, such is its significance that it is worthy of discussion separate from other marketing techniques. Sponsorship is not a separate marketing communication strategy. Instead, it is a specific marketing relationship that is designed to be beneficial to both the sponsored and the sponsor, which can contribute to a range of communication strategies (Rowley and Williams 2008). As noted in Chapter 3, social marketing's embrace of sponsorship arrangements has grown as the result of many governments' interest in promoting public–private partnerships and the development of network governance arrangements as a result of cutbacks or redirections in government spending (Polonsky and Speed 2001; Seitanidi and Ryan 2007; Madill and O'Reilly 2010).

For the corporate sponsor the primary benefit from sponsorship is the ability to clearly target a specific region, a specific type of person, or a specific customer or client while simultaneously boosting corporate brand and image (Jalleh *et al.* 2002; Bhattacharya *et al.* 2009). Sponsorship may come in many forms, e.g., financial assistance, advertising and promotion, facilities, provision of event infrastructure, management skills and labour (Madill and O'Reilly 2010). Sponsors often perceive social marketing opportunities as a means of raising corporate profile, promoting particular products through enhanced profile and image, obtaining lowers costs per impression than those achieved by standard advertising, improving sales and in being seen as good corporate citizens and exercising their social responsibilities. Nevertheless, from the perspective of the change agency and the integrity of their activities it is essential that the potential sponsor be appropriate to the needs and image of the organisation and/or intervention. Mismatching of product and sponsors will cause problems for both sponsor and the product. In addition, it must be recognised that some sponsors will want to influence the nature of the intervention while nearly all will expect a return of some description from their investment in the form of greater product and/or corporate recognition (Daellenbach *et al.* 2006; O'Reilly and Madill 2007).

Table 4.6 identifies the stages of the corporate sponsorship process. Benefits from sponsorship should accrue to both sponsor and sponsored and change agencies increasingly recognise that companies are seeking returns on their investments. Decisions about the suitability of a product for sponsorship are based by businesses on a number of criteria including brand, sales and marketing return on investment as well any desire to act as a good corporate citizen (see also Table 3.3). Regardless of the size of the sponsorship that is sought, proposals must be detailed, professionally presented and designed to meet company philosophies and objectives.

TABLE 4.6 Stages in the corporate sponsorship process

Stage	*Characteristics*
1. Research	Research to identify suitable company for change agency and/or behavioural intervention.
2. Preparation	Preparation of sponsorship proposal which includes: • details of specific product(s) for which sponsorship is sought; • details of relationship of product(s) to any broader themes or generic product; • identification of potential benefits for sponsor; and • clearly identified set of legal, financial, managerial and marketing responsibilities for both the change agency and the sponsor.
3. Consideration	Consideration by potential sponsor: • initial contact; • informal discussions with marketing manager/members of marketing division; • formal presentation to marketing manager/members of marketing division; and • if large sponsorship, formal presentation to board.
4. Decision	If no resume search, if yes proceed to next stage.
5. Agreement	Legal agreement between corporate sponsor and change agency detailing responsibilities of both parties.
6. Implementation	Operationalise sponsorship through promotion of product.
7. Evaluation and feedback	Feedback to company that provides for evaluation of the success of the product /intervention and the sponsorship, who will then decide to continue or discontinue sponsorship arrangements. Return to early stages of process.

BOX 4.6 LIVE EARTH, SPONSOR RECOGNITION AND CLIMATE CHANGE BEHAVIOUR

In 2007 Lightspeed Research conducted a mobile survey during the July 2007 seven-day-long Live Earth concerts held on seven continents for the Ethical Reputation Index. They surveyed people aged 18–45 who were aware of the Live Earth event, 200 in the UK and Australia, and 600 in the US. Questions focused on combating climate change, the Live Earth concerts and artists, and awareness of event sponsors. When asked to identify the sponsors of the Live Earth concerts, many respondents struggled to identify the companies that were actually support- ing the event. MSN and Pepsi had the highest awareness of brands in connection with the Live Earth concerts, as did non-sponsors Yahoo and Coca-Cola. The majority of respondents felt that Live Earth was unlikely to encourage them to do more to combat climate change, although those watching the event responded more positively. Although reusing and recy- cling were shown to be common activities, fewer respondents were willing to reduce car or air travel, or seek greener product/service alternatives (Mobile Marketing Association 2007).

BOX 4.7 CIVIC CROWDFUNDING

Public donations to fund civic projects for the public good, such as parks, memorials and recreation centres, is nothing new. However, the Internet age has seen the development of new means of public fundraising. Inspired by Kickstarter, a crowdfunding site that helps innovators and artists find investors and patrons for their projects, a new generation of crowdfunding start-ups are helping to raise funds for public projects.

Spacehive, a UK site for urban projects, has raised funds for art gallery and commu- nity centre development. Donors are charged only when the project reaches its funding target, with Spacehive taking a small percentage of funds raised. In the US, Citizinvestor only promotes projects that are put forward by local councils.

Advocates of the approach see crowdfunding as a means of leveraging funds from larger corporate sponsors, while also being a means of improving the quality of local gov- ernment projects and interventions as only relatively popular projects will receive funding. Bryan Boyer of Brickstarter in Finland 'would like to "turn NIMBYS into YIMBYS" (Yes In My Backyard). He hopes crowdfunding will not only help residents plan small developments, but also finance the surveys and audits to persuade governments to consider bigger ones' (Economist 2013a: 54).

However, critics contend that crowdfunding may be more difficult for boring but func- tional infrastructure plus the availability of money from crowdfunders may lead to councils cutting back in their funding of public space (Economist 2013a), affecting some of the poorest neighbourhoods in particular, which may lack some of the funds and expertise to support crowdfunding, but which may most need public park and leisure facilities.

Brickstarter: http://brickstarter.org/
Citizinvestor: www.citizinvestor.com/
Neighbor.ly: The Civic Crowdfunding Platform: http://neighbor.ly/
Spacehive: https://spacehive.com/

Implement and monitor intervention programme

The implementation and monitoring of interventions is crucial to success although implementation is often given insufficient attention in intervention development. Implementation is the process by which policy and strategy is translated into action. A good working definition of implementation can be taken from the seminal work by Pressman and Wildavsky (1979: xxi) in which implementation 'may be viewed as a process of interaction between the setting of goals and actions geared to achieve them'. Indeed, much of the focus in implementation research is on closing the 'implementation gap' or 'deficit' between policy and action (Treuren and Lane 2003). Implementation therefore implies a linkage between policy and action (Barrett and Fudge 1981), with implementation arguably being the most important in terms of the actual outcomes of policies and programmes (usually conceived in socio-economic and/or environmental terms) as compared to the physical documents or statements of intention that represent the policy outputs (Northway *et al.* 2007), a point of difference usually lost in most studies of policy in tourism (Hall 1999). Nevertheless, one of the greatest difficulties in examining the relationships between policy and action is that if they are examined from a dynamic, as opposed to a static or 'one-shot' perspective, then policy and action appear inseparable. As Pressman and Wildavsky (1979: xxi) observed:

> Our working definition of implementation will do as a sketch of the earliest stages of the program, but the passage of time wreaks havoc with efforts to maintain tidy distinctions ... In the midst of action the distinction between the initial conditions and the subsequent chain of causality begins to erode ... The longer the chain of causality, the more numerous the reciprocal relationships among the links and the more complex implementation becomes.

Policy and implementation are therefore two sides of the same coin (Hall 2008a). One cannot effectively consider action without considering policy/policies and policy cannot be understood unless there is an awareness of how it will be actioned. Table 4.7 indicates some of the factors influencing selection of policy implementation instrument. Hence there is, or should be, an ongoing process of feedback between the different stages of the social marketing process as well as appropriate monitoring to see that goals are being accomplished. Therefore, for the communication dimension and work plan, key questions are (Turning Point 2007):

- Are respective audiences, benefits and messages clear and supported by prior research?
- Does each of the activities support the overall strategy?
- Are the respective materials, delivery channels and partner roles clear and feasible?
- Is the plan for pre-testing the messages and materials clear and feasible?
- Are roles and responsibilities clear?
- Do the timelines, budgets and resources required appear reasonable and work to schedules?
- Are necessary review/ethical clearances and procurement mechanisms clear and in place?

TABLE 4.7 Factors influencing selection of policy implementation instruments

Factor	Criteria
Measure of effectiveness	An instrument must be capable of attaining its objective in a reliable and consistent fashion, whilst being adaptable to changing circumstances over time and sensitive to differences in local conditions.
	An instrument should be compatible with other policy approaches.
	Compliance costs need to be factored in to policy considerations.
Measure of efficiency	The instrument should be judged against costs relative to desired outcomes and the costs of other instruments.
	Compliance costs need to be factored in to policy considerations.
Political values	An instrument should be equitable in its impact across the target population of actors, i.e. of firms, organisations and/or individuals.
	An instrument should be politically acceptable, easy to operate and as transparent and understandable as possible.
	Compliance costs need to be factored in to policy considerations.

Source: After Hall (2008a, 2009b)

In the case of the fifth P of social marketing – politics – it is important to bear in mind that in the case of the more contentious interventions not only do groups and individuals influence policy but they also influence implementation. The actions of interests that try and influence policy making does not stop when a policy or plan is written, or funding provided, but will continue throughout the entire policy–action process. Such issues are inseparable from the task of 'doing implementation' (Hall 2008a), because

> any attempt to develop implementation … must face the difficulty – once it moves away from the attempt to develop checklists of pitfalls for the implementation process … of becoming involved with the wide range of questions which have been raised in relation to policy making and in the study of organisations.
>
> (Ham and Hill 1994: 115)

Evaluation

Evaluation is the 'final' stage that is usually identified in the social marketing process. Evaluation is guided by the impulse to understand and to make informed judgements and choices and helps realise the full potential of a plan or programme.

Evaluation is the process whereby individual and public judgement processes are harnessed for reflection on action. Evaluation is a systematic assessment of the effectiveness, efficiency and/or appropriateness of a programme or an intervention. Evaluation involves making judgements about the results of some sort of measurement against specific objectives. This is usually done by collecting and analysing information on the intervention, judging the worth of the intervention and making informed decisions for the future. There are many different legitimate and covert reasons for undertaking an evaluation (Table 4.8) (Theobald 1979; Hall and McArthur 1998), several of which are connected to the politics of social marketing (and which you often do not find mentioned in many texts!). Evaluation is broadly based around making assessments and decisions. Evaluation typically requires some form of research, which may include market, stakeholder or visitor research, but it may not. Whether evaluation uses market research, visitor research or monitoring entirely depends upon the objectives of the evaluation and its subject matter and approach (Table 4.9) (Bennett 2007), and is grounded in a number of ethical and moral issues (Table 4.10). The difference between evaluation, monitoring and the different forms of research may well be based on the intent of the programme and the time frame in which each is used. Some of the principles of evaluation that should be kept in mind at all times are (Hall and McArthur 1998):

- what needs to be measured is determined before the measurement technique;
- the only aspects assessed are those that will provide the critical information needed;
- stakeholders clearly understand the rationale and nature of the evaluation programme;
- what is to be evaluated already has some form of measurable objectives or performance criteria;
- relevant information can be collected;
- results are balanced and reliable, and recommendations are relevant, feasible and timely;
- information is presented in a way that increases the possibility of acceptance; and
- the right information reaches the right people in a way that reflects their interests and abilities (e.g., comprehension and cognitive).

Recommendations and decisions arising from an evaluation must relate to the programme's or interventions original objectives and the evaluation brief. Some of the ways in which a positive response to decisions can be achieved include:

- concentrating on refining the recommendations rather than making an extensive list of specific actions;
- sorting recommendations into common groups based on similar fields, stakeholders or issues;
- sorting recommendations according to the organisational scale in which they are being pitched, e.g. policy recommendations should be listed before specific actions;
- presenting a set of recommendations that reflect alternative courses of action; and
- delivering recommendations in a relevant manner to those expected to endorse and/or implement them.

When attempting to implement critical decisions arising from the evaluation among stakeholders it is sometimes useful to adopt the following initiatives:

- be non-defensive about the information and treat it as an indication of success or possible trouble rather than 'gospel';
- ensure the stakeholder has the information required to understand the rationale for the decision, and no other information likely to cloud it;
- present useful comparisons between the results covered and other similar situations;
- use existing channels of communication and decision making within the organisation; and
- build in encouragement for using the results and implementing the recommendations.

TABLE 4.8 Legitimate and covert purposes of using evaluation

Legitimate purposes	Explanation of legitimate purposes
Testing management assumptions	Determine whether assumptions that many social marketing approaches and interventions rely on are valid or appropriate to the problem and organisational setting
Increasing accountability	Assess and demonstrate the degree to which a policy, programme or intervention is meeting its objectives
Improving decision making	Access and integrate relevant information that improves the quality of decision-making in areas such as resource allocation, marketing media, segmentation, and other policy and programme directions
Reviewing performance indicators	Consider whether the original objectives or desired outcomes remain realistic and appropriate
Meeting sponsor and grant requirements	Evaluation of programme objectives may be required as part of funding programmes, especially those generated externally
Covert purposes	Explanation of covert purposes
Postponing decisions	Putting off a difficult decision until the situation dies down or until the problem partially solves itself
Avoiding responsibility	Commission consultants or other staff to undertake an evaluation of the problem so that a difficult decision can be displaced to them
Manipulating public perceptions	Use positive evaluations to promote the merits of a policy or programme to stakeholders or other decision makers, or bury or discredit negative reports, being selective in the content and method of evaluation is also a mechanism used to achieve this purpose
Meeting grant requirements	Evaluation of programme objectives may be required as part of funding programmes, especially those generated externally (this is only a covert purpose if it is selective in content and/or method to maximise a positive spin on the results of the intervention)
Eliminating the administrator	Tie a programme evaluation to the performance of a decision maker, then load the evaluation so that the programme appears to be failing to meet expectations, then recommend that a dismissal is the only way to change the situation

Source: Adapted from Theobald (1979); Hall and McArthur (1998)

Re-definition

Once the evaluation has been conducted decisions then need to be made with respect as to whether to continue the intervention as is or change it for the same target market, or whether to abandon or change the nature of the intervention altogether. Such decisions are made, at least in part, because the behaviour problem itself changes over time as a result of shifts in knowledge as a result of exposure to new theories, research and experiences, changes in the external environment, and the relationality between the intervention and the target audience in which the actions of each become interrelated or 'entangled' over time. The change over time as the process of social marketing occurs therefore means that it is impossible to avoid some sort of change to the definition of the intervention problem and the nature of intervention.

TABLE 4.9 Models of programme evaluation

Model	Emphasis
Goal oriented	Assessing progress towards goals
	Assessing the effectiveness of innovations
Decision oriented	Assisting decision makers to make intelligent judgements
Responsive	Depicting programme and intervention processes and the value perspectives of stakeholders
Evaluation research	Focusing on explaining effects, identifying causes of effects
	Generating generalisations about programme or intervention effectiveness
Goal-free	Assessing the effects of a programme or intervention using criteria not represented in the programme's own conceptual framework
Advocacy-adversary	Assessing contrasting points of view
Utilisation oriented	Increasing the utility of findings for specific stakeholders and users

TABLE 4.10 Ethical and moral issues in evaluation

Issue	Explanation
Realism	Being realistic about the limitations and potential outcomes of an evaluation helps stakeholders to adjust their expectations and input to the evaluation process.
Privacy	Privacy implies assuring anonymity and confidentiality if it is required. Anonymity implies that none of the data gathering will pick up names, positions and contacts, while confidentiality implies that the evaluator may know them but not make them available to others.
Non-coercion	People should never be forced to take part in an evaluation unless involvement is a necessary prerequisite that is understood and accepted by the participant. In some instances, such as when involving children, written consent may be needed.
Avoidance of harm upon others	An evaluation should not pose physical or psychological harm to an individual.
Avoidance of preconceived perceptions	An evaluator will usually have an idea of what the likely outcome may be before starting the evaluation. While this can be extremely useful in streamlining the approach, it should not influence the evaluator to centre the evaluation on proving the preconceptions through avoiding procedures or adding extra ones.
Objective procedure	An objective procedure requires the evaluation's objectives to be clearly communicated, the methods to reflect the objectives, the data samples to be representative and the analysis to be accurate.
Avoidance of positional influence	The evaluator must not abuse the strong position they are in to influence the entire evaluation, and must also avoid influences from people with position, such as employers, stakeholders, colleagues or friends.

Issue	Explanation
Truthful information	Sometimes evaluations reveal what managers and evaluators do not want to hear. It is vital to present results as objectively as possible. It is also important to outline the approach used so that stakeholders understand the context of the evaluation.
Fairness in reporting information	It is critical to ensure that all stakeholders have access to the results of an evaluation, not just those sympathetic to the organisation or results generated. The way an evaluation is communicated will also affect who has genuine access to it e.g. language, length, complexity, written or verbal presentation and timing.
Timeliness of the dissemination of information	An evaluation can be rendered nearly useless if it is not made available when needed, or at least when it was promised.

Source: Hall and McArthur (1998); French (2008)

In some cases within market economies a redefinition of the problem may even lead to the abandonment of social marketing with its role being taken by commercial marketing as the behavioural change that social marketing sought to introduce takes hold and becomes the 'new norm' (Menegaki 2012). For example, if social marketing is successful with respect to the promotion of energy efficient appliances and measures in the tourism and hospitality industry as the use of such appliances becomes the industry standard, then the need for behavioural change interventions diminishes and commercial marketing becomes standard as commercial companies take over the promotion of efficient appliances and the use of renewable energy. The role and process of social marketing therefore also needs to be understood within the life-course of a product or behaviour that social marketing promoted (Figure 4.4). However, it is important to note that the extent to which a behaviour becomes a norm and is therefore transformed to becoming an everyday occurrence in the realm of commercial marketing will vary from situation to situation, especially as in some situations it may be highly desirable not to commoditise behaviours.

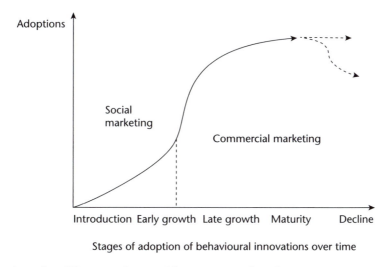

FIGURE 4.4 A product life-course from social to commercial marketing

Chapter summary

This chapter has outlined the stages of the social marketing process. However, it is important to stress that this is an idealised process, and that other marketing and social marketing books and guides may divide up the stages slightly differently although many common elements do exist. The key point being that social marketing needs to be undertaken systematically and that it is part of a cyclical iterative process. An important issue that is stressed in the chapter is the on-going significance of the fifth P of politics, here understood in a broad sense, given the influence of various stakeholders in programme development and the acceptability of interventions. Furthermore, marketers are faced with important ethical decisions with respect to the various different types of interventions that are available, including approaches such as guerrilla and viral marketing and the role of the Internet and social networks, as well as the undertaking of evaluations.

The relationship between commercial and social and non-profit marketing is discussed further in the next chapter before examining a series of thematic case studies. We will come back again to the relationship between commercial and social marketing and the implications for the application of social marketing in the final chapter.

Further reading and websites

Useful explanations of the processes of social marketing in a general sense can be found in:

French, J. (2008) *Procurement Guide for Social Marketing Services*. London: National Centre for Social Marketing. (This is also extremely helpful with respect to knowing what questions to ask and how to manage a social marketing intervention without actually being a social marketer yourself.)

Turning Point Social Marketing National Excellence Collaborative (2007) *The Basics of Social Marketing: How to Use Marketing to Change Behavior*. Seattle, WA: Turning Point.

A community approach to social marketing, which closely parallels some of the community-based tourism planning literature (see Chapter 8), is discussed in:

McKenzie-Mohr, D. (2011) *Fostering Sustainable Behavior: An Introduction to Community-Based Social Marketing*. Gabriola Island: New Society Publishers.

Also refer to the extremely useful Tools of Change website, which has a wide range of social marketing material including case studies:

www.toolsofchange.com/en/home

On the interplay between commercial and social marketing, including with respect to the relationships between commercial entities and non-profit change agencies, see:

Andreasen, A. R. (2012) 'Rethinking the relationship between social/nonprofit marketing and commercial marketing', *Journal of Public Policy and Marketing*, 31(1): 36–41.

Henley, N., Raffin, S. and Caemmerer, B. (2011) 'The application of marketing principles to a social marketing campaign', *Marketing Intelligence and Planning*, 29(7): 697–706.

Wymer Jr, W. W. and Samu, S. (2003) 'Dimensions of business and nonprofit collaborative relationships', *Journal of Nonprofit and Public Sector Marketing*, 11(1): 3–22.

A useful study on the effects of three alternative strategic marketing orientations: market orientation, sales orientation and product orientation on museums is:

Izquierdo, C. C. and Samaniego, M. J. G. (2007) 'How alternative marketing strategies impact the performance of Spanish museums', *Journal of Management Development*, 26(9): 809–831.

On branding issues for non-profit organisations see:

Keller, E. W., Datoon, M. C. and Shaw, D. (2010) 'NPO branding: Preliminary lessons from major players', *International Journal of Nonprofit and Voluntary Sector Marketing*, 15(2): 105–121.

For a more specific brand example with respect to the relationship between events and sponsors see:

Rowley, J. and Williams, C. (2008) 'The impact of brand sponsorship of music festivals', *Marketing Intelligence and Planning*, 26(7): 781–792.

On evaluation see:

Bennett, R. (2007) 'The use of marketing metrics by British fundraising charities: a survey of current practice', *Journal of Marketing Management*, 23(9–10): 959–989.
Hall, C. M. and McArthur, S. (1998) *Integrated Heritage Management*. Norwich: The Stationery Office.
Theobald, W. F. (1979) *Evaluation of Recreation and Park Programs*. New York: John Wiley & Sons. (An excellent book if you can locate it.)
Weiler, B. and Ham, S. H. (2010) 'Development of a research instrument for evaluating the visitor outcomes of face-to-face interpretation', *Visitor Studies*, 13(2): 187–205.

BOX 4.8 WAS SAFE SEX CAMPAIGN 'GIMMICKY ADVERTISING' AND 'WASTED MONEY'?

Sex is a leisure activity that is a major focus of social marketing campaigns. A UK Department for Children, Schools and Families safer sex campaign aimed at teenagers was branded a 'gimmicky' waste of taxpayers' money in 2009. The 'Want respect? Use a condom' campaign included a specially commissioned drama series, called *Thmbnls*, described as 'the world's first interactive made-for-mobile drama' (Bublik 2009), which cost £250,000 and involved 22 one-minute-long episodes featuring a group of teenagers discussing relationships and attitudes to contraception. The intervention was targeted at sexually active 16–19 year olds; the wider campaign 'Want respect? Use a condom' aimed to reduce the levels of teenage pregnancy and the incidence of sexually transmitted infections in young adults by associating condom use with respect (Bublik 2009).

The 22-part drama, broadcast weekly to teens' mobiles, incorporated subtle safe sex messages. Public relations, social networking, mobile and online advertising drove sign-ups, and was supported by a dedicated website with additional multimedia content. Zero-rated data charges were negotiated with operators and audio personalisation was used to help build dialogue with the target audience. However, only 5,576 mobile phone users signed up for downloads of the videos in the four months after it was launched, which meant it cost £45 per subscriber when set against the cost of the film (Mackenzie 2009). Episodes were also posted on YouTube.

According to the government the campaign was a success and the number of subscribers had exceeded its own targets. Nevertheless, the government was accused of 'gimmicky' advertising and marketing. Susie Squire from the Taxpayers' Alliance said:

> Too often the government engages with gimmicky marketing and gimmicky advertising because they think they are going to reach a new audience ... I think when it comes to spending taxpayers' money, particularly on healthcare issues, they should be going for the most effective approach, not the most fashionable.
>
> (Quoted in Mackenzie 2009)

In the previous year, the UK government's spending on digital media had increased by 57 per cent to £35 million (Mackenzie 2009). However, questions were asked as to whether the money is being used wisely. Toby Beresford, commercial director of London-based agency Nudge, told BBC News:

> With quarter of a million pounds, I'd be looking at least half a million people to sign-up, to engage with that campaign ... We see social media marketing as still a high risk marketing area. You can get massive uplift and massive success. However those are still the minority of social media campaigns. We would still expect government departments to take a step back from the more sort-of 'let's get a viral out there' risky approach.
>
> (Quoted in Mackenzie 2009)

A spokesperson for the Department for Children, Schools and Families said: 'The Thmbnls project was designed as a pilot to test an innovative approach to using personal media, in this case mobile phone technology, in delivering messages to notoriously hard to reach audiences' (quoted in Mackenzie 2009).

The spokesperson said the government would be carrying out a project evaluation looking at the impact of Thmbnls, but stated that the number of subscribers exceeded its own target (Mackenzie 2009). What the BBC report did not mention was that as of the 26 March 2009:

> The mobile drama from the COI and Department for Children, Schools and Families, has had its trailer viewed 188,000 times. The 22-week campaign, currently in its 11th week, has seen over 220,000 visitors to the dedicated website with 44,000 clicking through to the sign-up page. A Facebook profile, which went live on 3 March, has attracted 65 fans.
>
> (NMA Staff 2009)

However, O'Sullivan (2009) writing several weeks earlier also suggested that the experiment had not been a success:

> This story is not an 'I told you so', it's just worth noting the channels that fail. There's so much clamour around mobile TV this year that it's important to remind everyone how things can go belly-up. This isn't the first mobile TV failure this year, and I doubt it will be the last. Just throwing money at these kinds of project because they're new and

interesting isn't going to get anywhere fast. Mobile TV has been a wildly unpredictable industry. I very much suspect that the road to success will be slow and careful, and will be littered with burning wrecks like this.

Sources: Bublik (2009); Mackenzie (2009); NMA Staff (2009); O'Sullivan (2009)

Questions for reflection:

- To what extent does a case such as this reflect the fifth P of social marketing?
- How should success be judged for social marketing interventions?
- How might criticism of new initiatives potentially affect the use by change agencies of new technologies or marketing approaches?
- How would you design a safe sex campaign that promoted condom use to teenagers? What communication channels would you use?
- What personal ethical issues might arise if when working on a safe sex campaign? To what extent is it possible to reconcile personal beliefs versus professional demands?

5

THE CRAFT AND PRACTICE
OF SOCIAL MARKETING

This short chapter serves to link the background chapters with respect to the development of social marketing and application to tourism, theories of behavioural change and governance in the selection of social marketing interventions, and the process of social marketing, with the application of social marketing principles. It is divided into four main sections:

- The relationship between commercial and social marketing applications in tourism.
- The criteria for identifying social marketing interventions.
- The craft of social marketing.
- Social marketing and the issue-attention cycle.

The relationship between commercial and social marketing applications in tourism

Tourism studies is often treated by many disciplines as a sub-set or specialised case of an existing discipline or as an interdisciplinary or post-disciplinary field of study. Unfortunately this approach plays down the complexity of not only *doing* tourism research but also the *application* of tourism knowledge, especially with respect to the tourism system. Yet in many ways tourism management, marketing and planning is much more complex than the usual applications of business-related theory. This is especially because of the multiple product nature of tourism so that even though there often is a business selling a specific tourism product it is still embedded in a wider customer value chain that includes a destination product as well as a trip product (which is sometimes packaged for tourists). This situation means that tourism businesses, as well as destination management and marketing organisations need to place a great deal of emphasis on network relationships in order to be able to attract customers as well as having substantial geographical reach to be able to access the customer who, often by definition, is not located in the home environment of the business.

Yet the social marketing application of tourism is even more complicated as not only is there a potential focus on the often mobile tourist and the various dimension of the tourism product and its externalities, but also on other stakeholders, such as destination residents, businesses, management bodies, industry associations and government agencies. This issue of complexity is also recognised in the social marketing literature. Andreasen argues:

> nonprofit and social marketing do not comprise a special (and minor) set of marketing applications … the managerial challenges that nonprofit and social marketing managers face are significantly more complex than those faced in the commercial sector. Such managers typically must simultaneously promote sales (e.g., Goodwill clothing, charity T-shirts, opera attendance), corporate support, volunteering, individual giving and grants, and contracts from foundations and government agencies. The targets of each of these marketing challenges respond to different and often unique tactics and strategies and are evaluated in terms of different outcomes.
>
> (Andreasen 2012: 37)

Andreasen (2012) therefore suggests that it is important to reorder social and non-profit marketing so that it is not just regarded as a special case and that it instead has a range of characteristics that could be usefully translated back to commercial marketing because of its focus on behavioural change, what he admittedly described somewhat felicitously as the 'social-dominant logic' of social marketing (for similar strains of argument see also Andreasen 2003; Peattie and Peattie 2003; Waters *et al.* 2011; Wymer 2011; Farrell and Gordon 2012; Gordon 2012; Lefebvre 2012). Nevertheless, identifying the similarities and differences between commercial and social marketing is important as it suggests that when examining the application of social marketing in a tourism context we are looking not just at the straight transfer of commercial marketing tools, as important as these may be, but we are also looking at significantly different emphases with respect to internal and external organisational demands as well as measures of success.

Drawing on the work of Andreasen (2012) and Andreasen and Kotler (2007) Table 5.1 highlights some of the differences and similarities between commercial and social marketing. Commercial and social marketing organisations have different goals even though they may use some similar marketing tools to achieve them, a situation that exists in tourism as well (Dinan and Sargeant 2000). However, the resource base for social marketing organisations is usually reliant on fundraising initiatives, such as donations, government funding and sponsorships, rather than sales (Brady *et al.* 2011; Kim *et al.* 2011), and is also often extremely dependent on the work of volunteers and work with partnership organisations (Riecken *et al.* 1995; Briggs *et al.* 2010; Hager and Brudney 2011; Waikayi *et al.* 2012). Furthermore, the results of the social marketing exchange may take many years before they are recognised, which is substantially different from the immediate purchase of foods and services from commercial organisations. The value chain of social marketing is therefore substantially different from that of commercial marketing.

TABLE 5.1 Comparisons between commercial and social marketing

Element	Commercial marketing	Social marketing
Primary target audience	Customers	Downstream consumers and upstream institutions and organisations
Secondary target audience	Supply chain members Media Other identified stakeholders	Media Volunteers Donors and sponsors Partners Governments Public
Inputs	Organisational budgets Staffing Internal support	Organisational budgets Staffing Volunteers Donations and sponsorship Partnering
Budgets	Substantial	Minimal
Strategy creation and execution	Few limits with restricted public scrutiny	Substantial limits and close public scrutiny
Organisational outputs	Sales campaigns (of various kinds)	Behaviour change Volunteer retention Donation, funding and sponsorship levels and loyalty Collaboration with businesses, government and other NGOs and non-profit organisations Sales campaigns (for some non-profits)
Limits on offerings	Few	Often considerable
Key behaviour of target markets	Often low involvement Audience generally indifferent or positive	Often high involvement Audience generally indifferent or opposed (with the exception of some non-profit niches such as arts, culture and heritage)
Target audience benefits	Immediate or near term	From short-term to long-term with many interventions not having results until distant time horizons (e.g. sustainability, environmental conservation)
Results management	Sales figures Market share Shareholder satisfaction	Behaviour change Reduction in externalities Volunteer retention Donation, funding and sponsorship levels and loyalty Collaboration levels Stakeholder satisfaction Sales figures
Outcomes	Profit levels Return on Investment	Behavioural change Reductions in externalities Return on investment Programme growth
Impacts	Consumption change Externalities	Behavioural change Reduction in externalities

Source: After Andreasen and Kotler (2007); Andreasen (2012)

BOX 5.1 DONOR SWITCHING: A SOCIAL MARKETING EXCHANGE CHALLENGE

Bennett (2009) examined the question of why donors to charitable organisations often switch their support from one charity to another. This is a critical question for charities and social marketing organisations as their activities are often highly reliant on personal and corporate donations. This study found that a person's image congruence with a specific charity, involvement with the first organisation, boredom and over-familiarity with a charity's communications, and the attractiveness of a second charity's campaigns in relation to the first, all exerted highly significant influences. An individual's innate need for variation also affected the number of switches he or she had concluded and whether switches were likely to concern a second charity in the same or a different sector; although this did not influence the strength of the urge to switch support. A person's perception that all charities were basically alike similarly influenced the number and character of switch decisions but not the desire itself to switch. In what is potentially a major issue of the marketing exchange relationship between social marketing organisations and donors Bennett (2009) also found that satisfaction with the first charity's work and with the quality of its communications did not exert significant impacts on any of the dependent variables.

As Andreasen (2012) points out the substantial differences in the transactions involved in non-profit and social marketing as compared with commercial marketing therefore have important implications for effective marketing management (see also Henley *et al.* 2011; Farrell and Gordon 2012). In the case of social marketing:

- Financial performance signals come from multiple sources.
- There are a variety of non-financial performance signals: e.g. volunteering, level of in-kind support, partnering.
- Competition between organisations is not just over behavioural outcomes, as in the private sector, but over the resources needed to achieve such outcomes.
- It is extremely difficult to discern clear market signals, i.e. when can it be said that behavioural change is a success?
- If government funding is involved success may be measurable more by meeting financial reporting indicators than behavioural change information. In addition, political considerations will also be significant in evaluating performance.

In response to these issues Andreasen (2012) suggests that new marketing management models need to be developed that explicitly incorporate the range of different exchanges that occur in social marketing of which commercial exchanges of products/services for (eventual) cash is only a special case, as in the example of many non-profit tourist attractions in the arts, cultural and heritage sector (Bennett and Sargeant 2005; Goodall 2006; Rowley and Williams 2008; Siano *et al.* 2010), as well as national parks and reserves (Hall and McArthur 1998; Zegre *et al.* 2012). In this context commercial outcomes are only one of many impacts necessary for the survival and growth of change agencies. Indeed, Becker and Fleur (2010) in a study of the funding and maintenance of aviation museum operations identified three operational strategies: the community partnership, the philanthropic proprietorship and the controlling sponsorship. Nevertheless, it is important to note that although certain non-profit visitor attractions are subsidised and supported by government and other funders, in some cases this is a form of cross-subsidy from tourism businesses and government tax takings as a result of the role of such attractions drawing tourists to a destination. Therefore in such circumstances they are best understood as non-profit elements of a commercial destination tourist system, with its accompanying set of management pressures to attract more visitors (Quinn 2002; Wiener *et al.* 2009; Zegre *et al.* 2012). Of course, in other circumstances support comes because they are seen as a public and community good rather than a destination good.

In response to some of these issues Andreasen (2012) suggests a change in terminology so that in social marketing we are best to refer to 'target audiences' rather than 'customers' or 'consumers'. Similarly, such notions could be applied in the case of universities where the focus should be on 'students' instead of 'customers', and in government where the focus should be on 'citizens' rather than 'customers' and 'consumers'. In addition, Andreasen (2012) highlights that the 'value proposition' of social marketing is not necessarily embedded in a specific product or service. Instead, it lies in behaviours. Therefore, he highlights a number of behavioural objectives that lie at the heart of what social marketing is trying to achieve

- *start a behaviour:* e.g., volunteer to guide visitors around your home town, label local foods on menus;
- *switch or substitute a behaviour:* e.g. use a train to get to your holiday destination rather than a plane, use sustainable fair trade coffee and tea rather than non fair trade coffee and tea in restaurants, cafés and hotels;
- *stop a behaviour:* e.g. stop holidaying in countries with poor human rights records, make sure that all electrical appliances are turned off in a room when it is not occupied;
- *not start a behaviour:* e.g. do not pollute lakes and rivers when camping and hiking, do not purchase hotel uniforms from any company that does not have child labour protection safeguards in its supply chain;
- *continue a behaviour:* e.g. continue to separate rubbish into organics, waste and recyclables, use energy-efficient lighting;
- *increase a behaviour:* e.g. take your family and friends to visit your local museum and art gallery more, use more local food in restaurant menus;
- *decrease a behaviour:* e.g. take fewer long-distance flights, use less energy and water.

(Adapted from Andreasen 2012; examples are this author's)

Andreasen's behavioural focus provides a useful framework to understand not only the broader sphere of marketing but also the application of social marketing to a tourism context. However, given that there are a large number of disciplines and academic approaches that seek behavioural change how can we identify interventions as social marketing or not? Therefore the next sections discuss the ways in which the social marketing process and approach may be benchmarked.

BOX 5.2 USING TOURISM AS AN INCENTIVE FOR SEXUALLY TRANSMITTED DISEASE TESTING

In 2008 six primary health care trusts in the North East of England gave young people aged between 16 and 24 the chance to win a holiday if they got themselves tested for Chlamydia, a sexually transmitted disease. One in 10 people have the disease, which left untreated can cause infertility. A large number of cases of Chlamydia go undiagnosed because around 50 per cent of infected men and 70 per cent of infected women do not have any symptoms. Anyone who was tested, and encouraged three friends to be tested, were entered into a holiday competition. The competition was designed with the help of Newcastle-based social marketing firm Foundry Media who donated the four first-prize holidays (BBC News 2008).

Newcastle's director of public health, Danny Ruta, said the NHS had looked at the marketing techniques the commercial sector was using to target young people:

> I can't stress enough what serious consequences having undiagnosed chlamydia could have for a young person – it could devastate their future plans to have a family.

> We've been on all university and college campuses, in night clubs and many other places with our peer advisors who explain to young people what's involved in taking a chlamydia test.

> This holiday competition is a tried and tested way commercial organisations market to young people and given the serious implications undiagnosed chlamydia can have, the NHS must give it a go.

(Quoted in BBC News 2008)

Benchmarking social marketing practices

As discussed in Chapter 1, and as also noted by Truong and Hall (2013), despite the interest in tourism in changing behaviours, there are few publications that have been directly written on social marketing and tourism. Therefore, determining the social marketing dimensions of tourism projects, for example, can be extremely difficult without being clear about what exactly makes social marketing, well, social marketing! In part this is, of course, difficult because as discussed in Chapter 1 there is no single widely accepted definition of social marketing (see also Dann 2010). As Truong and Hall (2013) reported it is also difficult to identify social marketing interventions in tourism because usually such projects are not labelled social marketing in their information and/or evaluation reports. 'Consequently, results obtained from a search strategy that is simplistically based on the social marketing label are most likely to be insufficient and even flawed' (Truong and Hall 2013: 115).

Andreasen (2002: 7) proposed a number of benchmarks 'for identifying an approach that could be legitimately called social marketing'. Notwithstanding Andreasen's (2012) more recent comments with respect to the language of social marketing (see the previous section), he argued that:

> what makes social marketing potentially unique is that it (1) holds behavior change as its 'bottom line,' (2) therefore is fanatically customer-driven, and (3) emphasizes creating attractive exchanges that encourage behavior (the benefits are so compelling and the costs so minimal that everyone will comply). These tenets, in turn, imply central roles for consumer research, pretesting, and monitoring; for careful market segmentation; and for strategies that seek to provide beneficial, popular, and easy-to-implement exchanges to target audience members.
>
> (Andreasen 2002: 7)

On this basis six benchmarks were identified by Andreasen (2002):

1 *Behaviour change* as 'the benchmark used to design and evaluate interventions' (Andreasen 2002: 7).
2 *Audience research* to understand target audiences, and pre-test and monitor interventions.
3 *Segmentation* of target audiences.
4 Attractive and motivational *exchanges* with target audience.
5 Attempts to use all of the four Ps of the *marketing mix*.
6 *Competition* for desired behaviour of target audience.

These benchmarks have been influential in a number of social marketing applications (e.g. McDermott *et al.* 2005; Gordon *et al.* 2006; De Meyrick 2007; Stead *et al.* 2007; Mah *et al.* 2008; Luca and Suggs 2010, 2013; Wettstein *et al.* 2012). Nevertheless, as Truong and Hall (2013) note, a sole focus on individuals (downstream level) would substantially limit the examination of social marketing's effectiveness given the interest in social marketing to also seek change to the upstream organisations, institutional arrangements and structures that also affect individual behaviours. Therefore in Truong and Hall's (2013) study of the use of social marketing in pro-poor tourism projects in Vietnam upstream targeting was also included as a benchmark while audience research and segmentation was combined given their close similarities (Table 5.2).

In Truong and Hall's (2013) study 21 pro-poor tourism projects in Vietnam were judged to pass the six social marketing benchmarks (see also Truong 2013). Primarily downstream behaviour change goals included preventing or mitigating illegal logging, hunting, forest burning, promoting the conservation of natural resources in tourist destinations, encouraging environmentally and socially responsible/sustainable tourism and motivating local people to actively participate in tourism. More upstream goals included improving cooperation among various stakeholders and motivating local authorities to establish and enforce conservation laws and regulations. Audience research primarily consisted of community needs assessment, training assessment, interviews, focus groups or piloting of project interventions. All selected projects used more than one element of the marketing mix and considered tangible (new farming techniques, new rice varieties) and intangible (community pride) exchanges and barriers (competition) to change. Truong and Hall reported:

> Behavior change outcomes were often combined with other results or reported by the improved awareness in or increased involvement of the target audience as noted above. Although behavior change outcomes were not always clearly reported, changes in the target audience's awareness, cognition, or perception of value might to a greater or lesser extent influence their choice of behavior in the long term.
>
> (Truong and Hall 2013: 132)

TABLE 5.2 Social marketing benchmark criteria

Benchmarks	Description
Behaviour change goal	Behaviour change considered as an objective of intervention and evaluation measures.
Audience research and segmentation	Interventions are designed based on understanding of audience needs and wants. Formative research is conducted and intervention elements pretested. The audience is segmented.
Social marketing mix	Interventions attempt to use the set of 4Ps of the marketing mix. Interventions that only use the promotion element are social advertising or communications. Other Ps may include people and policy. The use of these elements is flexible.
Exchange	Something the target audience are interested in or want is offered to motivate behaviour change that may be tangible (financial incentives, rewards) or intangible (emotional satisfaction, community pride).
Upstream targeting	Programme interventions seek to influence other individuals and organisations that influence target audience behaviour (e.g., local authorities, professional organisations, policy makers).
Competition	Competing internal behaviours (e.g. current behaviour) and external factors (e.g. policies) are considered in programme interventions. Strategies are used to eliminate or minimise these factors.

Source: Adapted from Truong and Hall (2013) after Andreasen (2002); McDermott *et al.* (2005); Stead *et al.* (2007)

Yet one of the most important findings was that although some tourism-related projects used all elements of the social marketing concept, they did not refer explicitly to the field. No project labelled itself under the term social marketing, a finding that is also consistent with public health-related behavioural intervention projects (Stead *et al.* 2007). Although projects suggested positive results it was also observed that evaluation procedures were not based on long-term assessment of change and monitoring and evaluation procedures were generally qualitative and impressionistic (see the discussion on evaluation in Chapter 4).

Another influential set of benchmarks developed from Andreasen's (2002) work is that of the UK National Social Marketing Centre (NSMC) (Table 5.3). According to the NSMC:

> The benchmarks were selected by reviewing successful social marketing projects and identifying the common elements that contributed to their success. The benchmarks are not a social marketing process, but the elements that can improve the impact of a social marketing intervention.
>
> (National Social Marketing Centre 2010a)

One significant difference in the NSMC benchmarks is the explicit recognition of theory informed interventions. However, there is otherwise a high degree of overlap between the various benchmarks. Several of the elements of benchmarks will therefore be used in the following chapters to illustrate the application of social marketing to the tourism context (see Chapter 6). Such an approach further adapts Andreasen's (2002) perspective:

TABLE 5.3 Benchmark criteria for social marketing interventions

Criteria	Explanation
Behaviour	Does the intervention aim to change people's actual behaviour?
Customer orientation	Does the intervention focus on the audience and attempt to fully understand their lives, behaviour and the issue(s) under investigation using a mix of data sources and research methods?
Informed by theory	Does the intervention use behavioural theories to understand behaviour and inform the intervention?
Insight	Does 'customer research' identify 'actionable insights', i.e. the understandings that will lead intervention development?
Exchange	Does the intervention consider the benefits and costs of adopting and maintaining a new behaviour and maximise the benefits and minimises the costs to create an attractive offer?
Competition	Does the intervention seek to understand what competes for the audience's time, attention and inclination to behave in a particular way?
Segmentation	Does the intervention avoid a 'one-size-fits-all' approach? Does it identify audience 'segments' that have common characteristics and then tailors interventions appropriately?
Methods mix	Does the intervention use a mix of methods to bring about behaviour change and not rely solely on raising awareness?

Source: After French (2008); National Social Marketing Centre (2010a)

I do not argue that programs must have all six elements in strong measure to qualify for the label 'social marketing.' It is inevitable that many will have heavy doses of advertising – because this is one thing marketers do well – and more limited roles for other elements of the marketing mix. However, campaigns that are purely communications campaigns are not social marketing. Indeed, it is when campaigns move beyond mere advertising that the power of the approach is manifested.

(Andreasen 2002: 7)

Social marketing as craft

On the whole, the difficult thing about persuading others is not that one lacks the knowledge needed to state his case nor the audacity to exercise his abilities to the full. On the whole, the difficult thing about persuasion is to know the mind of the person one is trying to persuade and to be able to fit one's words to it.

(Han Fei Tzu, quoted in Meltsner 1980: 125–126)

As this and the previous chapter have indicated there are a number of approaches to behaviour change that come under the rubric of social marketing. Nevertheless, differences remain over the subject's definition and, as Chapter 2 pointed out, many of the behavioural change theories that inform social marketing are never actually formally used or tested in social marketing research. Many social marketing interventions make no mention of theory at all (Luca and Suggs 2013). How then does it work?

One way in which this can be tackled is with respect to the role of persuasion in policy and planning and the notion of such activities as being based on a craft approach. The craft approach and its emphasis on argument and persuasion of stakeholders has had some influence on tourism planning and policy making (e.g., Hall and Jenkins 1995; Tyler and Dinan 2001; Hall 2008a), but given its links to public policy making, surprisingly none at all on the social marketing literature. Nevertheless, as will be discussed below, such an approach is potentially extremely relevant in explaining how social marketing is approached in practice as well as the selection of interventions.

It should never be assumed that organisations, including governmental ones, are rational and will automatically recognise and adopt the most appropriate policy and intervention responses or reflect the needs of their constituencies (Haas 2004). The dominant or received view of much marketing and management education (as well as neo-classical economic education), with its focus on technical and economic efficiency and a one-one-one correspondence between the stages of the process and the phases of analysis, is a set of prescriptive theories of thinking and decision making. This situation can create difficulties for approaches that may lay outside of dominant ways of thinking about problems as well as their solutions. Indeed, Majone's observation with respect to the contemporary state of policy and economic analysis:

> Significant advances in techniques (or at least using techniques developed in other disciplines), breadth of research interests, and curricula, coexist with naïve faith in the latest managerial 'fix,' and an almost total disregard for the skills traditionally considered essential accomplishments of good policy advisors, such as the ability to argue, communicate, and evaluate evidence.
>
> (Majone 1980: 161)

Remains as relevant to the present day as when it was originally written. However, to decide, even if to decide rationally, is not enough. Decisions must be accepted and carried out; in addition to the organisational process for implementation, there must be a parallel intellectual process of elaboration on and development of the original policy idea and new arguments are constantly needed to give the different components of a policy the greatest possible fit to changing external conditions (Majone 1980). This therefore requires the knowledge received by decision makers to be usable, that is information that is accurate, politically tractable and usable for its users (Haas 2004).

Clark and Majone (1985) suggest four criteria of usable knowledge:

- *adequacy* – all the relevant knowledge or facts germane to the matter at hand;
- *value* – contributing to further understanding and meaningful policy;
- *legitimacy* – its acceptance by others outside the community that developed it;
- *effectiveness* – its ability to shape the agenda or advance the state of the debate, and, ultimately, improve the quality of the environment and/or well-being.

Similarly, the Center for International Climate and Environmental Research (CICERO) applies three requirements for a solution design model to be considered adequate and which appear directly relevant to 'real world' social marketing interventions:

- It must be capable of mobilising sufficient political support to produce agreement.
- It must be capable of generating solutions that can be implemented.
- It must be capable of generating solutions that are instrumental towards solving the problems for which they were designed.

(CICERO 1999 in Haas 2004: 575)

Such an approach with a focus on the political acceptability of the solutions offered as well as their effectiveness and capacity to be implemented bear a close relationship to the craft approach to policy analysis, which also shares a concern with shaping and communicating advice to stakeholders so that it is accepted. As Dye (1987: 7) noted: '[T]he skills of rhetoric, persuasion, organization and activism' influence the decision and policy-making processes. Similarly, Geva-May and Wildavsky (1997: 142) characterise the communication function as 'articulated persuasion' – the argumentation and advocacy efforts for a particular position that are undertaken, not in the analytical realm, but on a 'political and sociological platform'. This 'persuasion perspective' – 'the ethical attempt to persuade a decision maker of the value of an analysis and/or recommendations' (Longo 2007: 2) – is therefore fundamental in framing the process of communicating policy and/or intervention analysis to decision makers.

In craftwork 'successful performance depends on possessing a clear understanding of the possibilities and limitations of materials and tools, and on establishing a highly personal relationship between the person and his or her task' (Majone 1980: 170) and is grounded in the classical Aristotelian analysis of craftwork in the *Nichomachean Ethics*, which involves four constituents of the task of craftwork:

- *material* – what is being worked on, i.e., the data, information and conceptual constructs used in defining the problem to be analysed (see also Weimer 1998);
- *efficient* – the agent and the tools he or she uses in shaping the material, i.e. tools, techniques and theories of behavioural change;
- *formal* – the shape the material acquires, i.e., the evidence that is cited and from which a conclusion about what forms of intervention are to be used and which target audience are drawn; and
- *final* – the purpose of the activity, which is the creation of a specific object or the services it provides, i.e., the conclusion itself and the related activities of communication to stakeholders and its implementation.

This scheme provides a valuable alternative way of describing the structure of the social marketer's task as well as reflecting some of Andreasen's (2002) concerns as to the need to be marketing social marketing. As Majone (1980: 171) observed: '[T]he conception of analysis as craft provides categories (data, information, tools, evidence, argument) that are applicable to any type and style of analysis'. Moreover the role of argument in craftwork gives a realistic perspective of the way in which social marketing processes are shaped both within change agencies and when the need for a particular type of intervention (and the resources that need to go with it) is argued to governments, sponsors and donors as well as, in some cases, the wider public and the target audience itself. Interestingly, a craft approach also potentially suggests why sometimes theory is left out of social marketing interventions as what is regarded as acceptable may lie more in 'common-sense' approaches to behavioural change, or ones that lie within a certain construction of 'what works' than what may be demonstrated by provision of competing scientific theories or evidence (Shove 2010). As Haas (2004: 571) suggests: 'Politicians don't want science; they want a justification for pre-existing political programs which are driven principally by political anticipations of gain'.

Many decision makers are likely to be much more familiar with marketing concepts than they are with behavioural change theories. Prior experience and the approaches used in previous projects, and their success, is therefore potentially a much more persuasive instrument than the provision of theoretical discussions. Of course, this does depend on the training education and backgrounds of those who ultimately decide on interventions and their funding but for those without appropriate backgrounds there is a clear challenge to make the science of behaviour change simple and persuasive. 'Harry Truman is supposed to have complained about his economist advisers who would say "on the one hand" and "on the other hand". Truman said, just give me a one-handed economist' (Haas 2004: 573).

It is therefore also important to recognise that interventions also imply non-interventions. In other words there is a much wider range of potential interventions that could be used than what is actually used. Decisions as to the selection of an intervention and its implementation therefore suggests that non-decisions and non-interventions (or non-selections) also exist. Such considerations, and the reasons why potential interventions are not used, including their political acceptability, need far greater recognition in the social marketing process (Webster 1975; Levin and Ziglio 1996; Jones 2011; Jones et al. 2011; Devlin-Foltz et al. 2012; Hughes et al. 2012), including with respect to tourism (Weiler et al. 2009; Hall 2011b).

Argument is the link between the data and the conclusion that is reached. 'The structure of the argument will typically be a complex blend of factual statements and subjective evaluations. Along with mathematical and logical deductions, it will include statistical, empirical, and analogical inferences, references to expert opinion, estimates of benefits and costs, and caveats and provisos of different kinds' (Majone 1980: 171). This is, in short, the classical social marketing report! It is also important to bear in mind that evidence does not occur in abstract form 'out there'. Instead, information and data is selected to support an argument in order to persuade an audience.

> Selecting inappropriate data or models, placing them at the wrong point in the argument, or choosing a style of presentation which is not appropriate for the intended audience, can destroy the effectiveness of information used as evidence, regardless of intrinsic cognitive value.
>
> (Majone 1980: 171–172)

Social marketing can therefore neither be performed competently, nor used properly without an appreciation of its craft dimensions.

The craft approach also helps make more sense of the problem of 'speaking truth to power (Wildavsky 1987) or as Bardach (2002) put it, the task of 'educating the client'. As Haas (2004: 571) suggests: '[T]he path from truth to power is a circuitous route at best … Power doesn't care about truth anyhow'. Yet what remains in and what is left out of any social marketing programme required value judgements 'which must be explained and justified' (Majone 1989: 21) as well as considerations of personal and professional ethics. If persuasion is 'a method of mutual learning through discourse' (Majone 1989: 173) then not only is there a need to understand clients and the political and stakeholder context within which the social marketing process occurs, but also oneself.

BOX 5.3 THOMPSON'S (2008) RULES TO MAKE ARGUMENTATION MORE EFFECTIVE

1 Practice inquiry before advocacy. Be open to a variety of points of view before you embrace any one of them.
2 Know your subject [do your homework].
3 Be honest about what you know and don't know [don't invent].
4 Try to tell the truth as you perceive it [don't lie or distort].
5 Don't oversimplify.
6 Acknowledge possible weaknesses in your position. Be honest about your own ambivalence or uncertainty.
7 Avoid irrelevant emotional appeals or diversionary tactics.
8 Appeal to the best motives of your colleagues, not their worst.
9 Be prepared to lose if winning means doing psychological harm to others and demeaning yourself in the bargain.

(Thompson 2008: 6–7)

PLATE 5.1 Help Save Our Market! Stallkeeper campaign for the Oxford covered markets, July 2013

Social marketing, the issue-attention cycle and agenda setting

The linkages between the craft of social marketing, including the relationship to policy influence and governance, and social marketing being seen as a 'solution' to a 'problem' is an important one as it helps provide a further context for reasons why social marketing may be applied in one situation and not another. Andreasen (2006) suggested that the processes of how social problems climb social agendas to become problems that require resolution – the process of agenda setting – was significant for social marketing.

It has long been recognised that public perceptions of the relative importance of an issue are largely determined by the news media (Wood and Peake 1998) whether directly to the receiver of the media communication or by word of mouth. The media interprets issues, giving them more or less significance through the amount or type of coverage provided. The amount of media coverage of an issue may not reflect its actual importance in real terms. For example, in the case of tourism, the SARS or avian flu outbreaks in the 2000s, while important health issues (Lee and Basnyat 2013), pails into significance each year when compared to the number of deaths from diseases such as dengue fever or malaria carriers, which also travel back to their home country.

The media, particularly television news, also focus attention on specific events through this same interpretive function (Iyengar and Kinder 1987). However, not only does the media influence general public opinions, it also plays a major part in informing consumer's images of destinations and transport modes, their relative safety and security, either directly in terms of being read, heard or watched, or indirectly through the advice given by friends, relatives and other sources of WOM information (Fodness and Murray 1997). Moreover, with global communication events can be played out live on the television, computer and smartphone screens; there is the potential for having an even greater impact on the viewing public. Yet the media serves to filter which events are shown and which are not.

These issues highlight the importance for understanding the means by which tourism and social marketing related issues and events get onto media or policy agenda. Agenda-setting research focuses not on the opinions surrounding issues, but on issue salience. Cohen (1963) was the first to state what has become the central public agenda-setting hypothesis: the press 'may not be successful much of the time in telling people what to think, but it is stunningly successful in telling its readers what to think about' (Cohen 1963: 13). Following from Cohen's discussion, public agenda-setting work demonstrated that increased issue salience for the media leads to increased issue salience for the public – in agenda-setting terms, that the media agenda has an impact on the public agenda, where an agenda is a ranking of the relative importance of various public issues (Dearing and Rogers 1996).

Several hypotheses have been put forward with respect to agenda setting and issue salience. One of the most significant concepts in understanding the relationships between the media and the issue agenda is the concept of the issue-attention cycle (Downs 1972). According to Downs, modern publics attend to many issues in a cyclical fashion. A problem 'leaps into prominence, remains there for a short time, and then, though still largely unresolved, gradually fades from the center of public attention' (1972: 38). Originally applied to an understanding of social and environmental issues, the notion of an issue-attention cycle has also been found to be extremely important in explaining the relationship between domestic and foreign policy decisions, the media and the level of public interest in certain issues (Cohen 1963; Walker 1977; Peters and Hogwood 1985; Iyengar and Kinder 1987;

Henry and Gordon 2001; Shih *et al.* 2008). The issue-attention cycle is divided into five stages that may vary in duration depending upon the particular issue involved, but which almost always occur in the following sequence:

1   the pre-problem stage;
2   alarmed discovery and euphoric enthusiasm;
3   realising the cost of significant progress;
4   gradual decline of intense public interest;
5   the post-problem stage.

Hall (2002) applied the issue-attention cycle to understanding the policy agenda and related consumer perspectives on travel security following the terrorist attacks of 11 September 2001, and argued that these stages not only described recent efforts with respect to travel safety measures and policies but were also indicative of wider public opinions towards issues associated with travel safety and subsequent political interventions. Hall (2002) noted in particular that travel security problems were clearly recognised by experts prior to 11 September but that they had a low media profile and that it took the events of that day for them to become an important policy issue and provided for subsequent interventions, including for example the use of social marketing with respect to encouraging appropriate security promoting travel behaviour when flying. However, the issue-attention cycle has been connected to the salience of a number of social marketing issues including climate change and tourism entrepreneurs attitudes (Hall 2006b), public attitudes to climate change (McDonald 2009), health improvement projects (Hubbell and Dearing 2003), skin cancer (Stryker *et al.* 2005), the market for green consumer products (Thøgersen 2006), clothing sweatshops (Greenberg and Knight 2004), flu pandemics (Shih *et al.* 2008; Lee and Basnyat 2013) and obesity (Barry *et al.* 2012).

Other significant hypotheses regarding agenda setting include Zucker (1978) who suggested that it was likely the more individuals experience an issue event directly, the less potential there is for media effects on public opinion. Similarly, Yagade and Dozier, (1990) argued that 'concrete' issues should be more open to media effects than 'abstract' issues. Arguably this may at least be a partial explanation for the importance of perceptions of health and safety as a determinant in travel decision making as opposed to other 'crises' in destinations that may be economic or financial in nature. Other authors, such as MacKuen and Coombs (1981) and Wanta and Hu (1993), have argued that issues that involve dramatic events or conflict should also increase the potential for media attention and have consequent effects on public opinion. From a social marketing perspective Andreasen (2006) proposed that issues are transformed into high-priority problems through eight stages:

1   *Inattention*: the problem exists, but has not yet become a widespread concern.
2   *Discovery*: the problem comes to citizens' and policy-makers' attention and it may be examined in greater detail.
3   *Climbing the agenda*: advocacy groups, politicians and other actors, including the media, raise the issue as a problem that needs to be addressed.
4   *Outlining the choices*: actors debate how the problem may be addressed.
5   *Choosing courses of action*: actors debate the costs of action or inaction, affected parties, impacts and other relevant factors.

6   *Launching initial interventions*: governments and other change agencies launch early pioneering efforts to address the problem.
7   *Reassessing and redirecting*: after interventions have been running for some time, actors assess interventions and adjust them depending on formal evaluations, and perceptions of success and failure (both of actors and the wider public).
8   *Success, failure, or neglect*: outcomes occur after an extended period of time when solutions may or may not have been found for the problems, or when other issues have climbed up the agenda and shifted the initial problem to a lower priority.

Andreasen's (2006) staging of issue salience is also significant because it also suggests that social marketing not only responds to the issue-attention cycle but may also seek to actively influence it when looking to affect public and political opinion about the importance of an issue as well as the need to intervene to 'solve' it. Indeed, if media and public opinion is important to influence political decision making, funding and intervention selection, then such an approach may be vital to influence upstream as well as downstream behavioural change. Nevertheless, regardless of the factor behind issue salience, the carrying capacity of the media means that the ecological competition between issues leads to a situation in which new issues arise replacing the other issues in terms of extent and quality of coverage. Media coverage becomes diminished and routinised over time with only sporadic review or anniversary stories that mark the effects of the original event on policy and administrative processes. As issues move towards the media horizon they also decline in importance as a consumer concern (Hall and O'Sullivan 1996). Given such a situation it is apparent that unless a crisis continues for a substantial length of time then it is extremely unlikely to have permanent impacts on destination perceptions or policy and issue agendas (Hall 2010d).

The challenge facing those who have to deal with the implications of certain issues and concerns being salient in the public or policy mind is do they have strategies in place to influence media presentation and ranking of issues? Ultimately this is not just a question of media management but also social marketing strategy.

Chapter summary

The chapter has examined the craft and practice of social marketing. In revisiting the question of the relationship between commercial and social marketing that we initially encountered in the first chapter it reinforced the importance of behaviour change as the central thrust of social marketing. However, this also raised questions about the extent to which social marketing could be 'benchmarked' so that social marketing interventions could be more readily identified. One of the outcomes of this is that the exercise of social marketing approaches is sometimes not labelled as such (Truong and Hall 2013). Thereby also recalling Andreasen's (2002) suggestions as to the importance of 'marketing social marketing in the social change marketplace.'

The chapter then went on to discuss the importance of craft approaches to social marketing because of the extent to which social marketers seek to argue their case in the social change marketplace so that interventions can be supported. It was noted that a craft approach has a number of requirements with respect to the activities of social marketers especially in relation to being aware of the perceptions and requirements of the audience of social marketing proposals and initiatives. It was also noted that, at times, craft approaches may not require the formal inclusion of behavioural change theory into the social marketing process. In fact, in some cases where the audience already has certain predispositions and attitudes towards the nature of the problem, selection of intervention, and 'what works' and is politically acceptable, a craft approach may work against formal use of theory.

BOX 5.4 ALCOHOL AND SHOCK ADVERTISING

In 2010 NHS Northamptonshire decided to air a 'shock' television advertisement to try to reduce binge drinking among young people. Broadcast after 9pm, 'Another Night Wasted' was aimed at 18- to 24-year-olds and showed a man unconscious by a public toilet. NHS Northamptonshire said it had thought 'long and hard' about making the 'extremely shocking TV advert'. Alcohol-related hospital admissions had increased by 109 per cent since 2002 with alcohol also being connected to violent crime, including domestic abuse. Heidi King, head of social marketing for NHS Northamptonshire, said:

> Our research shows that people aged 18 to 24 are 44% more likely than any other age group to binge drink … Factor in the World Cup, music festivals and the long summer evenings and there is an increase in alcohol consumption and the pressure on the health system is considerable.

(BBC News Northampton 2010)

The point of the advertisement was not to tell people to stop drinking but to consider drinking less for fear of missing some of the most important moments of the summer.

Questions for self-reflection:

1 Alcohol is a legally sanctioned drug in most jurisdictions. How does the fact that it is legal affect the capacity to undertake social marketing campaigns to reduce consumption?
2 What role should the tourism and hospitality industry take with respect to encouraging responsible drinking? How does this role conflict with the need for businesses to make a profit?
3 What factors would put alcohol high on the issue agenda and what difference might this make for policy making?
4 How effective might a 'shock' television advertisement shown after 9pm be in encouraging responsible drinking?
5 What would be the main elements of any marketing campaign that you would propose to encourage 18- to 24-year-olds to drink responsibly?

Further reading and websites

With respect to benchmarking in social marketing see:

Andreasen, A. R. (2002) 'Marketing social marketing in the social change marketplace', *Journal of Public Policy and Marketing*, 21: 3–13.

Luca, N. R. and Suggs, L. S. (2010) 'Strategies for the social marketing mix: A systematic review', *Social Marketing Quarterly*, 16(4): 122–149.

Truong, V. D. and Hall, C. M. (2013) 'Social marketing and tourism: What Is the evidence?' *Social Marketing Quarterly*, 19(2): 110–135.

On craft approaches as well as persuasion see:

Geva-May, I. (2002) 'Cultural theory: The neglected variable in the craft of policy analysis', *Journal of Comparative Policy Analysis*, 4(3), 243–265.

Geva-May, I. and Wildavsky, A. (1997) *An Operational Approach to Policy Analysis: The Craft. Prescriptions for Better Analysis*. Boston, MA: Kluwer Academic Publishers.

Majone, G. (1989) *Evidence, Argument, and Persuasion in the Policy Process*. New Haven, CT: Yale University Press.

Thompson, F. (2008) 'The three faces of public management', *International Public Management Review*, 9(1), http://www.ipmr.net.

Wildavsky, A. B. (1987) *Speaking Truth to Power: The Art and Craft of Policy Analysis*. New Brunswick, NJ: Transaction Books.

With respect to issue salience refer to work on the issue-attention cycle:

Downs, A. (1972) 'Up and down with ecology – the issue attention cycle', *The Public Interest*, 28: 38–50.

McDonald, S. (2009) 'Changing climate, changing minds: Applying the literature on media effects, public opinion, and the issue-attention cycle to increase public understanding of climate change', *International Journal of Sustainability Communication*, 4: 45–63.

With respect to issues of issue salience in a tourism context see:

Hall, C. M. (2002) 'Travel safety, terrorism and the media: The significance of the issue-attention cycle', *Current Issues in Tourism*, 5(5): 458–466.

Hall, C. M. (2010) 'Crisis events in tourism: Subjects of crisis in tourism', *Current Issues in Tourism*, 13(5): 401–417.

On issues associated with volunteering in social marketing see:

Briggs, E., Peterson, M. and Gregory, G. (2010) 'Toward a better understanding of volunteering for nonprofit organizations: Explaining volunteers' pro-social attitudes', *Journal of Macromarketing*, 30(1): 61–76.

Hager, M. A., and Brudney, J. L. (2011) 'Problems recruiting volunteers: Nature versus nurture', *Nonprofit Management and Leadership*, 22(2): 137–157.

A good case study of volunteer management within a social marketing organisation is:

Waikayi, L., Fearon, C., Morris, L. and McLaughlin, H. (2012) 'Volunteer management: An exploratory case study within the British Red Cross', *Management Decision*, 50(3): 349–367.

6

THE DEMARKETING OF TOURISM ATTRACTIONS, ACTIVITIES AND DESTINATIONS

Demarketing has long been regarded as a special case of social marketing, particularly with respect to reducing consumption (Peattie and Peattie 2009; Gössling 2010), and its application in tourism has been surprisingly limited (Beeton and Benfield 2002; Armstrong and Kern 2011; Truong and Hall 2013), especially given that tourism was one of the examples used in the original article by Kotler and Levy (1971). Although demarketing has been interpreted by some tourism commentators as meaning a reduction in visitor numbers to a destination or attraction it is actually a far more sophisticated concept that refers to reducing and managing demand while still achieving economic and other goals. Beeton and Benfield (2002: 499) with respect to its use as a visitor and environmental management tool suggest that demarketing 'has the potential to provide planners and managers with a range of constructive tools and techniques that, when applied to areas in a proactive manner, can result in positive and successful results'. After an introduction to the concept of demarketing this chapter provides a number of cases on demarketing from the tourism literature. Table 6.1 provides an overview of the social marketing context of the cases studies. Cases are provided at different scales and include Sissinghurst Castle in the UK, Cyprus, and the Blue Mountains and Uluru National Parks in Australia.

Defining demarketing

Kotler and Levy (1971: 76) defined demarketing as 'that aspect of marketing that deals with discouraging customers in general or a certain class of customers in particular on either a temporary or permanent basis'. Kotler and Levy (1971) identified four different types of demarketing: general, selective, ostensible and unintentional. General demarketing is used when the goal is to reduce the total demand. Selective demarketing is used when demand from a specific market segment or group of consumers needs to be reduced. Ostensible demarketing gives the appearance of aiming to reduce product demand when it is actually seeking to initiate an increase in demand. Unintentional demarketing occurs when attempts to increase demand manage to drive customers away (Kotler and Levy 1971). Demarketing is therefore not the opposite of marketing, but a specific application of marketing principles

TABLE 6.1 Overview of demarketing cases discussed in Chapter 6

Case	System stage(s) of tourism	Behaviour change goal	Audience research and segmentation	Social marketing mix	Exchange	Downstream (customer)/upstream focus	Competition	Theory of behaviour change	Long-term effectiveness
Sissinghurst Castle Garden (National Trust attraction)	• Destination (at attraction) • Consumer decision making	Better allocation of visitor numbers in the garden by demarketing	Visitor survey	• Reduction in promotion of garden as an attraction • Use of promotion	• Improved experience of the garden as a result of lower number of visitors	Customer	None in a narrow sense	Communication and education	Good; the approach has been very successful in managing the high visitor demands
Cyprus (national government)	• Destination • Consumer decision making	Change nature of market by focusing more on high-end tourists	Market research	All four Ps were applied		• Customer • Some concern for communities	Other destinations		None
Blue Mountains National Park (state government)	• Destination (at attraction)	Spread visitor pressures more evenly in park and improve visitor experience	Some market research available	Promotion (via signage)	• Improved visitor experience	Customer	None in a narrow sense	Communication and education	Marginal, as it was a latent form of demarketing
Uluru, Uluru National Park (national parks agency)	• Destination (at attraction)	Encourage visitors not to climb Uluru	Target audiences identified for future demarketing campaigns	Primarily product and promotion. Also significant broad policy issues	• Satisfaction of knowing that not climbing Uluru meets Aboriginal cultural concerns	Customer with some potential to market tour companies and encourage them to provide appropriate advice to visitors	Experience of reaching the top of Uluru	Behavioural learning? Communication and education	Potentially good though change will take a long time while voluntary

(Shama 1978; Kindra and Taylor 1995; Wall 2005). Kotler and Levy (1971) suggested that marketing is as relevant to controlling and/or reducing demand as it is for increasing demand. The role of marketing in influencing levels of demand led to Kotler (1973) identifying eight different states based on the level of actual versus desired demand. These are presented in a modified form in Table 6.2, which also recognises seasonal demand as an additional state to that proposed by Kotler (1973), given that most seasonal demand as well with supply is often highly regular in nature.

The different states of demand are extremely relevant for attraction and destination-related social marketing as they highlight the different states of demand that social marketing may try and influence. Although much commercial tourism marketing is geared towards trying to increase levels of demand, social marketing may not only seek to increase demand in some circumstances but is also just as likely to be used as a tool to reduce or minimise demand. The state of full demand may well be appropriate for the sustainable balance between visitor numbers, behaviour and the qualities of the attraction in some heritage sites. However, where there are too many visitors social marketing may be used as a tool to reduce numbers to an appropriate level. In other cases unwholesome demand may be a focus, for example seeking to ensure that visitors engage in appropriate behaviours at religious heritage sites, burial sites or other culturally and host community sensitive locations.

TABLE 6.2 States of actual versus desired demand

Nature of demand	Characteristics
Negative demand	Most or all of the important segments of the potential market dislike the product and in fact might conceivably pay a price to avoid it.
No demand	All or important segments of a potential market are indifferent or uninterested to a particular product.
Latent demand	A substantial number of people share a need for something that does not exist as an actual product.
Faltering demand	Demand for a product is less than its former level and further decline is expected in the absence of revision of the target market, product characteristics and/or marketing.
Full demand	The current level and timing of demand is equal to the desired level and timing of demand.
Irregular demand	The current pattern of demand is marked by volatile fluctuations that depart from the pattern of supply.
Seasonal demand	The pattern of demand over time is marked by regular fluctuations in demand that are relatively consistent with the pattern of supply.
Overfull/excess demand	Demand exceeds the level at which the marketer feels able or motivated to supply it.
Unwholesome/ inappropriate demand	Any positive level of demand is regarded as excessive because of undesirable qualities associated with the product, e.g. child sex tourism.

Source: After Kotler (1973)

Table 6.3 illustrates the relationship between four of the demand states identified in Table 6.2 and connects them to a tourism context and some facets of social marketing. Demarketing can be used to permanently or temporarily discourage current and potential customers in order to respond to issues of overfull demand. This may be especially important for problems of excess demand or overuse of national parks and heritage sites (Groff 1998; Kern 2006). Countermarketing is sometimes equated with demarketing and the latter is often used to refer to the former (Moore 2005; Wall 2005). However, they differ with respect to the nature of demand and/or behaviours that they are trying to reduce. Countermarketing refers to situations where the product is inherently inappropriate or unwholesome and where the marketer aims to destroy demand. In the broader social marketing context, for example, this would characterise the attempts to reduce demand for tobacco. In the case of tourism examples would be campaigns to prevent child sex tourism or unsafe drug and sexual practices when travelling. In contrast, the aim of demarketing, as Kotler and Armstrong (2001: 14) emphasise, 'is not to destroy demand but only to reduce or shift it'. Demarketing is therefore often used when product demand is perceived to be too high, usually by the supplier, e.g. with respect to sustainable levels of energy or water demand, but in some cases, such as that of crowding, by the customer.

One of the more interesting examples of demarketing in tourism is that of Beeton and Pinge (2003) who proposed demarketing gambling in order to encourage local tourism. In seeking to maximise benefits to tourism destinations and reduce the community health impacts of gambling Beeton and Pinge (2003: 310) suggested that 'if gambling expenditure can be limited, with that money being shifted to local tourism, local communities stand to benefit'. Beeton and Pinge (2003) argued that at the same time that gambling was demarketed to the target market so tourism should be marketed as a substitute leisure activity. In keeping with a range of previous measures and research on gambling Beeton and Pinge (2003: 317) suggested several gambling demarketing measures that could be applied in the Australian context:

- limiting the supply of the product, e.g. number of gaming machines, time limits on machines, reducing opening hours and enforcing breaks;
- making access to venues more difficult, e.g. limited street frontage, limited entrances direct from street;
- reducing promotion of gaming venues;
- discouraging tied promotion of gambling venues with other, more benign products, such as shopping;
- providing better information to gamblers, e.g. duration of play and time of day, odds of winning, amounts lost; and a cross-marketing measure of
- promoting local tourism opportunities at gambling venues.

Beeton and Pinge's (2003) suggestions with respect to using tourism as an alternative 'leisure attraction' to gambling have not been implemented, and although there is greater awareness of problem gambling in Australia, measures to restrict gambling activities are restricted by the political influence of clubs that have gaming machines as well as the tax returns to government from gambling.

TABLE 6.3 Connecting product demand levels to social marketing

Demand state	Characteristic	Tourism context	Facet of marketing / social marketing
Overfull demand	'A state in which demand exceeds the level at which the [organisation] feels able or motivated to supply it' (Kotler 1973: 47).	Tourist demand for a site or experience reaches a level that results in negative environmental and/or social impacts and the degradation of the visitor experience.	*Demarketing* The marketing task is to permanently or temporarily discourage customers.
Seasonal demand	The pattern of demand over time is marked by regular fluctuations in demand that are relatively consistent with the pattern of supply, although excess capacity to supply the product will exist at certain times of the year.	Although demand has a regular pattern over time there are often periods at which infrastructure and resources are under-utilised. Therefore marketing can be used to improve ROI and/or provide benefits over a longer period of time.	*Synchromarketing* The task of social marketing is to bring the movements of supply and demand into better synchronisation. This may be done by seeking ways of extending shoulder seasons or hosting special events or lowering prices in periods of otherwise low demand.
Irregular demand	'A state in which the current timing pattern of demand is marked by … volatile fluctuations that depart from the timing pattern of supply' (Kotler 1973: 46).	Unexpected variations in demand can lead to problems of temporary overfull or faltering demand, e.g. those created by crisis events.	*Synchromarketing* The task of social marketing is to bring the movements of supply and demand into better synchronisation. This is often done by changing product, promotion or price characteristics.
Unwholesome/ inappropriate demand	'A state in which any positive level of demand is felt to be excessive because of undesirable qualities associated with the product' (Kotler 1973: 47).	Examples include site use or user behaviours that are inappropriate in their local or wider context, e.g. vandalism of heritage sites.	*Countermarketing (unselling)* The task of social marketing is to minimise the extent of inappropriate demand through various interventions

Source: After Kotler (1973); Groff (1998)

Although the use of social marketing to curb gambling is a significant area of tourism-related demarketing some attention has also been given to its role in maintaining environmental and visitor values in protected areas. Groff (1998: 130) observed that 'Many national parks, public lands and natural resource areas in the United States and other countries are facing excess demand for one or more types of recreation or visitor experiences'. Groff (1998) identified three specific situations of excess demand in national parks and outdoor recreation management in which agencies could apply demarketing measures:

- *temporary shortages*: as a result of lack of supply of sites, programmes and/or experiences given the level of unexpected or seasonal peak visitor demand;
- *chronic overpopularity*: the popularity of attraction or experience can threaten the quality of the visitor experience and also damage the natural resource that attracts the visitors; and
- *conflicting use*: issues surrounding visitor safety, compatibility of use with resources, potential conflicts between different user groups, and the different uses and programmes demanded by visitors and the community.

These three situations are similar to those identified by Wearing and Archer (2001: 39) who suggest the use of demarketing in specific circumstances: 'In situations of excess demand, lack of supply or conflicting use, demarketing strategies are appropriate in order to discourage the level of demand for a particular setting or activity'. Table 6.4 notes Wearing and

TABLE 6.4 Relationship of marketing mix to protected area demarketing measures

Demarketing measure	*Elements of marketing mix*
Increasing prices in a manner so they increase disproportionately as time spent in the park management destination increases	Price
Creating a queuing system to increase the time and opportunity costs of the experience	Price
Limiting the main promotional strategy to select and specialised media channels	Promotion, place
Promoting the need to conserve the area through minimal impact and sustainable development	Promotion
Highlighting the environmental degradation that could occur if too many people frequent the area	Promotion, place
Highlighting any restrictions or difficulties associated with travel to the area	Promotion, place
Provide alternative locations or experiences for visitors and communicate them	Place, product, promotion
Zoning policies are applied to limit activities to some locations and not others; in some cases this may be undertaken on a seasonal basis	Place
Utilise interpretation as a management tool to reduce some undesirable and inappropriate behaviours and develop new understandings of the product in order to reduce visitor pressures	Promotion, product

Source: Measures 1–6 from Wearing and Archer (2001: 36); 7–9 from Hall and McArthur (1998)

Archer's (2001) suggested strategies for protected areas in the context of the marketing mix (see Chapter 4). The use of interpretation as a form of demarketing to counteract inappropriate visitor behaviour (Hall and McArthur 1998; Archer and Wearing 2002; see also Groff 1998) is regarded by Kern (2006) as a countermarketing measure rather than a form of demarketing. *However*, in certain circumstances interpretation can also be regarded as a means of demarketing when it encourages visitors to utilise substitute experiences thereby reducing visitor pressure on some protected areas and heritage attractions. Similarly, Benfield (2001) also suggests that offering alternatives for activities that have been rationed helps to maintain visitor satisfaction (see the Sissinghurst Castle case below).

BOX 6.1 DEMARKETING CHILD SEX TOURISM

Sex tourism is 'tourism where the main purpose or motivation is to consummate commercial sexual relations' (Hall 1992; see also Ryan and Hall 2001). The growth of child sex tourism in particular has seen attention turn to active demarketing campaigns aimed at discouraging such behaviours amongst tourists. Negative impacts that have arisen as a direct result of sex tourism include human trafficking, kidnapping, organised crime and the sexual exploitation of both women and children (Black 2010), leading to an array of physical, emotional and mental consequences (Black 2010; Glover 2006). Black (2010) studied sex tourism in the context of social marketing campaigns, and found that there was a gap that existed in terms of social marketing literature and case-based studies in this area. This led to the proposition of the Sex Tourism Destination Competitiveness (STDC) Model (Black 2010). The premise behind this model was that the STDC of a country 'refers to the ability of a country to attract tourists for sex or sex-related purposes under free and fair market conditions' (Black 2010: 33).

Donovan and Henley (2003: 21) note that 'a major concern of social marketing must be to bring about changes in the social structural factors that impinge on an individual's opportunities, capacities, and right to have a healthy and fulfilling life', and in order to address this Black (2010: 38) argues that 'social marketing may be utilised to distinguish tourism from sex tourism'. Intervention in government policymaking (Black 2010) and using advertising to promote the negative consequences of child sex tourism (Glover 2006) are two areas where such strategies have been applied successfully.

It is noted by Black (2010: 34) that 'policy intervention is more applicable in the case of created and supporting resources of the country that include safety, hotels, transportation, or entertainment in the country'. This creates somewhat of a dilemma for social marketing campaigns; the sex industry in many countries is tied closely to both historical and cultural traditions (Black 2010), which makes political interference difficult. Referring to this situation, Black (2010: 39) also decrees 'this is an uncontrollable variable for marketers, making it difficult to intervene. Unless economics and social conditions improve the supply-side, the conditions will continue to favour the sex industry in poor countries'.

Case studies

Mass tourism at Sissinghurst Castle Garden, Kent

The advent of mass tourism at Sissinghurst Castle Garden, Kent, which is arguably one of the most famous public gardens in the United Kingdom, presents a prime example of how if managed correctly the impacts of tourist visitation can actually be controlled very effectively. Benfield (2001) investigated tourist flows at Sissinghurst Castle Garden as part of a case study into sustainable tourism, and found that management had set limits on visitation based upon a working knowledge of what they viewed as sustainable best practice in order to negate damage to the gardens themselves. This case study was also based on the ideas put forward by Butler (1999) who argued that the core to the concept of sustainability lay in the application of limits, particularly in terms of carrying capacity. Butler (1999) argued that whilst research into such limits lay in the origins of earlier research in tourism and recreation (e.g., Clawson and Knetsch 1966; Lime and Stankey 1975), little research had focused on the management of tourism areas and facilities in which the effectiveness of managerial policy had been analysed in order to see what controls and regulations had worked in terms of setting visitor limits.

Benfield (2001: 213) noted that 'at certain peak times, visitors were becoming unable to negotiate the paths and were spilling over onto the grass and over gardens, in the process destroying the very features they had come to observe'. Clearly, this situation was untenable if Sissinghurst Castle Garden was going to pursue long-term commercial viability as well as maintain its gardening and cultural heritage, and some form of control needed to be put in place in order to address this situation.

The decision made by management to limit the carry capacity of Sissinghurst Castle Garden to 400 visitors at any point was made in 1989, which relied on self-regulation on the part of visitors (Benfield 2001). This system where 'a large notice at the entrance to the garden warning that the garden was currently crowded and that appreciation of the garden might be impaired by the presence of large numbers of fellow visitors' (Benfield 2001: 213) was ineffective as visitors continued to access the garden even once the carry capacity had been reached. The solution to this problem was the use of a timed-entry system that was first introduced in 1992, as well as obligatory reservations for tour buses, a booking system for tour groups, and reducing and then discontinuing any paid advertising, which had stopped completely by 1997. Furthermore, media features on Sissinghurst 'were edited, where possible, to stress the sensitivity of the garden and the restrictions that were in place' (Benfield 2001: 215).

A visitor survey referred to by Benfield (2001) in this particular case illustrated that limiting the areas in which tourists were able to access and controlling visitor access through timed entry had actually worked. The introduction of these measures along with the provision of relevant information before visiting had allowed visitors to actually engage more with the history behind Sissinghurst Castle and expand beyond the garden as being the main visitor focus. As part of the process of utilising the pre-visit and 'travel to' stage of tourism the National Trust also provided 'waiting visitors with complimentary access to the oast houses where there are static displays interpreting the garden's founding and current issues in horticulture' (Benfield 2001: 214). However, Benfield (2001: 25) notes that this case study also shows clearly that 'self-management does not work in the context of mass tourism in public gardens. By contrast, control, when initiated with a receptive and knowledgeable audience, can not only benefit the facility but can also accrue other side benefit'.

Demarketing in the Republic of Cyprus

As a popular tourist destination, the Republic of Cyprus had seen a rapid growth in visitor numbers since it became fashionable as a destination in the late 1960s (Clements 1989). This growth in local tourism also brought with it a decline in the standard of tourist behaviour (Modiano 1988), which resulted in the application of demarketing tactics designed to actively target certain segments of the tourist population whilst discouraging others (Clements 1989). The case study by Clements (1989: 91) focused on how the four Ps (price, product, place, promotion) were manipulated in Cyprus through demarketing. Measures that were used included strict control over the place and product attributes of tourism, such as discouraging cheap self-catering apartments and nightclubs, increasing prices for tourism services and discouraging discounting, and reducing promotion in specific markets:

> To minimise potential destabilising effects, the tourism strategy was to attract to the island older high and middle income groups to the exclusion of other groups normally associated with mass tourism. The establishment of a prestige holiday destination could be achieved through selective advertising and promotion, and quality accommodation, supported by higher than average prices.

Whilst noting that such a selective demarketing process did serve to improve the reputation of tourist behaviour in Cyprus, Clements (1989) observed that these formerly undesirable elements who have been discouraged from visiting through demarketing strategies will be displaced to other destinations. With respect to control of the promotional channels Clements (1989: 91) suggested that the Cyprus Tourism Organization

> is monitoring standards of information presentation at the points of tourist departure. Agencies report directly to [the Cyprus Tourism Organization] on how Cyprus is being presented in local media and how holidays are being offered ... efforts are made to ensure that travel and tour operators do not deviate from 'acceptable promotional policies'.

Importantly, Clements (1989) also suggested that fluctuations in tourism demand may mean that maintaining a successful demarketing policy could be affected, as in order to be fiscally successful destinations are still required to meet a minimum threshold in terms of basic tourist capacity. Indeed, a long-term issue in Cyprus as well as with such approaches overall is that the definition of what is economically appropriate with respect to returns from tourism will change over time – often in relation to the success of other sectors in the economy as well as changes in government or government policy.

The challenges presented by the emphasis on sustainable practices in tourism marketing have served to highlight the need for both innovative responses and long-term strategic thinking from the perspective of marketers. The focus on carrying capacity at tourist destinations in tandem with demarketing practices, which aim to create sustainable outcomes, both highlight that attempts have been made in part at addressing these challenges. One example of the strategies and responses designed to address these challenges in action can be seen through the establishment of a carrying capacity threshold on the East Coast of the Republic of Cyprus (Saveriades 2000).

In a bid to examine whether the development of tourism on the East Coast of the Republic of Cyprus had altered the social character of this particular area as a tourist destination,

Saveriades (2000) focused on tourist flows through the study area and argued that the positive or negative nature of these changes is directly correlated to the ability of a destination to be able to withstand the volume of tourist activity that it allows. The premise of this argument was grounded in the hypothesis that 'sustainability of a specific level of tourist development and use within a specified region, over development in many destinations resulted in socio-cultural as well as environmental deterioration, or in a decline in the quality of the overall tourist experience' (Saveriades 2000: 147).

Carrying capacity specifically refers to the volume of tourist activity experienced within a given destination (Sowman 1987), and in this study Saveriades (2000) argued that carrying capacity is determined by two factors; the first factor being the ability of the host community to absorb tourism development before negative effects are experienced, and the second factor being the decline of tourist flows resulting from the carrying capacity threshold being met, rendering the destination unable to either satisfy or attract further visitor traffic (Saveriades 2000). The importance of carrying capacity as a tourism management and planning tool was seen to be of particular importance when considering the environment in Cyprus; the casual approach exhibited by regional planners towards tourism development in the 1970s had created a situation whereby it 'became apparent that unplanned development could transform or even permanently destroy the character of natural and cultural resources and result in loss of tourism demand' (Saveriades 2000: 147).

Saveriades (2000) found that although the perceived level of frustration exhibited by locals towards tourists visiting the East Coast of Cyprus was found to be insignificant, there was a level of concern that the economic benefits derived from tourism could be affected if carrying capacity was not closely monitored. The creation of a monitoring system for the Republic of Cyprus would serve to 'ensure that tourism development is carried out within the context of the optimum *overall* capacity level, thus ensuring its sustainability' (Saveriades 2000: 147). It was therefore recommended that 'carrying capacity findings should be used to facilitate the process of continuous monitoring of tourism by making adjustments to plans as needed' (Saveriades 2000: 147) in order to control mass tourism, a seeming continuation of the process suggested over a decade earlier by Clements (1989) and that clearly had not been successful in the longer term.

The Blue Mountains National Park, Australia

The Blue Mountains National Park to the west of Sydney in Australia is an important draw-card for both domestic and international tourists. The park is a World Heritage Site as well as a national park of New South Wales and is widely used in tourist promotion. Kern (2006: 13) succinctly describes the dilemma confronting national park management in the context of demarketing:

> On the one hand, tourism and recreation are *one raison d'être* for national parks, as they justify in economic terms the retention of relatively undisturbed natural areas. On the other, national parks are under increasing pressure from tourism and recreation.

Armstrong and Kern (2011) investigated the application of demarketing to control excess tourist demand within the Blue Mountains National Park, and found that while no holistic or systematically planned demarketing existed the demarketing measures that were employed were not consciously viewed as deliberate attempts to control tourist demand. They suggested that this was in part due to the fact that the '*latent* use of demarketing may be that marketing in general has only recently established itself as a valued concept in Australian protected areas' (Armstrong and Kern 2011: 139). In order to address this situation the collection of comprehensive visitor information that could be used to inform demarketing practices was recommended; with the collection of this data being seen by Armstrong and Kern (2011: 140) as vital because to 'systematically develop limitations on visitation there are two prerequisites: establishing carrying capacities and methodically collecting and monitoring visitor data'. The need for the management of Blue Mountains National Park to also educate visitors in terms of environmental protection was also found by Armstrong and Kern (2011: 140) to be a pertinent issue as 'while limits for certain locations are currently applied, total limits on the number of licences issued for particular activities do not exist in the park at present'.

The long-term benefits of demarketing within the Blue Mountains National Park were found to exist within the application of basic cost-effective plans as 'providing limited signage or not signposting certain sites or features was found to be employed to demarket specific places to keep them pristine and for reasons of visitor safety' (Armstrong and Kern 2011: 140). Solutions such as this do need to take into account the need for the park to provide visitor-friendly alternatives though, as the abrupt application of such demarketing situation can serve to confuse visitors (Kern 2006).

Inappropriate tourist behaviour at contested sites: the case of Uluru, Australia

McKercher, Weber and du Cros (2008) examined tourist behaviour at Uluru (formerly known as Ayers Rock) in Australia in a case study that was aimed to investigate what, if any, future demarketing activities should be applied in order to curb insensitive forms of behaviour. With the climb of Uluru itself being viewed as increasingly culturally insensitive and socially unacceptable (McKercher *et al.* 2008), a solution to this problem was sought by stakeholders as

> the contested nature of the place can also produce a certain level of moral ambiguity about what constitutes appropriate behaviour. Mixed signals can be transmitted by stakeholders with divergent value sets leading to confusion about what is and what is not acceptable behaviour.
>
> (McKercher *et al.* 2008: 369)

With the climb attracting over 150,000 tourists per year (McKercher *et al.* 2008), it has been suggested that the reasons for the varying levels of tourist behaviour at the site can be explained by one of three categories with the first of these categories being visitors who rely on their own cultural norms in terms of how they behave (Hall and McArthur 1998). Conversely, Selanniemi (2003, as cited in McKercher *et al.* 2008: 369) argues that 'an anarchic behaviour style may emerge, in recognition that tourism is a liminal activity where normal social time and structure stops and is replaced, at least temporarily, by an anti-structure that frees the individual from social norms'. The third category of visitors were identified as those who may participate yet at the same time be aware that their behaviour is at odds with the likely social norms of the destination (McKercher *et al.* 2008). This particular case study also suggested:

Members of the first group and many in the second may see nothing inherently wrong with their actions. However, members of the third group and some members of the second group, retrospectively, may be aware that their actions are inappropriate at some level and will, consequently, need to rationalise their choices to assuage guilt or personal culpability.

(McKercher *et al.* 2008: 369)

Those visitors who climbed Uluru and fell into the aforementioned second and third categories were viewed as the tourist groups that needed to be the focus of future demarketing campaigns in order to discourage them from attempting the climb (McKercher *et al.* 2008). It remains to be seen whether such demarketing strategies have had a positive effect on tourist behaviour at Uluru, and if so, whether such strategies are able to be maintained in the long term.

Chapter summary and conclusions

This chapter has outlined the concept of demarketing as a specific application of social marketing and has provided four case studies to illustrate its application. In referring to the use of demarketing to reduce car-based travel behaviours Wall (2005: 426) argues that 'whilst demarketing can be seen to work, it needs to be well planned and integrated with other government initiatives in order for it to be fully effective'. Wall's observation with respect to government demarketing in general applies equally well to its application in a tourism context. Of the four cases only the Sissinghurst example indicates the long-term success of a demarketing approach in achieving organisational objectives. Scale, in fact, may be a crucial element in the success of social marketing as being of a limited size as well as having a clear set of management objectives may provide a greater degree of control over the marketing mix. The capacity of the National Trust to manage and limit access to Sissinghurst is relatively clear as opposed to the more complex situation of many national parks and destinations, which will have a greater range of interests and stakeholders to satisfy.

The lack of control over promotional channels was an issue with Cyprus's attempts to demarket itself as well as with the national parks. In the case of parks and protected areas:

While protected area managers may be able to control the messages conveyed to visitors on-site, such as through signage, maps and leaflets, they have far less control over any external promotion and messages circulating about the Protected Areas through film, guide-books, tourist brochures and the like.

(Wearing and Nelson 2004: 10)

The lack of control over promotional channels means that external promotional messages can counteract demarketing efforts by park management agencies. However, the 'lack of control over mass and other media sources used by visitors' Wearing and Archer (2005: 14) is an issue not just for the marketing of protected areas but for any tourist attraction or destination that seeks to demarket itself and/or communicate particular information. In the case of many attractions for example, while attraction managers may wish to restrict access or focus on particular groups of consumers other destination actors may seek to continue to use the attraction in promotion in order to increase numbers of visitors to the region.

As in other areas of social marketing some aspects of demarketing have also become ethically controversial. Indeed, even Kotler and Levy (1971: 81) noted that the general and selective demarketing of certain products and services 'may raise thorny issues in social ethics' with respect to rights and access. For example, in a health case context MacStravic (1995) suggests that limiting access to emergency rooms and discouraging inpatient stays after delivery of a child in order to reduce 'overuse' and costs of health and medical facilities is 'pragmatically risky and ethically questionable' (MacStravic 1995: 57). He instead recommends that in such circumstances there is a need for 'remarketing' to ensure that alternative options are available so as to ensure user well-being. One of the ironies of the application of demarketing measures in some public health services in the developed world is that, in seeking to reduce demand for some health services, for example by increasing costs passed on to the consumer or increasing waiting lists, it has driven some people to engage in medical tourism by travelling to cheaper locations to have health-related treatment. Indeed, in the case of health care Mark and Elliot (1997: 300) suggest that demarketing 'will only really become credible if it develops as a demand-side activity'.

Beeton and Benfield (2002: 510) also suggest that the negative side of some demarketing measures are

> issues of equity and access (especially if too much focus is on using price as a demarketing tool or if there is a lack of awareness that limitations on visitation are in place and potential visitors have come a long way only to be barred entry).

Rights to access, particularly to publicly funded attractions, is a major political issue in many jurisdictions, especially if access has been free historically. For example, Buckley *et al.* (2003: 58) argue in the Australian context that 'where parks want to restrict visitor numbers or activities for environmental or social reasons, they generally use non-economic mechanisms rather than raise fees, for reasons of social equity'. Elsewhere Buckley (2003: 60) has suggested that if people have been able to visit protected areas in the past without paying user fees 'then they may raise strong objections to newly introduced fees, to the point of political action' and may even see such pricing as a means of 'double taxation'. Such observations only serve to reinforce Wall's (2005) observations that pricing is one of the most politically unattractive demarketing and social marketing tools even if it is extremely effective in achieving policy objectives.

Acceptability of demarketing and countermarketing measures, as with other social marketing tools, is heavily dependent on political support in the long-term, especially if economic conditions change and/or there are shifts in policy direction. Restricting access and reducing demand for 'public' tourism resources will always remain politically contentious while even private tourism attractions may lose stakeholder support if they feel excluded from access. Nevertheless, given population growth and the ongoing increase in domestic and international tourist numbers in most parts of the world it seems likely that demarketing will remain a potentially important part of any integrated social marketing strategy that seeks to better match supply and demand or reduce inappropriate behaviours.

BOX 6.2 DEMARKETING THE SISTINE CHAPEL?

The Sistine Chapel (*Sacellum Sixtinum* in Latin) is the best-known chapel in the Apostolic Palace, the official residence of the Pope in the Vatican City, Rome. The chapel receives over five million visitors a year to see its Renaissance frescoes and especially the iconic image of the hand of God giving life to Adam, which is part of the ceiling painted by Michelangelo between 1508 and 1512 (Graham-Dixon 2008). Although visited by an estimated 20,000 tourists and pilgrims a day the chapel is still used for religious services, although it is also the location for the Papal Conclave of the College of Cardinals that selects new popes. The amount of visitors is acknowledged as affecting the artworks in the chapel serving to both increase the air temperature and humidity as well as create dust and other pollution, leading to one of Italy's most respected writers, Pietro Citati, to describe the situation as an 'unimaginable disaster' where tourists resemble 'drunken herds' (Kingston 2012).

In an article in *Corriere della Sera* in September 2012, Pietro Citati demanded that the Vatican limit access to the Sistine chapel, claiming it would save the frescoes from damage and restore some decorum to the consecrated site. Describing a visit, Citati claimed that 'in the universal confusion, no one saw anything' and 'any form of contemplation was impossible'. The answer, he said, was to reduce the number of visitors drastically. 'The church needs money for its various activities, but these monstrous conditions are not possible'. Antonio Paolucci, the manager of the Vatican museums, which include the Sistine chapel, replied in the pages of the Holy See's daily paper, *L'Osservatore Romano*:

> The days when only Russian grand dukes and English lords or [American art expert] Bernard Berenson could gain access to the great masterpieces are definitely over … We have entered the era of large-scale tourism, and millions want to enjoy our historical culture … Limiting numbers is unthinkable.
>
> (Kingston 2012)

Paolucci said because the chapel was a place of prayer, timed visits were impossible. 'This chapel is a compendium of theology, a catechism in images. Could you limit access to Lourdes?' But Citati told the *Observer* newspaper: 'Why can't you limit numbers at a holy place if it is at risk? We are condemning it to disaster' (Kingston 2012).

Questions for self-reflection:

- How could demarketing principles be applied to the Sistine Chapel?
- Is it appropriate to limit visitor access to religious sites? Should access be allowed only to people on a pilgrimage or from that religion?
- Is charging an appropriate way to limit access to public sites with high visitor numbers?

Further reading and websites

The seminal paper on demarketing is:

Kotler, P. and Levy, S. J. (1971) 'Demarketing? Yes, demarketing!' *Harvard Business Review*, 49(6): 74–80.

In tourism some of the most interesting applications of demarketing are to be found in:

Armstrong, E. K. and Kern, C. L. (2011) 'Demarketing manages visitor demand in the Blue Mountains National Park', *Journal of Ecotourism,* 10: 21–37.
Beeton, S. and Pinge, I. (2003) 'Casting the holiday dice: Demarketing gambling to encourage local tourism', *Current Issues in Tourism*, 6: 309–322.
Benfield, R. W. (2001) '"Good things come to those who wait": Sustainable tourism and timed entry at Sissinghurst Castle Garden, Kent', *Tourism Geographies,* 3: 207–217.
McKercher, B., Weber, K. and du Cros, H. (2008) 'Rationalising inappropriate behaviour at contested sites', *Journal of Sustainable Tourism*, 16(4): 369–385.

For Sissinghurst see: www.nationaltrust.org.uk/sissinghurst-castle.

For the Sistine Chapel see Vatican Museums Online, the Sistine Chapel: http://mv.vatican.va/3_EN/pages/CSN/CSN_Main.html.

7

TOURIST- AND VISITOR-FOCUSED SOCIAL MARKETING

Cases and issues

This chapter examines a number of cases in which social marketing is utilised in which the primary focus of the intervention is the visitor. These include voluntary carbon offsetting, modifications to visitor behaviour, volunteer tourism, the prevention of youth problem gambling and reducing barriers to sun protection. Health has long been a major focal point of social marketing as well as being an individual and community concern in its own right. Much of the focus in health-related social marketing in the tourism context is on risk reduction by visitors, although it should be noted that there are a number of campaign areas, such as those related to sex and drugs, in which the development of marketing campaigns and strategies is substantially influenced by non-health interests. However, nearly all of the case studies in this chapter are affect by the fifth 'P' of social marketing – politics – to various degrees.

There is also a substantial emphasis on the potential of social marketing to encourage pro-environmental behaviours. This has often been focused on on-site behaviour but more recently has shifted towards encouraging behavioural change before commencing journeys, such as in the case of engaging in carbon offsetting.

Table 7.1 relates the case studies to some of the various dimensions of social marketing.

Voluntary carbon offsetting in the aviation sector: can tourists be persuaded to adopt pro-environmental behaviours?

There are substantial concerns regarding the impact of air travel on global carbon emissions and consequent climate change (Becken 2004; Gössling et al. 2007; Hares et al. 2010; Smith and Rodger 2009; McKercher et al. 2010; Gössling and Upham 2012) (Box 7.1). These concerns have led to the introduction of projects to encourage pro-environmental behaviours such as carbon offsetting schemes, which have grown rapidly since 2000 (Gössling et al. 2007). These voluntary offsetting schemes are designed to encourage pro-environmental behaviours at both an individual and an organisational level (Sterk and Bunse 2004; Lecocq and Capoor 2005). The reasons for participation in voluntary schemes vary. Lynes and Dredge (2006) note that on an individual level participation can be based on an increased awareness of the everyday behaviours that can reduce environmental impact, while at an organisational level voluntary schemes form an important part of environmental management and social responsibility programmes for the companies involved.

TABLE 7.1 Overview of social marketing cases and issues discussed in Chapter 7

Case	System stage(s) of tourism	Behaviour change goal	Audience research and segmentation	Social marketing mix
Voluntary carbon-offsetting in the aviation sector	Decision to travel, travel to and from a destination	Get customers to participate in carbon offsetting	Substantial amount of consumer research	Promotion, some elements of price
Sustainable tourism attractions in Devon	Destination (attraction)	Improve visitor environmental behaviour	Survey of visitors to three attractions	Promotion, product
Volunteer tourism	Decision to travel/volunteer, activities at destination	Behaviour change may be with the assistance of volunteers to undertake interventions; or may also occur for the volunteer	Growing research base with respect to volunteer characteristics	Product, place
Problem gambling	Destination, decision about attractions	Reduce rates of youth gambling	Substantial amounts of consumer research. Identification of most at-risk groups	Promotion product price
Sun protection	Tends to be at destination although can have elements at all stages and is in fact potentially best approached prior to decision to engage in travel or leisure activity or in the recollection stage, particularly if having been affected by sunburn	Take measures that reduce the immediate risk of sunburn and the long-term risk of skin cancer	Substantial amounts of consumer research. Identification of most at-risk groups	Promotion price (cost of not taking protective health measures)
Intangible: doing something for the well-being of the planet	Primarily customer focused, although some attention given to airlines to encourage them to have such schemes	Cheaper trip not having to pay offsets		Little apparent change in percentage of travellers engaging in such schemes

Case	System stage(s) of tourism	Behaviour change goal	Audience research and segmentation	Social marketing mix
Tangible: improving environmental qualities of attraction Intangible: positive personal feelings	Customer focused	Business as usual		Unknown
Intangible: doing something for the well-being of others	Customer focused; although with some attention given to the possibilities of community or environmental change	Full-time work (for volunteers)	Some use of exchange theory	Volunteer tourism continues to be popular however its long-term contribution to interventions is unknown
Long-term benefits in terms of self, relationships and economic and social well-being	Customer focused; some attention given to casinos to have problem gambler programmes; upstream actions by health professionals in terms of persuading governments to take problem gambling seriously as a health and social measure	Experience of gambling		Focus on de-normalisation has some effects Social marketing has to be part of an integrated strategy
Short and long-term health benefits	Customer focus; upstream actions by health professionals in terms of persuading governments to take sun-protection campaigns seriously as a health measure	Presumed immediate positive self-image and status in having a sun tan	Few evaluations describe the theoretical base of interventions, although many publications specify theories that have guided their programmes, including learning theory, message framing and fear arousal, stages of change, and social cognitive theory	There has been a gradual increase in sunburn avoidance behaviour in some target segments

Pro-environmental behaviours have been found to be grounded in the concept of self-identity (Cook *et al.* 2002; McKenzie-Mohr 2000a), and are influenced both by personal motivations such as self-esteem as well as social pressures grounded in the expectations of others (Tajfel and Turner 1986; Stryker and Burke 2000; Ellemers *et al.* 2002) and under which individuals act (Bem 1967). Self-identity also defines the values, beliefs and behaviours of the social groups to which an individual belongs (Christensen *et al.* 2004), which can be witnessed through attempts to 'establish consistency in our attitudes and actions and continuity across experiences, and therefore appears to be highly relevant in exploring consistency (and, ultimately, spill-over effects) across pro-environmental behaviours' (Whitmarsh and O'Neill 2010: 306).

BOX 7.1 CARBON OFFSETTING IN AVIATION

'In general, an offset is a compensating equivalent, as an activity it can mean to balance, cancel out or neutralise' (IATA 2008: 6). In the context of addressing climate change concerns, offsetting is an action by companies or individuals to compensate for greenhouse gas emissions during their use of commercial aviation (IATA 2008). Six principles of carbon offsetting are identified by IATA (2008): complementarity, additionality, verification, registration, traceability and guarantee, to help people and organisations gain confidence in the purchase and use of carbon offsets and ensure the quality of offset programmes.

With regard to the carbon offsetting types, there is a vital distinction between projects in the voluntary market, which generate offsets called VERs (Verified or Voluntary Emission Reductions), and projects in the Kyoto market, which generate offsets called CERs (Certified Emission Reductions). A key difference is that VERs rely on third party verification while CERs are formally certified under Kyoto rules (IATA 2008).

Voluntary offsetting schemes have grown rapidly since 2000 due to the interest of companies, organisations, event managers and individuals to offset their emissions even in the absence of legal demands (Gössling 2010). However, a number of concerns have been raised about the unregulated voluntary carbon-offset market, including calculation methods, the principle of additionality, the possibility of double-counting and multiple sales of the same carbon credits, the lack of standards for verification, the time scales and location of projects, and the ethics of some projects (Gössling and Peeters 2007). Even though with the lowest level of credibility in terms of meeting acclaimed emission reductions and additionality, VERs are currently the most common type of offset sold in the voluntary market (Gössling 2010). To achieve transparency and standardisation it is desirable that VERs evolve to CERs or MERs (Mandatory Emission Reductions) in the future.

Several case studies have attempted to examine whether pro-environmental behaviours have been responsible for carbon offsetting behaviour in international air travel, with Gössling, Haglund *et al.* (2009) focusing on Swedish air travellers, and Cohen and Higham (2011) analysing the perceptions of tourists who travel on long-haul flights from the UK to New Zealand. Both studies indicated evidence that tourists are exhibiting increased awareness of the effects of carbon emissions caused by air travel (Gössling, Haglund *et al.* 2009; Cohen and Higham 2011). In their survey of Swedish air travellers' knowledge and attitudes to air travel, climate change and voluntary carbon offsetting, Gössling, Haglund *et al.* (2009) found that whilst most participants perceived flying to be an important part of their lifestyle and questioned whether it was necessary to reduce their amount of personal air travel, approximately a quarter of the respondents expressed a willingness to fly less as their individual contribution towards carbon offsetting, which is also consistent with the findings of prior research by Gössling, Peeters and Scott (2008: 875) who stated that 'pro-environmental concerns are clearly emerging among consumers, and may play a significant role in travel decisions in the future'. Conversely, Cohen and Higham (2011) discovered that whilst some participants in their study were unaware of the impact with regard to climate change from the carbon emissions resulting from air travel (and as a result were reluctant to cut down the amount of travel that they did), a majority of those who were surveyed stated that they 'were aware of the impact and were beginning to consume air travel with a carbon conscience' (Cohen and Higham 2011: 22).

Cohen and Higham's (2011) study also points towards the possibility of a less than ideal economic scenario for destinations that are geared towards long-haul travel markets. As government departure taxes are raised and more travellers become concerned about climate change and are conscious of environmental initiatives designed to alleviate the effects of carbon emissions, so tourist numbers may shift. Cohen and Higham (2011: 22) use the New Zealand example to suggest the prospect of what might lie ahead as a challenge to airlines who depend on the long haul market for a significant portion of their revenue:

> [Whilst] New Zealand's largest long haul market may not yet be redirecting their holidays away from New Zealand because of climate concern over air travel, any further movement within this source market towards consuming air travel with a conscience could pose significant challenges for NZ tourism. This may especially be the case if the UK strengthens initiatives to further education and media messages about air travel's climate impact.

It is clear from this statement that any social marketing campaigns conducted in the UK towards air travel to New Zealand could be particularly damaging to New Zealand tourism and that of other long-haul destinations. Indeed, the UK's increase in the level of their air passenger duty (APD), ostensibly because of reasons related to emissions reduction, indicates the extent to which long-haul destinations feel vulnerable to changes in tourist travel behaviour. For example, the Australian Tourism Export Council (ATEC), suggested 'this new charge will significantly impact travel to Australia from the United Kingdom, and is a critical trade barrier between the UK and Australia and New Zealand', and also accused the UK of using the climate change debate 'to disguise this protectionist departure tax in "greenwash"'. ATEC also suggested that the APD would 'also impact on developing nations – for example those in the South Pacific – who are reliant on inbound tourism to generate much of their export income' (TravelMole 2008). PATA Regional Director (Pacific) Chris Flynn claimed that the APD would do more environmental harm than good:

> The long haul tourism industry has helped to preserve natural environments because of the income generated for regional governments ... Threats to tourism revenue will lead to pressure on natural resources as locals look to other sources of income – and that's bound to include the leveraging of these resources.

> (PATA 2010)

A spokeswoman for the New Zealand prime minister said that, according to the New Zealand Ministry of Transport, the amount of duty per economy class passenger to New Zealand is around five times what it should be if the tax was simply aimed at offsetting the cost of carbon emissions: 'It's hard to find an environmental justification for this. Travellers to distant locations like New Zealand should not be disproportionately penalised' (Krause 2010). However, a contrary position was put by the spokesperson for the travel agency House of Travel, a major New Zealand chain, who suggested that any cost increase is never well received by the public, 'but the reality is these are only quite small increases to the overall cost of travelling from Britain to New Zealand' (TVNZ 2010). Both New Zealand and Australia have government-mandated departure taxes, but they are not priced according to distance travelled and instead are flat fees (Scott *et al.* 2012a: 138).

Modifying visitor behaviour through social marketing: the case of sustainable tourism attractions in Devon, England

The concept of the 'sustainable tourist' (Croall 1995) has been identified by Dinan and Sargeant (2000: 7) as a tourist having the attributes of someone who 'appreciates the notion that they are a visitor in another person's culture, society, environment and economy, and respects this feature of travel'. Andreasen (1995) suggests that one of the key aims of social marketing is to encourage modification of existing consumer behaviour (see also Chapters 1 and 5), and this notion led Dinan and Sargeant (2000) to explore behavioural modifications in the context of sustainable tourism attractions situated in close proximity to the popular tourist destination of Devon. The study is also significant as it was one of the first attempts to explicitly link social marketing with tourism.

In 1997 Dinan and Sargeant (2000) conducted a survey of 540 visitors to three tourist attractions that actively employed sustainable tourism strategies in Devon, during the peak visitor season of July and August. In order to facilitate the collection of data, each attraction was situated in a different part of the West Country region (east, south and north), with the first attraction (a museum and interpretation centre) in an urban setting, the second (a cycle and walking route) situated in a semi-rural urban setting, and the third attraction (a farm and wildlife attraction) in a completely rural setting. Visitors were asked whether they would willingly adopt a code of conduct that was aimed at encouraging sustainable visitor behaviours at each of the three attractions, and were also posed a series of questions regarding their attitudes towards pro-environmental behaviours such as recycling and their willingness to buy sustainable local products. Each of these variables were then rated on a scale from zero through to six that enabled Dinan and Sargeant (2000) to develop a sustainability index to see whether there was a relationship between pro-environmental behaviours in everyday life and the willingness to follow a sustainable code of conduct once inside a tourist attraction.

The initial predictor variables utilised by Dinan and Sargeant (2000) in this study were the individuals' motives to visit the region, their awareness of issues surrounding sustainable tourism and the degree of exposure that they had experienced of unsustainable tourist behaviours. Through the use of CHAID (chi-squared automatic intervention detection) analysis, the results of this survey revealed that the majority of respondents expected a code of conduct to be distributed by either the management of the attraction concerned or tour operators themselves (Dinan and Sargeant 2000). Two-thirds of respondents stated that they did not visit tourist attractions in the West Country if they did not appear to offer sustainable tourism options. However, with respect to recycling Dinan and Sargeant (2000: 10) found that 'only when evidence of non-sustainable behaviour is clearly visible will many individuals finally accept that it is time to modify their own behaviour'. This was exhibited through respondents stating that only when they saw evidence of litter at the attraction that they were visiting did they think about their own behaviour in regards to this aspect within a code of conduct; if there was no evidence of litter then they would be less likely to follow a code of conduct.

The results of this particular study emphasised the need for future social marketing campaigns in the West Country to focus on dimensions of utility, which Andreasen (1995) states are vital in terms of changing the behaviours of tourists and illustrating the benefits of these changes, which ultimately leads towards more sustainable outcomes. Dinan and Sargeant (2000: 12) indicates that future marketing campaigns need to concentrate on 'exposing individuals to negative environmental impacts, [which] could well help stimulate preventative behaviours' but also notes that tourist attractions would not have either the budgets or resources to carry out such campaigns in isolation. As a result of this, greater levels of collaboration are suggested by Dinan and Sargeant (2000: 12) on both a regional and national level so that campaigns that are based around social marketing concepts can be 'effective in developing it to its full potential, while at the same time minimising the economic, social and physical impacts of enhanced visitor numbers on the host region'.

Volunteer tourism

Volunteering is an important element of non-profit and social marketing (see Chapter 4) as well as increasingly tourism and leisure (Stebbins and Graham 2004), where people, often those who have recently finished a programme of study, travel overseas to assist in development, conservation, scientific or social projects. Volunteering is non-coerced assistance or service offered either formally or informally with no or, at most, token pay done for the benefit of both the people and the volunteer. As well as assisting others, Stebbins (1992) suggests that volunteering bears durable benefits for the volunteer such as self-actualisation, self-enrichment, recreation or renewal of self, feelings of accomplishment, enhancement of self-image, self-expression, social interaction and belongingness. Thoits and Hewitt (2001) examined how volunteering affects six different dimensions of well-being: levels of happiness; life satisfaction; self-esteem; sense of control over life; physical health; and depression.

Described as a niche market that is 'an inevitable consequence of a restless society, jaded from the homogenous nature of traditional tourism products and seeking alternative tourism experiences' (Callahan and Thomas 2005: 185), volunteer tourism has risen to the fore as a way for tourists to simultaneously give back to the environment whilst developing a sense of self (Wearing 1998, 2001). As Bussell and Forbes (2002: 246) state 'a volunteer must have some altruistic motive' that needs to be addressed; and the predictability of a package holiday fails to satisfy such altruistic needs (Callahan and Thomas 2005). However, this form of tourism activity, which is also a social marketing strategy, requires sensitivity to the cultural and social norms of the host communities involved (McGehee and Andereck 2009) as a lack of knowledge of these can be harmful. Wearing (2001: 1) defines the concept of volunteer tourism as:

> Those tourists, who, for various reasons, volunteer in an organised way to undertake holidays that might involve aiding or alleviating the material poverty of some groups in society, [and] the restoration of certain environments or research into aspects of society or the environment.

McGehee and Santos (2005: 760) redefined this definition one step further by suggesting volunteer tourism to be 'utilising discretionary time and income to travel out of the sphere of regular activity to assist others in need'. Volunteer tourism is, therefore, seen by some to provide a more reciprocally beneficial form of travel in which both the volunteer and the host communities are able to gain from the experience. The concept of volunteer tourism has, therefore, come to be strongly related to concepts of sustainable tourism and sustainable development, especially with respect to pro-poor tourism and ecotourism.

While the concept of international volunteering is by no means a new phenomenon (e.g. early examples include missionary movements), in recent years there has been a rapid increase in the number of individuals taking part in short-term, organised volunteer tourism programmes (VTPs). The increasing demand for VTPs has been paralleled by an increase in sending organisations, which promote, sell and organise programmes for volunteer tourists. Sending organisations now offer a large variety of options depending on volunteer tourists' preferred activity, location and duration (Callanan and Thomas 2005), and provides greater opportunities for interaction and exchange between volunteer tourists and host communities.

Crabtree's (1998) study of volunteer tourists on a 'service learning' programme in El Salvador and Nicaragua argues that volunteer tourism leads to 'global citizenry – interdependence and mutual responsibility' (Crabtree 1998: 187). Crabtree's (1998) research also inadvertently provides an example of how volunteer tourism may represent a form of social marketing intervention that could be described as 'reconciliation tourism' (see Higgins-Desbiolles 2003). A quote from an American volunteer tourist in El Salvador illustrates this:

> Cleaning up your own mess: I guess that's what we're doing here. Much of the situation here is, to some degree or another, our mess. That's part of the poetic justice. We're rebuilding a school that our tax dollars destroyed … It seems like the right thing to do.
>
> (Volunteer journal excerpt in Crabtree 1998: 195)

Simpson (2005b: 191) highlights the sense of 'long-term social agenda' apparent in several gap-year projects. Evidence of this underlying 'social agenda' can also be found with regard to the way in which certain sending organisations name and promote themselves.

However, other literature, particularly relating to the UK gap year, challenges such views. Simpson (2004, 2005b) suggests that gap-year sending organisations impose a simplistic view of 'the other' so that 'difference' can be sold and consumed. This occurs through the use of sweeping generalisations of destination communities in promotional materials and continues throughout the VTP due to a lack of critical engagement with the experience (Simpson 2005a, 2005b). Consequently, it has been argued that working as a volunteer tourist cannot be assumed to contribute to a deeper understanding of other cultures. Instead, volunteer tourism, as with other forms of tourism, can sometimes be used as an opportunity for people to confirm, rather than question, previously conceived ideas (Simpson 2005b).

Volunteer tourism that takes place in developing countries may also not always generate a genuine awareness of the issues facing host communities. Simpson (2005b) argues that poverty is often trivialised in sending organisations' marketing, and, subsequently, by volunteer tourists themselves. In many cases, volunteer tourists' previously formulated perceptions of poverty may be reinforced by their experiences if they are not encouraged to question the broader processes behind such issues. This can then lead to assumptions that host communities accept their poverty: 'They don't have TVs but it doesn't bother them because they don't expect one' (interviewee, in Simpson 2005b: 213). Alternatively, some volunteer tourists may adopt a 'lotto logic' in which differences between countries are primarily attributed to 'luck' (Simpson 2005b).

Such criticisms are based on the argument that it cannot be assumed that by merely facilitating contact with the 'other', this will lead to long-term international understanding and respect. Indeed, Griffin (2004: 70) argues that 'the assumption that "seeing" equates to "knowing" means stereotypes in the mind of the observer could perhaps be strengthened rather than challenged'. Despite such perceptions, Raymond and Hall (2008) suggests that even where cross-cultural appreciation does occur at an individual level, this does not necessarily lead to changes in broader perceptions of nationalities or cultures. Several interviewees in their research implied that the positive relationships they had developed with individuals from different countries were simply 'exceptions to the rule'. For example, by claiming that American volunteer tourists are 'not your normal American tourist' (Repeat volunteer), previously held ideas and stereotypes associated with the 'normal' American were maintained. Although this concept has not been directly discussed in literature regarding volunteer tourism, it supports research relating to work and study exchanges. Richards (2006) suggests that while such experiences do lead to increased cultural tolerance, more deeply embedded attitudes are less likely to be affected. Indeed, such a situation may exist with both the volunteer and the host community. An examination of this phenomenon saw social–cultural and economic tourism provide the focus for a case study by McGehee and Andereck (2009) who examined residents' attitudes towards volunteer tourism in Tijuana, Mexico.

The case of Tijuana, Mexico

McGehee and Andereck (2009) utilised social exchange theory (Ap 1992) and applied it to volunteer tourism in Tijuana, Mexico. This theory has been defined by Ap (1992: 668) as 'a general sociological theory concerned with understanding the exchange of resources between individuals and groups in an interaction situation'. Using this definition, McGehee and Andereck (2009: 42) suggested the following in relation to volunteer tourism:

> Perceived personal benefit will be a strong predictor of support for additional volunteer tourism, and conversely, lack of perceived benefit would predicate lack of support. Perceived personal benefit should also predict perceived negative and positive impacts from volunteer tourism, as well as general support for volunteer tourism development within a community.

Wearing (2001: 11) has argued that 'ecotourism – and by default volunteer tourism – is mass tourism in its early pre-tourism development stage'. McGehee and Andereck (2009) also noted that this was a possible cause of tension from the local residents, which was found with respect to volunteer tourism that took place in Tijuna, although they suggested that 'depending on the volunteer tourism organization with whom they are involved, volunteer tourists may require resources such as accommodation, food and transportation in a different, more sustainable form from mass tourists' (McGehee and Andereck 2009: 48), which nevertheless impacts on the daily lives of the residents of Tijuna. Callahan and Thomas (2005: 187) point out that 'the motive for tour operators and many other businesses to get involved in social and community projects is to promote an image of ethical and social responsibility', yet if these motivations run in parallel or in opposition to the needs of local residents, then McGehee and Andereck (2009) suggest that there is very little difference between volunteer tourism and the undesirable impacts caused by mass tourism.

In order to address the possible negative impacts of volunteer tourism it has been suggested that appropriate levels of consideration need to be given to the residents of the host destination (McGehee and Andereck 2009). Of interest here is the fact that this is also consistent with the findings of McGehee and Andereck (2004) who used the same model but with a focus on mass tourism instead of volunteer tourism. As McGehee and Andereck (2009: 48) suggest 'the prospective negative impacts of tourism certainly would argue in favour of appropriate planning, and even those who are supportive of added volunteer tourism development recognize the need to enhance voluntourism using a deliberate and thoughtful approach'.

Cultural and religious divides were found to be two areas in which McGehee and Andereck (2009) noted that further research was needed in the context of volunteer tourism as they found that there was 'a strong connection between religion and the motivation for volunteer activities on the part of the tourists, but there was some resistance by residents to faith-based organisations as being the major suppliers of volunteer tourists' (McGehee and Andereck 2009: 49). As suggested by Wearing (2001), the seemingly altruistic motivations of those who participate in volunteer tourism can actually run the risk of offending those who are the hosts; this shows that greater sensitivity is required on the part of organisations who engage in such endeavours, a point also taken up in Raymond and Hall's work on the role of sending organisations in volunteer tourism.

The role of sending organisations in volunteer tourism

Although the responsibility of developing cross-cultural understanding cannot be solely attributed to the sending organisation, Raymond and Hall (2008) suggests that through careful planning and management, these organisations can have an influence at a number of stages. Three key recommendations were made for sending organisations seeking to improve cultural and social relations through their programmes.

First, sending organisations need to carefully consider the type of work in which their volunteer tourists should be involved in when they develop their programmes: 'It's about getting the volunteers to fit in and match their skills with the needs of the community rather than just as some companies do, getting the volunteers and then dumping them on a project' (director of sending organisation in Raymond and Hall 2008).

The importance of finding appropriate work is particularly significant when considering arguments that claim that certain VTPs may represent a form of neo-colonialism in which participants use developing countries as 'training grounds' for future professionals (Roberts 2004: 46). In order to move away from such criticism, it is, therefore, essential that volunteers are appropriately qualified and prepared so that they are perceived positively by their hosts and can make a genuine contribution, rather than simply absorb time and resources.

Raymond and Hall (2008) also highlighted the importance of developing programmes with local people so that volunteers are involved in work that does not undermine the value of local staff. This supports work by Ellis (2003) who noted that some people may associate rising levels of volunteering with employment losses. This was recognised by one host organisation that suggested that volunteer tourists could potentially replace local employees if programmes were not carefully managed:

I do want to emphasise that we do take care not undercutting the market price ... So you can see how when they [the volunteers] come in I can involve them in the planting side of it ... and in the mean time of course I've got contractors coming in behind and doing the maintenance. So it means everyone's getting a piece of the action but the whole process is happening perhaps twice the rate to what it would have otherwise happened at.

(Representative of host organisation in Raymond and Hall 2008)

Clearly, this is important not only for ethical reasons but also to ensure that positive economic and social relationships develop between volunteer tourists and the host organisations with which they are working. In addition, it is essential that host communities are in control of the programme to ensure that projects are not inappropriately imposed on host communities. This will also help to ensure that an environment of shared power and purpose develops between 'host' and 'guest'.

Second, Raymond and Hall's (2008) research reinforces the importance of experiential learning and the inaccuracy of assuming that contact with the 'other' will automatically result in a broadening of horizons and a greater understanding of host communities (e.g. Crabtree 1998; Simpson 2005a, 2005b). The sending organisations involved in Raymond and Hall's research used a range of different techniques to encourage reflection amongst their participants. These included encouraging volunteers to keep a journal so that they would reflect during their VTP (through writing) and after their VTP (through reading). In addition, some sending organisations had written requirements such as applications, essays and/or evaluations. In several group VTPs, group discussions were conducted to explore broader issues surrounding the project and role plays were carried out to encourage volunteers to identify with local people.

Third, sending organisation should recognise that if cross-cultural understanding is to develop, their volunteers need to be exposed to other cultures. This can occur in two key ways: through having a group of volunteers of a variety of nationalities and background and/or through creating opportunities for volunteers to interact with members of the host communities. In addition, volunteers and members of host communities should be provided with opportunities for interaction and exchange. While this occurs naturally to some extent through volunteers' work, several sending organisations involved in Raymond and Hall's (2008) research highlighted the importance of deliberately creating opportunities for exchange between volunteers and their hosts. This research points to a number of options for facilitating interaction between local people and volunteer tourists. One opportunity involves placing volunteer tourists in host families in order to enable greater immersion into the local community. In some cases, living with a host family was not only seen as a means to integrate into the culture, but also as an important part of the challenge of the volunteering experience. In the case of one programme especially, the fact that their volunteers lived with local families was perceived as an essential component of the programme:

People staying in a pension or a hotel or a youth hostel with other kids, they're not integrated into society, they're not really understanding the culture on a different level ... Living with these families ... you can't replace that with anything else ... I think it's quintessential because also those kids living in that environment see the reality of people that they also grow to care about and ... it's a source of motivation for a lot of them also to really work hard and make a difference.

(Programme coordinator in Raymond and Hall 2008)

In addition, interaction can be facilitated where volunteer tourists work alongside local volunteers. However, although this is valued by volunteer tourists, developing such a programme presents a number of challenges. Whereas volunteers both in developed and developing countries generally only work part-time (Anheier and Salamon 1999), volunteer tourists, for the most part, work full-time. As a result, it can be difficult to find local people who are able to take part in a full-time programme. For example, while one organisations' weekday projects involve both local and international volunteers, it is much more difficult to find local volunteers who can participate on longer 'residential' projects:

> Ideally I think we would like them to work alongside Australian volunteers more but … the only Australians who can do that are people who are unemployed or perhaps students during school holidays. So for a lot of the time there are not a lot of Australian volunteers on projects, maybe some retirees.
>
> (Representative of sending organisation)

A further option for facilitating interaction between volunteers and local people is to create social occasions in which both volunteers and local people participate. For example, on the final day of one volunteer programme, hosts and volunteers were both involved in culturally representative performances that included singing, dancing and storytelling. Through such activities, this programme was able to move away from the typical forms of cultural consumption associated with conventional tourism to an exchange model based on mutual cultural appreciation (Raymond and Hall 2008).

Volunteer tourism potentially provides the opportunity to develop cross-cultural understanding. However, it cannot be assumed that cross-cultural understanding automatically results from sending individuals to participate in VTPs. While this does not mean that volunteer tourism is without value for the volunteers and the communities they visit, it does suggest that it is essential for programmes to be carefully developed and managed. Where individuals volunteer through sending organisations, these organisations can play an important role in ensuring that stereotypes are broken rather than reinforced (Raymond and Hall 2008).

Social marketing campaigns aimed at the prevention of youth problem gambling

Social marketing programmes designed to prevent or reduce the risk from recognised high-risk behaviours, such as those that result from tobacco and drug use, have already been in place for several decades (Chapter 1). One area of what is sometimes described as 'deviant leisure' (Sullivan 2006), which has not received the same level of attention with regard to social marketing campaigns, is the issue of problem gambling (Messerlian and Derevensky 2006), although the use of casino development as a destination marketing or regeneration tool has provided a tourism-related focus on the negative issues associated with gambling (Morgan 2010). Problem gambling has in itself become a significant public health issue (Korn and Shaffer 1999; Shaffer and Kidman 2003; Lemarié and Chebat 2013) that affects all sectors of society. Even though the prevention of problem gambling has been incorporated into many advertising campaigns aimed at adults, Derevensky *et al.* (2003) suggest that there are few interventions that have been specifically designed to target the youth market.

Although there is little evidence currently available of prevention initiatives that have been undertaken, progress has been made towards developing an understanding of the motivations behind youth gambling (Derevensky and Gupta 2000; Hardoon and Derevensky 2002). Research has highlighted that most youth report having gambled during their lifetime (National Research Council 1999), while Byrne *et al.* (2005: 682) suggest that there is an estimated 'probable pathological gambling rate of between 4–6% of youth under 18 years of age'. A further 10–15 per cent of youth on top of this figure have been found to be at risk of developing a gambling addiction as well (Derevensky and Gupta 2000; National Research Council 1999). Even though there are significant gaps in the current literature on problem gambling and adolescents, one issue that is clearly evident is that this particular sector of the market is perhaps the most vulnerable to the development of high-risk behaviours (Derevensky and Gupta 2000; Gupta and Derevensky 2000; National Research Council 1999). Internet gambling has become popular with many young people who frequent Internet gambling websites (Derevensky and Gupta 2007; Messerlian *et al.* 2005). This is a phenomenon which, as Messerlian *et al.* (2004) observe, is caused in part due to the presence of policies that create a situation where the barriers to entry are far less of a challenge than those that exist when visiting an actual casino in real life.

In order to determine which themes would be most appealing for use in problem gambling campaigns that were specifically aimed at adolescents, Messerlian and Derevensky (2006) conducted 30 focus groups consisting of 175 participants from nine Canadian schools situated in south-eastern Ontario and Montreal. The aim of each focus group was to identify campaign strategies used in prior social marketing campaigns that had tackled the prevention of health-compromising behaviours such as tobacco and drug use in order to determine if these campaign strategies would be applicable in the context of a youth problem gambling campaign (Messerlian and Derevensky 2006). Research by Byrne *et al.* (2005), which focused on health-related social marketing campaigns, found that strategies that emphasised negative effects and also utilised denormalisation tactics proved to be the most successful methods in terms of attempting to change youth attitudes and behaviours towards substance abuse. Earle (2000) acknowledges the potential that social marketing possesses in terms of being able to reach a large number of youths regarding the risks of excessive gambling through the use of tactics such as prevention messages.

The results obtained from the focus groups conducted by Messerlian and Derevensky (2006) showed that there were a number of campaign strategies that were considered ineffective by participants. Campaigns that were based around messages that used a 'don't do it' approach were rejected as they were seen to be both 'imposing and patronizing' (Messerlian and Derevensky 2006: 303), and campaigns that took an unbalanced approach were also viewed with suspicion. The most effective campaigns were found to be those that took an informative approach or attempted to actively engage youths without appearing to preach to them (Messerlian and Derevensky 2006). The way in which messages in social marketing campaigns were delivered also came under scrutiny, with Messerlian and Derevensky (2006: 303) stating as a result of their findings in this area that 'it is recommended that campaigns communicate the risks of gambling in an unbiased, realistic and fair method, given adolescents' criticism of ads that focus primarily on the negative/harmful aspects of the behaviour'.

The tone used in the communication of prevention messages was found to be a critical factor in how participants viewed social marketing campaigns (Messerlian and Derevensky 2006). Excessive use of humour or drama was shown by Messerlian and Derevensky (2006) as potentially rendering some campaigns ineffective. The frequency of exposure to prevention messages was also deemed to be a crucial factor as oversaturation could 'lead to desensitisation and habituation toward ads' (Messerlian and Derevensky 2006: 303). Noting the importance of how youth view prevention campaigns in the context of social marketing is absolutely imperative if a campaign is to be successful. This is one area of debate amongst academics where there has been very little agreement, a fact that Byrne *et al.* (2005: 6) note by stating that 'the effectiveness of Youth Substance Use Social Marketing Campaigns (YSSMCs), and SMCs in general, on health outcomes has been a long-standing debate in the community of public health specialists'. The results obtained from this study demonstrate that when it comes to targeting the youth market through prevention campaigns there is very little room for error when ensuring that all elements of the campaign combine to work as a unified whole. On this note, Messerlian and Derevensky (2006: 305) conclude that 'social marketing as a public health strategy needs to be part of an integrated youth gambling prevention approach that includes the implementation of healthy public and social policy as well as the development of science-based prevention programs'.

Reducing barriers to sun protection: application of a holistic model for social marketing

Although the opportunity to gain a suntan is a major part of beach tourism and other types of tourism that focus on sun and surf or sun and skiing, there is increasing recognition that overexposure to the sun can be harmful, especially with respect to a long-term increase in skin cancer. Therefore, a growing number of countries around the world are now actively engaged in social marketing interventions to reduce the risks of skin cancer and create awareness and behavioural change of people when they are outdoors and exposed to the sun (Clarke *et al.* 2001; McLeod *et al.* 2011). Many of these primary prevention social marketing campaigns utilise various mass media channels (McLeod *et al.* 2011).

These campaigns often focus on the application of social marketing at both the micro- and macro-environmental levels to minimise the remaining barriers to sun protection in order to get their message heard (McLeod *et al.* 2011). At the macro-level are those campaigns that are physical, social, environmental and climate-related, while at the micro-level are those that deal with the individual's own progression through each of these macro-level stages (McLeod *et al.* 2011).

Social marketing campaigns aimed at reducing the incidence of sunburn have been conducted successfully in Australia, Canada, New Zealand and the UK. McLeod *et al.* (2011) suggest that probably the best known of these campaigns is the 'Slip, Slop, Slap' campaign that was first put together by the Anti-Cancer Council of Victoria, Australia: 'Slip! [*slip on a shirt*], Slop! [*slop on some sunscreen*], Slap! [*slap on a hat*]' (Anti-Cancer Council of Victoria 1989). Over time, two new messages were added to the slogan, 'Seek! [*seek shade*]' and 'Slide! [*slide on some sunglasses*]' and was aimed at reducing consumers' exposure to UV rays (Bauman *et al.* 2002). There was also a second tier of social marketing campaigns that were based on similar themes but focused on early detection of skin cancer (Borland *et al.* 1990). The combination of very high skin cancer rates with high general practitioner visits (> 1 million per annum) has resulted in skin cancer being the cancer posing the most costly burden on the Australian health system (Tan *et al.* 2012). In 1987, a broad-based multifaceted programme called SunSmart was developed with the support of state government funding from the Victorian Health Promotion Foundation.

PLATE 7.1 Sunsmart campaign information on lifeguard seat, Vancouver

The SunSmart programme tries to influence the knowledge, attitudes and intentions of individuals, along with social and cultural norms in an attempt to promote sun-protection behaviour. The programme aims to increase public awareness of the link between sun exposure and skin cancer through education, settings-based interventions and public communication. It also attempts to change the desirability of a tan. The SunSmart programme has conducted activities across a broad range of settings including schools, community groups, leisure facilities, workplaces and child care centres.

(Tan *et al.* 2012: 71)

This case study looks in detail at the SunSmart campaign in New Zealand before concluding with a comment on the need to develop more integrated social marketing approaches with respect to the promotion of sun protection.

SunSmart in New Zealand

Skin cancer is by far the most common form of cancer affecting New Zealanders. This includes melanoma, squamous cell carcinoma, basal cell carcinoma and sunspots. Every year a total of about 67,000 new skin cancers are diagnosed, compared to around 16,000 for all other cancers (Cancer Society of New Zealand 2008). To combat issues surrounding skin cancer in New Zealand, a number of campaigns have been designed to communicate the potential risks associated with skin cancer to people and get them to act proactively.

In New Zealand there are two main organisations that partnered to combat skin cancer. The first organisation is the Health Sponsorship Council (HSC). This is a government agency that was formed in the early 1990s to promote healthy living and was originally focused on anti-smoking measures (Ministry of Health 2009). The main functions of the HSC are:

- promoting and maintaining health brand identities reflecting New Zealand's public health priorities;
- promoting health messages and behaviours utilising a range of communication tools, including sponsorship;
- providing a national resource to assist organisations contracting, marketing or delivering products or services bearing HSC or complementary public health brands.

(Ministry of Health 2009)

The second organisation is the Cancer Society of New Zealand. This is a non-profit organisation that has worked with and alongside cancer patients to offer support and ultimately focus on reducing all aspects related to the damage caused by cancer. In the early 1980s they began to focus on skin cancer and how it can be prevented (Cancer Society of New Zealand 2008). In addition to communication campaigns on the message of preventative forms of protection from skin cancer they have worked alongside many organisations on different campaigns that relate to cancer. These include Smokefree initiatives, breast cancer awareness and creating events such as the 'relay for life' to raise money for cancer patients and research into curing cancer.

In 2001 a New Zealand Skin Cancer Control Steering Group (NZCCSG) was formed that included the Cancer Society, HSC and other experts, which would work to prevent skin cancer. The main goal of the NZCCSG is to reduce the proportion of New Zealanders who develop and die from skin cancer (Skin Cancer Control Steering Committee 2008).

In 2001 the partnership between HSC and the Cancer Society began as the key marketing group for the SunSmart campaign to effectively campaign toward the following goals set by the NZCCSG:

- *diagnosis and treatment*: increase effectiveness of skin cancer diagnosis and treatment to reduce morbidity and mortality;
- *detection*: improve early detection of skin cancer, particularly melanoma, to reduce mortality;
- *prevention*: improve prevention of skin cancer, particularly melanoma, to reduce incidence.

(Skin Cancer Control Steering Committee 2008: 5)

Other countries such at the United Kingdom and Australia are using similar campaigns. Australia has had campaigns running since the early 1980s such as 'Slip, Slop and Slap' (ensuring that individuals wear a hat and sunscreen/sunblock) and the SunSmart campaign from 1988 (Borland *et al.* 2001). New Zealand has adapted these campaigns in an effort to reduce the amount of skin cancer. Success in these campaigns has been measured by changes in sunburn trends, positive sun protection behaviour, structural or organisational changes in preventative actions against sunburn, reduced use of sun beds, and sport and leisure groups being actively SunSmart. There is evidence suggesting that skin cancer 'incidence rates are beginning to plateau after decades of increase. The rates of (skin cancer) in younger cohorts are falling, and the earlier detection of SC is leading to better treatment and long-term outcomes' (Borland *et al.* 2001: 292). However, skin cancer reduction is regarded as a long-term behavioural change programme.

Target market

The SunSmart campaign aims to change the attitudes of the younger generation as it is well recognised that sunburn at a young age can cause skin cancer later in life. This age group is targeted at primary school right up to secondary school. The focus is also on parents and caregivers to practice the SunSmart rules. However, priority audiences differ according to the prevention, detection or diagnosis/treatment pathways.

For the prevention pathway, the Committee identified that primary audiences included those under the age of 20. However, within this group, it was agreed that the priority audiences needed to be broken down further. It was identified that the primary audience were young children (0 to 12-year-olds) and their parents and caregivers. In addition, adolescents (13 to 18-year-olds) were identified as a secondary audience. The importance of audience segmentation was also discussed.

(Skin Cancer Control Steering Committee 2008: 5)

Goal

The goal of the SunSmart campaign is to get the target audience and in general the whole population using proactive methods of skin cancer prevention. This includes changing the behaviour of what people wear, how often they are in the sun, pro-tanning culture and the ability to identify early signs of skin cancer. The following goals were part of the strategic framework of the skin cancer control steering committee for the period 2008–11:

1 Reduce risks associated with sun bed use, particularly those to do with technological change.
2 Maintain knowledge and improve quality of information to people 50 years and older.
3 Increase knowledge and understanding among health workers.
4 Increase knowledge and understanding among health professionals.
5 Develop Trans-Tasman guidelines to inform action/implementation.
6 Support international and national efforts to better understand, and communicate, the current UV environment in New Zealand.
7 Reduce time exposed to harmful UVR.
8 Increase (effective) use of sun protection strategies.
9 Improve efficacy of sun protection tools and products.
10 Reduce prevalence of cumulative harmful exposure to UVR (key audience: outdoor workers).
11 Reduce incidence of sunburn, particularly acute intermittent. (Key audience: <20 years.)

(Skin Cancer Control Steering Committee 2008: 6)

Strategies

The SunSmart campaign uses many strategies to advertise to the target market. They have a range of merchandise such as hats, sunglasses, sun block, Frisbees and more. They use television media to advise the public the damage sunburn can do to young children. One of the advertisements advises: 'Never let your child get sun burnt' (Health Sponsorship Council 2006), as sunburn can cause melanoma later on in life.

The tiger prawn has been used as a character that would appeal to children on how to be SunSmart. It is also used in television campaigns and on posters and radio announcements. The SunSmart campaign also works closely with surf lifesaving teams at beaches in summer. The campaign emphasises the need for everyone on the beach to protect themselves (Health Sponsorship Council 2006).

SunSmart has partnerships with the Pharmacy Guild that provides SunSmart window displays in summer. Weather and news services also use the aid of the UV index – a measure of how long it is 'safe' to be in the sun without getting sunburn, in order to get people to 'slip, slop and slap' during summertime (Health Sponsorship Council 2006).

SunSmart offers information to education providers about how to become a SunSmart accredited school. This means actively involving teachers to change habits so children do not get burnt. A 'no hat, play in the shade' policy emphasises that schools need to implement hats, shade and make sure children are not in the sun at high risk times between 11am and 4pm (Cancer Society of New Zealand 2008). They also offer programmes for each year level to educate them about the sun and how harmful it can be and what can be done if sunburn does occur. Local government has also been targeted with guidelines available to help increase safety at swimming pools, parks, outdoor facilities (i.e. sports grounds), building regulations and for any outdoor workers.

Evaluation

As noted above the SunSmart campaign is a long-term social marketing intervention. Research showed that sunscreen use was significantly higher in 2006 than in 2003. There is also a significant increase in use of hats worn to protect people in the sun from 38 per cent of respondents to 45 per cent. The use of sunglasses in the sun has also significantly increased since 1994 (Health Sponsorship Council 2006).

Research was also conducted on the effectiveness of the marketing campaign. Respondents were asked to recall if they had seen any advertising or promotional material warning about the danger of sun exposure. The trend has been mixed. There was a significant increase in awareness in 2006 compared to 2003 but it was still significantly lower than in 1994 after the campaign first commenced. The general message that seemed to be interpreted by around 40 per cent of respondents was to 'always use/ wear sunscreen' followed by 'cover up/protect yourself' (Health Sponsorship Council 2006: 9). This information seemed to be best communicated through television media as 74 per cent of respondents remembered hearing the SunSmart advertisement material on the television.

Another study has shown that

> strategies to encourage the early detection of melanoma in New Zealand have not yet reduced the incidence of thick melanomas. This may be because it is too soon to see the impact of early detection or because early detection strategies predominantly identify melanomas that are unlikely to progress, but miss thicker nodular melanomas.
>
> (Cox *et al.* 2008: 18)

Cox *et al.* (2008) believed that it would be another 20 years or so before we can see any effect campaigns such as the SunSmart movement have on the population of people with skin cancer. Nevertheless, significant challenges remain as even though the SunSmart campaign has been active for over two decades, a majority of the population are still not actively protecting themselves from the sun, with less than two-thirds of builders and horticulturalists wearing sunscreen and only 5 per cent wearing a hat (Reeder 2009).

As the above results reinforce, McLeod *et al.* (2011) found that population studies had revealed that the incidence of sunburn was still particularly high, especially amongst adolescents (Davis *et al.* 2002), despite there having been social marketing campaigns conducted to reduce consumers' exposure to ultraviolet rays. Large budget expenditures on social marketing campaigns designed to reduce such risks were found by McLeod *et al.* (2011) to have failed to change the behaviours of those consumers who were the target of these advertisements. Therefore McLeod *et al.* (2011) suggested that future campaigns needed to target at-risk groups given that a more targeted approach concerning sun protection has been found to have a better chance of success (Lombard *et al.* 1991; Jones and Leary 1994).

BOX 7.2 THE SOLAR UV INDEX: SLIP, SLOP, SLAP, SEEK AND SLIDE

Cancer councils across Australia have worked very closely with the Australian Bureau of Meteorology to promote a solar UV index along guidelines issued by the World Health Organization. The UV index is an international standard measurement of how strong UV radiation from the sun is at a particular place on a particular day. The UV index ranges from 0 to 11+ and the higher the number the greater the risk of skin and eye damage. The SunSmart UV Alert is a communications tool that can be used to determine when it is necessary for individuals to protect themselves from UV radiation and when sun protection is not required. SunSmart UV Alert times are issued throughout the year by the Bureau of Meteorology when the UV index is forecast to reach three or above. When the UV index reaches three and above, the following five steps are recommended for protection against sun damage: (i) Slip on some protective clothing; (ii) Slop on sun protection factor (SPF) 30+ sunscreen – make sure it is broad spectrum and water resistant, and apply 20 minutes before you go outdoors and re-apply every two hours; (iii) Slap on a hat; (iv) Seek shade; and, (v) Slide on some sunglasses – make sure they meet appropriate standards (Tan *et al.* 2012).

Source: World Health Organization, World Meteorological Organization, United Nations Environment Programme and International Commission on Non-Ionizing Radiation Protection (2002)

Chapter summary

This chapter has provided a series of case studies that examine how social marketing has been used to influence behaviour. One of the issues that they raise is the question of what is the difference between influencing tourist behaviour and that of non-tourists. In some cases, such as that of problem gambling or sun protection, the answer may be very little, whereby the intervention is one that is aimed at the general at-risk population before they even engage in specific tourism or leisure behaviour. However, increasingly, as in the case of sun protection, there is a realisation that improved target marketing may increase the likelihood of behavioural change. Indeed, there is widespread awareness in the health literature that in the case of both gambling and sunbathing that tourism is a major driver of these activities, with increased leisure time and international tourism being regarded as significant contributing factors to such risky behaviour (Eiser *et al.* 1995; Eiser and Arnold 1999; Sjöberg *et al.* 2004; Peattie *et al.* 2005; Garside *et al.* 2010; Tan *et al.* 2012).

In the case of volunteer tourism, carbon offsetting and behaviour at tourist attractions case studies, the three case studies are specifically focused on the tourist market. A common element in these cases is that the ideal intervention point is before the tourist begins their trip or enters the attraction. Indeed, understanding of the stages of the tourism experience is potentially an extremely important component of tourist-related social marketing interventions that appears not to be fully utilised (refer to Figure 4.2). For example, discussion of health-related social marketing interventions in tourism often do not identify the best points in a trip at which to communicate information to consumers in terms of the effectiveness of any campaign. A further common issue, including with respect to health interventions, is that the theoretical underpinnings of any intervention is either often not stated or stated only in broad terms. Indeed, Saraiya *et al.*'s (2004) observation with respect to all studies of interventions to prevent skin cancer by reducing exposure to ultraviolet radiation can be easily applied to the cases and literature discussed in this chapter and throughout much of the book:

> Research to improve the use of ... theories of message development, especially in terms of instruments and message templates, could benefit interventions to increase sun-protective behaviors. In all studies, messages were assumed, rather than tested, to possess the characteristics that they were intended to have.
>
> (Saraiya *et al.* 2004: 443)

Furthermore, with the exception of sun-protection-related studies there is a lack of long-term data on the effectiveness of interventions, while in the case of the SunSmart campaigns it appears that even after over 30 years of social marketing many people still do not change their behaviour substantially.

Further reading and websites

The SunSmart campaign is one of the most readily available social marketing campaigns that relates to tourist behaviour, see:

SunSmart New Zealand: http://sunsmart.org.nz/
SunSmart Victoria Australia: www.sunsmart.com.au/
Slip, Slop, Slap, video of original campaign with Sid the Seagull: www.youtube.com/watch?v=tGgn 5nwYtj0

SunSmart Victoria videos on YouTube are useful to watch with respect to change over time in advertising, the variety of issues they address, as well as issues associated with lay knowledge and skin cancer protection, such as how to put suntan lotion on: www.youtube.com/user/SunSmartAus?feature=watch.

Useful review papers include:

Garside, R., Pearson, M. and Moxham, T. (2010) 'What influences the uptake of information to prevent skin cancer? A systematic review and synthesis of qualitative research,' *Health Education Research*, 25(1): 162–182.
Glanz, K., Halpern, A. C. and Saraiya, M. (2006) 'Behavioral and community interventions to prevent skin cancer: What works?' *Archives of Dermatology*, 142(3): 356–360.

With respect to carbon offsetting and other forms of interventions in carbon-related behaviour in tourism see the excellent:

Gössling, S. (2010) *Carbon Management in Tourism: Mitigating the Impacts on Climate Change.* London: Routledge.

There are numerous works on volunteering in tourism. The case study in this chapter was drawn on material developed with Eliza Raymond, in particular:

Raymond, E. M. and Hall, C. M. (2008) 'The development of cross-cultural (mis)understanding through volunteer tourism', *Journal of Sustainable Tourism*, 16: 530–543.

On the research approach adopted by Eliza see:

Raymond, E. M. and Hall, C. M. (2008) 'The potential for appreciative inquiry in tourism research,' *Current Issues in Tourism*, 11: 281–292.

A useful profile of the motivations of the volunteer vacation market is:

Brown, S. and Lehto, X. (2005) 'Travelling with a purpose: Understanding the motives and benefits of volunteer vacationers', *Current Issues in Tourism*, 8: 479–496.

BOX 7.3 SELF-REFLECTIVE QUESTIONS

- How do you perceive a tanned skin with respect to notions of health and identity?
- How can social marketing overcome issues of fashion and identity with respect to sun protection campaigns? Or are people just lazy?

8

DESTINATION AND COMMUNITY-BASED TOURISM AND SOCIAL MARKETING

Cases and issues

Destinations are the focal point for much tourism research as well as for much of the tourism experience. They serve as one of the main reasons for being a tourist. Although some tourism marketers and promoters and, perhaps, even tourism planners may sometimes seem to propose otherwise, a destination is not just another 'product' or 'commodity' (Hall 2008a). Although destinations are places of tourist consumption they are also places in which people live, work and play and to which they may have a strong sense of attachment and ownership, what is usually described as a sense of place: the term that is used to refer to the subjective, personal and emotional attachments and relationships people have to a place (Cresswell 2004). Although, in many cases, people might only consciously notice the unique qualities of places when they are away from them, when a place is being rapidly altered, or when a place is being marketed and promoted in a way they do not relate to.

Because destinations are such a focal point for tourism it is not surprising that much of the work that connects social marketing to tourism is destination based. Destinations have long been the focal point for awareness of the negative social and environmental impacts of tourism (Hall and Lew 2009) so it is therefore not surprising that many social marketing interventions in tourism are geared towards trying to maintain destination qualities. In addition, because of the attention that has come to be given to the negative environmental, cultural and personal impacts of tourism and the social context within which they occur since the 1970s, a particular focus has developed in tourism planning on destination communities and development of community-based approaches to tourism.

One of the earliest and most influential statements of the community approach to tourism development is to be found in Peter Murphy's (1985) book *Tourism: A Community Approach*. Murphy (1985) advocated the use of an ecological approach to tourism planning that emphasised the need for local control over the development process. One of the key components of the approach is the notion that in satisfying local needs it may also be possible to satisfy the needs of the tourist, a 'win–win' philosophy that is intuitively immensely attractive. Nevertheless, despite the undoubted conceptual attraction to many destinations of the establishment of a community approach to tourism planning, substantial problems remain in the way such a process may operate and be implemented (Singh *et al.* 2003). Indeed, even in the case of Murphy's work local control was often expressed through the role of interest groups, particularly business groups, rather than a broader degree of community control.

Community tourism planning is a response to the need to develop more socially acceptable guidelines for tourism. Cooke's (1982) seminal work on social sensitivity to tourism in British Columbia provides important insights into the manner in which the social impacts of tourism on a community can be ameliorated through appropriate planning measures. Cooke (1982) identified several conditions that are appropriate to local tourism development and that remain relevant to the present day:

- Tourists respect local cultural and ethnic traditions and values.
- Opportunities for extensive local involvement in the tourism industry through decisions made by local government; community–wide support for volunteer tourism programmes; and active participation in the direction of tourist development.
- Tourism is an economic mainstay, compatible with other economic sectors, or is viewed as a desirable alternative to other industries.
- Themes and events that attract tourists are supported and developed by the local community.

Conditions associated with locally inappropriate tourism development include (Cooke 1982):

- Tourists do not respect local or ethnic traditions and values.
- Uncertainties about the future direction of tourism development with local people feeling that they have little control.
- Residents feel that visitors are catered to ahead of locals, and that infrastructure and facilities have been designed for the benefit of tourists rather than the local community.
- Growth in the host community is proceeding faster than what the residents feel appropriate.
- Perceived or actual conflicts over natural resource use.

Cooke (1982) recommended that all tourism planning be based on the goals and priorities of residents. Indeed, she even went further and recommended that local attractions be promoted only when endorsed by residents. While many readers may have sympathy with this approach and while this idea underlies much of the community development literature (Singh *et al.* 2003), its practical exercise will have substantial implications for tourism that could even mean stopping certain types of development that may be favoured by certain stakeholders in the planning process (Hall 2008a).

A community approach to tourism planning is therefore a 'bottom–up' form of planning, which emphasises development in the community rather than development of the community. Under this approach, residents are regarded as the focal point of the tourism planning exercise, not the tourists, and the community, which is often equated with a region of local government, is regarded as the basic unit of governance or planning (see Chapter 3). However, substantial difficulties arise in attempting to implement the concept of community planning in tourist destinations given the political nature of the planning process (Singh *et al.* 2003). Indeed, Hall (2008a) suggests that communities rarely have the opportunity to say no to tourism development. Nevertheless, the community-based tourism approach has been extremely influential with respect to thinking about what communities desire from tourism and the relationship of tourism development to the enhancement of the quality of life of residents and the maintenance of the amenity values of destinations. Therefore, social marketing issues such as poverty and quality of life (QOL) are significant in a community context (Zapata *et al.* 2011). In addition, a focus on communities and their well-being is arguably integral to the process of social marketing, especially the people and partnership dimensions (Chapter 4), and members of a community acting as change agents is integral to concepts of community-based social marketing (McKenzie-Mohr 2011). This chapter therefore examines how social marketing may be able to assist in the development of sustainable communities in the developed and less developed countries as well as campaigns focused on community members and tourists at the destination. Case studies range from pro-poor tourism initiatives, through to environmental programmes as well as destination-based approaches that examine attempts to change community behaviours (Table 8.1)

BOX 8.1 HOSTING WORLD CUPS AS A SOCIAL MARKETING OPPORTUNITY?

The public unrest in Brazil that occurred in 2014 at the time of hosting the Confederations Cup, and the concerns of many poorer people that the money used for the development of stadia to host the FIFA World Cup could have been better spent on community services and infrastructure, served as a high-profile reminder of the issues associated with hosting mega-sporting events. As Rio de Janeiro's mayor Eduardo Paes told the BBC, Brazil should have seized the occasion to invest in healthcare, education and transport: 'Brazil has lost a great opportunity with the World Cup. Fifa asked for stadiums and Brazil has only delivered stadiums ... We should have used the opportunity to deliver good services too' (quoted in BBC News Latin America & Caribbean 2013). However, somewhat prescient comments in the light of both the Brazilian and South African experiences made at the time of the 2018 World Cup bids suggested that the hosting of World Cups could even be seen as a social marketing opportunity. In referring to the failed England bid Professor Simon Chadwick, chair at Coventry University Centre for the International Business of Sport, suggested:

> [I]t is almost like a piece of political marketing, rather than social marketing ... They are trying to sell it as a good place to host the World Cup, but I think they should focus more on social marketing that ties in more with Fifa's message; highlighting the potential social development of hosting the event ... As part of the global football movement, they should be stressing the social side more, I feel – that is what these guys who decide the host county will want to hear.

(Quoted in Wilson 2010)

Protest-hit Brazil 'missed chance' to improve services (YouTube):
www.youtube.com/watch?v=envyxqrMwoE

TABLE 8.1 Overview of social marketing cases and issues discussed in Chapter 8

Case	System stage(s) of tourism	Behaviour change goal	Audience research and segmentation	Social marketing mix	Exchange	Downstream (customer)/ upstream focus	Competition	Theory	Long-term effectiveness
PPT initiatives in India	• Destination (at attraction) • Consumer decision-making	Using the attraction of pro-poor tourists as a community economic development mechanism to improve quality of life	None	• Use of promotion • Product	Increased community well-being	• Customer • Upstream (with respect to desire to attract such a market as well as the development of standards)	Other projects that may attract tourists		Unknown; institutional arrangements will be essential
Community based tourism, La Fortuna, Costa Rica	• Destination	Developing a particular community tourism product is regarded as beneficial to community and will attract a particular market	None	• Product • Place • People (in the community) • Partnership (between community organisations)	Increased community well-being	Local (internal to community) focus	Alternative modes of tourism development		Unknown; long-term prospects will depend on power relationships and structures, and governance capacities
Chilean land restoration program	Destination community-based	• Allowing land access tor research to be conducted on ecosystem degradation • Improved partnership	Interviews with stakeholder groups	• Partnership • People	Long term and relatively intangible; ideas on exchange differed between stakeholders	Both, depending on nature of stakeholder	Ease of not collaborating		Good long-term prospects though collaboration is harder when projects move to implementation of research recommendations stage

Case	System stage(s) of tourism	Behaviour change goal	Audience research and segmentation	Social marketing mix	Exchange	Downstream (customer)/ upstream focus	Competition	Theory	Long-term effectiveness
Deliberately lit fires in the southern Welsh Hills	Destination community	Reduce firelighting behaviour of local people	Market research	• Promotion • People	Other activities. Increase pride in landscape	• Local community members	Business as usual		Appears likely
Place promotion	• Decision to travel • Destination • Recollection	• Improve place image externally and internally • Encourage residence to feel more positive about where they live and become good 'place brand ambassadors'	Consumer, stakeholder and resident research	Promotion Product People Partnership	Increased community pride	• Local community members	Competing place destinations as well as other images of place		Can work well but campaigns have to be believable and relevant and sustained over time.
Social justice and politics on a local level: the case of Desa Senaru, Indonesia	Destination community	• Meaningful community participation in decision-making		People	Involvement in community	• Local community members; family members	Economic development goals and timeframe		Unknown

Case studies

Quality of life through responsible tourism and sustainability

The rapid growth of tourism in developing nations, many of whom suffer from widespread poverty, has seen a school of thought emerge that views tourism as a catalyst for poverty alleviation (Chok *et al.* 2007) usually referred to as pro-poor tourism (PPT) and as a result improving quality of life (QOL). Although often not specifically labelled as social marketing programmes Truong and Hall (2013) illustrate that many PPT projects have all the core elements of social marketing interventions. The beginnings of responsible tourism lie within linkages to other sustainability based initiatives such as 'alternative' tourism (Butler 1990), ecotourism (Cater and Lowman 1994; Hall and Lew 1998), green tourism (Wheeler 1991; McKercher 1993) and pro-poor tourism (Hall 2007b; Harrison 2008). The assumption that mass tourism could 'elevate QOL through the direct and indirect regeneration of revenue and employment' (Weaver 2012: 389) has been shown to be something of an illusion, however; the often failure of mass tourism to create such benefits for the poorest members of host communities has resulted in both activists and academics alike adopting a cautious approach towards the belief that these benefits actually exist (Zapata *et al.* 2011). Pleuramom (1999) has cited that in developing nations over two-thirds of revenue raised by tourism activities does not actually reach the local economy due to foreign exchange leakages. If this perspective holds true it is hardly surprising that an air of caution permeates the very notion of tourism improving QOL at all.

Kumarakom in Kerala, India

Case studies by Michot (2010) and Chettiparamb and Kokkranikal (2012) have both focused on Kumarakom in Kerala, India as an example of tourism as a contributor to QOL. Kerala is noted as being 'a pioneer in the field of pro-poor tourism' (Michot 2010: 3) largely due to the adoption in 2006 of the Responsible Tourism Initiative whereby state tourism policies embraced PPT (Michot 2010; Chettiparamb and Kokkranikal 2012), and Kumarakom was used as the pilot project to conduct an evaluation of responsible tourism (Chettiparamb and Kokkranikal 2012; Michot 2010). Of note here is that although both case studies focused on the same area, each study suggested different reasons for the successful application of responsible tourism and the long-term perspective. Chettiparamb and Kokkranikal (2012) argued that the principles applied in Kerala showed that in order for responsible tourism policies to be successful then it was recommended that they should not be prescriptive in nature. In contrast, Michot (2010) argued that Kerala benefited from favourable initial conditions that allowed pro-poor tourism policies to be readily adopted, although the communication of these policies from the state sector and what they meant was seen as an issue. Michot (2010: 20) states the following in relation to this:

> PPT measures have to be economically viable but the lack of communication over the PPT programme in Kerala might be a considerable issue in the long run. If the tourists knew more about it, they may openly ask for it, and the industry and the governments would probably take the issue more seriously. In order to increase the popularity of PPT and of socio-economic dimensions of tourism more generally, it is relevant to create an international label for tourism businesses and destinations that respect established guidelines.

Michot (2010: 19) also points to the favourable conditions for the establishment of PPT in Kerala; the 'traditional left-wing orientation of the citizen, the well-organised and powerful civil society, the existence of Tourism Institutes such as KITTS and of poverty reduction organisations such as Kudumbashree and the well-educated population' were all cited as reasons why this particular pilot programme had been initially successful. Conversely, Chettiparamb and Kokkranikal (2012) suggest that the case of Kerala might actually provide a somewhat artificial result for the success of PPT, and put forward the idea that only when this success is compared with other forms of sustainable tourism in the same area could it actually then be considered as a flagship programme for future PPT initiatives.

Supplementing rural livelihoods and supporting green tourism: the case of homestays at Korzok

Ladakh is located in the Indian Himalayas, and since opening to tourism in 1974 this destination has experienced rapid growth from adventure tourists eager to experience the unique landscape, biodiversity and culture on offer (Anand *et al.* 2012). With this growth, however, has not only come pronounced economic and social changes, but also negative environmental impacts (Anand *et al.* 2012), and this has led to the Snow Leopard Conservancy introducing a homestay model in Ladakh, which was designed to integrate both development and conservation goals in the area (Jackson and Wangchuk 2004). As Hvenegaard (1994) points out, ecotourism is widely viewed as an ecologically, economically and culturally sustainable alternative to traditional tourism activities that do not operate in a manner sensitive to local culture and the environment. With this idealism in mind, organisations and institutions working in the Ladakh area initiated sustainable community-based tourism projects that operated on two distinct levels; first, these initiatives were aimed at protecting local wildlife and natural resources, while second these projects also offered alternative livelihood opportunities for local residents (Anand *et al.* 2012).

The introduction of homestays in Ladakh was also seen as an effective model by the World Wide Fund For Nature (WWF-India) who built their own similar development in Korzok, which is situated in the Ramsar wetland of Tsomoriri (Anand *et al.* 2012). With a diverse range of stakeholder interests to take into account, this initiative by the WWF-India served to illustrate just how community development can operate alongside conservation goals, which Anand *et al.* (2012: 133) summarise:

> Ensuring participation and representation of the community in tourism has helped them secure rights, in this case, through the assistance of a nongovernmental organization and the state government; the benefits of tourism were not monopolized by affluent outside actors. Entrusting responsibilities to the villagers of Korzok for running the enterprise has allowed for a more equitable, steady and sustainable flow of monetary benefits.

The successful outcome of this programme also supports the findings of Chhatre and Agrawal (2008) who noted that the establishment of locally based monitoring programmes and the enforcement of how resources were utilised in turn generates not only a strong sense of ownership amongst local communities, but also results in generally positive conservation outcomes. This trend also looks set to continue in the region; Anand *et al.* (2012: 134) note that 'inspired by the Korzok model, the Changpa inhabitants of Tso Kar, a high-altitude wetland in Changthang, have shown interest in developing a project along similar lines'. This suggests that in certain circumstances community-based tourism can become a socially equitable approach in recognising the threats posed by unplanned tourism, and addressing the issues involved as more tourists look for low-impact, environmentally sensitive ways in which to travel and also search for destinations that embrace these concepts (Kiss 2004; Jones 2005; Nelson 2007).

Community agency and sustainable tourism development: the case of La Fortuna, Costa Rica

Some research on community-based tourism has demonstrated that the economic benefits of tourism can simultaneously provide a sense of both empowerment and ownership for participants (Scheyvens 2002; Tao and Wall 2009). The ability of community-based tourism to foster initiatives that are designed to mitigate undesirable impact from tourism activities whilst also allowing for participants to achieve economic, social and environmental goals designed to encourage sustainable conservation practices is therefore potentially significant for sustainable tourism development (Stem *et al.* 2003; Kruger 2005; Stronza and Gordillo 2008). There are two schools of thought that exist, however, on whether community-based tourism does in fact lead to sustainable tourism; Okazaki (2008) along with Roberts and Tribe (2008) believe that the two concepts are linked, while Akama (1996), Li (2006) and Stem *et al.* (2003) argue the opposite.

For sustainable tourism practices to be successfully implemented, Matarrita-Cascante *et al.* (2010: 736) state that 'communities engaged in tourism development must present an array of particular attitudinal, organisational and behavioural characteristics'. This statement ties in with the social marketing concept put forward by Andreasen (1995), which illustrates that community-based tourism has real potential to provide evidence of whether social marketing practices can actually help facilitate community engagement in order to advance the development of locally based sustainable initiatives. Using a field-theoretical perspective, Matarrita-Cascante *et al.* (2010) focused on the town of La Fortuna in Costa Rica as a case study of community-based tourism in action.

La Fortuna is a relatively new township, and the first documented settlers arrived in 1915. Since 1980 the local economy has shifted towards tourism activities due to a national downturn in the agricultural sector coupled with growth in the state-sponsored promotion of tourism (Hill 1990). Utilising interviews with key local community figures and participant observation, Matarrita-Cascante *et al.* (2010) illustrated how economic, social and environmentally sustainable practices were made a reality through 'a process of building relationships that increase the capacity of local people to unite, act and adapt to changing conditions' (Matarrita-Cascante *et al.* 2010: 738). Key factors considered vital to enable these relationships were found to be the strong intra- and extra-community interactions that existed in La Fortuna, and these factors were both aided and augmented by systems of open communication, participation, distributive justice and tolerance, which were seen to exist within the community (Matarrita-Cascante *et al.* 2010).

There has been much discussion amongst academics regarding the advantages that can be gained through the community-led management of local resources (Zapata *et al.* 2011). The case of La Fortuna illustrates that such community-level approaches 'can allow for the design of policies and practices sensitive to the opportunities, constraints and uniquenesses' (Matarrita-Cascante *et al.* 2010: 738), which can also mean that goals that are tailored towards sustainability can also be designed to adapt to the differing environmental conditions within the communities concerned (Tosun and Timothy 2003; Cole 2006a, 2006b). Policies designed to protect the sustainable aims of community-based tourism in La Fortuna were clearly evident as Matarrita-Cascante *et al.* (2010: 747) notes that many participants 'consistently mentioned their opposition to the establishment of tourism enterprises dedicated to gaming, gambling and sex – all seen as detrimental to social life in La Fortuna'. Such enterprises were viewed as being counterproductive to the protection of the social environment goals that were the cornerstone of projecting a sustainable image of La Fortuna to visitors, and were not only seen as relevant for improved community life, but also as being key to the protection of the social environment that attracts tourism to the area (Matarrita-Cascante *et al.* 2010).

The role of social marketing in environmental policymaking: the case of the Chilean land restoration programme

Westley, Holmgren and Scheffer (2010) focused on the role of social marketing, particularly in the context of stakeholder groups, in garnering the acceptance of an innovative experimental approach towards the restoration of semi-arid shrub land in Chile based within eco-regions referred to as matarrols (Myers *et al.* 2000). This land restoration programme involved the use of controlled scientific experiments designed to promote herbivore control. Whilst the results of the initial series of experiments conducted had proved promising, Westley *et al.* (2010) noted they were yet to be formally introduced into local ecosystem management approaches. It is also important to note that Chile's environmental protection has suffered the instability of several political regimes, which have left CONAF (the ministry responsible for conserving Chile's native forests) with considerably less clout compared to industrial and even agricultural stakeholders (Westley *et al.* 2010). The purpose of this case study therefore was to demonstrate how social marketing could be used to help gain an understanding of a variety of stakeholders' differing motivations whilst also attempting to suggest a possible framework in which best practice strategies could be developed for diffusing scientific research into future regional environmental management programmes (Brechin *et al.* 2002; Westley *et al.* 2010).

Westley *et al.* (2010: 3) contend that in some areas of social marketing, such as campaigns aimed at health care, that part of the problem with dealing with multiple groups of stakeholders lay in the fact that 'there has been a tendency to forget that marketing is fundamentally about exchange', and cite one of the fundamental tenets of social marketing set out by Kotler and Roberto (1989: 24) who originally stated that social marketing was designed for 'encouraging voluntary behaviour of the target audience by offering benefits they want, reducing barriers they are concerned about and by using persuasion to motivate their participation in program activity'. There is an exception to this; Westley *et al.* (2010) point towards the work of Rothschild (1999) who declared that exchange is more difficult to define when a clear link between behavioural change and self-interest is not present, or when there is a substantial delay between the exchange taking place and obtaining any form of reward. Westley *et al.* (2010: 3) argue that this demonstrates that social marketing amongst stakeholders needs more than just a persuasive element 'as persuasion alone may be of limited value' in the eyes of some stakeholder groups.

Bearing the work of Rothschild (1999) in mind, Westley *et al.* (2010) conducted a series of interviews to identify the range of possible barriers and benefits for turning experimentation into adaptive management. This was done through the selection of five different stakeholder groups who were based in the central valley south of Fray Jorge National Park, which was one of the areas where controlled scientific experiments had taken place. These stakeholder groups consisted of three park scientists who were already involved in the experiments, two private landowners, two small farmers involved in local agricultural collectives, three mining industry executives and two government policy makers from Santiago. It was assumed by Westley *et al.* (2010: 4) that 'different groups who control potential experimental sites would be motivated to "buy" the concept for different reasons'.

Analysis of the exploratory interviews conducted suggested that the likelihood of collaboration amongst the different stakeholder groups varied significantly across the five groups that were sampled. Large landowners were found to have the ability and the opportunity to provide sites for experimentation, whilst farmers' cooperatives neither had the opportunity or the ability to turn over land for experimentation, basing their motivations for participation in some form of exchange, which Westley *et al.* (2010: 11) states would usually be 'not just in the form of a subsidy but also in the form of expertise'. It was also found that the stakeholder group who were most likely to support collaboration were the international mining companies 'if they felt they could gain political support and greater freedom of action by participating' (Westley *et al.* 2010: 11).

Case studies from other areas of the world are noted by Westley *et al.* (2010) as suggesting that the involvement and cooperation of local stakeholder groups in restoration projects that focus on degraded ecosystems is feasible, but is also difficult to maintain over the long-term. It is possible, however, via planning processes and also through the involvement of local groups to 'build social capital by linking local groups together' (Westley *et al.* 2010: 11) whilst simultaneously helping to facilitate an approach that Pinkerton (1999) suggests could be broad enough to satisfy the interests of multiple groups of stakeholders. Unfortunately for those stakeholders who place a high value on environmental aspects of this deal, Westley *et al.* (2010: 10) demonstrate that it would appear that Chilean policymakers 'concede that pressure from the international community has the greatest potential to influence policy in the near future'.

In order to counteract this situation, Wesley *et al.* (2010) suggest that the answer to this dilemma lies with the application of ongoing pressure from both the international scientific community and NGOs. It would seem that such pressure would 'be necessary to increase the value of such legislation for the policy makers themselves' (Wesley *et al.* 2010: 13). Local landowners and collectives were noted as being offered the least incentive to participate in the restoration programme as it presently stood, but Wesley *et al.* (2010: 13) suggested that in this area 'a legislative change to reward restoration would help tip the balance'.

Multiple groups of stakeholders will each have differing motivations in terms of the outcomes that they value from conservation programmes. Westley *et al.* (2010: 13) states the following with regard to this in the context of social marketing:

> Social marketing is not a panacea. Nonetheless, it needs to be added to the development literature like other approaches that are better documented, such as participatory management and community-based management. Its contribution, however, is that it reveals the significant differences in motivation that characterise different social groups concerned with or affected by conservation imperatives. As such, social marketing can provide a source of further insight for those dedicated to restoration in complex social contexts.

It is noted in this case study that when motivation does coincide with skill and opportunity that 'very little education, marketing or coercion is needed. In the complex world of conservation, however, this is seldom the case' (Westley *et al.* 2010: 4). Rothschild (1999) also points towards the value that can be gained in a broader social context when education is added to the social marketing mix – this can aid in the selling of intangible concepts or ideas in particular, which Westley *et al.* (2010) demonstrate is possible in this case, provided stakeholders are prepared to wait.

Deliberately lit fires in the Southern Wales hills

The deliberate lighting of grass fires in southern Wales is a major problem that affects the region's tourism industry as well as being an environmental and social nuisance. In 2009 there were approximately 7,000 such fires costing £7 million a year to control in south Wales, one-fifth of the UK total. In May 2011 an important wildlife habitat, a Site of Special Scientific Interest (SSSI) and a priority habitat, was 'wiped out' by the worst grass fire for 30 years in the Brecon Beacons National Park. For three days, nearly 2,000 acres of upland common and peat bog had been burning in the Beacons between Trapp, Brynamman and Llandeilo. The fire destroyed hundreds of eggs from nesting birds, and red grouse, voles, mice, hares, moles, lizards and hen harriers perished in the flames (BBC News Wales 2011).

Dave Ansell, station manager within the South Wales Fire and Rescue Service community safety and partnerships department, told BBC Radio Wales that he believed those figures suggested that in some areas setting grass fires was almost socially acceptable.

> Tom Jones made a song very famous once – *The Green Green Grass of Home*. I speak to a lot of people who are very proud to be Welsh and proud to be from the valleys and yet they're quite happy, or appear to be quite happy, to allow their mountains to burn. … People need to realise that this isn't risk-free naughtiness, that it is affecting somebody, that it is affecting the places they live, that it's affecting bringing tourism and industry into the area.
>
> (Quoted in Fairclough 2011)

Mr Ansell said that he saw parallels between the work he oversees to prevent grass fires in the first place and earlier campaigns to tackle drink-driving.

> I speak to a lot of people who are very proud to be Welsh and … from the valleys and yet they're quite happy, or appear to be quite happy, to allow their mountains to burn … 40 or 50 years ago, drink-driving was almost acceptable and allowed and people did drink and drive. By changing the law, by using marketing and the media it's totally socially unacceptable to drink and drive these days. I think it's exactly the same way forward with the grass fires. We have to change people's attitudes, we have to change their behaviour.

To tackle these problems, South Wales Fire and Rescue Service has developed a new marketing and communications campaign using social marketing techniques. According to Dr Sue Peattie:

> The perpetrators were mostly young males between seven and 17. The drivers seemed to be very much peer pressure, natural curiosity, boredom and thrill-seeking. So it was a case of developing activities that would satisfy those. But that alone would not have worked by itself. We needed to ensure that the community realised that this was not harmless fun and that this sort of behaviour was no longer going to be tolerated.
>
> (Quoted in Fairclough 2011)

Based on Dr Peattie's research, South Wales Fire and Rescue Service launched Project Bernie in 2010 with a cartoon sheep as its mascot and the slogan 'Grass is Green; Fire is Mean' (Peattie *et al.* 2012). For a six-week period around Easter, the Tonypandy area was used as a test bed for a variety of inter-linked initiatives including diversionary activities for youngsters and high-visibility, zero-tolerance patrols in areas at risk. A series of activities including the 'chance to be a fire fighter for a day' are being staged to divert youngsters from starting grass fires. Activities range from writing songs and recording a CD to learning bush craft survival skills. The campaign also used bill boards, street stencils, posters and flyers. According to Sue Peattie: 'This approach goes beyond just raising awareness on the dangers of deliberately set-ting grass fires. It is about stepping into the shoes of the target audience, listening to them, understanding them and deciding the most appropriate action' (quoted in BBC News 2010). With a 46 per cent decrease in grass fires over the Easter 2010 period and a wider decrease in anti-social behaviour, Project Bernie's debut was judged a success and at Easter 2011 its approach was rolled out further (Fairclough 2011; Peattie *et al.* 2012).

Station manager Dave Ansell is in no doubt that the scheme is beginning to have an effect:

> For many many years we've almost accepted grass fires internally as well. Just raising the awareness internally that we're no longer going to stand for it has made a huge difference within the service. I believe the high number of calls we've been getting in the control room are also due to the awareness raising that we've done – making people aware of it, that they're not going to stand for it any more.
>
> (Quoted in Fairclough 2011)

PLATE 8.1 The seaside town of Margate in the UK has been revitalised by the development of the Turner Gallery and accompanying place promotion

PLATE 8.2 The Old Town Square of Margate has now become a location for tourists to visit again

Social marketing in the context of place promotion and development: the cases of branding Logan City and Absolutely Positively Wellington

Place marketing campaigns are as much internal as they are external. When competing against other places it is important to consider both indigenous and exogenous factors that can influence tourist reasons for selecting a destination as well as the perceptions of local people. Indigenous factors include decisions about strategy, images, support, resources and the value of facilities. Exogenous factors can influence tourism in the location of the place/destination in relation to markets and various other destinations or attractions.

Russell, Mort and Hume (2009) investigated how social marketing principles can be applied in the context of place branding and promotion through a case study that focused on Logan City in Queensland, Australia. Logan is a relatively young city that was established in the late 1970s (Russell *et al*. 2009). Employing the narrative analysis technique (Czarniawska 2004; Gabriel 2000; Rhodes and Brown 2005), the case study investigated how the management of Logan City Council were seeking to position the city using 'a novel combination of place branding, re-imaging, social capital enhancement and community development linked to economic development' (Russell *et al*. 2009: 236).

The Logan City Council is described by Russell *et al*. (2009: 232) as a 'large non-profit organisation operating at the regional level with a defined history, diverse stakeholders, numerous challenges and substantial involvement with the whole community'. The branding used in this campaign was intended to promote a positive image of the City of Logan through utilising billboard advertising in an attempt to change attitudes and perceptions amongst the community of the city. The overall aim of the campaign was to create 'positive community self-perception – perhaps even brotherhood' (Russell *et al.* 2009: 236). In taking this approach Russell *et al.* (2009) argue that the aim of the Branding Logan City campaign is grounded in the broader context of social marketing consistent with the initial concepts in this area advocated by Wiebe (1952) and Kotler and Zaltman (1971) where ideas and social issues were the focus of campaigns, rather than later social marketing campaigns that have focused on behavioural change on the part of individuals (Andreasen 1995).

While experts within the domain of social marketing emphasise that successful campaigns need to be fully integrated, coherent and undertaken over a reasonable period of time (Andreasen 1995; Hastings 2007; Kotler *et al.* 2002) there is also a school of thought were it is noted that persistence and long time frames are the key to such success (Walsh *et al.* 1993). This latter belief was clearly evident in the Branding Logan City campaign where the advertising used moved through several phases, moving 'from merely images of identity to images of action – showing for example diverse activities being engaged in as part of embracing life in Logan' (Russell *et al.* 2009: 236). Early stages of the campaign focused on images of individuals engaged in a variety of differing activities around the city, and then moved on to images that solely focused on the local facilities around Logan with the absence of any individuals present in these particular photographs with the theme 'Logan: a great place', while specific taglines for this stage were 'A great place to shop'; 'A great place to relax'; and 'A great place for culture' (Russell *et al.* 2009). This stage of the campaign was grounded in destination marketing themes (Morgan *et al.* 2002) that utilised place-based imagery, while the final stage emphasised locally based economic activities, a theme that was in part due to an upcoming local Council election, with the 'Get it in Logan' phase of the campaign (Russell *et al.* 2009). With regards to their being a lack of a specific behavioural focus (Andreasen 1995) in the Branding Logan City campaign Russell *et al.* (2009: 236) write that 'within this campaign's social marketing approach, in the campaign the traditional approaches to place marketing and re-imaging that are "other directed" are subverted by making them "self-directed".' The final stage of this campaign was successful enough that the Logan City Council was able to report back that economic growth had actually increased in the region, which illustrated that even though the campaign had been run over a long period of time, the outcome was ultimately successful in financial terms (Russell *et al.* 2009).

By embracing and adapting the familiar rhetoric that normally forms the focus of place and re-imaging campaigns through the use of place-base imagery, Russell *et al.* (2009: 236) suggested that the Branding Logan City campaign 'provides new insight into the application of social marketing to important though neglected fields of social change – the social change needed for a distressed locality to become revitalised and to move forward confidently to build a productive and caring community'. Russell *et al.*'s (2009) focus on this case study was to demonstrate that their belief that social marketing needs to be considered as more than just a tool to change behaviour and attitudes; the case of Branding Logan City shows that it is possible to instil non-behavioural dimensions such as civic pride as well.

Absolutely Positively Wellington or 'Wellington is dying and we don't know how to turn it around'

In May 2013 New Zealand Prime Minister John Key commented at a meeting to business people in the Auckland suburb of Takapuna that the capital city of New Zealand 'Wellington is dying and we don't know how to turn it around'. Key later apologised for the remarks and tried to soften his message by saying that rather than dying, 'I should have said "under sustained pressure"' (quoted in Schouten 2013). Mr Key came under substantial criticism for his remarks. The remarks sparked a call from Property Council Wellington President Ian Cassels for the national government to support efforts to encourage economic growth in Wellington: 'As a major stakeholder in the city, the Government should focus its attention on Wellington's economic activity and support the efforts of local residents and businesses' (quoted in Schouten 2013). However, Mr Key's comments also led to suggestions that the city should revisit a place marketing campaign, the Absolutely Positively Wellington brand, created in 1991, which was aimed at rebranding the city as well as making Wellingtonians feel much better about the city at a time when it was undergoing major economic restructuring.

Rather than create a new brand for the city, Positively Wellington Tourism (PWT), the Wellington City Council (WCC) body responsible for tourism, event and retail promotion planned to rejuvenate the Absolutely Positively Wellington campaign, to promote the capital as a 'city that creates its own positive energy'. PWT planned to launch a marketing campaign with the 'Wellington Story' as a cornerstone that will include a paragraph PWT had written, promoting the city: 'Packed with creators, thinkers, dreamers, doers and lovers of life, it's the one place in the country – in the world – where everything is possible' (quoted in Chapman and Cowlishaw 2013).

'Absolutely Positively Wellington' was a branding campaign launched in 1991. It began with a newspaper advertising campaign by Saatchi & Saatchi featuring successful Wellingtonians. It was hugely successful with respect to recognition and impact and also spawned an iconic television commercial. In 1993 the slogan was officially adopted as the city's brand by the WCC after being gifted by Wellington Newspapers, who ran a newspaper, the *Evening Post*, which had given Saatchi & Saatchi the space to run the original campaign (Brabazon 2009). As of 2013 the logo was still featured on WCC rubbish bags and parking tickets (Chapman and Cowlishaw 2013).

The council's economic growth manager, Katie Sadleir, said the plan was for the council to act as facilitator, PWT to focus on marketing, and business development organisation Grow Wellington to focus on 'converting' opportunities. PWT chief executive David Perks told councillors the brand was still relevant, but the city had to start singing its own praises, and make sure residents and businesses were doing the same. 'We need our people and our businesses to get their swagger back ... we need to go further than the jingle of the 90s' (quoted in Chapman and Cowlishaw 2013).

According to Kim Wicksteed, the general manager of Saatchi & Saatchi in Wellington, when he was asked by *The Evening Post* for 'something positive' to promote the city, the campaign was still the envy of other towns and cities and rejuvenating the slogan was a great idea after Prime Minister John Key's comments about the city 'dying': 'The advertisements had this little logo that the city really adopted ... It was the first sort of attitudinal leap in the country as far as a town or a city is concerned, and Wellington just embraced it. I still smile when I get my rates bill and see the logo' (quoted in Chapman and Cowlishaw 2013).

Social justice and politics on a local level: the case of Desa Senaru, Indonesia

Butler and Hinch (2007) suggest that governments generally support indigenous tourism as a social and economic development mechanism in impoverished regions, however, 'meaningful participation' (Schellhorn 2010: 116) by all stakeholders is often constrained through differences in educational, political and cultural influences (Zeppel 2006). Nevertheless, 'the fact that tourism can alter relationships within the host society, including the power balance amongst different community subgroups, is often overlooked' (Schellhorn 2010: 132).

In order to examine the effects of tourism on social and political relationships at a regional level, Schellhorn (2010) conducted research on the Sasak village of Desa Senaru, adjacent to Gunung Rinjani National Park in Indonesia. This location is an important gateway to the Segara Anak caldera, which is a crater lake directly below Mount Rinjani, and attracts thousands of pilgrims and tourists every year. The competition for tourism revenue in this particular area is very intense and it is suggested by Schellhorn (2010: 125) that this situation is because 'the competitive nature of this industry is partly a result of rural poverty, [and] it is also a direct effect of the entrepreneurial structure of Senaru's tourism economy'.

The political situation within which local tourism operators in Senaru conduct their business does not fall into the familiar Western model of individualism. Family-based support networks operate in a collectivist manner where it 'seems that the notion of professional competitiveness in chase of the tourist dollar does not balance with the reciprocal friendship concept and ideology of generosity' (Schellhorn 2010: 127) that permeates business relationships. As a result of this, Schellhorn (2010: 132) writes that 'native people will only benefit from the development of their resources if this process enables them to realise their own aspirations' and that this realisation may require changing the goals of short-term economic development in the Senaru region in order to bring these goals into lie with heritage conservation and social development aims. This could, in turn, allow for the adoption of an integrated approach towards tourism development that takes into account all stakeholders concerned (Schellhorn 2010).

In terms of social justice, it would seem, as Schellhorn (2010: 132) states, that although the situation in Desa Senaru was effective in terms of 'raising awareness of the triple bottom line of economic, social and environmental objectives, it neglected its crucial cultural component'. This created a scenario where those entrepreneurs who already possessed local knowledge and a ready skill base at hand were able to exploit opportunities offered by tourism development programmes and funds provided by donors to operate such schemes. There has been much discussion on the need to strengthen indigenous participation in tourism development (Scheyvens 2002; Cole 2006a, 2006b; Zeppel 2006). What this particular case study found was that the case of Desa Senaru demonstrated that there were perhaps greater degrees of limitations placed on the involvement of some native populations in tourism development that had been previously suspected; Schellhorn (2010: 132) contends that these 'emerge from institutional processes, their dynamic conditions and subtle effects rather than from readily identifiable barriers'.

Advocating a proactive development approach that embraces both training and education programmes that encourage indigenous participation, and that are also constantly monitored and evaluated by the people of Desa Senaru, is what Schellhorn (2010) believes would be the optimal solution for the predicament illustrated in this situation. Providing opportunities for all and not just skilled opportunists could use social justice to counter 'the informal albeit powerful structure of the local tourism industry [which] indicates a socially inefficient development process' (Schellhorn 2010: 132).

Chapter summary

This chapter has provided a number of case studies of community-based tourism and social marketing. In several cases, such as that of pro-poor tourism, interventions might not even have been considered as social marketing although they do have a number of the characteristics (Truong and Hall 2013). Although 'the local' and 'the community' are clearly of great significance in tourism and social marketing it is vital not to romanticise them; communities are not the embodiment of innocence (Hall 2008a). 'On the contrary, they are complex and self- serving entities, as much driven by grievances, prejudices, inequalities, and struggles for power as they are united by kinship, reciprocity, and interdependence' (Millar and Aiken 1995: 629). Such observations reinforce O'Brien *et al.*'s (2008: 18) observation: 'Approaches that treat communities as homogeneous (i.e., able to adapt or reduce risks as a group) are prone to failure'.

A key issue in both acceptance and effective use of social marketing knowledge and interventions in communities is the issue of trust. Where trust is absent community-based social marketing initiatives are virtually impossible to achieve. This also highlights that relevant information is individually and socially contextualised and actioned. 'Concepts and tools do not necessarily motivate behaviour change where individuals are not motivated to change or perceive barriers to doing so' (Whitmarsh *et al.* 2011: 58). Although changes in attitudes may be encouraging, if communities wait for an event to 'make them believe' in the need for behaviour change then the prospects for engendering more sustainable and resilient communities are not good. Communications are therefore rightly highlighted as extremely important, 'which suggests an emphasis on presenting knowledge in a community's own language, through innovative media' (O'Brien *et al.* 2008: 20).

BOX 8.2 ENCOURAGING PEOPLE TO STAYCATION

In 2010 at the height of the global financial crisis the tourism industry in many destinations were starting to focus on the concept of a 'staycation', i.e. encouraging people to travel locally or at least domestically rather than travel internationally. From a social marketing perspective such campaigns tended to focus on price, promotion and product but were competing against the habit or normalcy of travelling further afield. Such 'buy local' campaigns although often strongly supported in the area of attractions like farmers' markets may be harder to achieve with respect to holiday travel. In the case of the Isle of Wight in England marketing staff hoped to harness social networking websites to encourage more visitors to come – and to stay longer. A Facebook page was set up to encourage visitors to upload photos and share memories of their trips to the island. According to Claire Robertson, Isle of Wight Council's strategic manager for communications:

> In the past we've used tried and traditional methods – poster advertising, magazine advertising and so on, but this year we're also looking to put a significant amount of resource into online marketing, as that's obviously a growing source of influence on visitors coming to the island

(Quoted in Sinclair 2010)

Questions for self-reflection

- What barriers exist in trying to encourage people to holiday locally?
- To what extent might a Facebook page and online marketing give a destination a competitive advantage in trying to encourage people to visit?
- What role might the VFR market have in encouraging staycations and more local forms of travel?

Further reading and websites

A community approach to social marketing, which closely parallels some of the community-based tourism planning literature (see Chapter 8), is discussed in:

McKenzie-Mohr, D. (2011) *Fostering Sustainable Behavior: An Introduction to Community-Based Social Marketing*. Gabriola Island: New Society Publishers.

Also refer to the extremely useful Tools of Change website, which has a wide range of social marketing material including case studies:

www.toolsofchange.com/en/home

A useful online toolkit to encourage public participation is:

Health Canada Policy Toolkit for Public Involvement in Decision Making (Health Canada 2000): www.hc-sc.gc.ca/ahc-asc/pubs/_public-consult/2000decision/index-eng.php

Useful readings with respect to the operation of community-based tourism and social marketing include:

Peattie, S., Peattie, K. and Thomas, R. (2012) 'Social marketing as transformational marketing in public services: The case of Project Bernie', *Public Management Review*, 14(7): 987–1010.
Troung, V. D. and Hall, C. M. (2013) 'Social marketing and tourism: What is the evidence?' *Social Marketing Quarterly*, 19(2): 110–135.
Zapata, M. J., Hall, C. M., Lindo, P. and Vanderschaeghen, M. (2011) 'Can community-based tourism contribute to development and poverty alleviation?' *Current Issues in Tourism*, 14(8): 725–749.

9

SUSTAINABLE TOURISM CONSUMPTION AND SOCIAL MARKETING

Towards behavioural change?

Chapter 9 brings together a number of themes in the previous chapters within contemporary concerns for sustainable consumption. The chapter discusses some of the various dimensions and potential paradoxes in tourism-related sustainable consumption and the importance of marketing in promotion and communication as well as the development of marketing strategies. A significant concept examined in the chapter is the notion of 'degrowing' tourism and the way in which marketing may assist this, particularly through the encouragement of new localised and low emissions/energy forms of consumption. However, critically the chapter suggests that different approaches to intervention and consumer change are bound up with different ways of thinking about governance and the relative significance of agency and individual responsibility and capacity as compared with the role of structure and the actual capabilities of individuals to make change.

Sustainable consumption

Sustainable consumption is a global issue with importance for all individuals, but none more so than for marketers. The Norwegian Ministry of the Environment (1994) defines sustainable consumption as:

> [T]he use of services and related products which respond to basic needs and bring a better quality of life while minimising the use of natural resources and toxic materials as well as emissions of waste and pollutants over the life cycle of the service or product so as not to jeopardise the needs of future generations.

The three immediate goals of sustainable consumption can be simplified as 'less', 'more' and 'ethical' (Manoochehri 2001). 'Less' proposes the radical reduction of aggregate material throughput in developed economies. 'More' advocates sustainable economic development in developing countries that responds to needs and 'ethical' proposes changes in global patterns of consumption, based on reconsidered values and cultural practices in the North (developed economies), and access and redistribution in the South (developing economies). Through the third goal, Manoochehri (2001) highlights the inequalities between developed and developing countries. For example the obesity epidemic observed in developed countries (as a consequence of over-consumption) is in strict contrast to the inadequate conditions (shelter, water, food) experienced by millions of individuals in developing countries.

In the case of tourism sustainable consumption is potentially an extremely significant idea because tourism, in real terms, is less sustainable than ever. The Brundtland definition, that 'sustainable development is development that meets the needs of the present without compromising the ability of future generations to meet their own needs' (WCED 1987: 49), has come to feature in many a tourism textbook and student essay, even though tourism was hardly mentioned in the report at all (Hall 2008a). Yet, despite the ongoing series of statements of concern from organisations such as the UNWTO and the WTTC the fundamental reality is that in terms of resource use, land use change, biodiversity loss and pollution, tourism's negative effects are getting worse not better. Several authors have tried to identify the global dimensions of tourism-related environmental change (e.g. Gössling 2002; Gössling and Hall 2006a) with Gössling's (2002) study providing a benchmark for later estimates (Hall and Lew 2009).

Many models, theories and studies of sustainable tourism, sustainable mobility and sustainable consumption, including with respect to tourism and climate change, contain underlying assumptions about an individual's capacity to act. These assumptions relate to behaviour, behavioural change and governance, given that the range of policy measures that the state utilises to achieve its policy goals are based on assumptions regarding individual and collective behavior (Hall 2011b) (see Chapter 3). Although usually not explicitly stated, such assumptions are contained not only in public policy positions but also in the recommendations of industry, institutions, consultants and academics on how to improve the sustainability of tourism because they implicitly suggest that by engaging policy setting or intervention A consumers will do B. Therefore, the chapter aims to apply our understanding of tourism and social marketing with respect to the carbon capability of consumers (Whitmarsh *et al.* 2011), i.e. downstream change, to also suggest that theories, paradigms and understandings of behavior and how change might occur also frames the extent to which governance is actually capable of making change, i.e. is upstream change also required. The chapter first gives an overview of the environmental challenges provided by tourism so as to provide a context as to why change is required. It highlights that sustainable consumption responses to the unsustainability of present-day tourism is based upon efficiency and sufficiency type approaches, the latter being reliant on changes in consumer behaviour and therefore providing a direct link to social marketing imperatives. The chapter then goes on to outline three different approaches to consumer change before examining how the framing of behavioural capacity is connected to policy learning and the way in which such framing has led not only to dominance of the paradigm of 'ABC' (attitude, behaviour and choice) in favoring certain behavioural approaches to sustainable tourism but also the ignorance of others that frame consumer behaviour.

PLATE 9.1 Photograph taken in a Marks & Spencer store in Oxford in July 2013 juxtaposing a travel advertisement with the M&S goal of becoming carbon neutral. The picture highlights the issue of where you draw the boundary with respect to becoming carbon neutral and the relative responsibilities of individuals and businesses.

The environmental impacts of tourism

The amount of tourist trips is increasing not only in absolute terms but, when compared with growth in world population, also in relative terms (also see Hall 2005b, who similarly indicated that international tourism mobility was increasing faster than population growth). Such growth is significant not only in terms of the economic dimensions of tourism but also in the growth of emissions with the rate of growth outstripping improvements in energy efficiency and emissions reduction per tourist (Gössling, Hall and Scott 2009; Scott *et al.* 2012a, 2012b).

Carbon dioxide (CO_2) is the most significant greenhouse gas (GHG), accounting for 77 per cent of global anthropogenic global warming (Stern 2006). CO_2 emissions from tourism have grown to an estimated level of about 5.0 per cent of all anthropogenic emissions of CO_2 in 2005, with most of this (40 per cent) from aviation. Globally, an average tourist trip lasts 4.15 days (average length for all international and domestic tourist trips) and generates average emissions of 0.25 tonnes of CO_2 per traveller (Scott *et al.* 2008). The vast majority of trips produce low emissions, but it is the small proportion of long-haul trips that are highly emission–intense. Long–haul travel between the five world regions the UNWTO use for statistical aggregation purposes (Africa, Americas, Asia–Pacific, Europe and the Middle East) accounts for only 2.7 per cent of all tourist trips, but contributes 17 per cent of global tourist emissions (UNWTO and UNEP 2008).

Trips by coach (bus) and rail account for 34 per cent of all trips worldwide, but comprise only 13 per cent of global CO_2 emissions (including emissions from accommodation and activities). Although air-based trips comprise only 17 per cent of all tourist trips, they cause about 40 per cent of all tourism-related CO_2 emissions, and 54–75 per cent of radiative forcing (the change in the balance between radiation coming into the atmosphere and radiation going out). While the average trip generates 0.25 tonnes of CO_2, long-haul trips and luxury cruises can generate up to 9 tonnes of CO_2 per person per trip (35 times the emissions caused by an average trip) (Scott *et al.* 2008). Even 'ecotourism' holidays that are supposedly environmentally friendly, such as dive holidays, will cause high emissions in the range of 1.2 to 6.8 tonnes of CO_2 due to emission from air, automobile and boat travel (Gössling *et al.* 2007). The impact of aviation-based long-haul travel on the environment becomes even more significant when it is recognised that such trips can generate higher per person emissions in a single holiday than the annual per capita emissions of the average world citizen (4.3 tonnes of CO_2), or even the higher average of an EU citizen (9 tonnes of CO_2) (Peeters *et al.* 2007).

Travel between and within the more economically developed regions of the world (Europe plus parts of the Americas and the Asia-Pacific) is the most significant contribution to emissions, comprising 67 per cent of international trips worldwide and 50 per cent of all passenger kilometres (pkm) travelled globally. In contrast, Africa is the least important destination for travellers from the developed countries, receiving just 2.2 per cent of all trips from Europe and the Americas (3.3 per cent of CO_2 emissions from tourism). Long-haul (interregional) tourism from Europe represents 18 per cent of all international trips, and 49 per cent of all CO_2 emissions from travel. Long-haul travel within and between the world's most industrialised countries, therefore, causes most of tourism's greenhouse gas emissions (UNWTO and UNEP 2008), although it is the least developed countries that will have the greatest problems in adapting to the effects of climate change. Because of such issues there is substantial debate about how international transport emissions can and should be incorporated into climate change mitigation and adaptation schemes, who should pay and how future transport infrastructure should be developed (Gössling, Hall and Scott 2009).

The impacts of tourism at a global scale affects not only the atmosphere but also land use. Gössling (2002) calculated that globally, leisure-related land use might amount to 515,000 km^2 (200,000 mi^2), representing 0.34 per cent of the terrestrial surface of the Earth and 0.5 per cent of its biologically productive area. Less than 1 per cent of leisure-induced land alteration was due to accommodation, with traffic infrastructure accounting for 97 per cent of change. Leisure-induced land alterations, however, are often concentrated in ecologically sensitive or significant environments. Tourism urbanisation tends to be focused in high-value amenity environments and is closely associated with other forms of amenity-related urbanisation, such as retirement and lifestyle migration, particularly in coastal areas (Hall 2006a). Furthermore, it should also be stressed that Gössling's calculations are extremely conservative, including only commercial accommodation and not second homes or other secondary dimensions of tourism-related urbanisation in destination and resort areas (Hall and Lew 2009).

Another significant dimension of global environmental change that is related to increased tourism mobility is the unplanned movement of biota and disease from one location to another via transport and people (Hall and Baird 2013). Humans are significant vectors for disease, as well as being carriers of pests, which may also host diseases that affect humans, plants and animals.

> In terms of its rate and geographical extent, its potential for synergistic disruption and the scope of its evolutionary consequences, the current mass invasion event [of biota] is without precedent and should be regarded as a unique form of global change.
>
> (Ricciardi 2007: 335)

The extent of global biotic exchange is such that alien invasions are included as 'Threats to Biodiversity' in the Convention on Biological Diversity's (CBD) framework (McGeoch *et al.* 2006). Even though biosecurity measures are in place in many airports prohibited items still get through. For example, in Australia it has been estimated that the leakage rates for airline passengers arriving in Australia, which measures the percentage of all items that have crossed the border but which still contain or possess sizeable material, has been relatively stable since 1998 at between 3 and 4 per cent (Hall 2005b). The impacts of the introduction of exotic species can be substantial. Pimentel *et al.* (2001) examined the economic and environmental threats from alien plant, animal and microbe invasions in the US, UK, Australia, South Africa, India and Brazil, and estimated that over 120,000 non-native species had invaded the six countries and are causing more than US$314 billion per year in damages.

In the light of global health scares such as SARS, increasing attention is also given to the role of international travel as a channel for the spread of infectious disease, what Morse (1993) described as *viral traffic*. According to Hall (2005b) the increase in air travel has also increased the potential for diseases to spread for two reasons: first, the increased speed of travel means that people can travel and pass through airports before disease symptoms become evident; and, second, the increased size of modern aircraft. For example, drawing on the travel medicine literature, Hall (2005b) postulated a hypothetical situation in which the chance of one person in the travelling population having a communicable disease in the infectious stage was one in 10,000. With a 200-passenger aircraft, the probability of having an infected passenger aboard (x) is 0.02 (200/10,000 = 0.02) and the number of potential contacts (y) is 199. If homogeneous mixing is assumed, this means a combined risk factor (xy) of 3.98 (a 3.98 per cent chance of being exposed to n infectious disease). If the aircraft size is doubled to 400 passengers, then the corresponding figures are x = 0.04, y = 399 and xy = 15.96. In the case of the double-decker

Airbus A380 that came into service in 2007, the passenger configuration ranges from 550 to almost 800 seats if placed into an all economy class configuration. If we assume a 600-seat aircraft, then the corresponding figures are x = 0.06, y = 599 and xy = 35.94. In other words, tripling the number of seats available increases the risk factor nine-fold, from a 4 per cent to a 36 per cent chance of being exposed to an infectious communicable disease.

Potentially the one positive contribution of tourism to the global environment has been the use of tourism as a justification for the establishment of national parks and protected areas, what can be referred to as the global conservation estate (Hall and Lew 2009). The global conservation estate has grown enormously since the first *United Nations List of Protected Areas* was published in 1962 with just over 1,000 protected areas. In 1997 there were over 12,754 sites, and 102,102 sites covering 18.8 million km² (7.25 million mi²) by 2003, a figure equivalent to 12.65 per cent of the Earth's land surface (Chape *et al.* 2003: 21). Of the total area protected, it is estimated that 17.1 million km² (6.6 million mi²) constitute terrestrial protected areas, or 11.5 per cent of the global land surface. However, some biomes, such as lake systems and temperate grasslands, are poorly represented, while marine areas are significantly under-represented (Frost and Hall 2009).

The bottom line of this litany of environmental change is that tourism cannot be regarded as an 'environmentally friendly' industry and may even be behind a number of other industries with respect to the overall level of environmental activity and the provision of environmentally sound alternatives (Martens and Spaargaren 2005). Figure 9.1 provides a representation of the relative level of environmental activities and the provision and adoption of environmentally sound alternatives for different consumption activities in developed countries (Hall and Lew 2009). Tourism is therefore like any other form of development, it has its costs and benefits (Gössling, Hall and Weaver 2009). However, the tourism industry often seems to regard itself as different and continues to portray itself as a positive contributor to the environment via ecotourism and pro-poor tourism in some destinations while seemingly ignoring the global environmental changes it contributes too. Almost any first year university student understands the notion of a tourism system whereby tourism influences not only the destination but also the tourism generating area and the transit region(s) in which the tourist travels to and from the destination (Hall and Lew 2009). Yet these extra-destination impacts often seem to be glossed over by industry and government actors in seeking to account for tourism's environmental affects. Ironically, when it comes to assessing tourism's economic impacts, such as through Tourism Satellite Account modelling, there seems to have been great enthusiasm in demonstrating the extent of its economic reach. The promotion of a similar research programme that matches tourism to its considerable environmental effects has not been as forthcoming.

Because of tourism's impacts on environmental quality, tourism is subject to something akin to Hardin's (1968) 'tragedy of the commons', whereby free access and unrestricted demand for a finite natural resource ultimately structurally dooms the resource through over-exploitation. The 'solution' has been to manage the problems of the commons via various means, such as regulation, applying the polluter pays principle, and even corporatisation or privatisation of what was previously an unregulated public resource. In the case of some of the commons properties, such as the air or the sea, regulation and polluter pays policies are often substantially resisted by the tourism industry. The industry typically refers to the wider 'public good' that their economic activity generates as a justification to minimise regulatory constraints. Of course, such arguments are nonsense, as all businesses contribute to a common economic good via their purchasing and employment capacities, and yet common public goods (such as air and roads) still need to be managed to avoid the effects of overuse (Hall and Page 2006).

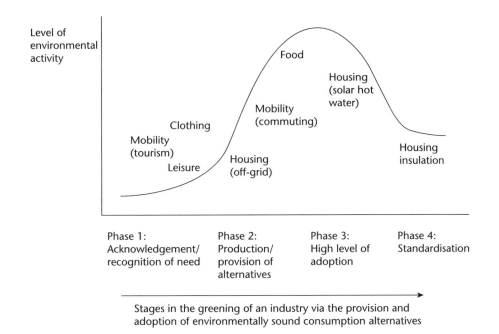

FIGURE 9.1 The relative level of environmental activities and the provision and adoption of environmentally sound alternatives for different consumption domains in developed countries (after Hall 2007c, 2009a)

There are very few tourists who deliberately aim to abuse the destination they are visiting and the social and environmental resources they are consuming. Many visitors are even seeking to make environmentally and socially friendly tourism purchasing decisions. However, as in the tragedy of the commons, individual travellers generally do not believe that their consumption is going to lead to negative impacts. In fact, most will likely believe being a tourist is good for a destination because of the employment it creates. Nevertheless, it is the totality of all the individual tourist consumption and production decisions that are causing undesirable economic, social and environmental change (Hall and Lew 2009).

Unfortunately, there are no easy solutions to these challenges, as preventing people from travelling will create political problems, while all that consumption (and subsequent pollution) may just be shifted elsewhere. Instead, solutions lie in the realm of the sub-title of Hardin's (1968) famous essay, in that measures require a 'fundamental extension in morality'. The issue is not just one for tourism, significant as it is, but is grounded with respect to morality in terms of self-reflexive, conscious considerations of what and why we consume. If we accept the moral principle derived from Kant's ([1785] 1996) categorical imperative – act in the way you would be willing for it to become a general law that everyone else should act in the same situation – then proper levels of consumption would mean a lifestyle, including tourism, recreation and leisure, that everyone can enjoy and that the global environment can cope with without undesirable change (White 2008). However, this is the very problem with much contemporary tourism: there is just not enough world for everyone to be the average North American or European long-haul tourist. Undoubtedly, some steps have been taken with respect to better understanding how we can do this, but globally tourism has neither become a 'force for peace' nor fulfilled the initial hope of sustainable tourism and ecotourism. Instead, global tourism presents as much 'greenwashing' (Medina 2005) as do many of the other multinational industries that are promoting themselves as becoming more energy efficient and purveyors of green solutions, such as the coal, oil and nuclear industries, multinational car firms and aircraft manufacturers. Indeed, the energy and transport industries have a mutually reinforcing role with respect to the development of medium- and long-distance tourism. Yet, if the contributions of tourism to these sectors is to be acknowledged as part of the economic benefits of tourism then so should the environmental impacts.

BOX 9.1 WE ALL HAVE TO CONSUME, BUT DO WE REALLY HAVE TO TRAVEL SO MUCH TO BE HAPPY?

We all have to consume. Consumption is an ecological necessity and is inherent in biological systems. The issue really is the nature of that consumption, and from whose – or what – perspective we are taking with respect to its appropriateness. In the case of tourism we are fundamentally dealing with two different, though related, aspects of consumption. First, there is the socio-economic dimension in which tourism is part of economic, cultural and lifestyle concerns that centre on economic, social and mobility capital. Second, there is the extent to which tourism consumes the non-human environment, what may be referred to as natural or ecological capital. Both aspects of consumption are deeply embedded within contemporary capitalism

Tourism, as we would recognise it, existed well before the onset of the industrial age of tourism. However, the industrial revolution and the rapid growth of capitalist society clearly marked a radical change in the rate, nature, and the promotion of consumption. Tourism, in the sense of travel for travel's sake, was intimately associated with this process as a new form of mass consumption and production that changed both people and places. In addition, tourism consumption came to be linked with identity (Baranowski and Furlough 2001). By this we understand that consumers combined, adapted and personalised different travel and tourism discourses as a way of negotiating key existential and psychological tensions.

It has, of course, long been recognised that contemporary tourism activity must be understood within the context of contemporary capitalism (Britton 1991), although this essential relationship is perhaps at times not to the forefront of thinking in tourism studies as it should be, particularly given its critical institutional role in the setting of economic, social and environmental relations. However, it may well be the case that capitalism, and especially its current neo-liberal form, is now so institutionalised in the academy that the capacity to think other, let alone do other, has been significantly reduced (Slaughter and Rhoades 2004). Nevertheless, there are significant lines of resistance to some of the dimensions of contemporary capitalism in tourism, especially with respect to alternative forms of tourism and leisure consumption and the desire by some to 'tread lightly' on our planet. Indeed, concern over anthropogenic global environmental change probably provides the most urgent driver for improving our understanding of consumption and consumptive practices.

Assessments of consumption can be subjective or objective in form. Subjective assessments are usually value judgements as to the appropriateness of tourism behaviour as well as to the extent of travel. This is often bound up in notions of cultural and local appropriateness, good form and concerns over deviant behaviour, e.g. concerns over drug and alcohol consumption in some holiday destinations. A personal observation here would be that the academy has tended to focus on 'middle-class' tourism forms rather than much of what would be regarded as mass tourism. This is not to argue of course that such matters as heritage, cultural attractions and events, convention centres, national parks and wine and food are unimportant, but perhaps it does neglect the reality that for many people tourism really is about fun and sun, getting away and having a pleasurable time – and doing it cheaply. Of course, the academy may also be reflecting its own, predominantly white, highly mobile, middle-class concerns that what it does is travel and what other people do is tourism. Furthermore, the vast majority of work in tourism studies is fundamentally about getting people to consume more. The tourism academy could be loosely described as a bunch of relatively time and money rich people trying to find ways of getting other relatively time and money rich people to travel and travel more, sometimes with a good cause in mind like conserving heritage or creating jobs for the poor, but it is still about encouraging consumption (Hall 2011c).

What is to be done?

If tourism is to make a genuine contribution to sustainability then it becomes vital that there is greater public acknowledgement by industry and government of what the positive and negative impacts of tourism are, and thereby to see tourism as part of the larger socio-economic and bio-physical system (Hall and Lew 2009). To modify Goodland and Daly (1996), sustainable tourism development is tourism development without growth in throughput of matter and energy beyond regenerative and absorptive capacities. Although often referred to as a service industry, tourism's impacts are not intangible. In order to reduce its environmental footprint, tourism needs to become part of a circular economy rather than a linear one, so that inputs of virgin raw material and energy and outputs in the form of emissions and waste requiring disposal are reduced (Hall 2009b). Such a change is often categorised, as noted at the start of the chapter, as sustainable consumption.

Within tourism there are two main approaches to encouraging this approach (Figure 9.2). First is the efficiency approach, which seeks to reduce the rate of consumption by using materials more productively. Eco-efficiency stresses the technological link between value creation in economic activities and environmental quality. This approach places more focus on recycling, using energy more efficiently, eco-innovation and reducing emissions, but otherwise operating in a 'business as usual' manner, that encourage so called 'green growth'. Examples of this include efforts to produce more fuel-efficient aircraft.

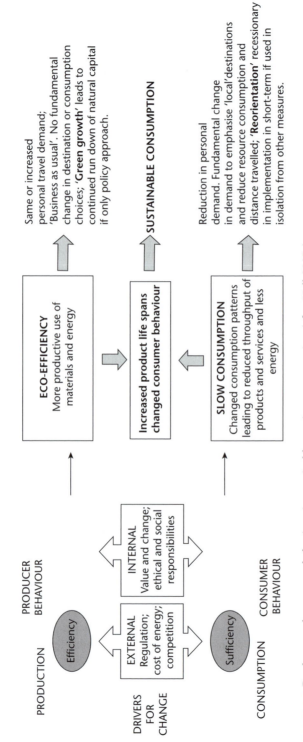

FIGURE 9.2 Producer and consumer behaviour in sustainable tourism consumption (after Hall 2007c)

The second approach may be referred to as 'slow consumption' or a 'sufficiency' approach, and includes consumer activism and change as well as industry and public policy initiatives. This approach is of major significance to this book because it focuses on behavioural change. Examples of a sufficiency approach include (Hall 2007c, 2009a):

- The development of environmental standards at the regional, national and international scales, e.g. such as the Nordic Swan label (Bohdanowicz 2009) (also utilised under the efficiency approach).
- The development of 'short' supply chains. These include relocalisation schemes such as farmers markets and 'local diets' that reinforce the potential economic, social and environmental benefits of purchasing, consuming and producing locally (e.g. Hall and Sharples 2008), as well as projects such as Fair Trade, which seeks to create a more direct relationship between producers and consumers.
- Ethical consumption, through ethical and responsible tourism (e.g. Goodwin and Francis 2003).
- The so-called 'new politics of consumption' such as anti-consumerism and culture jamming (e.g. White 2008).

BOX 9.2 ANTI-CONSUMPTION BEHAVIOUR AND ATTITUDINAL CHANGE: THE CASE OF THE 2009 SOUTH AUSTRALIAN SINGLE-USE POLYETHYLENE PLASTIC BAG BAN

Lee *et al.* (2009) contend that the very nature of anti-consumption forces consumers to change their perspectives and focus in the context of habitual behaviours. Sharp, Høj and Wheeler (2010) put this notion to the test when they examined whether the prohibition of an item associated with habitual consumption can actually serve as a catalyst for the development of anti-consumption attitudes and behaviours. Their research focused on the 2009 South Australian legislated retail ban on single-use polyethylene plastic bags (Sharp *et al.* 2010). This study involved 1,167 interviews that were conducted with shoppers before the ban was announced, during the demarketing campaign that was conducted during the four months that the phasing-out period ran for, and also when the ban was in full effect (Sharp *et al.* 2010). In order to allow for the identification of individual-level attitudinal and behavioural change, Sharp *et al.* (2010) also conducted a further 253 interviews that were repeated with the same individuals to see what effect the ban on single-use polyethylene plastic bags had created in terms of anti-consumption behaviours.

Demarketing campaigns that feature high levels of information have been found by McKenzie-Mohr (2000a, 2000b) as being responsible for actually failing to change consumption behaviours. Wall (2005) notes that direct bans in the form of outright prohibition, such as the South Australian plastic shopping bag ban, have been seen to be equally if not more effective than just employing pure demarketing measures in isolation. Sharp *et al.* (2010) noted in their research that in order to promote behavioural change on a large scale in terms of anti-consumption usually requires some form of intervention, which Geller (1989) cites as normally occurring at the level of public policymaking. Convery *et al.* (2007) supports this by stating that these consumption reduction programmes have commonly been through environmental taxes associated with air, water energy and waste.

Past research by Hayabuchi *et al.* (2005) has observed that voluntary anti-consumption of store-provided bags is relatively low, with only 25 per cent of shoppers voluntarily refusing to take store-provided bags (Hayabuchi *et al.* 2005). Sharp *et al.* (2010) grouped shoppers according to their level of voluntary anti-consumption of plastic bags before the ban took place in South Australia, and found that shoppers who voluntarily showed anti-consumption behaviour were the only group showing any shift in anti-consumption behaviours during the subsequent demarketing campaign that was run during the four month phasing-out period. Also of note was the fact that this group of shoppers were very supportive of forcing others to also participate in anti-consumption, while shoppers that showed little or no voluntary anti-consumption were found to exhibit low levels of behavioural and attitudinal resistance (Sharp *et al.* 2010).

These findings demonstrate that banning an item that is used as part of everyday habitual consumption does help to achieve anti-consumption behaviours in relation to the object concerned (in this case plastic shopping bags); however, prohibition of such items does not necessarily mean that participants will adopt consistent attitudes towards anti-consumption in other areas of their daily routines (Sharp *et al.* 2010). The evidence provided by this case suggests that demarketing campaigns alone are not enough to reduce socially undesirable behaviours in the context of anti-consumption. If the accompanying negative reinforcement of such habitual behaviours is missing, then a demarketing campaign by itself is simply not adequate to achieve long-lasting and widespread behavioural change that embraces sustainability.

The slow consumption approach is also closely related to the concept of 'décroissance' or 'degrowth' that has entered the lexicon of green economics since 2000. Despite how it sounds degrowth is not a theory of contraction equivalent to theories of growth. It is a term created by critics of growth theory that seeks to provide an alternative to the dominant doctrines of 'economism' in which growth is regarded as the ultimate good. Instead the concept of 'degrowth' proposes the development of a form of economics that is bound by the sustainable limits of humankind's ecological footprint on the planet's natural resources (Latouche 2004). Degrowth is therefore not so much connected to downsizing per se but to the notion of right-sizing and the creation of a steady state economy, components of which include:

- Reducing the global ecological footprint (including the carbon footprint) to a sustainable level.
- In countries where the per capita footprint is greater than the sustainable global level, reducing to this level within a reasonable timeframe.
- Increasing consumption by those in severe poverty as quickly as possible, in a sustainable way, to a level adequate for a decent life, following locally determined poverty-reduction paths rather than externally imposed development policies.
- Increasing economic activity in some cases; but redistribution of income and wealth both within and between countries as a more essential part of poverty reduction.

(Flipo and Schneider 2008)

BOX 9.3 DECLARATION OF THE FIRST INTERNATIONAL CONFERENCE ON ECONOMIC DEGROWTH HELD IN 2008

The process of degrowth should be characterised by:

- an emphasis on quality of life rather than quantity of consumption;
- the fulfilment of basic human needs for all;
- societal change based on a range of diverse individual and collective actions and policies;
- substantially reduced dependence on economic activity, and an increase in free time, unremunerated activity, conviviality, sense of community, and individual and collective health;
- encouragement of self-reflection, balance, creativity, flexibility, diversity, good citizenship, generosity and non-materialism;
- observation of the principles of equity, participatory democracy, respect for human rights and respect for cultural differences.

(Flipo and Schneider 2008: 318)

Tourism has not been a focal point of degrowth research (Bourdeau and Berthelot 2008). However, tourism research has engaged with elements of the concept given that its goals are similar to those of sustainable consumption. Areas of commonality with specific tourism studies includes not only the broader discourse of tourism within the development of a just and materially responsible society (Hall and Brown 2006), but also the relationship between tourism and Slow Food (e.g. Hall and Sharples 2008), and Fair Trade (e.g. Clevedon and Kalisch 2000), with the Slow Food movement in particular, as the name implies, being regarded as an exemplar of slow consumption.

The consumption behaviour 'sufficiency' approach to sustainability and the production-oriented 'efficiency' approach mirror broader alternatives with respect to sustainable development. However, both are ultimately required in the transformation to a steady state economy. Slow consumption alone may just provide recession or, at worst, economic chaos (Jackson 2005), at least in the short term – as perhaps witnessed in the 2008–12 global economic and financial recession. Increasing product life spans and decreased energy use may also enable both efficiency and sufficiency (Cooper 2005; Jackson 2005). This includes means by which materials are used more productively (i.e., the same quantity providing a longer service) and throughput is slowed (i.e., products are replaced less frequently, plus, in the case of travel, reducing distance of trip or having a 'staycation'). Such lifecycle thinking has been brought to other sectors, such as manufacturing, but it would be environmentally appropriate to utilise this approach in tourism. Research and thinking on tourism and its impacts therefore needs to broaden attention to visitor consumption beyond the point of purchase to all phases in the life of the tourism product and experience, from start to finish and from conception to final disposal.

Sustainable tourism consumption does not necessarily mean people holidaying or travelling less, although in the case of long-distance air travel there would almost certainly be a decline. Instead, it would mean people travelling more locally and, when people do travel long distance, potentially staying longer, travelling by the most efficient means and/or paying substantially more so as to reduce the overall environmental effects of their trip in terms of emissions, energy consumption and environmental damage (Hall and Lew 2009). Although some isolated destinations distant from their origin markets will be affected many destinations and some tourism sectors would actually benefit. Furthermore, a number of tourism businesses are already seeking to develop more efficient buildings and products. Fundamental to the application of degrowth principles to tourism is the internalisation of external diseconomies – those costs incurred by the activity of one actor but borne by the community at large. This idea is ostensibly in keeping with orthodox economics. But Latouche (2006) argues that it would clear the way towards more sustainable consumption as it would place the costs of our social and environmental problems on the books of the companies responsible for them. In one sense this means fully applying the principle of polluter pays in order to ensure that costs as well as benefits are demonstrated in economic activities rather than being externalised. In tourism this means accounting for the environmental effects of tourism not just at the destination, as significant as they might be, but throughout the entire course of the consumption and production of a tourist trip. And in the context of tourism that will therefore bring a strong focus on the activities of the transport sector, and airlines in particular.

BOX 9.4 VOLUNTARY SIMPLICITY

In contemporary society, consumption is no longer used just to serve basic needs, but is instead used to encourage the purchase of luxury and other goods that are being for purposes of status or fashion and the often short-term term belief that they will contribute to a sense of well-being (see Chapter 2). This situation has led many consumers to re-evaluate their consumption choices (Shaw and Newholm 2002). During this process, a movement known as 'voluntary simplicity' or 'simple living' can influence individuals. The Voluntary Simplicity Movement can be understood broadly as a diverse social movement made up of people who are resisting high-consumption lifestyles and who are seeking, in various ways, a lower consumption but higher quality-of-life alternative (Alexander and Ussher 2012).

A desire for more sustainable or appropriate consumption patterns is not new and, in the West, has its roots in Quakerism, Transcendentalism and even elements of Puritanism (Shi 1986), while in a more modern form it also finds expression in the countercultures of the 1960s (Musgrove 1974). More recently, it also has found expression in the notion of voluntary simplicity, which refers to 'the choice out of free will (rather than being coerced by poverty, government austerity programs, or being imprisoned) to limit expenditures on consumer goods and to cultivate non-materialistic sources of satisfaction and meaning' (Etzioni 2003: 7), so that an individual can free up money and time to focus on other aspects of their life (Shaw and Newholm 2002). Alexander (2011) states that people who live simply base both their personal and social progress on developing and fostering relationships and increasing richness through means other than consumption, rather than defining themselves by wealth and status. Another important aspect of voluntary simplicity is reflection, whereby if a person thinks more about what in life they actually need, they will live a simpler lifestyle through spending less (Kronenberg and Lida 2011). Essentially voluntary simplicity is about discovering what is really needed in life in order to live happily, by knowing how much consumption is truly enough (Alexander 2011). This potentially avoids becoming trapped on the hedonic treadmill or becoming part of the material rat race as individuals are not trying to keep up materialistic pursuits and instead find happiness through other sources.

People choose to simplify their lives at different levels, from moderate to strong simplification. Etzioni (1998) defines three different types of simplifiers, known as downshifters; where people choose to give up few luxuries in their life, strong simplifiers; where high-paying jobs are given up in order to free up time and diminish stress, and the simple living movement; where people adjust their whole life in order to live simply. In order to live this lifestyle, Craig-Lees and Hill (2002) state that people must have access to alternatives of high income such as wealth, education or unique skills. This is because individuals tend to trade down their income, therefore these alternatives are needed in order to live. This is not so important in downshifters, as jobs are not usually given up, however, it becomes very important in strong simplifiers and the simple living movement as jobs are either reduced or given up.

Motivations behind embracing voluntary simplicity suggest that people choose to live simply because they have come to a realisation that money is not the answer to happiness. Alexander (2011) states that people often think that high income and large consumption will create higher levels of well-being. When trapped in a work and spend cycle however, people often forget about what it is that is good in their lives. This cycle has no end and provides no means of lasting satisfaction. Through voluntary simplicity, especially in strong simplifiers and simple livers, individuals try to break this work and spend cycle by quitting their high-paying and stressful jobs in order to free up their time and participate in activities that create fulfilment and meaning (Etzioni 1998). When simplifiers in Melbourne, Australia, were asked what was the main reason that led them towards voluntary simplicity, all stated that they came to the realisation that consuming is not what makes people happy, and that having more is not the answer to happiness (Penn 2010).

However, before individuals turn to simple living, they tend to have lived with relatively high income levels. Etzioni (1998) describes downshifters as a group who can afford to buy luxury items, but choose not to. Zavestoski (2002) found that people who were considering simple living tended to be well paid and highly educated. These individuals have the money to live a high materialistic lifestyle, however, when people turn to voluntary simplicity, it is usually because of the development of anti-consumption attitudes or as a way to de-stress their life (Huneke 2005). They change their lives by reducing working hours or giving up work all together, and live on a substantially smaller income. The conception that more money creates greater happiness does not hold true in this situation, as people are actively giving up money in a quest to find greater happiness. Binswanger (2006) concluded his paper on why income growth fails to make people happy by suggesting that people would be a lot happier if they lived with less money but had more free time.

Alexander and Ussher (2012) conducted a survey with respect to how happy participants were who had made the transition to simple living; 89 per cent of respondents stated that their transition towards a simpler lifestyle had increased their happiness and only 0.2 per cent stated that they were less happy. Penn's (2010) study on urban simplifiers in Melbourne found that voluntary simplicity had enriched their lives because it had allowed them to live in line with their values, had given them more ability to control their own lives, and they are now better able to appreciate what they have. Research on voluntary simplifiers in America stated that a particular individual's comment on the lifestyle seemed to illustrate a general consensus when she said 'the more I simplify my life the better it becomes' (Huneke 2005: 21). This suggests that a life that is not based around consumption and materialism can be a source for happiness.

The concerns of voluntary simplicity and sustainable consumption suggest that we should be interested as much in the quality of the tourism experience as the quantity. Despite the best efforts of neo-liberal economists, marketers, corporations and governments to persuade others, the promise of consumerism, that the more goods and services – including travel and tourism – a person uses, the more satisfied that person will be, is not true. Money and materialism does not buy happiness. Research on income and subjective well-being shows that among the non-poor, increased income has little or no lasting impact on happiness (Myers 1993, 2003; Ahuvia 2008). There is a clear necessity to ensure that basic material needs as well as health and education are met, both between and within countries. But the transfer of intensive consumerism to the newly and less developed countries only appears to be creating new sets of problems rather than providing solutions. As Myers (2003) noted in the American context:

> We have bigger houses and broken homes, higher income and lower morale, more mental health professionals and less well-being. We excel at making a living but often fail at making a life ... The evidence leads to a startling conclusion: our becoming much better off over the past four decades has not been accompanied by one iota of increased psychological well-being. Economic growth has provided no boost to our collective morale.
>
> (Myers 2003: 50)

PLATE 9.2 Freiburg in Germany has an enviable reputation as a green city because of its public transport system and its encouragement of solar energy production and green design

PLATE 9.3 Protests in Freiburg aimed at the extent to which the city fulfils its green image

Approaches to behavioural change

In seeking to understand the different modes of policy intervention in changing behaviours with respect to sustainable consumption there is a need to understand the situated meanings associated with sustainability, mobility and environmental behaviours. That is, how individuals translate and apply knowledge in their daily lives and decision making (Whitmarsh *et al.* 2011), including with respect to travel and tourism (Gössling *et al.* 2012a), as well as the different forms of governance (Hall 2011b). This section will highlight these issues primarily with respect to individual responses to climate change in a tourism context.

In the case of sustainable tourism mobility, the vast majority of individuals are not yet willing to give up international travel or change their travel markedly (Cohen and Higham 2011; Mair 2011; Gössling *et al.* 2012a; Scott *et al.* 2012b; Kroesen 2013), despite enthusiasm by governments and industry to encourage voluntary changes in consumer behaviour. As the UK Sustainable Consumption Roundtable (2006b: 35) reported:

> Consumers struggle with the idea of flying less. They candidly acknowledge that the prospect of cutting back on flights was extremely unattractive ... flying abroad represents a major aspiration for consumers ... In addition, cutting back on flying is also very unattractive as consumers feel that there are few alternatives.

Even the most environmentally aware tourists might not be more willing to alter travel behaviour and may even be among the most active travellers (Gössling, Haglund *et al.* 2009; Barr *et al.* 2010; McKercher *et al.* 2010). Such a situation reflects the importance of recognising that relevant information is individually and socially contextualised and actioned. 'Concepts and tools do not necessarily motivate behaviour change where individuals are not motivated to change or perceive barriers to doing so. ... amongst users of carbon calculators, many (though by no means all) use such tools to *offset* their emissions rather than to *change* their energy consumption behavior' (Whitmarsh *et al.* 2011: 58).

For the majority of people, issues of climate change, energy, sustainable consumption and sustainable mobility have a relatively low salience in day-to-day activities, choices and actions (Sustainable Consumption Roundtable 2006a, 2006b; Weber 2006; Whitmarsh 2009; Whitmarsh *et al.* 2011). Awareness of environmental problems at an abstract level is usually not translated into personally relevant cognitions or motivating attitudes. For the majority of people the understanding about environmental issues tends to be limited to abstract or vague concepts. Whitmarsh *et al.* (2011: 57) argue that climate change poses major challenges to communicators and educators as '[i]t is a risk "buried" in familiar natural processes such as temperature change and weather fluctuations ... and has low salience as a risk issue because it cannot be directly experienced' (see also Weber 2006). Interestingly there is some evidence to support this observation given that research suggests that the attitudes of tour operators as well as the general public change when they experience weather events that they believe are associated with climate change (Hall 2006b; Tervo-Kankare *et al.* 2012). For example, in December 2012 after the impacts of Hurricane Sandy the results of a US poll by the Associated Press-GfK found rising concern about climate change among Americans, with 80 per cent citing it as a serious problem for the US, up from 73 per cent in 2009. According to Goldenberg (2012): 'Some of the doubters said in follow-up interviews that they were persuaded by personal experience: such as record temperatures, flooding of New York City subway tunnels, and news of sea ice melt in the Arctic and extreme drought in the mid-west'.

The suggestion by Whitmarsh *et al.* (2009) that there are currently low levels of 'carbon capability' among the UK population is arguably one that can be transferred to a wide range of individual and social contexts (see also Waitt *et al.* 2012). Carbon capability is '[t]he ability to make informed judgments and to take effective decisions regarding the use and management of carbon, through both individual behavior change and collective action' (Whitmarsh *et al.* 2009: 2). Carbon capability is not defined in a narrow individualistic sense of solely knowledge, skills and motivations (although these are important components). Instead, it suggests that a carbon capable individual, or family (Waitt *et al.* 2012), have an understanding of the limits of individual action and where these encounter societal institutions, infrastructure and systems of provision that act as barriers to low-carbon lifestyles, including travel and tourism, then they can recognise the need for collective action and other governance solutions (Whitmarsh *et al.* 2009, 2011). Carbon capability is also regarded as an analogue to financial capability as applied to anthropogenic climate change, and similarly involved budget management, planning, staying informed and making choices (Lorenzoni *et al.* 2011). Carbon capability has three core dimensions:

- *decision-making/cognitive/evaluative* (technical, material and social aspects of knowledge, skills, motivations, understandings and judgments);
- *individual behaviour or 'practices'* (e.g., energy conservation, sustainable or slow travel); and
- *broader engagement with systems of provision and governance* (e.g., lobbying, voting, protesting, creating alternative social infrastructures of provision).

Under a carbon literacy approach the assumption is that as an individual gains knowledge, perhaps as a result of educational and social marketing campaigns, they may change individual behaviours and practices (Figure 9.3). In contrast, a carbon capability approach argues that that much consumption (and hence contribution to resource use and emissions) is inconspicuous, habitual and routine, rather than the result of conscious decision making. This means that individual cognitive decisions about consumption are mediated through socially shaped lifestyle choices, resulting in sets of socio-environmental practices that are, in turn, delimited by social systems of provision and the rules and resources of macro-level structures and institutions (Giddens 1984; Whitmarsh *et al.* 2009) (Figure 9.4). Carbon capability does not imply that education and social marketing trying to encourage behaviour change is without value. Rather it highlights that the capacity for behavioural change needs to be understood in a much wider context.

Approaches to consumer change

The notion of carbon capability therefore inherently suggests a need to move beyond an understanding of environmental behavioural change that suggests that just providing information is sufficient for consumers to make 'rational' or 'appropriate' choices. However, it also raises the need to understand the underlying assumptions of different approaches to behaviour change. Three major contemporary approaches can be recognised in approaching issues of sustainability tourism mobility, as well as other areas of sustainable consumption: utilitarian, social/psychological and systems of provision/institutional (Seyfang 2011). An overview of these approaches is provided in Table 9.1 and is discussed below.

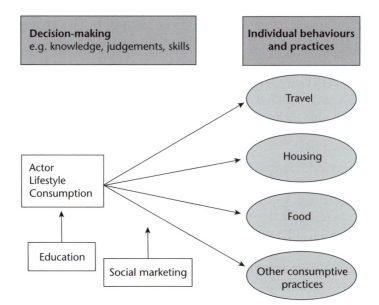

FIGURE 9.3 Dimensions of carbon literacy

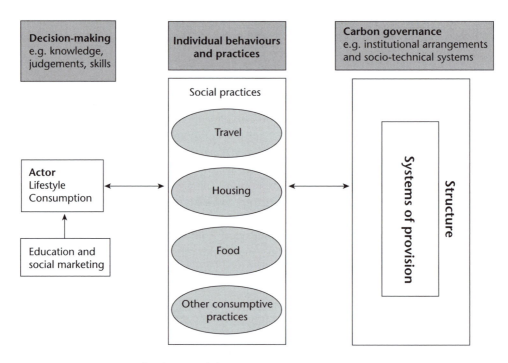

FIGURE 9.4 Dimensions of carbon capability

TABLE 9.1 Approaches to consumer change

Approach	Scale	Understanding of consumer decision making	Consumption is …	Tools to achieve sustainable consumption	Dominant forms of governance
Utilitarian (green economics)	Individual	Cognitive information processing on basis of rational utility maximisation	The means for increasing utility	Green labelling, tax incentives, pricing (including carbon trading), education	Markets (marketisation and privatisation of state instruments)
Social and psychological (behavioural economics/ nudging/social marketing/ green consumer behaviour/ ABC model)	Individual	Response to psychological needs, behaviour and social contexts. Dominant paradigm of 'ABC': attitude, behaviour and choice	Satisfier of psychological needs; cultural differentiator; marker of social meaning and identity	Nudging – making better choices through manipulating a consumer's environment. Social marketing in order to encourage behavioural change and promote sustainable lifestyles and behaviour	Markets (marketisation and privatisation of state instruments). Networks (public–private partnerships)
Systems of provision/ Institutions (degrowth, steady-state tourism)	Community, society, network	Constrained/shaped by socio-technical infrastructure and institutions	Routine habit, inconspicuous rather than conspicuous	Short supply chains, local food, local tourism	Hierarchies (nation state and supranational institutions). Communities (public–private partnerships, communities)

Sources: Seyfang (2011); Hall (2009a, 2011a, 2011b); Burgess (2012); Gössling and Hall (2013)

Utilitarian approach

The utilitarian approach to behavioural change utilises a conventional neo-classical micro-economic view of consumption by individuals as rational utility-maximisers. The approach assumes that individuals consume goods and services in free markets with perfect competition and information to decide a course of action that delivers the greatest utility to the individual. Even though the intellectual basis of neo-classical economics has been severely criticised, especially in terms of the relationship of its assumptions to real world economic behaviour (Keen 2011), the approach underlies much contemporary neo-liberal economic policy and has influenced the socio-political construction of rational utility maximising the neo-liberal consumer (McGuigan 2006; Bone 2010). From this perspective, efforts to promote sustainable mobility and consumption tend to rely on government intervention (or self-regulation) to correct 'market failure' and ensure that private and corporate individuals have greater information on which to base their decisions. The approach aims to appeal to rational actors with information to overcome an 'information deficit' and encourage 'rational behaviour'. However, access to information and education about climate change and more sustainable forms of consumption has not led to substantially improved sustainability behaviour (Christie 2010; Ockwell *et al.* 2010; Gadenne *et al.* 2011). Addressing the issues of 'value-action gap' and consumer awareness has not been matched by wholesale behavioural change (Seyfang 2011).

Social/psychological approaches: nudging and social marketing

The failure of neo-classical economic models to increase levels of sustainability behaviour has led to the realisation that behaviour does not change simply because of better quality information (Whitmarsh 2009; Whitmarsh *et al.*, 2009). The critique of neo-classical/rational models has primarily come from two social/psychological sources: behavioural economics and consumption studies.

Behavioural economics recognises that individuals have bounded rationality (Conlisk 1996) and often engage in satisficing behaviour (Simon 1959, 1965) as well as the role of social norms and routines that are not subject to rational cost–benefit calculations, including notions of community and fairness in economic outcomes (Folmer and Johansson-Stenman 2011). Significantly, with respect to the manner of influencing behaviour it also stresses that too much choice in the market leads to information overload and subsequent difficulties in decision making (Seyfang 2011). The focus on satisficing is not new and has long been influential with respect to policy making (Simon 1965); however, it has recently assumed renewed significance with respect to climate change solutions (Thynne 2008), including transition management (Gössling *et al.* 2012b). However, it has become an underlying dimension of the recent interest of behavioural economics in 'nudging' (Cialdini 2007; Amir and Lobel 2008; Thaler and Sunstein 2008).

The focus of nudging is in reconfiguring the 'choice architecture' to encourage beneficial decision making by consumers. The approach suggests that the goal of public policy making should be to steer citizens towards making positive decisions as individuals and for society while preserving individual choice. Acting as 'choice architects' policy makers organise the context, process and environment in which individuals make decisions and, in so doing, they exploit 'cognitive biases' to manipulate people's choices (Alemanno 2012). According to Bovens (2009) and Alemanno (2012) a policy instrument qualifies as a nudge when it satisfies the following:

- the intervention must not restrict individual choice;
- it must be in the interest of the person being nudged;
- it should involve a change in the architecture or environment of choice;
- it implies the strategic use of cognitive biases; and
- the action it targets does not stem from a fully autonomous choice (e.g. lack of full knowledge about the context in which the choice is made).

In the UK nudging has become a centre-piece of the Cameron coalition government, with David Cameron reportedly making *Nudge* (Thaler and Sunstein 2008) obligatory reading for his colleagues before the election, while in the US Sunstein became head of the Office of Regulatory Affairs in the Obama administration (Burgess 2012). An example of the kind of solutions being explored are schemes that attempt to reduce electricity consumption by providing feedback to households on their own and neighbours' usage (Burgess 2012). In the UK the influence on the concept on policy initiatives, including emissions reduction and changes in travel behaviour, is seen in the MINDSPACE report (Dolan *et al.* 2010), which although published during the tenure of the Cameron government had been commissioned by the previous Labour government, thereby illustrating the broad political attraction of the approach. Indeed, Box 9.5 outlines how the Labour government under Prime Minister Tony Blair had already positioned the role of the state in health interventions with respect to the use of social marketing in the mid-2000s.

In terms of its attractiveness, the MINDSPACE report suggests 'approaches based on "changing contexts" – the environment within which we make decisions and respond to cues – have the potential to bring about significant changes in behaviour at relatively low cost' (Dolan *et al.* 2010: 8). MINDSPACE is a mnemonic 'which can be used as a quick checklist when making policy' (Dolan *et al.* 2010: 8; see also Dolan *et al.* 2012):

1 *Messenger* we are heavily influenced by who communicates information.
2 *Incentives* our responses to incentives are shaped by predictable mental shortcuts such as strongly avoiding losses.
3 *Norms* we are strongly influenced by what others do.
4 *Defaults* we 'go with the flow' of pre-set options.
5 *Salience* our attention is drawn to what is novel and seems relevant to us.
6 *Priming* our acts are often influenced by sub-conscious cues.
7 *Affect* our emotional associations can powerfully shape our actions.
8 *Commitments* we seek to be consistent with our public promises, and reciprocate acts.
9 *Ego* we act in ways that make us feel better about ourselves.

A key insight of such an approach is that people do not act as isolated individuals, and instead consumption is socially situated and is often deeply embedded with habits and norms being significant. An insight that is shared with studies of consumption that recognise that consumption is a multilayered phenomena that is full of meaning including its role as a signifier of identity, cultural and social affiliations (consumption tribes), and relationships (Goldstein *et al.* 2008; Seyfang 2011). The symbolic value of consumption and its function for social distinction as well as self-expression are long recognised as being important for tourism and leisure consumption (Miles 1998; Chen and Hu 2010), including specifically with respect to sustainable consumption (Goldstein *et al.* 2008; Barr *et al.* 2011; Hall 2011c).

BOX 9.5 FROM DICTATORIAL NANNY STATE TO INDIVIDUAL RESPONSIBILITY?

Tony Blair in his 2006 end-of-term speech focused on the health sector and raised the issue of how far the state can intervene and at what point individual responsibility kicks in. Blair set out a vision whereby the government merely creates the right environment for individuals to make healthy choices rather than being more 'dictatorial' in directing interventions. According to Dr Fiona Adshead, the government's deputy Chief Medical Officer for England, the drive was born out of a need to be realistic about how people live their lives and the government is embracing social marketing to get people to make healthy choices.

> We have to understand how people live their lives. We can't approach it from the fantasy of how we would want them to. Some people will not always make the healthy choices. But I think if we can get the message across that a small change can make a big difference, and it is up to the individual to take responsibility for that, anything is achievable. What we can do is create the conditions for individuals to do that. Clear food labelling is one way this can be done, but we have to look to tailor approaches to individuals.
>
> (Quoted in Triggle 2006)

Meanwhile, others believed the government should not be afraid of being accused of being a nanny state and needed to take a tough stance on health issues, as had occurred with respect to the smoking ban in pubs. Kevin Barron, chairman of the House of Commons Health Select Committee, said ministers were 'too nervous': 'I think that what all governments have to do is to think about what's good for the public, getting the right messages out, and then just getting on with it basically. Put right, argued properly, we shouldn't be scared of somebody shouting to us "nanny state"' (quoted in Triggle 2006). But Professor Ian Philp, a health expert at Sheffield University and national director for older people, said the government should be careful about being too heavy-handed. 'The real challenge is that people don't want to hear messages from government on television campaigns but people will listen to messages in sources like lifestyle magazines or watching on soaps and so on' (quoted in Triggle 2006).

The main focus of behavioural change from a consumption studies perspective is via the tool of social marketing. The potential of social marketing to influence sustainable behaviours in relation to climate change has become increasingly argued (Downing and Ballantyne 2007; Peattie and Peattie 2009; Peattie *et al.* 2009), including with respect to tourism (Gössling, Hall *et al.* 2008; Barr *et al.* 2010, 2011; George and Frey 2010), although the actual conduct of such tourism–specific campaigns is limited (Truong and Hall 2013). However, although social/psychological approaches recognise the need to make major changes and while social norms are often cited as driving factors, there is little scope for wondering about how needs and aspirations come to be as they are, i.e. they do not fundamentally question structures and paradigms (Shove 2010), which is not the case with the systems of provision approach.

Social marketing and climate change: the case of the Act on CO$_2$ campaign

Addressing climate change through the promotion of pro-environmental behaviours has become a growing area of concern within social marketing (McKenzie-Mohr 2000a, 2000b; Peattie and Peattie 2009; Corner and Randall 2011) and the psychology of climate change communication in general (American Psychological Association 2009; Spence and Pidgeon 2009; Climate Change Communication Advisory Group 2010). One example of the issues associated with climate change communication is Britain's *Act on CO$_2$* campaign from the mid-1990s, which employed two different television campaign strategies in order to increase public awareness about climate change whilst suggesting behavioural changes that could be made on the part of the viewer (Department of Energy and Climate Change 2012). The first of these strategies was an advertisement entitled 'Bedtime Stories', which utilised a fear-based approach to the issue through depicting scenarios that could result from not practicing pro-environmental behaviours, and offered the viewer the chance to re-write the ending to this story through practicing environmentally conscious behaviours; the second strategy conversely took a more pragmatic approach and suggested that viewers should consider driving five miles less a week in a bid to help decrease CO$_2$ gas emissions (Department of Energy and Climate Change 2012). The fear-based tactics that were featured in the first strategy came under attack in a critical analysis by the Climate Change Communication Advisory Group (2010), which, citing empirical evidence from research conducted by Hoog *et al.* (2005), stated that the use of such tactics in social marketing campaigns actually were ineffective in generating the desired behavioural response from viewers and that the 'Bedtime Stories' advertisement had failed as a result of this (Climate Change Communication Advisory Group 2010).

The need to approach the strategies employed in social marketing campaigns with care when attempting to promote the concept of 'environmental citizenship' (Corner and Randall 2011: 1012) has been noted by Lorenzoni *et al.* (2007) as a significant challenge, especially when attempting to engage with the public in order to drive some form of behavioural change. Corner and Randall (2011: 1012) address this dilemma for marketers with the following:

> Fostering a sense of pro-environmental identity or environmental citizenship among the general population is important if pro-environmental behavioural changes are to be embraced and maintained. Social marketing techniques may be able to play a role in achieving these aims, but they must be anchored in the deeper notions of identity and citizenship if they are to have a meaningful influence on promoting a proportional response to climate change.

The criticisms levelled at the *Act on CO$_2$* campaign clearly indicate that while education can provide a foundation for pro-environmental campaigns, the use of social marketing in isolation was not enough to influence widespread behavioural change in this instance. This key finding derived from Corner and Randall's (2011) research demonstrates that there are some limitations evident when social marketing is applied in order to increase public engagement with climate change issues, and as a result of this several alternative approaches designed to circumvent these limitations were suggested in this particular case. These approaches were based around four core principles that were found to enhance public engagement when considering climate change issues; these principles were increased environmental education, value-based engagement and the enhancement of both social capital and citizenship (Corner and Randall 2011). These principles each revolved around the nexus of the overarching theme, which was that 'motivating a proportional response to climate change (i.e. more than piecemeal changes in pro-environmental behaviour) will involve engaging people at a deeper level (and in a broader capacity) than is possible with the techniques of social marketing' (Corner and Randall 2011: 1012).

An attempt to establish what motivates pro-environmental behaviours regarding climate change led to Wolf *et al.* (2009) also conducting research in this particular area. This study found that the desire for some form of civic responsibility was one of the key primary drivers of such behaviour (Wolf *et al.* 2009). Clearly, capitalising on this idea of civic responsibility is somewhat difficult given the intangibility of such a concept. Bearing this in mind, Brulle (2010) argues that the scope of some environmental campaigns can suffer as a direct result of myopia denying the fact that 'the public sphere and the institutions of civil society are the crucial mechanisms for affecting change' (Corner and Randall 2011: 1012). The professional nature of pro-environmental campaigns has also been the subject of criticism by Brulle (2010) who suggests that one of the real dangers present lies with the current way in which campaigns are presented, and how their presentation can actually serve to reinforce existing perceptions of power and equality. Following on from Brulle's (2010) arguments, Corner and Randall (2011: 1012) suggests that the solution to this dilemma indicates that 'what is needed is a communication process that promotes civic engagement and public dialogue, rather than passive receptiveness to small-scale behavioural change'. Dobson (2010) also offers support to this viewpoint by pointing out that the commitment to both the values and principles that underscore the basis of pro-environmental behaviours at the individual and community level are what motivate these behaviours, rather than reasons such as procuring financial benefits derived from practicing such behaviours.

Corner and Randall (2011) contend that although campaigns such as *Act on CO$_2$* have been criticised for failing to meet their goals this does not necessarily mean that there is no place for social marketing within the context of attempting to redress the level of public engagement regarding climate change issues. With respect as to how social marketing could be utilised in future environmental campaigns as a potential tool to counter this scepticism, Corner and Randall (2011: 1013) offer the following:

> Climate change is somewhat different, in that the challenge of public engagement often involves promoting particular behavioural changes, or building support for policies – so it is not simply the science of climate change that is being communicated. But there is no reason that 'selling' climate change will be any more effective than attempts to sell other scientific topics.

Systems of provision/institutional approaches

The third approach takes a more structural perspective on the organisation of systems of consumption and provision, and focuses on the contextual collective societal institutions, norms, rules, structures and infrastructure that constrain individual decision making, consumption and lifestyle practices. These are referred to variously as 'infrastructures of provision' (Southerton *et al.* 2004a), institutions and 'systems of provision': the vertical commodity chains comprising production, finance, marketing, advertising, distribution, retail and consumption that 'entails a more comprehensive chain of activities between the two extremes of production and consumption, each link of which plays a potentially significant role in the social construction of the commodity both in its material and cultural aspects' (Fine and Leopold 1993: 33).

The significance of the systems of provision approach is that it highlights that particular socio-technical systems constrain choice to that available within the system of provision, and can therefore 'lock in' consumers to particular ways of behaving and consuming (Lorenzoni *et al.* 2007; Maréchal, 2007, 2010; Seyfang 2011; Unruh 2000), including potentially with respect to travel and tourism (Becken 2007; Hares *et al.* 2010; Verbeek and Mommaas 2008). The approach provides a profound critique of the other two approaches for several reasons. First, it suggests that positioning the problem of sustainable mobility and consumption as a problem of personal choice fails to appreciate the socially situated and structured nature of consumption and is an 'arguably suspect theory of choice' given that it assumes

> that people could and would act differently if only they knew what damage they were doing. Such ideas inform programmes of research into the relationship between environmental belief and action, and the design of policy initiatives geared around the provision of more and better information.
>
> (Southerton *et al.* 2004b: 4)

Second, much research on consumption fails to recognise that consumers do not consume resources, they consume the services that are made possible by resources. Third, a focus on the end consumer serves to 'obscure important questions about the production and manufacturing of options and the intersection between, design, demand and use' (Southerton *et al.* 2004b: 5). Fourth, the socially sustainable dimensions of consumption, such as distribution and equity effects, are often ignored in government and institutional reports and decision making (Hall 2009a). Finally, it suggests that socio-technical systems, institutions and structures are not neutral, in that their formation and constitution is likely to sway behaviours more in one direction than others.

The systems of provision approach has focused on alternative systems of provision, with one notable area for tourism being the development of alternative food networks such as farmers' markets and short supply chains, such as Fair Trade. The emphasis on localism and short supply chains has been influential in the hospitality and restaurant sector together with the Slow Food movement and the growing interest in forms of slow tourism (Fullagar *et al.* 2012; Gössling and Hall 2013). Some aspects of the approach also focus on anti-consumption measures, such as voluntary simplicity or the more active notion of culture jamming – 'the innovative and alternative ways in which people are offering a form of creative, non-violent resistance against the way we view the world, either for the sake of the interruption or for getting an alternative message across' (Woodside 2001: 9) – which provides significant alternatives to contemporary consumer culture (Hall 2011c).

BOX 9.6 THE WAY TO ENGAGE PEOPLE IN COMPLEX ISSUES SUCH AS CLIMATE CHANGE IS NOT ON BILLBOARDS OR TV SCREENS

In contrast to the suggestions in Box 9.5 with respect to the use of social marketing in health interventions so as to encourage greater personal responsibility, Corner (2012) suggests that the way to engage people in complex issues, such as climate change, is not on billboards or standard television programming. Corner (2012) noted that the US Heartland Institute (climate-denial lobbyists) billboard advertising campaign that compared those who accept the science of climate change to the Unabomber Ted Kaczynski was an unmitigated public relations disaster, exposing their marginal position in the debate and losing them hundreds of thousands of dollars of corporate sponsorship. Several major corporations (including PepsiCo) rushed to distance themselves from Heartland's extremist position and cut their financial links. As Corner (2012) observed:

> While it is worth asking why a household name such as this – with public carbon reduction commitments – was still involved with a group like Heartland, its response demonstrated a simple but important point: no credible organisation wants to be caught on the wrong side of the climate debate.

Nevertheless, he also emphasised that some of the most high-profile advertisements selling climate change have also not fared much better than the billboards at the centre of the Heartland fiasco. For example, the UK government television advertisement 'Bedtime Stories' (see above) was withdrawn following complaints to the Advertising Standards Authority about newspaper adverts that accompanied it. The advert depicted a young girl being read a scary story about climate change as cartoon sea levels rose around her house, but was criticised by climate change communication specialists on the basis that using scare tactics is not an especially good way of encouraging sustainable behaviour. Similarly, the No Pressure video, released by the campaign group 10:10, despite starring a cast of A-list celebrities, was also a communications disaster. In one scene, children in a classroom were shown 'exploding' for expressing climate sceptic views. Obviously, climate sceptic groups condemned the campaign, although that didn't stop Heartland going several steps further with its own 'serial killer' advertisements.

As Corner (2012) suggests, these examples suggest that there have been some ill-advised attempts at climate change communication. But more importantly, selling a complex issue such as climate change through fairly superficial media such as posters or short films is not necessarily a good idea. Corner argues that although social marketing has been found to produce measureable changes in well-defined behaviours, such as use of public transport,

> there are serious question marks about whether social marketing offers the right set of tools for catalysing the individual, social and political shifts necessary to make the transition to a low carbon society. In particular, although social marketing may be effective in achieving short term goals in changing behaviour, it embodies a way of looking at the world which privileges consumers over citizens, targets individuals rather than social groups or communities, and pays little attention to the sorts of values that – in

the long term – are likely to generate much greater environmental engagement. In short, while the tools of the marketing industry might be useful for developing the green consumer economy, they are limited in their capacity to produce more substantive engagement … Given the evidence that the materialistic values promoted by the vast majority of adverts (even those that seek to sell green products) are ultimately counterproductive in generating a society-wide response to climate change that is proportionate to the scale of the challenge, perhaps the most effective advertising for climate change could be no advertising at all.

10:10 No Pressure: www.youtube.com/watch?v=PDXQsnkuBCM
Act on CO_2 Campaign: Bedtime Story: www.youtube.com/watch?v=0dOfBEm5DZU
Billboard Compares Climate Change Believers to Unabomber:
www.youtube.com/watch?v=eQ2tM9Hfe0w

Linking change approaches in consumption and governance

The three different approaches to behaviour change discussed above have different sets of assumptions and work within different paradigmatic frames. Acknowledging these assumptions may in itself be useful for improving dialogue on the problems of achieving sustainable consumption and mobility with the academic community. However, it is also important to recognise that the different approaches are also intimately related to different understandings of governance, the role of the state and policy learning.

Both the utilitarian (green labelling, tax incentives, pricing, education) and social/psychological (nudging, social marketing) approaches to encouraging sustainable consumption are grounded in the ABC model. Social change is thought to depend upon values and attitudes (A), which are believed to drive the kinds of behaviour (B) that individuals choose (C) to adopt. The ABC model resonates with current widely shared ideas about individual agency and media influence. 'The combination of A and B and C generates a very clear agenda for effective policy, the conceptual and practical task of which is to identify and affect the determinants of pro-environmental behavior' (Shove 2010: 1275). Shove reinforces the perspective of Southerton *et al.* (2004b), noted above, when she comments that present strategies of state intervention 'presume that environmental damage is a consequence of individual action and that given better information or more appropriate incentives damaging individuals could choose to act more responsibly and could choose to adopt "pro-environmental behaviours"'. But in so doing they do not fundamentally question structures/paradigms and their role in influencing how and why environmentally problematic lifestyles and patterns of consumption are reproduced and how they change.

Instead, the third approach suggests that explanations of patterns of behaviour and consumption lie within socio-technical systems and structures. Such explanations 'do not deny the possibility of meaningful policy action, but at a minimum they recognise that effect is never in isolation and that interventions go on within, not outside, the processes they seek to shape' (Shove 2010: 1278). This also suggests that in order to encourage sustainable mobility the system itself, and the 'rules of the game' need to change (Hall 2011a). However, the difficulty for this in policy terms is that it represents a direct challenge to the status quo.

TABLE 9.2 Relationship of dimensions of carbon capability to orders of change in policy learning

Policy learning	Characteristics	Carbon capability	Intervention
1st order change	Incremental, routine behaviour that is based around government officials and policy experts that leads to a change in the levels (or settings) of the basic instruments of policy, e.g. codes of conduct, voluntary instruments, new indicators	Focus on individual decision making and behaviour, e.g. knowledge, judgements, skills	Education
2nd order change	Selection of new policy instruments and techniques and policy settings as a result of previous policy experience but the overarching policy goals remain the same – more strategic, e.g. green growth	Individual behaviour/practices	Social marketing, nudging
3rd order change	Policy paradigm shift, occurs when a new goal hierarchy is adopted by policy makers because the coherence of existing policy paradigm has been undermined, e.g. regulation and intervention, institutional change	Broader engagement with carbon and consumption governance	Lobbying, voting, protesting, regulatory change, creating alternative social infrastructures of provision

Source: After Hall, P. A. (1993); Whitmarsh *et al.* (2009, 2011); Hall (2010a, 2011b).

The three approaches to consumer change and carbon capability have analogues in the policy learning literature (Hall 2011a) (Table 9.2). First-order change tends to be characterised by incremental, routinised, satisficing behaviour that is based around government officials and policy experts that leads to a change in the 'levels (or settings) of the basic instruments of ... policy' (Hall, P. A. 1993: 279). Second-order change is characterised by the selection of new policy instruments and techniques and policy settings due to previous policy experience but the overarching policy goals remain the same. Second-order change is more strategic although officials and policy experts still remain relatively isolated from external political pressures. Third-order change, or a policy paradigm shift, takes place when a new goal hierarchy is adopted by policy makers because the coherence of existing policy paradigm(s) has been undermined, 'Where experiment and perceived policy failure has resulted in discrepancies or inconsistencies appearing which cannot be explained within the existing paradigm' (Greener 2001: 135). In situations where existing institutions and policies cease to be relevant to policy problems, policy failure may also lead the state to search for policy advice outside of previous internal and external sources, including academia, think tanks and non-government organisations (Pierre and Peters 2000).

The adoption of social/psychological approaches, such as nudging and social marketing, rather than simply providing education or relying on market mechanisms to encourage sustainable consumption, only represents a second order change. It is a continuation of the ABC approach and not a fundamental reassessment or paradigm shift in thinking about policy intervention. As the MINDSPACE report itself states:

> Some leading proponents have portrayed the application of behavioural economics as a radical 'third way' between liberal and paternalistic approaches to government. Others have tended to dismiss the approach as a distraction to the robust application of 'normal' economics to policy. In crude terms, the first camp says the way to reduce carbon

emissions is through harnessing the power of techniques such as comparisons with our neighbours' emissions; for the second camp, it is simply to get the price of carbon right, and then to let markets sort it out.

Our position sits between the two camps. The application of behavioural economics does not imply a paradigm shift in policy-making. It certainly does not mean giving up on conventional policy tools such as regulation, price signals and better information.

(Dolan *et al.* 2010: 77)

One of the appeals of behavioural economics approaches for policy making, such as nudging, is the promise of cost effectiveness; achieving 'more for less', particularly in public services. The practical emphasis is on 'smart' solutions that supposedly do not involve more resources; an imperative in recessionary times with many governments committed to reducing spending (Burgess 2012). It also reinforces the interests of some stakeholders in continuing the process of deregulation while Burgess (2012) also suggests that society-wide application of behavioural solutions assumes a fundamentally pliant and passive population that attaches limited value to individual liberty and autonomy in modern 'risk society'. Selinger and Powys White (2012) support Burgess's (2012) critique of nudging but go on to suggest that the cause-and-effect relations of even seemingly straight-forward nudge proposals are not nearly as predictable as expected. Indeed, they are regarded as incapable of 'solving' 'wicked problems' such as sustainable consumption and climate change 'occurring at a "whole earth level" in which multiple systems, operating with different norms and at different scales, interact with one another to produce emergent behavior that can be exceptionally difficult, if not impossible, to predict' (Selinger and Powys White 2012: 29). As they go on to note:

[A]lthough discussions abound about how nudging can reduce energy consumption, nudge proponents do not even attempt to discuss at all the complex interventions that are needed to shift diverse citizens in diverse parts of the world away from a CO_2 intensive society or adapt to the changes that might accompany the perpetuation of CO_2 intensive industries, infrastructures, and lifestyles.

(Selinger and Powys White 2012: 29)

A further significant and complicating issue with respect to the social/psychological approach is that 'Given that the ABC is the dominant paradigm in contemporary environmental policy, the scope of *relevant* social science is typically restricted to that which is theoretically consistent with it' (Shove 2010: 1280) (this author's emphasis). Policy makers fund and legitimise lines of enquiry that generate results that they can accept and manage, even if they do not necessarily provide the 'solution' to the policy problem. The result is a self-fulfilling cycle of credibility (Latour and Woolgar 1986), in which evidence of relevance and value to policy makers helps in securing additional resources for that approach. As Shove acknowledges, the ABC paradigm is not just a theory of behavioural change:

[I]t is also a template for intervention which locates citizens as consumers and decision makers and which positions governments and other institutions as enablers whose role is to induce people to make pro-environmental decisions for themselves and deter them from opting for other, less desired, courses of action.

(Shove 2010: 1280)

Yet, it is also possible that the vocabulary of ABC is required in order to keep a very particular understanding of governance in place.

It is, nonetheless, clear that policy makers are highly selective in the models of change on which they draw, and that their tastes in social theory are anything but random. An emphasis on individual choice has significant political advantages and in this context, to probe further, to ask how options are structured, or to inquire into the ways in which governments maintain infrastructures and economic institutions, is perhaps too challenging to be useful (Shove 2010: 1283).

What would it take to go beyond the first three letters of the alphabet?

This chapter has highlighted that different approaches to behavioural change are based on different assumptions about the problem of sustainable consumption and the relative importance of the role of individual agency and structure. It has emphasised that while social/psychological approaches, including behavioural economics and social marketing, do acknowledge the importance of social norms and routines, and identity and status in consumption behaviour, they do not necessarily interrogate the systems of provision that give rise to the social practices of consumption of travel and tourism. The chapter does not deny the value of nudging and social marketing, which are at times indistinguishable (Burgess 2012). However, it suggests that without also facing up to the implications of structure and institutions then the likelihood of being 'locked-in' to socio-technical systems of provision is greatly increased. Interestingly such issues have become an important issue within social marketing because of the debate between downstream interventions, which look at consumer change (Figure 9.3), and upstream interventions, which seek to change business and organisational behaviours and, from a more radical perspective, structural and system behaviour (Andreasen 2006; see also Chapter 5) (Figure 9.5).

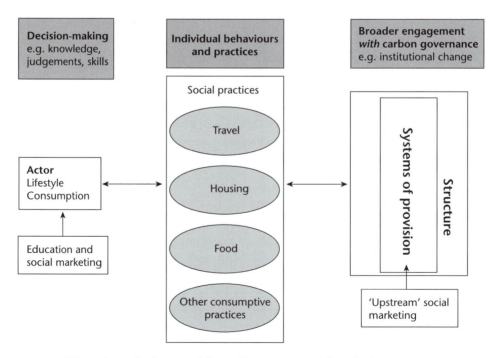

FIGURE 9.5 Dimensions of carbon capability with upstream social marketing

Just as significantly the chapter has emphasised that different ways of understanding behavioural change, and the approaches used to implement them, relate to the different forms of governance discussed in Chapter 3. Some of the characteristics of the key elements of these so-called 'new' modes of governance were indicated in Table 9.1. Each of the conceptualisations of governance structures is related to the use of particular sets of policy instruments (Hall 2011b). Given the artificiality of any policy–action divide (Barrett and Fudge 1981), these instruments and modes of governance can also be connected to different conceptual approaches to implementation (Hall 2009b). In something of a chicken-and-egg situation it is not really possible to say what came first – the mode of governance or the intervention mechanism for behavioural change that implements public policies. What is important to stress therefore is that the mode of governance and the manner of intervention become mutually reinforcing. One cannot be adequately understood without the other, even if this often the case in the many academic, institutional and governmental papers that propose methods to improve sustainable behaviours by tourists (usually while still travelling in increasing numbers to tourist destinations) (Hall 2011a). Yet the mutual reinforcement between modes of governance and intervention also creates a path dependency in which solutions to sustainable tourism mobility are only identified within 'green growth' arguments for greater efficiency and market-based solutions, yet with continued focus on growth in both GDP and tourism numbers, and an ideology that frames the problem of sustainable consumption in terms of individual consumption and responsibility (Bailey and Wilson 2009; Shove 2010; Whitmarsh *et al.* 2011).

'Lock-in' to a particular socio-technical system of provision has been recognised as a major constraint to emissions reduction and avoidance of dangerous climate change (Maréchal 2007, 2010), except perhaps by those that believe in and promote the neoliberal, technocentric and ecological modernisation values underpinning the carbon economy (Bailey and Wilson 2009). In such a situation policy learning is extremely difficult (Hall 2011a), with changes occurring only at the margin or in limited terms, such as the development of nudging, but without challenging the basic paradigm (see Table 9.2). Such an observation has implications for academic work as well as for policy problems and their solution. As Shove suggests:

> [P]aradigms and approaches which lie beyond the pale of the ABC are doomed to be forever marginal no matter how interactive or how policy-engaged their advocates might be. To break through this log jam it would be necessary to reopen a set of basic questions about the role of the state, the allocation of responsibility, and in very practical terms the meaning of manageability, within climate-change policy.
>
> (Shove 2010: 1283)

Yet, the public policy system and much of the research that feeds into it is not necessarily conducive to breakthroughs and rapid paradigm shifts. Hall (2011a), for example, noted that in research on tourism governance far too much attention has been given to the assumption that a well-designed institution is 'good' because it facilitates cooperation and networking rather actually focusing on the norms and implications of institutional arrangements and their potential outcomes. What, after all, is the point of encouraging governance mechanisms such as partnerships, network development, self-regulation and individual responsibility if they continue to have no practical effect on the sustainability of tourism and consumption? If the ethical value of 'individual choice' leads to increased emissions and worsening environmental change then how ethical is it?

This is not to suggest that there is no value in nudging and social marketing, and even education and market-based solutions. They are part of the suite of approaches that need to be used together *with* a fundamental examination of the socio-technical system itself if there is to be a sustainable post-carbon transition (Gössling *et al.* 2012b). Change can occur within the first and second orders of policy learning and with limited regulatory shifts. As the MINDSPACE discussion paper reported:

> [M]ost policymakers are focused on this bigger picture – often known as culture change … There may be occasions when the power of argument alone can eventually such culture change, such as gender equality or race relations. But generally the broader sweep of policy history suggests that such change is driven by a mix of both broad social argument and small policy steps. Smoking is perhaps the most familiar example. Over several decades the behavioural equilibrium has shifted from widespread smoking to today's status as an increasingly minority activity. Better information; powerful advertising (and the prohibition of pro-smoking advertising); expanding bans; and changing social norms have formed a mutually reinforcing thread of influence to change the behavioural equilibrium. There is every reason to think that is a pattern that we will see repeated in many other areas of behaviour too, from sexual behaviour to carbon emissions.
>
> (Dolan *et al.* 2010: 77)

In the case of smoking, education, social marketing and limited regulation has had a substantial impact on lowering the proportion of the population that smokes on a regular basis. The problem is:

- it has taken generations to achieve 'cultural change' in developed countries;
- it has been challenged by vested industrial and political interests along the way;
- it has taken many years for counter-institutional research to be accepted; and
- even then smoking still kills millions of people a year within an uneven pattern of regulatory control across the world.

In the case of sustainable tourism mobility, emissions and climate change we do not have the luxury to wait that long for such an imperfect set of behavioural 'solutions'.

It has long been recognised of course that consumers do have a major role in changing consumption behaviour (Leonard-Barton 1981; Ebreo *et al.* 1999). This chapter agrees with this, but it does not regard a focus on consumer responsibility and consumer behaviour alone as adequate to the challenges facing contemporary tourism. As suggested above there remain real institutional barriers to change in consumer behaviour at different scales, whether they be political, industrial and/or cultural, as well as the dominant mode of economic thinking itself.

From this position there is also a need to reconcile the two dominant perspectives on symbolic consumption. The first perspective, 'sign experimentation', assumes that consumption is an 'expressive movement' (Levy 1981: 51), by which consumers distinguish themselves from alternative values and meanings by expressing desired symbolic statements (Murray 2002). In this interpretation symbolic consumption is associated with identity politics with agency often being expressed in 'new' social movements (Best and Kellner 1997) such as environmental activism, the Slow Food movement, Fair Trade and voluntary simplicity. In this context 'new' demotes the fragmentation of labour and class structural inequalities that accompanies the growth of contemporary consumer culture, and emphasises the development of social movements around fashion, style, identity and 'emotional communities' (Murray 2002).

The second perspective, what Murray (2002) refers to as 'sign domination', emphasises the elimination of agency in favour of structural processes, and is grounded in a more critical sociology of consumer society. The persistent demand by consumers to adopt the appropriate images and signs of the everyday reinforces Gramsci's notion of domination (Forgacs 2000), whereby 'without critical reflection, consent to hegemonic social structures is more likely than resistance' (Murray 2002: 428). From this perspective, socialisation within a consumer culture creates a mass of 'good consumers', all struggling for the signs that fuel corporate capitalism (Harvey 1990). 'Sign value' is thus an institutional practice that sits at the very foundation of values and social integration (Baudrillard 1981). Nevertheless, as Murray (2002: 428) suggests: 'The use of signs and radical imagery to resist the system only creates a feeling of resistance. As a way of managing crisis and change, radical identities are also fashioned by the system'. Such a view is significant as it suggests that much consumer research in tourism has not noted the political dimensions of consumption, and symbolic consumption in particular. The assumption of agency has emphasised the creative role of the consumer, which has only been reinforced by the current marketing fashion of reference to co-creation (Hall 2011c), while simultaneously turning away from the political and oppressive potential of the symbolic (Murray 2002).

Indeed, there is a real need to question the way in which concern with the present economic system is bound up by many in the tourism industry as a form of anti-consumption consumption, such as the promotion of green travel experiences in some foreign land that takes no account of the emissions in getting to and from the latest fashionable ecotourism destination. Let it be emphasised that this is not to suggest that green consumption is a fad or a fashion statement. There is clear evidence to suggest that some consumers are making decisions based on environmental and social concerns and are interested in transferring these to a tourism context (Miller 2003). However, there are often substantial systemic barriers to tourism products being as environmentally and socially friendly as they could be. This includes not only the lack of independent capacity to monitor green claims but also the relatively weak regulation of such businesses. Moreover, a belief that green growth via greater efficiency is the most appropriate way forward to reduce tourism's contribution to climate emissions or that encouraging corporations to treat green consumers as an attractive market (Kleanhous and Peck 2006), without dealing with the fundamental implications of consumerism and consumption, means that tourism's contribution to global environmental change will continue to grow.

Nevertheless, it is also important to recognise the link between consumption and identity. Particularly as identity is forged as much by the meanings the consumer 'feels impelled to resist as by those that are tacitly embraced' (Thompson and Haytko 1997: 38). A responsible tourist is still a tourist after all. As noted above, there are attempts by consumers to escape the 'totalizing logic of the market' by attempting to construct localised 'emancipated spaces' that are constructed by 'engaging in improbable behaviors, contingencies, and discontinuities' (Firat and Venkatesh 1995: 255). Such improbable behaviours include distinguishing acts that appear to be outside the logic of commercialisation, such as voluntary simplicity and anti-consumption. These are all part of the new politics of consumption (Schor 2003). Nevertheless, focusing on lifestyle alone, without challenge to the role of structure and the cultural forces of production, may well mean that alternative consumption paths become 'appropriated by experts, packaged, and sold, [and] loses its distinctive character. When this happens, even a lifestyle based on anti-consumption becomes defined in terms of commodities, possessions, sign value, and commercial success' (Murray 2002: 439). The breakage of the false nexus between consumerism and happiness and the potential realisation of improving quality of life through leisure, tourism and travel lies not just in the advocacy, communication and downstream social marketing of the benefits of sustainable consumption and voluntary simplicity. Instead, it will require a much more fundamental and overt critique of the tourism industry's and tourism academy's roles in reinforcing and supporting contemporary consumerism and neo-liberal forms of capitalism and its institutions than what has hitherto been the case. Agency and individual responsibility is important. But understanding it in the context of structure – and how structures continue to be replicated – is critical.

Further reading and websites

Earlier versions of sections of this chapter were presented at the workshop Psychological and Behavioual Approaches to Understanding and Governing Sustainable Tourism Mobility, Freiburg, Germany, 3–6 July 2012. Funding support was provided by the Freiburg Institute for Advanced Studies. See also:

Hall, C. M. (2013) 'Framing behavioural approaches to understanding and governing sustainable tourism consumption: Beyond neoliberalism, "nudging" and "green growth"?' *Journal of Sustainable Tourism*.
Hall, C. M. (2014) 'You can check out any time you like but you can never leave: Can ethical consumption in tourism ever be sustainable?', in C. Weeden and K. Boluk (eds) *Managing Ethical Consumption in Tourism: Compromise and Tension*, Abingdon: Routledge.

The latter provides an extension of these arguments with respect to ecotourism, ethical tourism and commodity fetishism.

On tourism and climate and environmental change see:

Araña, J.E., León, C.J., Moreno-Gil, S. and Zubiaurre, A. (2012) 'A comparison of tourists' valuation of climate change policy using different pricing frames,' *Journal of Travel Research*, DOI: 10.1177/0047287512457260.
Eijgelaar, E. and Peeters, P. (2014) 'The global footprint of tourism', in A. Lew, C. M. Hall and A. Williams (eds) *Companion to Tourism*. Oxford: Wiley-Blackwell.
Gössling, S., Scott, D. and Hall, C. M. (2013) 'Challenges of tourism in a low-carbon economy', *WIRES Climate Change*, 4(6): 525–528.
Gössling, S., Scott, D., Hall, C. M., Ceron, J. and Dubois, G. (2012) 'Consumer behaviour and demand response of tourists to climate change', *Annals of Tourism Research*, 39: 36–58.
Scott, D, Gössling, S. and Hall, C. M. (2012) 'International tourism and climate change', *WIRES Climate Change*, 3(3): 213–232.
Scott, D, Gössling, S. and Hall, C. M. (2012) *Tourism and Climate Change: Impacts, Adaptation and Mitigation*. Abingdon: Routledge.

Some very useful sites with respect to climate change communication and related topics include:

Climate Communication: www.climatecommunication.org/
George Mason University Center for Climate Change Communication: www.climatechange communication.org/

Guardian Sustainable Business – Ideas and Insights for Progressive Business Leaders: www.guardian. co.uk/sustainable-business?

Public Interest Research Centre: www.pirc.info/

Yale Project on Climate Change Communication: http://environment.yale.edu/climate-communication/

Some very good papers with respect to the issues associated with communicating climate change and other issues with respect to sustainability include:

Corner, A. and Randall, A. (2011) 'Selling climate change? The limitations of social marketing as a strategy for climate change public engagement', *Global Environmental Change*, 21(3): 1005–1014.

Demeritt, D. (2001) 'The construction of global warming and the politics of science', *Annals of the Association of American Geographers*, 91, 307–337.

Downing, P. and Ballantyne, J. (2007) *Tipping Point or Turning Point? Social Marketing and Climate Change*. London: Ipsos MORI Social Research Institute.

Ockwell, D., O'Neill, S. and Whitmarsh, L. (2010) 'Behavioural insights: Motivating individual emissions cuts through communication', in C. Lever-Tracey (ed.), *Routledge Handbook of Climate Change and Society*. London: Routledge.

Weber, E. U. (2006) 'Experience-based and description-based perceptions of long-term risk: Why global warming does not scare us (yet)', *Climatic Change*, 77: 103–120.

An extremely useful paper on the potential role of provincial norms in changing people's behaviour is:

Goldstein, A., Cialdini, R. B. and Griskevicius, V. (2008) 'A room with a viewpoint: Using social norms to motivate environmental conservation in hotels', *Journal of Consumer Research*, 35: 472–482.

Although not directly related to issues of tourism and sustainable consumption the following paper provides an excellent account of issues associated with communicating to the public over complex environmental and social issues:

Pidgeon, N. and Rogers-Hayden, T. (2007) 'Opening up nanotechnology dialogue with the publics: risk communication or "upstream engagement"?', *Health, Risk and Society*, 9(2): 191–210.

BOX 9.7 WHOSE INTERESTS AND VALUES DOES TOURISM AND TOURISM RESEARCH SERVE?

Consideration of the interplay between agency and structure, between power and interests, and asking basic questions such as who benefits, how and why in tourism forces one to consider issues of 'good' and 'bad'. If it could be treated in isolation, travel and tourism would be neither inherently bad or good. But things should not be treated in isolation. If tourism did bring benefits to destinations, individuals and the planet without also incurring substantial costs then it should be celebrated. Yet it does not. Instead, we need to recognise that the vast majority of commercial travel and tourism is inseparable from contemporary consumerism and neo-liberal capitalism. More often than not tourism is serving a system with a narrow range of political and economic interests in which wealth is ever concentrated, in which the gap between rich and poor is greater than ever, in which happiness is conflated with materialism and quality with quantity, and in which the rights of other species to exist are being denied. This is bad.

Tourism is not value free. There are no problems in recognising that tourism has values. The problem is in failing to see the implications of those values and how they are linked to interests and power. The fundamental question is not why we want to engage in leisure and travel. The question is why have so many people increasingly come to believe that consuming such mobility will somehow make them happier and improve their life (Hall 2011c)?

Questions for self-reflection:

- What are the implications of questioning the values that tourism promotes? What are these values?
- How do issues of ethical consumption affect your travel behaviour?
- If social marketing is seeking to change tourism behaviour so as to reduce emissions what are the main areas of meaning and identity that need to be addressed?

10

A SUSTAINABLE FUTURE FOR SOCIAL MARKETING

Towards a socially dominant logic?

This final chapter identifies a number of future issues in the tourism/social marketing nexus with particular respect to the political and ethical dimensions of consumption and product promotion. The chapter revisits some of the concerns and issues that have been raised throughout the book with respect to the nature and role of social marketing in tourism. The chapter therefore questions the extent to which marketing is value free and a 'neutral tool' for organisations, and the importance of the values of the persons and organisations engaged in marketing. The chapter argues that many dimensions of social marketing demonstrate the importance of the ethical positions of the researcher and the organisations involved in the development of marketing strategies. In addition the chapter notes that marketing alone is not enough to necessarily change behaviour or develop sustainable tourism and that regulation is also necessary. Nevertheless, social marketing will remain a vital component in the strategies used to develop sustainable tourism.

BOX 10.1 MOTIVATIONS FOR CORPORATE AND ENVIRONMENTAL SOCIAL RESPONSIBILITY: THE CASE OF SCANDINAVIAN AIRLINES

Lynes and Andrachuk (2008: 377) state that in the context of corporate social and environmental responsibility many corporations can be categorised as being 'torn between social consciousness and shareholder profits'. Whilst many studies have examined motivations for environmental responsibility (Annandale and Taplin 2003; Bansal and Roth 2000; Khanna and Anton 2002; Orlitzky *et al.* 2011) and those motivations that emphasise social responsibility (Anderson and Bieniaszewska 2005; Bendell *et al.* 2005; Bichta 2003; Flammer 2012; Tullberg 2005), there is an emergent trend in the literature on this topic that looks at both corporate social and environmental responsibility (CSER) and how each of these concepts operates in tandem with the other (Egri and Ralston 2008; Jenkins and Yakovleva 2006; Lund-Thomsen 2004). Lynes and Andrachuk (2008: 377) note that 'increasingly, however, corporations are realising – for varying reasons – that being environmentally and socially conscious makes good business sense'.

A key example of one prominent corporation that has struggled to bridge the gap between idealism and reality concerning CSER is can be seen in the case of Scandinavian Airlines (SAS). According to Lynes and Andrachuk (2008: 377) 'being a good corporate citizen is a strong driver at SAS with respect to social responsibility – however, the effort to promote this image is not as strong as with environmental issues'. Scandinavian Airlines' mandate in terms of its corporate social and environmental responsibility is based on the European Commission (2002) definition of corporate social responsibility (CSR) as the level of commitment (which is also voluntary) of firms to make a contribution to society in terms of social and environmental goals. The management of this particular mandate has been cited by Edström (1991) as being critical to not only creating a positive image for Scandinavian Airlines as a company, but also has been proven to be a powerful tool in terms of helping the company to 'achieve better negotiating power with the government' (Lynes and Andrachuk 2008: 383).

The potential political power that can be generated for the firm in terms of dealing with government organisations through maintaining and following a strict CSER programme provides a clear motivation for Scandinavian Airlines and how they attempt to manage the public perception of their company in terms of their social responsibility. Lynes and Andrachuk (2008: 386) state the following with regards to how motivation on this particular level works for large companies:

> The effect of the interaction of influences, motivations and catalysts leads a firm towards a given level of commitment to CSER. This commitment can be seen through pledges to take action (e.g. corporate policies), the action itself (e.g. tools and personnel), reporting and external validation of its actions as well as some form of measurement for improvement (e.g. internal indicators).

Several issues were found to directly impact on the implementation of environmental and social responsibility initiatives at SAS. The first issue that is particularly important in this case is that of culture (Lynes and Andrachuk 2008). As airlines obviously operate in multiple international settings, the value systems that operate in terms of CSER across different countries will vary, a fact that Lynes and Andrachuk (2008: 388) acknowledge in this case when they state that 'because of differing fundamental assumptions within other cultures of what being socially responsible is, as SAS expands its operations abroad, it is having to adjust its social reporting mechanisms to better reflect the airline's commitment towards social responsibility'. The degree to which Scandinavian Airlines could implement social responsibility initiatives also became an issue as initiatives were found to be directly affected by internal regulatory measures and a lack of union support; this industry reality is what Lynes and Andrachuk (2008) cited as having the ability to appear to act as a deterrent when airline management were attempting to choose the best options for the environmental responsibility initiatives. The final issue that was found in this case to have a substantial impact on environmental and social responsibility initiatives at SAS was lack of readily identifiable tangible financial benefits from social responsibility. Andersson and Bateman (2000) suggest that the relationship between financial imperatives and championing environment and green marketing concepts is often fraught with problems due to the intangible nature of such concepts, and as Lynes and Andrachuk (2008) contend this is a real problem when attempting to implement and market sustainable initiatives. Future research in this area may reveal new approaches that large organisations such as SAS could utilise to overcome resistance to their desire to be perceived as sustainable, but this remains to be seen; it appears that in this case social marketers well and truly have to reach for new ideas and expand the realms of existing thought within the discipline of social marketing itself in order to solve the issues at hand.

Responsible social marketing?

As discussed in Chapter 2 and highlighted again in Chapter 9, the application of theories to the design of social marketing interventions and public policies remains a challenge for researchers and programme planners and there is considerable debate concerning the effectiveness and usefulness of theory in informing intervention development (Eccles *et al.* 2005a, 2005b; Oxman *et al.* 2005; Munro *et al.* 2007). Although primarily related to health interventions the Improved Clinical Effectiveness through Behavioural Research Group and J. Francis (ICEBeRG and Francis 2006) explicitly address the role of theory in the role of the transfer of research findings into practice. They argue that a theoretical approach offers the advantage of a generalisable framework within which to represent the dimensions that implementation studies address. In doing so, it informs the development and delivery of interventions, guides their evaluation and allows exploration of potential causal mechanisms. However, in contradiction of this position Bhattacharyya *et al.* (2006) suggest that the assertion of the ICEBeRG authors is problematic for three primary reasons:

1   The presence of an underlying theory does not necessarily ease the task of judging the applicability of a piece of empirical evidence.
2   It is not necessarily clear how to translate theory reliably into intervention design, which undoubtedly involves the diluting effect of 'common sense'.
3   There are many theories, formal and informal, and it is not clear why any one should be given primacy.

They go on to argue that to determine whether explicitly theory-based interventions are, on average, more effective than those based on implicit theories, experience and craft skills, empirical evidence is required that demonstrates the superiority of theory-based interventions: 'The use of theory should not be used as a basis for assessing the value of implementation studies by research funders, ethics committees, editors or policy decision makers' (Bhattacharyya *et al.* 2006: 1). A position that perhaps reflects Munro *et al.*'s observation of many of the theories discussed in Chapter 2 with respect to interventions:

> Despite a variety of studies in a variety of fields, or perhaps because of this variation, we would argue that there is no clear evidence yet for the support of any of these theories within the field of adherence behaviours. This is not to say that these theories cannot be useful – rather, we have insufficient evidence to conclusively determine this.
>
> (Munro *et al.* 2007: 115–116)

234 A sustainable future

Similarly, Luca and Suggs (2013: 20) report:

> The existing literature suggests that theories and models can serve as valuable frameworks for the design and evaluation of health interventions. However, evidence on the use of theories and models in social marketing interventions is sparse. ... [our findings] highlight an ongoing lack of use or underreporting of the use of theory in social marketing campaigns and reinforce the call to action for applying and reporting theory to guide and evaluate interventions.

These are issues that face the broader field of social marketing and behaviour change not just the health sector.

Specific research is therefore required to examine some of the key questions with respect to the theory–intervention debate (Munro *et al.* 2007):

- Do sound theories result in effective interventions?
- Does an effective intervention constitute proof of a theory's value?
- How might theory be used to inform the design of an effective intervention?
- How can a theory be reliably tested?

These are fundamental questions that may not even be directly answerable in social scientific, as opposed to natural scientific, approaches to knowledge. Nevertheless, it would be appropriate for better 'theory development' to be undertaken including more effort to be put into identifying variables common to theories, including ensuring that there is greater commonality in construct definition, as well as appropriate theoretical integration (Michie and Abraham 2008; Michie *et al.* 2008, 2009). Yet the reality is that an explicit theoretical basis is not always necessary for a successful intervention and further examination is needed to determine whether theory-based social marketing and behavioural change interventions are more effective than those without an explicit theoretical foundation.

Indeed, a key point stressed in Chapter 5 is that social marketing, as with much marketing in general, is actually craft based, that is it is grounded with experience of 'what works' in practice and that which is embraced by clients rather than being explicitly grounded in theory. This may be fine on a case-by-case basis if the client is satisfied with the results, but it does raise issues with respect to replicating the results of interventions in other contexts as well as being able to explain why something has worked!

Visions of success

A fundamental yet often ignored issue in behavioural interventions is how we define what we mean when it is suggested that an intervention is successful and works. In reality that may mean that a client is willing to judge even small amounts of behavioural change as being a success. Yet, in the case of governments for example, such a judgement may also be exercised because they are unwilling to engage in more regulatory forms of intervention and so social marketing provides an ideologically acceptable alternative to direct state action because of the desire to promote notions of personal choice. Success then is to a great extent in the eye of the beholder. However, in many circumstances such an approach may prove unsatisfactory if the rate of behavioural change is behind that required to avoid a significant personal or collective risk. For example, if the rate at which the proportion of people who smoke regularly has been cut in Western societies thanks to social marketing interventions was to be applied to reducing tourism's contribution to climate change, then absolute emissions would potentially still continue to increase, while the point at which dangerous climate change was to be reached would almost certainly have been reached long before any significant decline in emissions. Their success in behavioural change is also connected to rates of change over time as well as to the existence of key benchmarks.

BOX 10.2 TOPICS IN THE 1971 SPECIAL ISSUE OF THE *JOURNAL OF MARKETING* ON MARKETING'S CHANGING SOCIAL/ ENVIRONMENTAL ROLE: HOW SUCCESSFUL HAVE WE BEEN?

In Chapter 1 we listed the contents page of the issue of *Journal of Marketing* (vol. 35, no. 3) in which the seminal social marketing article of Kotler and Zaltman on 'Social marketing: An approach to planned social change' appeared (Box 1.1). With reference to the various topics below that were included in that special issue consider the contributions that social marketing has made and the extent to which the problems have been 'solved' or not. If not why? What does this say about the potential of social marketing to create change after more than 40 years?

- Marketing and population problems.
- Recycling solid wastes.
- The relative cost and availability of food for rich and poor people.
- Consumer protection.
- Societal adaptation.
- Incorporating ecology into marketing strategy: the case of air pollution.

The issue of the acceptability of interventions as well as the means by which they are measured also raises broader concerns over the extent to which marketing is a neutral tool or not. As noted in Chapter 1 the issue of the relationship between commercial and non-commercial dimensions of social marketing raises some fundamental issues in understanding what social marketing is seeking to achieve as well as perhaps some cynicism that may exist with respect to the validity of marketing's role in influencing behaviours for worse – as well as for good. For example, it can be argued that much of the current focus on marketing, including tourism marketing, in university courses is on encouraging people to consume more, not to consume more appropriately. Many university courses on marketing in effect teach students how to consume and encourage others to do likewise. As Hastings (2007: 4) suggested: '[C]ommercial marketers are demonstrating … an enviable capacity to influence behaviour. They are past masters at getting us to do things – buy their products, visit their shops, attend to their messages, deliver their messages, buy their products again. And, crucially – for the most part at least – we cooperate voluntarily' (And can you imagine your university grades, especially if you are doing marketing in a business school, if you did not cooperate?) Similarly, in the case of all the talk with respect to sustainability in tourism almost every destination increases its target for the number of visitors it wishes to attract every year. While there are ethical consumption and sustainable tourism messages at one level, they are not being enacted at others.

The above perspective on commercial marketing is only reinforced by an *Economist* article that described the main task of marketing, 'pungently described by an ad exec: "to figure out and fuel consumer desires like they've never been fuelled before"' (Economist 2013b: 56). The definition of social marketing used by the UK National Social Marketing Centre (NSMC) appears to suggest that social marketing is 'different':

> Social marketing is an approach used to develop activities aimed at changing or maintaining people's behaviour for their benefit.
>
> (National Social Marketing Centre 1010b)

Whereas marketing in the commercial world ultimately seeks to influence consumer behaviour for profit, social marketing encourages behaviours that provide benefit for individuals and society as a whole.

Yet if it is different how is this to be expressed? Donovan and Henley (2003), for example, argue that social marketing is distinguishable from other areas of marketing in that campaigns to bring about social change that are directed towards lobbying manufacturers to change their practices can be regarded as a form of social marketing, while forming alliances with commercial partners in a campaign would not be social marketing. Donovan and Henley (2003) also extend Andreasen's (1995) definition of social marketing by its recognition of the United Nations Universal Declaration of Human Rights as the 'baseline with respect to the common good' (Donovan and Henley 2003: 6). However, given the increasing recognition of the rights of nature as an important 'good' to what extent may this change the moral basis of social marketing and marketing in the future? Moreover, to what extent do Donovan and Henley's position represent a more fundamental critique of the socio-economic system that produces over-consumption and under-democratisation in the first place?

Andreasen (2006) has argued that an overly narrow view of social marketing underestimates its potential and that its target audiences encompass more than just 'problem people'. Andreasen (2006: 7) suggested that the institutional 'downstream focus' was 'too narrow and too limiting' with such a focus detracting from where the focus should lie – upstream – the institutions and structures that may be contributing to social a environmental problems if not causing them in the first place. Yet if downstream interventions are to be regarded as often political then upstream system change must certainly be so as it implies not only choices between values and interests but must also represent a challenge to power structures and relations.

Unfortunately, and perhaps strongly influenced by right-wing and neoliberal thought, there is far too much emphasis in marketing, including social marketing, on the notion of freedom of choice. For example, Lefebvre (2011: 58) suggests that '[s]ocial marketing is focused on people, their wants and needs, aspirations, lifestyle, freedom of choice'. But freedom of choice to consume must also come with responsibilities with respect to the implications of one's consumption not only on oneself but, perhaps more importantly, on others. People do not exist in isolation, we live in communities and collectivities, no matter how fractured they have seemingly become at times. Furthermore, the notion of freedom of choice potentially wilfully ignores that we are always located within particular socio-economic systems that affect our freedom of choice and that are difficult to change or shift from. For example, the capacity to do other is affected not just by how much money one has but where you live. Institutions and their systems structure one's consumption. What are the food alternatives available? What are the public transport alternatives? What are the source of pleasure that I am legally able to engage in? How is energy supplied and who are the providers? Where does your information come from and what alternative sources readily exist?

Within tourism the notions of co-creation and service dominant (S-D) logic is currently extremely influential. 'In S-D logic, the roles of producers and consumers are not distinct, meaning that value is always co-created, jointly and reciprocally, in interactions among providers and beneficiaries through the integration of resources and application of competences' (Vargo *et al.* 2008: 146). From this approach value is co-created by a 'reciprocal and mutually beneficial relationship' (Vargo *et al.* 2008: 146). However, the approach has also been substantially criticised (e.g. Humphreys and Grayson 2008) not least because the creation of use value and the creation of exchange value remain so different from one another and potentially affect the way we envision capacities for change.

First, the two processes are different in orientation: the creation of use value is oriented toward the object (here used to also include service), while the creation of exchange value is oriented toward others. This difference means that a different kind of product results from each process. The aim of creating use value is to enjoy the outcome of the production process and, in some cases, including that of co-production, potentially also the production process itself. The resulting object is thus oriented toward the needs of a particular user. In contrast, the aim of creating exchange value is still to produce an object that can be sold to others, and the resulting object therefore tends to embody the social values and preferences of consumers and producers. The exchange process has therefore always been an inherently social process because it involves negotiation between social actors or the persuasion of one actor by another (Marx [1867] 2001: 122), although this does not mean that their relationship is inherently equal as perhaps the use of the prefix co-, as in co-production, co-consumption and co-creation, would appear to suggest.

Therefore, what Marx described as the 'sphere of consumption' and the 'sphere of exchange' have substantially different logics. The former focuses on personal pleasure as part of consumption, 'and thus tends to have an intrinsic orientation – whereas the latter focuses at least initially on pleasing someone else – and thus has more of an extrinsic orientation' (Humphreys and Grayson 2008: 12). This means that products, including those understood as service products, produced with exchange value in mind, are therefore likely to embody existing social realities. 'As projections of value to others, they merely reproduce social order' (Humphreys and Grayson 2008: 12), i.e. they reflect the prevailing socio-technical systems and associated institutions and structures. In contrast, the production of use value tends to be more idiosyncratic and aimed at the object–user relationship. Humphreys and Grayson (2008), therefore suggest that there is more critical potential in the creation of use value than there is in the creation of exchange value because the creation of use value is more likely to challenge existing social values by virtue of its idiosyncrasy.

Second, use value and exchange value have different relationships to the concepts of 'alienation' or 'estrangement'. Clearly, when consumers produce use value for themselves, by making something for example, they receive the full value from their labour and they often retain a strong personal relationship to the object. However, when they produce something for exchange it becomes separate from their labour – they become alienated from it – and personal meaning is lost or lowered. Notions of co-creation as well as 'prosumption', where the boundaries of consumption and production are blended or blurred, appear to suggest that meaning becomes retained. Yet Humphreys and Grayson

(2008: 12) suggest that consumption here can still 'lose its meaningfulness, its connection to practices of meaning making such as identity creation, symbolic manipulation, and social signification'. Instead, they suggest that the supposed 'reenchantment' of consumption via co-creation can easily shift into disenchantment when consumers become heavily involved in production, especially as consumption spaces become controlled, rationalised and serially reproduced (Ritzer 1999; Ritzer and Jurgenson 2010). Furthermore, significant issues arise over the extent to which the surplus economic value deriving from exchange is allocated. This is not just with respect to consumer-generated products such as advertising or design ideas but also the extent to which personal data and consumption preferences (including the 'meta-data' available from online relationships) ceases to be private and is instead able to be sold by companies to other businesses. As Humphreys and Grayson (2008: 14) note:

> [T]o the extent that the 'prosumer' or 'co-production' revolution is merely a source of free labor for companies, it seems to be an unsustainable revolution at best and exploitation at worst ... The ethics of these practices also remain an open question. Is consumer input into the production process a net positive; does it reconnect the laborer with the products of his or her labor? Or, is it exploitation twice over, once when the object is produced and twice when it is sold back for a profit? Ultimately, one might appeal to consumer attitudes: consumers seem to love consuming things they make, and companies simply act as a facilitator in the process. On the other hand, one might take the position that consumers aren't aware of the value they themselves generate for companies, revenue that they do not receive.

'So what?' I hear the reader complain. What does this have to do with social marketing? Answer: 'Everything!' It suggests that the so-called new focus of marketing on S-D logic and co-creation (and co-consumption and co-production) fails to deal with some of the fundamental issues that we have been trying to address in this book with respect to change. To treat individuals as unfettered actors with complete or even substantial freedom of choice as consumers ignores the constraints that exist on consumption decisions including that with respect to behaviour change. In some areas the exigencies of the market means that we do have more choice and selection than others but in many cases we do not – unless for example we have the stark choice between consuming electricity generated from non-renewable emission-producing resources or nuclear power *or* not consuming at all. Great choice! Moreover the emphasis on 'co-' appears to suggest that we have equal power to consume and engage in economic relations. Really?

Conclusion: the need to consider both agency and structure in social marketing and behaviour change

A pervasive problem with much of marketing is its ignorance of structure. Some areas of social marketing though are a clear exception to this. The fact that social marketing forces us to consider the appropriateness of ethical behaviours itself makes us think of the situatedness of consumption, i.e. given where we are located what alternatives are there? Moreover, how did we learn to consume and behave in such a way in the first place. As to think about changing behaviour change also means thinking about what led to those behaviours coming about. Social marketing's potential to focus on upstream issues as well as downstream ones therefore provides the basis for a more fundamental critique of what ails society and environment, and tourism's role within it. As noted in Chapter 1 upstream social marketing practices assist in enabling more information, policy focus and social pressure being placed on government as well as corporate interests. Yet, as Andreasen (2006) notes society should aim to fix the structures and processes upstream that help create problems in the first place; in some cases these will be the socio-technical structures and institutions noted in the previous chapter, and is clearly concerned with much more than the behaviours of individuals but deals with system change. To engage in this requires not so much a service dominant logic but a *social dominant logic*, which includes not only a concern for well-being and QOL in society and the natural environment but also a realisation of the way that social structures and social–technical systems serve to both constrain and enable individual behaviours.

In the history of social marketing thought such a step actually is not particularly radical. It does clearly mean that marketing must be seen much broader than being commercially focused but to a great extent that has been realised, though is perhaps not so well understood in public perceptions of marketing (see Chapter 1). But it also means that notions such as S-D logic and co-creation need to be framed to the extent that they are not just being adopted by some marketers as yet another way of selling more things to people that not only they may not need but, more particularly, do not lead to more sustainable forms of consumption and an increase in well-being and QOL. As Hastings (2007: 4) comments:

> [C]ommercial marketers are demonstrating … an enviable capacity to influence behaviour. They are past masters at getting us to do things – buy their products, visit their shops, attend to their messages, deliver their messages, buy their products again. And, crucially – for the most part at least – we cooperate voluntarily.

Indeed, as noted at the beginning of the book, Lazer and Kelley's (1973: ix) definition of social marketing – '*Social marketing is concerned with the application of marketing knowledge, concepts and techniques to enhance social as well as economic ends. It is also concerned with analysis of the social consequence of marketing policies, decisions and activities*' – provides a ready base with which to interrogate the role of tourism in contemporary society, assess its negative consequences, especially for the environment, and utilise the tools of social marketing to influence change, both upstream and downstream.

This approach therefore means that as social and tourism marketers there is a real need to become much more politically, socially, environmentally and economically aware of the consequences of one's marketing and personal actions. And, as we sometimes note with respect to the people and organisations we study, close the gap between our personal values and our actions and behaviours in our public and private lives. This will not be easy but will likely lead to a far greater engagement in influencing tourism behaviour and futures; a more rewarding professional life as a marketer; and hopefully more sustainable forms of tourism.

BOX 10.3 ANTI-CLUTTER ADVERTISING CAMPAIGNS: THE CASE OF ADBUSTERS AND ANTI-CONSUMPTION

Mendoza (1999) suggests that excessive cumulative exposure to advertising can lead to increased scepticism amongst consumers who begin to feel exploited by the relentless nature of some advertising campaigns. This has led to a rise of a certain type of consumer who now wishes to 'maintain some sort of measure of sovereignty over his/her psychic space' (Rumbo 2002: 128). This desire has been nurtured by what Rumbo (2002) suggests is the shift towards more service-oriented, consumer-based economies where 'the commercialisation of public life has eroded the discursive spaces in which rational debate could conceivably occur' (Rumbo 2002: 129). This has led to the rise of anti-consumerism and campaigns designed to counter the clutter and 'noise' that surrounds contemporary mass media and marketing (Bordwell 2002; Rumbo 2002; Cohen *et al.* 2005).

Anti-clutter advertising campaigns are one such example of a trend that has emerged in response to changes in technology and increased saturation by advertising campaigns that have been 'prompted by the increasing predictability of antiquated advertising conventions' (Rumbo 2002: 129). One such example of an anti-clutter campaign can be seen in the case of Adbusters, which focuses on environmental, social and psychological issues (Rumbo 2002). Based in Vancouver, Canada, the Adbusters Media Foundation (AMF) is a group 'that has made strides to problematise consumerism' (Cohen *et al.* 2005: 60) and has also increased awareness in anti-consumerism as a social movement (Bordwell 2002; Rumbo 2002) through the production of the *Adbusters* magazine. The approach taken here towards anti-consumerism by the AMF can be seen to not only have its roots in the social rebellion of 1960s counterculture (Cohen *et al.* 2005), but also has undertones of the Kotler *et al.* (2002: 394) definition of social marketing as 'the use of marketing principles and techniques to influence a target audience to voluntarily accept, reject, modify, or abandon a behaviour for the benefit of individuals, groups, or society as a whole'.

The key environmental, social and psychological issues that provide the foci for the Adbusters philosophy can be grouped into two main categories: those critiques of advertising and commodification that fall under 'the colonisation of spaces by marketing and mass media technologies' (Rumbo 2002: 138) represent the first category, while the 'degradation of natural environments rising from global economic growth and concomitant human consumption' (Rumbo 2002: 138) form the basis for the second category. This second category encompasses critiques of how global economic policies, advances in technology and consumerism have all contributed to the decline of natural environments (Rumbo 2002). Lasn (1999) popularised the term culture jamming (which was originally introduced by American group Negativland in 1985) as a way to explain what was viewed as being the next wave in the 'new war to reclaim public and private discursive places' (Rumbo 2002: 138).

Rumbo (2002) points out that culture jamming provides consumers with the opportunity to use 'social contradictions to undermine the dominant hegemony'. In the case of Adbusters the effects on the magazine readership in terms of changing consumption behaviours has been difficult to empirically verify (Rumbo 2002) in terms of participation, with the only clues being letters from readers themselves, which has opened up the magazine to some criticism (Rumbo 2002). These criticisms have also been used by the very marketers whom Adbusters oppose; this has presented a dilemma, which as Rumbo (2002) points out, has created a situation where 'although resistance by environmentally and politically motivated consumers can affect change, marketers also strengthen the consumerist hegemony by absorbing criticisms and converting such criticisms into reasons for consumption' (Rumbo 2002: 138).

Peattie and Peattie (2009: 267) suggest that 'the success of consumption reduction may lie in the extent to which it becomes viewed as normal'. Trends such as that of downshifting (Andrews and Holst 1998) and voluntary simplification (Craig-Lees and Hill 2002) could actually hold some merit for future social marketing campaigns as the rejection of a materialistic lifestyle towards one of consumption reduction, or right-sizing (Hall 2009a), becomes more commonplace. Sharif (2011: 210) notes that 'one of the advantages of social marketing as a technique is its versatility', and the ability of social marketing campaigns to utilise this versatility in order to influence key stakeholders other than the end consumers who are the target for behavioural change is what Andreasen (2006) states will help to create the supportive environment necessary in order to maintain these changed consumption behaviours. The main obstacle to this, as Sharif (2011: 210) points out, 'will be to find ways to make consumption reduction attractive to consumers, and acceptable in practice (as well as in principle) to policy makers'. In response to this Peattie and Peattie (2009) believe that the final word in whether downshifting (Andrews and Holst 1998) will ever gain traction lies within the ability of social marketing to elicit behavioural change. It is this belief that moved Peattie and Peattie (2009: 267) to point out that 'the challenge of promoting consumption restraint for altruistic reasons, and for the benefit of future generations, will be a much sterner test of social marketing's effectiveness'.

Adbusters: www.adbusters.org/ (The culture jamming
network is also available on Facebook)

Further reading and websites

Edited by the co-founder of Adbusters this work provides a creative critique of contemporary consumerism.

Lasn, K. (2012) *Meme Wars: The Creative Destruction of Neoclassical Economics: A Real World Economics Textbook*, ed. D. Fleet. London: Penguin.

On ethics in tourism see:

Burns, L. B. (2014) 'Ethics in Tourism', in C. M. Hall, S. Gössling and D. Scott (eds) *Routledge Handbook of Tourism and Sustainability*. Abingdon: Routledge.
Lovelock, B. and Lovelock, K. (2013) *The Ethics of Tourism: Critical and Applied Perspectives*. Abingdon: Routledge.
Smith, M. and Duffy, R. (2003) *The Ethics of Tourism Development*. London: Routledge.
Weeden, C. and Boluk, K. (eds) (2014) *Managing Ethical Consumption in Tourism: Compromise and Tension*. Abingdon: Routledge.

As an author I have continually placed great emphasis on the importance of reflexion, which I see as vital to personal and broader behavioural change as well as greater transparency in what we do. If interested see:

Hall, C. M. (2004) 'Reflexivity and tourism research: Situating myself and/with others,' in J. Phillimore and L. Goodson (eds) *Qualitative Research in Tourism: Ontologies, Epistemologies and Methodologies.* London: Routledge.

Hall, C. M. (2010) 'The life and opinions of C. Michael Hall, gent: A shandy or full beer? Volume the first', in S. Smith (ed.) *The Discovery of Tourism*, Bingley: Emerald Publishing Group. (The general editor of the series did not want the chapter published in the form it was. I gratefully thank Steve Smith the book editor for fighting for it on my behalf.)

Hall, C. M. (2011) 'Researching the political in tourism: Where knowledge meets power,' in C. M. Hall (ed.) *Fieldwork in Tourism: Methods, Issues and Reflections*, London: Routledge. (The entire book has some very useful personal reflections on fieldwork in tourism and the personal and professional issues that arise.)

Hall, C. M. (2013) 'Through a glass darkly: The future of tourism is personal', in J. Leigh, C. Webster and S. Ivanov (eds) *Future Tourism: Political, Social and Economic Challenges*. Abingdon: Routledge.

Academic web page as of time of writing (contains copies of publications, presentations and writings): http://canterbury-nz.academia.edu/CMichaelHall

---

BOX 10.4 OPENING THE BLACK BOX OF BEHAVIOURAL CHANGE AND BEING THE CHANGE YOU WANT TO BE

At the start of the book I outlined an exercise with respect to seeking to change your own behaviour as a means of reflecting on the issues associated with behaviour change in general. Although this book has taken far longer than ten weeks to complete, rudely interrupted as it was by the Christchurch earthquakes, I thought it unfair that as I complete the book that I didn't try to reflect on and change some of my own behaviours. So in the true spirit of transparency and struggle to change I thought I would reflect on what I have tried to change in the last ten weeks.

- I have started and more or less kept to the 5:2 diet.
- I resolved to play more football with my four-year-old. That didn't really work as well as hoped for but I have been playing more Lego!

Finally, I am trying to be more open in my professional thoughts and 'speak truth to power'. This is not necessarily easy. My current main institution (the University of Canterbury) is badly affected financially by the Christchurch earthquakes and is hoping for an influx of government funding. At the same time there are appalling (re)developments and a lack of democracy in the post-earthquake environment in Christchurch, which makes New Zealand look like a tin-pot Third World one-party state. In this environment there is a lack of attention to social housing and instead a focus on compulsory acquisition of land for commercial purposes and the enhancement of real estate values. This is not how liveable cities grow themselves. However, by speaking out and criticising what is probably the most right-wing government in New Zealand since the end of the

Second World War would I affect the possibility of financial support for my own faculty at a time when it is needed? I don't know. However, in reading the conclusion of one of my PhD students' thesis where he noted that he didn't speak up in a situation where he should have done a fundamental truth came home to me. To be silent and not say something because you are concerned about the consequences is probably one of the most fundamental expressions of the exercise of power that you can have. Therefore how can I write of the importance of upstream social marketing unless I also engage in it myself? And one consequence of this is that you have the conclusion you have here that is actually trying to say something about what is often not discussed in public. You may disagree with it. But the important thing is that by saying some things that may be uncomfortable to some, including oneself, a wider spread of opinion and knowledge is available from which hopefully better decisions, interventions and policies will result.

Self-reflection questions:

- How has your own behavioural change gone?
- What barriers did you encounter?
- What would have enabled you to have changed your behaviours further?

REFERENCES

Abratt, R. and Sacks, D. (1988) 'The marketing challenge: towards being profitable and socially responsible', *Journal of Business Ethics*, 7: 497–507.

Addis, M. and Podesta, S. (2005) 'Long life to marketing research: A post modern view', *European Journal of Marketing*, 39(3/4): 386–413.

Agrawal, A. (2001) 'Common property institutions and sustainable governance of resources', *World Development*, 29(10): 1649–1672.

Ahuvia, A. (2008) 'If money doesn't make us happy, why do we act as if it does?' *Journal of Economic Psychology*, 29: 491–507.

Ahuvia, A. C. and Friedman, D. C. (1998) 'Income, consumption, and subjective well-being: toward a composite macromarketing model', *Journal of Macromarketing*, 18: 153–168.

Airhihenbuwa, C. O. and Obregon, R. (2000) 'A critical assessment of theories/models used in health communication for HIV/AIDS', *Journal of Health Communication*, 5: 5–16.

Ajzen, I. (2012) 'Martin Fishbein's legacy the reasoned action approach', *The Annals of the American Academy of Political and Social Science*, 640(1): 11–27.

Ajzen, I. and Driver, B. L. (1992) 'Application of the theory of planned behavior to leisure choice', *Journal of Leisure Research*, 24(3): 207–224.

Akama, J. (1996) 'Western environmental values and nature-based tourism in Kenya', *Tourism Management*, 17: 567–574.

Alemanno, A. (2012) 'Nudging smokers – The behavioural turn of tobacco risk regulation', *European Journal of Risk Regulation*, 2012(1): 32–42.

Alessio, D. and Jóhannsdóttir, A. L. (2011) 'Geysers and 'girls': Gender, power and colonialism in Icelandic tourist imagery', *European Journal of Women's Studies*, 18(1): 35–50.

Alexander, S. (2011) 'Property beyond growth: Toward a politics of voluntary simplicity'. In D. Grinlinton and P. Taylor (eds) *Property Rights and Sustainability: The Evolution of Property Rights to Meet Ecological Challenges*. Leiden: Martinus Nijhoff Publishers.

Alexander, S. and Ussher, S. (2012) 'The Voluntary Simplicity Movement: A multi-national survey analysis in theoretical context', *Journal of Consumer Culture*, 12: 6–86.

Allen, S., Smith, H., Waples, K. and Harcourt, R. (2007) 'The voluntary code of conduct for dolphin watching in Port Stephens, Australia: is self-regulation an effective management tool?' *Journal of Cetacean Research and Management*, 9(2): 159–166.

Alves, H. (2010) 'The who, where, and when of social marketing', *Journal of Nonprofit and Public Sector Marketing*, 22(4): 288–311.

American Marketing Association (AMA) (2008) 'The American Marketing Association releases new definition of marketing', AMA, 14 January. Online. Available HTTP: www.marketingpower.com/aboutama/documents/american%20marketing%20association%20releases%20new%20definition%20for%20marketing.pdf (accessed 1 April 2013).

American Psychological Association (2009) *Psychology and Global Climate Change: Addressing a Multi-faceted Phenomenon and Set of Challenges*, Washington, DC: American Psychological Association.

Amir, O. and Lobel, O. (2008) 'Stumble, predict, nudge: How behavioral economics informs law and policy', *Columbia Law Review*, 108, 2098–2139.

Anand, P. and Lea, S. (2011) 'The psychology and behavioural economics of poverty', *Journal of Economic Psychology*, 32: 284–293.

Anand, A., Chandan, P. and Singh, R. B. (2012) 'Homestays at Korzok: Supplementing rural livelihoods and supporting green tourism in the Indian Himalayas', *Mountain Research and Development, 32*(2): 126–136.

Anastasiadou, C. (2008) 'Tourism interest groups in the EU policy arena: Characteristics, relationships and challenges', *Current Issues in Tourism*, 11: 24–62.

Anderson, E. (1998) 'Customer satisfaction and word of mouth', *Journal of Service Research,* 1(1): 5–17.

Anderson, C. L. and Bieniaszewska, R. L. (2005) 'The role of corporate social responsibility in an oil company's expansion into new territories', *Corporate Social Responsibility and Environmental Management,* 12: 1–9.

Andersson, L. M. and Bateman, T. S. (2000) 'Individual environmental initiative: championing natural environmental issues in U.S. business organizations', *Academy of Management Journal,* 43(4): 548–570.

Andersson, S., Hadelin, A., Nilsson, A. and Welander, C. (2004) 'Violent advertising in fashion marketing', *Journal of Fashion Marketing and Management*, 8(1): 96–112.

Andreasen, A. R. (1995) *Marketing Social Change: Changing Behaviour to Promote Health, Social Development, and the Environment*. San Francisco, CA: Jossey-Bass.

Andreasen, A. R. (ed.) (2001) *Ethics in Social Marketing*. Washington, DC: Georgetown University Press.

Andreasen, A. R. (2002) 'Marketing social marketing in the social change marketplace', *Journal of Public Policy and Marketing*, 21(1): 3–13.

Andreasen, A. R. (2003) 'The life trajectory of social marketing some implications', *Marketing Theory*, 3(3): 293–303.

Andreasen, A. R. (2006) *Social Marketing in the 21st Century*. Thousand Oaks, CA: Sage Publications.

Andreasen, A. R. (2012) 'Rethinking the relationship between social/nonprofit marketing and commercial marketing', *Journal of Public Policy and Marketing*, 31(1): 36–41.

Andreasen, A. R. and Kotler, P. (2007) *Strategic Marketing for Non-Profit Organizations*, seventh edition. Upper Saddle River, NJ: Prentice Hall.

Andrews, C. and Holst, C. B. (1998) 'The real meaning of "inwardly rich"', *Journal of Voluntary Simplicity*, 28 May.

Anheier, H. K. and Salamon, L. M. (1999). 'Volunteering in cross-national perspective: Initial comparisons', *Law and Contemporary Problems*, 62(4): 43–65.

Annandale, D. and Taplin, R. (2003) 'The determinants of mining company response to environmental approvals regulation: a report of Australian research', *Journal of Environmental Planning and Management*, 46(6): 887–909.

Ansell, C. and Gash, A. (2008) 'Collaborative governance in theory and practice', *Journal of Public Administration Research and Theory*, 18: 543–571.

Anti-Cancer Council of Victoria (ACCV) (1989) *SunSmart Evaluation Studies No. 1: The Anti-Cancer Council's Skin Cancer Control Program 1988–89*. Melbourne: ACCV.

Antimova, R., Nawijn, J. and Peeters, P. (2012) 'The awareness/attitude-gap in sustainable tourism: A theoretical perspective', *Tourism Review*, 67(3): 7–16.

Ap, J. (1992) 'Residents' perceptions on tourism impacts', *Annals of Tourism Research,* 19: 665–690.

Archer, D. and Wearing, S. W. (2002) 'Interpretation and marketing as management tools in national parks: Insights from Australia', *Journal of Leisure Property*, 2(1): 29–39.

Armitage, C. J. (2009) 'Is there utility in the transtheoretical model?' *British Journal of Health Psychology*, 14(2): 195–210.

Armitage, C. J. and Conner, M. (2001) 'Efficacy of the theory of planned behaviour: A meta-analytic review', *British Journal of Social Psychology*, 40: 471–499.

Armstrong, E. K. and Kern, C. L. (2011) 'Demarketing manages visitor demand in the Blue Mountains National Park', *Journal of Ecotourism*, 10: 21–37.

Ashworth, G. J. (2009) 'Do tourists destroy the heritage they have come to experience', *Tourism Recreation Research*, 34(1): 79–83.

Ashworth, G. J. and Voogd, H. (1988) 'Marketing the city: Concepts, processes and Dutch applications', *Town Planning Review*, 59(1): 65–79.

Assael, H. (1990) *Consumer Behaviour and Marketing Action*. Boston, MA: PWS-Kent.

Athey, V. L., Suckling, R. J., Tod, A. M., Walters, S. J. and Rogers, T. K. (2012) 'Early diagnosis of lung cancer: Evaluation of a community-based social marketing intervention', *Thorax*, 67(5): 412–417.

Atkinson, P. B. and Mullins, G. W. (1998) 'Applying social marketing to interpretation', *Journal of Interpretation Research*, 3(1): 49–53.

Ay, C., Aytekin, P. and Nardali, S. (2010) 'Guerilla marketing communication tools and ethical problems in guerilla advertising', *American Journal of Economics and Business Administration*, 2(3): 280–286.

Ayuso, S. (2007) 'Comparing voluntary policy instruments for sustainable tourism: The experience of the Spanish hotel sector', *Journal of Sustainable Tourism*, 15: 144–159.

Bache, I. and Flinders, M. (eds) (2004) *Multi-level Governance*. Oxford: Oxford University Press.

Bailey, I. and Wilson, G. A. (2009) 'Theorising transitional pathways in response to climate change: Technocentrism, ecocentrism, and the carbon economy', *Environment and Planning A*, 41: 2324–2341.

Bailey, J., Price, R., Esders, L. and McDonald, P. (2010) 'Daggy shirts, daggy slogans? Marketing unions to young people', *Journal of Industrial Relations*, 52(1): 43–60.

Bailey, K. D. (1994) *Typologies and Taxonomies: An Introduction to Classification Techniques*. Thousand Oaks, CA: Sage.

Baltes, G. and Leibing, I. (2007) 'Guerilla marketing for information services?' *New Library World*, 10(1/2): 46–55.

Bamberg, S., Fujii, S., Friman, M. and Gärling, T. (2011) 'Behaviour theory and soft transport policy measures', *Transport Policy*, 18(1): 228–235.

Bandura, A. (1977) 'Self-efficacy: Toward a unifying theory of behavioral change', *Psychological Review*, 84: 191–215.

Bandura, A. (2010) 'Self-efficacy', in I. B. Weiner and W. E. Craighard (eds) *Corsini Encyclopedia of Psychology*, fourth edition. Hoboken, NJ: John Wiley & Sons.

Bansal, P. and Roth, K. (2000) 'Why companies go green: A model of ecological responsiveness', *Academy of Management Journal*, 43(4): 717–747.

Baranowski, S. and Furlough, E. (eds) (2001) *Being Elsewhere: Tourism, Consumer Culture, and Identity In Modern Europe and North America*. Ann Arbor, MI: University of Michigan.

Bardach, E. (2002) 'Educating the client', *Journal of Policy Analysis and Management*, 21(1): 115–136.

Barnes, J. H. and Dotson, M. J. (1990) 'An exploratory investigation into the nature of offensive television advertising', *Journal of Advertising*, 19(3): 61–69.

Barr, S., Gilg, A. and Shaw, G. (2011) '"Helping people make better choices": Exploring the behaviour change agenda for environmental sustainability', *Applied Geography*, 31, 712–720.

Barr, S., Shaw, G., Coles, T. and Prillwitz, J. (2010) '"A holiday is a holiday": Practicing sustainability, home and away', *Journal of Transport Geography*, 18, 474–481.

Barrett, S. and Fudge, C. (1981) *Policy and Action*. London: Methuen.

Barrutia, J. M. and Echebarria, C. (2013) 'Networks: A social marketing tool', *European Journal of Marketing*, 47(1/2): 324–343.

Barry, C. L., Gollust, S. E. and Niederdeppe, J. (2012) 'Are Americans ready to solve the weight of the nation?' *New England Journal of Medicine*, 367(5): 389–391.

Baudrillard, J. (1981) *For a Critique of the Political Economy of the Sign*. St Louis, MO: Telos.

Bauman, A., Ferguson, C., McKenzie, J., Smith, B. and Vita, P. (2002) 'Impacts from repeated mass media campaigns to promote sun protection in Australia', *Health Promotion International*, 17(1): 51–60.

BBC News (2008) 'Holiday offer to get disease test', 28 May. Online. Available HTTP: http://news.bbc.co.uk/2/hi/uk_news/england/7423761.stm (accessed 10 October 2013).

BBC News (2010) 'Arts project tackles grass fires in Rhondda', 28 March. Online. Available HTTP: http://news.bbc.co.uk/2/hi/uk_news/wales/south_east/8586793.stm (accessed 10 October 2013).

BBC News Latin America & Caribbean (2013) 'Protest-hit Brazil "missed chance" to improve services', 28 June. Online. Available HTTP: www.bbc.co.uk/news/world-latin-america-23093630 (accessed 28 June 2013).

BBC News Northampton (2010) 'Advert aims to cut Northamptonshire binge drinking', 1 July. Online. Available HTTP: www.bbc.co.uk/news/10472719 (accessed 1 April 2013).

BBC News Wales (2011) 'Fire wipes out wildlife habitat in the Brecon Beacons', 6 May. Online. Available HTTP: www.bbc.co.uk/news/uk-wales-13308097 (accessed 1 April 2013).

Beaumont, N. and Dredge, D. (2010) 'Local tourism governance: a comparison of three network approaches', *Journal of Sustainable Tourism*, 18: 7–28.

Becken, S. (2004) 'How tourists and tourism experts perceive climate change and carbon offsetting schemes', *Journal of Sustainable Tourism*, 12: 332–345.

Becken, S. (2007) 'Tourists' perception of international air travel's impact on the global climate and potential climate change policies', *Journal of Sustainable Tourism*, 15: 351–368.

Becker, C. and Fleur, E. L. (2010) 'Process to prototype: Insights for museums and nonprofit attractions', *Tourism Analysis*, 15: 591–597.

Beeton, S. (2001) 'Smiling for the camera: The influence of film audiences on a budget tourism destination', *Tourism, Culture and Communication*, 3: 15–26.

Beeton, S. (2003) 'Swimming against the tide: Integrating marketing with environmental management via demarketing', *Journal of Hospitality and Tourism Management*, 10(2): 95–107.

Beeton, S. and Benfield, R. (2002) 'Demand control: The case for demarketing as a visitor and environmental management tool', *Journal of Sustainable Tourism*, 10: 479–513.

Beeton, S. and Pinge, I. (2003) 'Casting the holiday dice: Demarketing gambling to encourage local tourism', *Current Issues in Tourism*, 6: 309–322.

Bell, B. and Blakey, P. (2010) '"Do boys and girls go out to play?" Women's football and social marketing at Euro 2005', *International Journal of Sport Management and Marketing*, 7(3): 156–172.

Bell, S., Hindmoor, A. and Mols, F. (2010) 'Persuasion as governance: A state-centric relational perspective', *Public Administration*, 88(3): 851–870.

Bem, D. J. (1967) 'Self-perception: An alternative interpretation of cognitive dissonance phenomena', *Psychological Review*, 74(3): 183–200.

Bendell, J., Bendell, M., Kearins, K., Ives, K. and Visser, W. (2005) '2004 Lifeworth annual review of corporate responsibility'. Online. Available HTTP: www.lifeworth.net (accessed 19 November 2012).

Benfield, R. (2001) '"Good things come to those who wait": Sustainable tourism and timed entry at Sissinghurst Castle Garden, Kent', *Tourism Geographies,* 3: 207–217.

Bennett, R. (2007) 'The use of marketing metrics by British fundraising charities: A survey of current practice', *Journal of Marketing Management*, 23(9-10): 959–989.

Bennett, R. (2009) 'Factors influencing donation switching behaviour among charity supporters: An empirical investigation', *Journal of Customer Behaviour*, 8(4): 329–345.

Bernier, N. F. and Clavier, C. (2011) 'Public health policy research: Making the case for a political science approach', *Health Promotion International*, 26(1): 109–116.

Bennett, R. and Sargeant, A. (2005) 'The nonprofit marketing landscape: Guest editors' introduction to a special section', *Journal of Business Research*, 58(6): 797–805.

Best, S. and Kellner, D. (1997) *The Postmodern Turn*. New York: Guilford.

Bhattacharya, C. B., Korschun, D. and Sen, S. (2009) 'Strengthening stakeholder–company relationships through mutually beneficial corporate social responsibility initiatives', *Journal of Business Ethics*, 85(2): 257–272.

Bhattacharyya, O., Reeves, S., Garfinkel, S. and Zwarenstein, M. (2006) 'Designing theoretically-informed implementation interventions: Fine in theory, but evidence of effectiveness in practice is needed', *Implementation Science*, 1(5): 1–3.

Bichta, C. (2003) 'Corporate socially responsible (CSR) practices in the context of Greek industry', *Corporate Social Responsibility and Environmental Management*, 10: 12–24.

Bickel, W. K., Yi, R., Mueller, E. T., Jones, B. A. and Christensen, D. R. (2010) 'The behavioral economics of drug dependence: Towards the consilience of economics and behavioral neuroscience', in D. Self and J. K. S. Gottschalk (eds) *Behavioral Neuroscience of Drug Addiction*. Berlin: Springer.

Billson, J. M. (1988) 'Social change, social problems, and the search for identity: Canada's northern Native peoples in transition', *American Review of Canadian Studies*, 18: 295–316.

Binswanger, M. (2006) 'Why does income growth fail to make us happier? Searching for the treadmills behind the paradox of happiness', *Journal of Socio-Economics,* 35: 366–381.

BITC (Business in the Community) (2000) *Profitable Partnerships*. London: BITC.

Bjørnskov, C. (2010) 'How comparable are the Gallup World Poll life satisfaction data?' *Journal of Happiness Studies*, 11(1): 41–60.

Black, G. S. (2010) 'A social approach for de-marketing sex tourism', *The Business Review, Cambridge*, 15(2): 33–41.

Black, J. M. (1996) 'Constitutionalising self-regulation', *Modern Law Review*, 59: 24–55.

Blackwell, B. (1992) 'Compliance', *Psychotherapy and Psychosomatics*, 58(3-4): 161–169.

Blake, A. (2008) 'Tourism and income distribution in East Africa', *International Journal of Tourism Research*, 10: 511–524.

Blake, A., Arbache, J. S., Sinclair, M. T. and Teles, V. (2008) 'Tourism and poverty relief', *Annals of Tourism Research*, 35(1): 107–126.

Blamey, R. K. and Braithwaite, V. A. (1997) 'A social values segmentation of the potential ecotourism market', *Journal of Sustainable Tourism*, 5(1): 29–45.

Bode, I. (2006) 'Disorganized welfare mixes: Voluntary agencies and new governance regimes in Western Europe', *Journal of European Social Policy*, 16(4): 346–359.

Boekaerts, M., Pintrich, P. R. and Zeidner, M. (eds) (2005) *The Handbook of Self-regulation*. Burlington, VT: Elsevier Academic Press.

Bohdanowicz, P. (2009) 'Theory and practice of environmental management and monitoring in hotel chains', in S. Gössling, C.M. Hall and D. Weaver (eds) *Sustainable Tourism Futures: Perspectives on Systems, Restructuring and Innovations*. New York: Routledge.

Bolderdijk, J. W., Steg, L., Geller, E. S., Lehman, P. K. and Postmes, T. (2012) 'Comparing the effectiveness of monetary versus moral motives in environmental campaigning', *Nature Climate Change*, 3: 413–416.

Bone, J. D. (2010) 'Irrational capitalism: The social map, neoliberalism and the demodernization of the West', *Critical Sociology*, 36: 717–740.

Bordwell, M. (2002) 'Jamming culture: Adbusters' hip media campaign against consumerism', in T. Princen, M. Maniates and K. Conca (eds) *Confronting Consumption*, Cambridge: MIT Press.

Borland, R., Hill, D. and Noy, S. (1990) 'Being SunSmart: Changes in community awareness and reported behaviour following a primary prevention program for skin cancer control', *Behaviour Change,* 7(3): 126–135.

Borland, R., Montague, M. and Sinclair, C. (2001) 'Campaigning Slip! Slop! Slap! and SunSmart, 1980–2000: Skin cancer control and 20 years of population-based campaigning', *Journal of Health Education and Behavior*, 28: 290–292.

Bottema, M. J. M. and Bush, S. R. (2012) 'The durability of private sector-led marine conservation: A case study of two entrepreneurial marine protected areas in Indonesia', *Ocean and Coastal Management*, 61: 38–48.

Bourdeau, P. and Berthelot, L. (2008) 'Tourisme et Décroissance: de la critique à l'utopie?' In F. Flipo and F. Schneider (eds) *Proceedings of the First International Conference on Economic De-Growth for Ecological Sustainability and Social Equity*, Paris, 18–19 April.

Bovens, L. (2009) 'The ethics of nudge', in T. Grüne-Yanoff and S. Ove Hansson (eds), *Preference Change: Approaches from Philosophy, Economics and Psychology*. Berlin: Springer.

Bowes, J. E. (1997) *Communication and Community Development for Health Information: Constructs and Models for Evaluation*. Seattle, WA: National Network of Libraries of Medicine, Pacific Northwest Region.

Box-Steffensmeier, J. M., Brady, H. E. and Collier, D. (2008) 'Political science methodology', in J. M. Box-Steffensmeier, H. E. Brady and D. Collier (eds) *The Oxford Handbook of Political Methodology*. Oxford: Oxford University Press.

Brabazon, T. (2009) 'Brand Wellington: When city imaging is GLAM'ed: A personal view', *Place Branding and Public Diplomacy*, 5(4): 260–275.

Brabbs, C. (2000) 'Analysis: Which of these ads sells jumpers? Benetton's death row campaign has reopened the debate on shock ad tactics used by companies and charities', *Marketing*, 22 June. Online. Available HTTP: www.marketingmagazine.co.uk/article/68963/ANALYSIS-ads-sells-jumpers---Benetton-rsquos-death-row-campaign-reopened-debate-shock-ad-tactics-used-companies-charities-Cordelia-Brabbs-reports (accessed 1 April 2013).

Bradford, N. (2003) 'Public–private partnership? Shifting paradigms of economic governance in Ontario', *Canadian Journal of Political Science/Revue canadienne de science politique*, 36: 1005–1033.

Bradshaw, T. K. and Blakely, E. J. (1999) 'What are "third-wave" state economic development efforts? From incentives to industrial policy', *Economic Development Quarterly*, 13: 229–244.

Brady, E., Brace-Govan, J., Brennan, L. and Conduit, J. (2011) 'Market orientation and marketing in nonprofit organizations: Indications for fundraising from Victoria', *International Journal of Nonprofit and Voluntary Sector Marketing*, 16(1): 84–98.

Bramwell, B. (1991) 'Tourism environments and management', *Tourism Management*, 12: 363–364.

Bramwell, B. (2005) 'Interventions and policy instruments for sustainable tourism', in W. Theobold (ed.) *Global Tourism*, third edition. Oxford: Elsevier.

Bramwell, B. and Lane, B. (eds) (2000) *Tourism Collaboration and Partnerships: Politics, Practice and Sustainability*. Clevedon: Channel View Publishers.

Bramwell, B. and Lane, B. (2011) 'Critical research on the governance of tourism and sustainability', *Journal of Sustainable Tourism*, 19: 411–421.

Bramwell, B. and Rawding, L. (1994) 'Tourism marketing organizations in industrial cities: Organizations, objectives and urban governance', *Tourism Management*, 15: 425–434.

Bramwell, B. and Sharman, A. (1999) 'Collaboration in local tourism policymaking', *Annals of Tourism Research*, 26: 392–415.

Brechin, S. R., Wilshusen, P. R., Fortwangler, C. L. and West, P. C. (2002) 'Beyond the square wheel: Toward a more comprehensive understanding of biodiversity conservation as social and political process', *Society and Natural Resources* 15: 41–64.

Brenkert, G. G. (2002) 'Ethical challenges of social marketing', *Journal of Public Policy and Marketing*, 21(1): 14–25.

Briggs, E., Peterson, M. and Gregory, G. (2010) 'Toward a better understanding of volunteering for nonprofit organizations: Explaining volunteers' pro-social attitudes', *Journal of Macromarketing*, 30(1): 61–76.

Bright, A. D. (2000) 'The role of social marketing in leisure and recreation management', *Journal of Leisure Research,* 32(1): 12–17.

Britton, S. G. (1991) 'Tourism, capital and place: Towards a critical geography of tourism', *Environment and Planning D: Society and Space,* 9: 451–478.

Brown, J., Broderick, A. J. and Lee, N. (2007) 'Word of mouth communication within online communities: Conceptualizing the online social network', *Journal of Interactive Marketing*, 21(3): 2–20.

Brown, S. W., El-Ansary, A. I. and Darsey, N. (1976) 'The portrayal of women in advertising: An overlooked area of societal marketing', *Journal of the Academy of Marketing Science*, 4: 577–591.

Brug, J., Conner, M., Harre, N., Kremers, S., McKellar, S. and Whitelaw, S. (2005) 'The Transtheoretical Model and stages of change: A critique. Observations by five commentators on the paper by Adams, J. and White, M. (2004) Why don't stage-based activity promotion interventions work?' *Health Education Research*, 20: 244–258.

Brulle, R. J. (2010) 'From environmental campaigns to advancing the public dialog: Environmental communication to civic engagement', *Environmental Communication*, 4(1): 82–98.

Bublik, C. (2009) 'THMBNLS – the world's first interactive made-for-mobile drama (incentivated)', Mobile Marketing Association Case Studies, 1 June. Online, Available HTTP: www.mmaglobal. com/studies/thmbnls-%E2%80%93-world%E2%80%99s-first-interactive-made-mobile-drama-incentivated (accessed 1 April 2013).

Buchthal, O. V., Doff, A. L., Hsu, L. A., Silbanuz, A., Heinrich, K. M. and Maddock, J. E. (2011) 'Avoiding a knowledge gap in a multiethnic statewide social marketing campaign: is cultural tailoring sufficient?' *Journal of Health Communication*, 16(3): 314–327.

Buckley, R. (2003) 'Pay to play in parks: An Australian policy perspective on visitor fees in public protected areas', *Journal of Sustainable Tourism*, 11: 56–73.

Buckley, R., Witting, N. and Guest, M. (2003) 'Visitor fees, tour permits and asset and risk management by parks agencies: Australian case study', in R. Buckley, C. Pickering and D. Weaver (eds) *Nature-Based Tourism, Environment and Land Management*. Wallingford: CABI Publishing.

Burgess, A. (2012) '"Nudging" healthy lifestyles: The UK experiments with the behavioural alternative to regulation and the market', *European Journal of Risk Regulation*, 2012(1): 3–16.

Burton, D. and Klemm, M. (2011) 'Whiteness, ethnic minorities and advertising in travel brochures', *The Service Industries Journal*, 31: 679–693.

Bussell, H. and Forbes, D. (2002) 'Understanding the volunteer market: The what, where, who and why of volunteering', *International Journal of Non-profit and Voluntary Sector Marketing*, 7(3): 244–257.

Butler, R. W. (1990) 'Alternative tourism: Pious hope or Trojan horse?', *Journal of Travel Research*, 28(3): 40–45.

Butler, R. W. (1999) 'Sustainable tourism: A state of the art review', *Tourism Geographies,* 1: 7–25.

Butler, R. W. and Hinch, T. (2007) 'Introduction: Revisiting common ground', in R. Butler and T. Hinch (eds) *Tourism and Indigenous Peoples: Issues and Implications.* London: Butterworth-Heinemann.

Buurma, H. (2001) 'Public policy marketing: Marketing exchange in the public sector', *European Journal of Marketing*, 35: 1287–1302.

Byrne, A., Dickson, L., Derevensky, J., Gupta, R. and Lussier, I. (2005) 'An examination of social marketing campaigns for the prevention of youth problem gambling', *Journal of Health Communication*, 10: 681–700.

Cabrini L. (2012) *Tourism in the UN Green Economy*, Report, UNWTO High-level Regional Conference on Green Tourism, 3 May, Chiang Mai, Thailand. Online. Available HTTP: asiapacific.unwto.org/sites/all/files/.../2012may_chiangmai_lc_0.pdf.

Callahan, M. and Thomas, S. (2005) 'Volunteer tourism: Deconstructing volunteer activities within a dynamic environment', in M. Novelli (ed.) *Niche Tourism: Contemporary Issues, Trends, and Cases.* Oxford: Elsevier.

Cameron, L. and Leventhal, H. (eds) (2003) *The Self-Regulation of Health and Illness Behaviour.* London: Routledge.

Campos-Soria, J. A., Marchante-Mera, A. and Ropero-García, M. A. (2011) 'Patterns of occupational segregation by gender in the hospitality industry', *International Journal of Hospitality Management*, 30: 91–102.

Cancer Society of New Zealand (2008) 'Cancer information'. Online. Available HTTP: www.cancernz.org.nz/information (accessed 10 May 2009).

Carl, W. (2006) 'What's all the buzz about? Everyday communication and the relational basis of word-of-mouth and buzz marketing practices', *Management Communication Quarterly,* 19(4): 601–634.

Carrigan, M., Moraes, C. and Leek, S. (2011) 'Fostering responsible communities: A community social marketing approach to sustainable living', *Journal of Business Ethics*, 100: 515–534.

Carter, S. M. (2003) 'Going below the line: Creating transportable brands for Australia's dark market', *Tobacco Control,* 12(3): 87–94.

Carter, S. M., Rychetnik, L., Lloyd, B., Kerridge, I. H., Baur, L., Bauman, A., Hooker, C. and Zask, A. (2011) 'Evidence, ethics, and values: A framework for health promotion', *American Journal of Public Health*, 101(3): 465–472.

Cater, E. and Lowman, G. (1994) *Ecotourism: A Sustainable Option?* Chichester: John Wiley & Sons.

Caton, K. and Santos, C. A. (2009) 'Images of the other selling study abroad in a postcolonial world', *Journal of Travel Research*, 48: 191–204.

Chandon, P. and Wansink, B. (2012) 'Does food marketing need to make us fat? A review and solutions', *Nutrition Reviews*, 70(10): 571–593.

Chape, S., Blyth, S., Fish, L., Fox, P. and Spalding, M. (2003) *2003 United Nations List of Protected Areas*. Gland and Cambridge: IUCN and UNEP-WCMC.

Chapman, K. and Cowlishaw, S. (2013) 'Back to future to revive Wellington's vitality', *Dominion Post*, 10 May. Online. Available HTTP: www.stuff.co.nz/dominion-post/news/8655338/Back-to-future-to-revive-Wellingtons-vitality (accessed 11 May 2013).

Chartered Institute of Marketing (CIM) (2011) *Don't Stop Me Now: Marketing in Central Government*. London: CIM.

Chen, P. T. and Hu, H. H. (2010) 'How determinant attributes of service quality influence customer-perceived value: An empirical investigation of the Australian coffee outlet industry', *International Journal of Contemporary Hospitality Management*, 22: 535–551.

Cheng, T., Woon, D. K. and Lynes, J. K. (2011) 'The use of message framing in the promotion of environmentally sustainable behaviors', *Social Marketing Quarterly*, 17(2): 48–62.

Chettiparamb, A. and Kokkranikal, J. (2012) 'Responsible tourism and sustainability: The case of Kumarakom in Kerala, India', *Journal of Policy Research in Tourism, Leisure and Events*, 4(3): 320–326.

Chhabra, D. (2009) 'Proposing a sustainable marketing framework for heritage tourism', *Journal of Sustainable Tourism*, 17: 303–320.

Chhabra, D. (2010) *Sustainable Marketing of Cultural and Heritage Tourism*. London: Taylor & Francis.

Chhabra, D., Andereck, K., Yamanoi, K. and Plunkett, D. (2011) 'Gender equity and social marketing: An analysis of tourism advertisements', *Journal of Travel and Tourism Marketing*, 28: 111–128.

Chhatre, A. and Agrawal, A. (2008) 'Forest commons and local enforcement', *Proceedings of the National Academy of Sciences*, 105(36): 13,286–13,291.

Chok, S., Macbeth, J. and Warren, C. (2007) 'Tourism as a tool for poverty alleviation: A critical analysis of "pro-poor tourism" and implications for sustainability', *Current Issues in Tourism*, 10: 144–165.

Christensen, P. N., Rothgerber, H., Wood, W. and Matz, D. C. (2004) 'Social norms and identity relevance: A motivational approach to normative behaviour', *Personality and Social Psychology Bulletin*, 30: 1295–1309.

Christie, L. H. (2010) 'Understanding New Zealand homeowners apparent reluctance to adopt housing-sustainability innovations'. Unpublished thesis, Victoria University of Wellington.

Chu, S.-C. (2011) 'Viral advertising in social media: Participation in Facebook groups and responses among college-aged users', *Journal of Interactive Advertising*, 12(1): 30–43.

Cialdini, R. (2007) *Influence: The Psychology of Persuasion*. New York: HarperBusiness.

Cini, F., Leone, L. and Passafaro, P. (2012) 'Promoting ecotourism among young people a segmentation strategy', *Environment and Behavior*, 44(1): 87–106.

Cismaru, M. and Lavack, A. M. (2007) 'Interaction effects and combinatorial rules governing protection motivation theory variables: A new model', *Marketing Theory*, 7(3): 249–270.

Cismaru, M., Lavack, A. M. and Markewich, E. (2009) 'Social marketing campaigns aimed at preventing drunk driving: A review and recommendations', *International Marketing Review*, 26(3): 292–311.

Clark, C. F., Kotchen, M. J. and Moore, M. R. (2003) 'Internal and external influences on pro-environmental behavior: Participation in a green electricity program', *Journal of Environmental Psychology*, 23(3): 237–246.

Clark, W. C. and Majone, G. (1985) 'The critical appraisal of scientific inquiries with policy implications', *Science, Technology and Human Values*, 10(3): 6–19.

Clarke, P., Peattie, K. and Peattie, S. (2001) 'Skin cancer prevention: Reevaluating the public policy implications', *Journal of Public Policy and Marketing*, 20: 268–279.

Clawson, M. and Knetsch, J. L. (1966) *Economics of Outdoor Recreation*. Baltimore, MD: Johns Hopkins University Press.

Clemens, E. S. and Cook, J. M. (1999) 'Politics and institutionalism: Explaining durability and change', *Annual Review of Sociology*, 25: 441–466.

Clements, M. (1989) 'Selecting tourist traffic by demarketing', *Tourism Management*, 10(2): 89–94.

Clevedon, R. and Kalisch, A. (2000) 'Fair Trade in tourism', *International Journal of Tourism Research*, 2: 171–187.

Clifton, J., Etienne, M., Barnes, D. K. A., Barnes, R. S. K., Suggett, D. J. and Smith, D. J. (2012) 'Marine conservation policy in Seychelles: Current constraints and prospects for improvement', *Marine Policy*, 36: 823–831.

Climate Change Communication Advisory Group (2010) 'Communicating climate change to mass public audiences'. Online. Available HTTP: http://pirc.info/downloads/communicating_climate_mass_audiences.pdf (accessed 7 January 2013).

Coccossis, H. and Constantoglou, M. E. (2006) 'The use of typologies in tourism planning: Problems and conflicts'. 46th Congress of the European Regional Science Association (ERSA), Enlargement, Southern Europe and the Mediterranean, 30 August–1 September, University of Thessaly-Department of Planning and Regional Development.

Coccossis, H. and Constantoglou, M. E. (2008) 'The use of typologies in tourism planning: Problems and conflicts', in H. Coccossis and Y. Psycharis (eds) *Regional Analysis and Policy: The Greek Experience*. Heidelberg: Physica-Verlag.

Coddington, W. (1993) *Environmental Marketing*. New York: McGraw-Hill.

Cohen, B. (1963) *The Press and Foreign Policy*. Princeton, NJ: Princeton University

Cohen, S. A. and Higham, J. E. (2011) 'Eyes wide shut? UK consumer perceptions on aviation climate impacts and travel decisions to New Zealand', *Current Issues in Tourism*, 14: 323–335.

Cohen, M., Comrov, A. and Hoffner, B. (2005) 'The new politics of consumption: Promoting sustainability in the American marketplace', *Sustainability: Science, Practice, and Policy*, 1(1): 58–76.

Cohen, S. A., Higham, J. E. and Cavaliere, C. T. (2011) 'Binge flying: Behavioural addiction and climate change', *Annals of Tourism Research*, 38: 1070–1089.

Cole, S. (2006a) 'Cultural tourism, community participation and empowerment', in M. K. Smith and M. Robinson (eds.), *Cultural Tourism in a Changing World: Politics, Participation and (Re)presentation*. Clevedon: Channel View.

Cole, S. (2006b) 'Information and empowerment: The keys to achieving sustainable tourism', *Journal of Sustainable Tourism*, 14: 629–644.

Coles, T. and Hall, C. M. (ed.) (2008) *Tourism and International Business*. London: Routledge.

Collier, D., Laporte, J. and Seawright, D. (2008) 'Typologies: Forming concepts and creating categorical variables', in J. M. Box-Steffensmeier, H. E. Brady and D. Collier (eds) *The Oxford Handbook of Political Methodology*. Oxford: Oxford University Press.

Collins, K., Tapp, A. and Pressley, A. (2010) 'Social marketing and social influences: Using social ecology as a theoretical framework', *Journal of Marketing Management*, 26(13–14): 1181–1200.

Conlisk, J. (1996) Why bounded rationality? *Journal of Economic Literature*, 34: 669–700.

Conner, M. and Norman, P. (eds) (2005a) *Predicting Health Behaviour*, second edition. Maidenhead: Open University Press and McGraw-Hill Education.

Conner, M. and Norman, P. (2005b) 'Predicting health behaviour: A social cognition approach', in M. Conner and P. Norman (eds) *Predicting Health Behaviour*, second edition. Maidenhead: Open University Press and McGraw-Hill Education.

Convery, F., McDonnell, S. and Ferreira, S. (2007) 'The most popular tax in Europe? Lessons from the Irish plastic bags levy', *Environmental and Resource Economics*, 38(1): 1–11.

Cook, A. J., Kerr, G. N. and Moore, K. (2002) 'Attitudes and intentions towards purchasing GM food', *Journal of Economic Psychology*, 23: 557–572.

Cooke, K. (1982) 'Guidelines for socially appropriate tourism development in British Columbia', *Journal of Travel Research*, 21(1): 22–8.

Cooper, C. (2007) 'Successfully changing individual travel behavior: Applying community-based social marketing to travel choice', *Transportation Research Record: Journal of the Transportation Research Board*, 2021(1): 89–99.

Cooper, C. and Hall, C. M. (2013) *Contemporary Tourism: An International Approach*, second edition. Oxford: Goodfellow.

Cooper, T. (2005) 'Sustainable consumption: Reflections on product lifespans and "throwaway society"', *Journal of Industrial Ecology*, 9(1–2): 51–67.

Cornelissen, S. (2005) *The Global Tourism System: Governance, Development and Lessons from South Africa*. Aldershot: Ashgate.

Corner, A. (2012) 'The Heartland ads are not the only climate change messages to go wrong', *The Guardian*, 1 June. Online. Available HTTP: www.guardian.co.uk/sustainable-business/climate-change-heartland-ads-messages-wrong? (accessed 10 October 2013).

Corner, A. and Randall, A. (2011) 'Selling climate change? The limitations of social marketing as a strategy for climate change public engagement', *Global Environmental Change*, 21: 1005–1014.

Cowell, D. (1979) 'Marketing in local authority sport, leisure and recreation centres', *Local Government Studies*, 5(4): 31–43.

Cox, B., Fletcher, L., Reeder, A., Richardson, A. and Sneyd, M. (2008) 'The incidence and thickness of cutaneous malignant melanoma in New Zealand 1994–2004', *The New Zealand Medical Journal*, 121(1279): 18–26.

Cox, D. (2001) 'Notes on culture jamming', in G. Turner and M. Allen (eds) *Techno Culture. Media International Australia: Culture and Policy*. No. 98. Nathan: Australia Key Centre For Cultural and Media Policy.

Cox, R. (2013) *Environmental Communication and the Public Sphere*, third edition. Thousand Oaks, CA: Sage.

Crabtree, R. D. (1998) 'Mutual empowerment in cross-cultural participatory development and service learning: Lessons in communication and social justice from projects in El Salvador and Nicaragua', *Journal of Applied Communication Research,* 26: 182–209.

Craig-Lees, M. and Hill, C. (2002) 'Understanding voluntary simplifiers', *Psychology and Marketing*, 19: 187–210.

Crane, A. (2000) 'Marketing and the natural environment: What role for morality?' *Journal of Macromarketing*, 20: 144–154.

Cresswell, T. (2004) *Place: A Short Introduction*, Oxford: Blackwell.

Croall, J. (1995) *Preserve or Destroy: Tourism and the Environment*, London: Calouste Gulbenkian Foundation.

Cuccia, T. and Rizzo, I. (2011) 'Tourism seasonality in cultural destinations: Empirical evidence from Sicily', *Tourism Management*, 32: 589–595.

Cunningham, G. B. and Kwon, H. (2003) 'The theory of planned behaviour and intentions to attend a sport event', *Sport Management Review*, 6(2): 127–145.

Cunningham, P. H., Gallagher, K. and Jones, T. (2010) 'Violence in advertising: A multilayered content analysis', *Journal of Advertising*, 39(4): 11–36.

Czarniawska, B. (2004) *Narratives in Social Science Research*. London: Sage.

Daellenbach, K., Davies, J. and Ashill, N. J. (2006) 'Understanding sponsorship and sponsorship relationships—multiple frames and multiple perspectives', *International Journal of Nonprofit and Voluntary Sector Marketing*, 11(1): 73–87.

Dahl, D. W., Frankenberger, K. D. and Manchanda, R. V. (2003) 'Does it pay to shock? Reactions to shocking and nonshocking advertising content among university students', *Journal of Advertising Research*, 43(3): 268–280.

Dann, S. (2010) 'Redefining social marketing with contemporary commercial marketing definitions', *Journal of Business Research,* 63: 147–153.

Davis, K. J., Cokkinides, V. E., Weinstock, M. A., O'Connell, M. C. and Wingo, P. A. (2002). 'Summer sunburn and sun exposure among US youths ages 11 to 18: National prevalence and associated factors', *Pediatrics*, 110(1), 27–35.

Davy, P. (2009) 'Scenes of a shocking nature', *The Guardian*, 27 March. Online. Available HTTP: www.guardian.co.uk/society/joepublic/2009/mar/27/charity-advertising-shock (accessed 1 April 2013).

Dawes, J. and Brown, R. B. (2000) 'Postmodern marketing: Research issues for retail financial services', *Qualitative Market Research: An International Journal*, 3(2): 90–99.

Dawson, J. and Scott, D. (2010) 'Systems analysis of climate change vulnerability of the US Northeast ski sector', *Journal of Tourism and Hospitality Planning*, 7: 219–235.

De Groot, J. I. and Schuitema, G. (2012) 'How to make the unpopular popular? Policy characteristics, social norms and the acceptability of environmental policies', *Environmental Science and Policy*, 19: 100–107.

De Groot, J. I. and Steg, L. (2009) 'Morality and prosocial behavior: The role of awareness, responsibility, and norms in the Norm Activation Model', *The Journal of Social Psychology*, 149(4): 425–449.

Dearing, J. W. and Rogers, E. M. (1996) *Agenda Setting*. Thousand Oaks, CA: Sage.

Demeritt, D. (2001) 'The construction of global warming and the politics of science', *Annals of the Association of American Geographers*, 91: 307–337.

Demeritt, D. (2006) 'Science studies, climate change and the prospects for constructivist critique', *Economy and Society*, 35, 453–479.

Demetriou, M., Papasolomou, I. and Vrontis, D. (2009) 'Cause-related marketing: Building the corporate image while supporting worthwhile causes', *Journal of Brand Management*, 17(4): 266–278.

De Meyrick, J. (2007) 'One size no longer fits all: the application of Andreasen's six social marketing benchmarks in Australian antismoking programs'. Unpublished PhD, Department of Business, Macquarie University. Online. Available HTTP: Zhttp://hdl.handle.net/1959.14/87046 (accessed 1 April 2012).

Department of Energy and Climate Change (2012) 'Tackling climate change'. Online. Available HTTP: www.decc.gov.uk/en/content/cms/tackling/saving_energy/saving_energy.asp (accessed 7 January 2013).

Derevensky, J. L. and Gupta, R. (2007) 'Internet gambling amongst adolescents: A growing concern', *International Journal of Mental Health and Addiction*, 5(2): 93–101.

Derevensky, J. L., Gupta, R., Dickson, L., Hardoon, K. and Deguire, A. E. (2003) 'Understanding youth gambling problems: A conceptual framework', in D. Romer (ed.) *Reducing Adolescent Risk*, Thousand Oaks, CA: Sage.

De Ruyter, K. and Wetzels, M. (2000) 'With a little help from my fans: Extending models of prosocial behavior to explain "supporters" intentions to buy soccer club shares', *Journal of Economic Psychology*, 21: 387–409.

Desai, D. (2009) 'Role of relationship management and value co-creation in social marketing', *Social Marketing Quarterly*, 15(4): 112–125.

Detweiler-Bedell, J. B., Friedman, M. A., Leventhal, H., Miller, I. W. and Leventhal, E. A. (2008) 'Integrating co-morbid depression and chronic physical disease management: Identifying and resolving failures in self-regulation', *Clinical Psychology Review*, 28(8): 1426–1446.

Derevensky, J. L. and Gupta, R. (2000) 'Youth gambling: A clinical and research perspective', *Journal of Gambling Issues*, 2, doi: 10.4309/jgi.2000.2.3.

Devlin-Foltz, D., Fagen, M. C., Reed, E., Medina, R. and Neiger, B. L. (2012) 'Advocacy evaluation challenges and emerging trends', *Health Promotion Practice*, 13(5): 581–586.

Diehr, P., Hannon, P., Pizacani, B., Forehand, M., Meischke, H., Curry, S., Martin, D. P., Weaver, M. R. and Harris, J. (2011) 'Social marketing, stages of change, and public health smoking interventions', *Health Education and Behavior*, 38(2), 123–131.

Diener, E. (2000) 'Subjective well-being: The science of happiness and a proposal for a national index', *American Psychologist*, 55(1), 34–43.

Diener, E. and Biswas-Diener, R. (2002) 'Will money increase subjective well-being? A literature review and guide to needed research', *Social Indicators Research*, 57(2): 119–169.

Diener, E., Ng, W., Harter, J. and Arora, R. (2010) 'Wealth and happiness across the world: Material prosperity predicts life evaluation, whereas psychosocial prosperity predicts positive feeling', *Journal of Personality and Social Psychology*, 99(1): 52–61.

Diener, E., Suh, E. M., Lucas, R. E. and Smith, H. L. (1999) 'Subjective well-being: Three decades of progress', *Psychological Bulletin,* 125(2): 276–302.

Dinan, C. and Sargeant, A. (2000) 'Social marketing and sustainable tourism: Is there a match?' *International Journal of Tourism Research*, 2: 2–14.

Dobson, A. (2010) *Environmental Citizenship and Pro-environmental Behaviour: Rapid Research and Evidence Review*. London: Sustainable Development Research Review.

Dolan, P. (2002) 'The sustainability of "sustainable consumption"', *Journal of Macromarketing*, 22: 170–181

Dolan, P., Hallsworth, M., Halpern, D., King, D., Metcalfe, R. and Vlaev, I. (2012) 'Influencing behaviour: The mindspace way', *Journal of Economic Psychology*, 33: 264–277.

Dolan, P., Hallsworth, M., Halpern, D., King, D. and Vlaev, I. (2010) *MINDSPACE: Influencing Behaviour Through Public Policy*. London: Cabinet Office and Institute for Government.

Donovan, R. (2011) 'Social marketing's mythunderstandings', *Journal of Social Marketing*, 1(1): 8–16.

Donovan, R. J. and Henley, N. (1997) 'Negative outcomes, threats and threat appeals: Widening the conceptual framework for the study of fear and other emotions in social marketing communications', *Social Marketing Quarterly*, 4(1): 56–67.

Donovan, R. J and Henley, N. (2003) *Social Marketing: Principles and Practice*. Melbourne: IP Communication.

Dorsey, J. W. (2010) 'Lawn control, lawn culture, and the social marketing of sustainable behaviors', *Ecopsychology*, 2: 91–103.

Downing, P. and Ballantyne, J. (2007) *Tipping Point or Turning Point? Social Marketing and Climate Change*. London: Ipsos MORI Social Research Institute.

Downs, A. (1972) 'Up and down with ecology – the issue attention cycle', *The Public Interest*, 28: 38–50.

Dredge, D. (2001) 'Local government tourism planning and policy-making in New South Wales: Institutional development and historical legacies', *Current Issues in Tourism*, 4: 355–380.

Dredge, D. (2006a) 'Policy networks and the local organisation of tourism', *Tourism Management*, 27: 269–280.

Dredge, D. (2006b) 'Networks, conflict and collaborative communities', *Journal of Sustainable Tourism*, 14(6): 562–581.

Dredge, D. and Jenkins, J. M. (2003) 'Federal-state relations and tourism public policy, New South Wales, Australia', *Current Issues in Tourism*, 6: 415–443.

Dredge, D. and Jenkins, J. M. (2007) *Tourism Planning and Policy*. Chichester: John Wiley.

Dunbar, J. M., Marshall, G. D. and Hovell, F. (1979) 'Behavioural strategies for improving compliance', in R. B. Haynes, D. W. Taylor and D. L. Sackett (eds) *Compliance in Health Care*. Baltimore, MD: Johns Hopkins University Press.

Dutta-Bergman, M. J. (2005) 'Theory and practice in health communication campaigns: A critical interrogation', *Health Communication*, 18(2): 103–122.

Dye, T. R. (1987) *Understanding Public Policy: An Introduction*. Englewood Cliffs, NJ: Prentice Hall.

Eagle, L., McDowell, R. and Bird, S. (2011) 'Examining policy assumptions regarding public–private partnerships in contested social marketing domains: the case of alcohol moderation'. World Non-Profit and Social Marketing Conference. The 2nd World Non-Profit and Social Marketing Conference, 11–12 April, Dublin, Ireland.

Earl, P. E. (1990) 'Economics and psychology: A survey', *The Economic Journal*, 100(402): 718–755.

Earl, P. E. (2005) 'Economics and psychology in the twenty-first century', *Cambridge Journal of Economics*, 29(6): 909–926.

Earle, R. (2000) *The Art of Cause Marketing: How to Use Advertising to Change Personal Behaviour and Public Policy*. Chicago, IL: NTC Business.

Easterlin, R. A. (1973) 'Does money buy happiness?' *The Public Interest*, 30(10): 56–65.

Ebreo, A., Hershey, J. and Vining, J.(1999). 'Reducing solid waste: Linking recycling to environmentally responsible consumerism', *Environment and Behavior*, 31: 107–135.

Eccles, M., Grimshaw, J., Walker, A., Johnston, M. and Pitts, N. (2005a) 'Changing the behavior of healthcare professionals: The use of theory in promoting the uptake of research findings', *Journal of Clinical Epidemiology*, 58(2): 107–112.

Eccles, M., Grimshaw, J., Walker, A., Johnston, M. and Pitts, N. (2005b) 'Response to the OFF theory of research utilization', *Journal of Clinical Epidemiology*, 58(2): 117–118.

Economist (2013a) 'Breaking ground', *The Economist*, 18 May: 53–54.

Economist (2013b) 'Marketing: Less guff, more puff', *The Economist*, 18 May: 55–57.

Edström, A. (1991) 'Scandinavian Airlines Systems (SAS): Strategic reorientation and social change', in M. Maccoby (ed.) *Sweden at the Edge: Lessons for American and Swedish Managers.* Philadelphia, PA: University of Pennsylvania Press.

Egri, C. P. and Ralston, D. A. (2008) 'Corporate responsibility: A review of international management research from 1998 to 2007', *Journal of International Management*, 14(4): 319–339.

Eichhorn, V., Miller, G., Michopoulou, E. and Buhalis, D. (2008) 'Enabling access to tourism through information schemes?' *Annals of Tourism Research*, 35(1): 189–210.

Eiser, J. R. and Arnold, B. W. (1999) 'Out in the midday sun: Risk behaviour and optimistic beliefs among residents and visitors on Tenerife', *Psychology and Health*, 14: 529–544.

Eiser, J. R., Eiser, C., Sani, F., Sell, L. and Casas, R. M. (1995) 'Skin cancer attitudes: A cross-national comparison', *British Journal of Social Psychology*, 34: 23–30.

Ellemers, N., Spears, R. and Doosje, B. (2002) 'Self and social identity', *Annual Review of Psychology*, 53(1): 161–186.

Ellis, C. (2003) 'When volunteers pay to take a trip with scientists – Participatory environmental research tourism (PERT)', *Human Dimensions of Wildlife*, 8: 75–80.

Erkuș-Öztürk, H. and Eraydin, A. (2010) 'Environmental governance for sustainable tourism development: Collaborative networks and organisation building in the Antalya tourism region', *Tourism Management*, 31: 113–124.

Etzioni, A. (1998) 'Voluntary simplicity characterization, select psychological implications, and societal consequences', *Journal of Economic Psychology,* 19: 619–643.

Etzioni, A. (2003) 'Introduction: Voluntary simplicity – Psychological implications, societal consequences', in D. Doherty and A. Etzioni (eds) *Voluntary Simplicity: Responding to Consumer Culture.* Oxford: Rowman and Littlefield Publishers.

European Commission (2002) *Corporate Social Responsibility: A Business Contribution to Sustainable Development.* Paris: Directorate for Employment and Social Affairs.

Evans-Lacko, S., Malcolm, E., West, K., Rose, D., London, J., Rüsch, N., Little, K., Henderson, C. and Thornicroft, G. (2013) 'Influence of time to change's social marketing interventions on stigma in England 2009–2011', *The British Journal of Psychiatry*, 202(s55): s77–s88.

Evans, W. D. (2006) 'How social marketing works in health care', *British Medical Journal*, 332(7551): 1207–1210.

Fairclough, S. (2011) 'Grass fire setting acceptability "needs stamping out"', Eye on Wales, BBC Radio Wales, 15 May. Online. Available HTTP: www.bbc.co.uk/news/uk-wales-13392098 (accessed 10 October 2013).

Farquarson, A. (2000) 'Marketing campaigns impact on consumer habits', *The Guardian*, 15 November.

Farrell, T. and Gordon, R. (2012) 'Critical social marketing: Investigating alcohol marketing in the developing world', *Journal of Social Marketing*, 2(2): 138–156.

Feng, R. and Morrison, A. M. (2002) 'GIS applications in tourism and hospitality marketing: a case in Brown County, Indiana', *Anatolia*, 13(2): 127–143.

Fennell, D. A. (2008) 'Ecotourism and the myth of indigenous stewardship', *Journal of Sustainable Tourism*, 16: 129–149.

Ferguson, R. (2008) 'Word of mouth and viral marketing: Taking the temperature of the hottest trends in marketing', *Journal of Consumer Marketing,* 25(3): 179–182.

Ferrand, A. and Stotlar, D. K. (2010) 'Introduction: New perspectives in sport event marketing', *International Journal of Sport Management and Marketing*, 7(3): 145–155.

Fine, B. and Leopold, E. (1993) *The World of Consumption.* London: Routledge.

Firat, A. F. and Venkatesh, A. (1995) 'Liberatory postmodernism and the reenchantment of consumption', *Journal of Consumer Research*, 22: 239–267.

Fishbein M. and Ajzen, I. (1975) *Belief, Attitude, Intention and Behavior: An Introduction to Theory and Research.* Menlo Park, CA: Addison-Wesley.

Fishbein, M. and Ajzen, I. (2010) *Predicting and Changing Behavior.* New York: Psychology Press.

Fisher, J. D. and Fisher, W. A. (1992) 'Changing AIDS-risk behaviour', *Psychological Bulletin*, 111(3): 455–474.

Fisher, J. D., Fisher, W. A., Amico K. R. and Harman, J. J. (2006) 'An information-motivation-behavioral skills model of adherence to antiretroviral therapy', *Health Psychology*, 25(4): 462–473.

Fisk, G. (1973) 'Criteria for a theory of responsible consumption', *Journal of Marketing*, 37(2): 24–31.

Flammer, C. (2012) 'Corporate social responsibility and shareholder reaction: The environmental awareness of investors', *Academy of Management Journal*, 56(3): 758–781.

Flipo, F. and Schneider, F. (eds) *Proceedings of the First International Conference on Economic De-Growth for Ecological Sustainability and Social Equity, Paris, 18–19 April 2008*. Paris.

Fodness, D. and Murray, B. (1997) 'Tourist information search', *Annals of Tourism Research*, 24(3): 503–523.

Folke, C. Hahan, T., Olsson, P. and Norberg, J. (2005) 'Adaptive governance of social–ecological systems', *Annual Review of Environment and Resources*, 30: 441–473.

Folmer, H. and Johansson-Stenman, O. (2011) 'Does environmental economics produce aeroplanes without engines? On the need for an environmental social science', *Environmental and Resource Economics*, 48: 337–361.

Forgacs, D. (2000) *The Antonio Gramsci Reader: Selected Writings, 1916–1935*. New York: New York University Press.

Forsyth, T. (1995) 'Business attitudes to sustainable tourism: Self-regulation in the UK outgoing tourism industry', *Journal of Sustainable Tourism*, 3: 210–231.

Fox, K. F. A. and Kotler, P. (1980) 'The marketing of social causes: the first 10 years', *Journal of Marketing*, 44(4): 24–33.

Foxall, G. (1984) 'The meaning of marketing and leisure: Issues for research and development', *European Journal of Marketing*, 18(2): 23–32.

Foxall, G. R. (1986) 'Theoretical progress in consumer psychology: The contribution of a behavioural analysis of choice', *Journal of Economic Psychology*, 7: 393–414.

Foxall, G. R. (1992) 'The consumer situation: An integrative model for research in marketing', *Journal of Marketing Management*, 8(4), 383–404.

Foxall, G. R. (1993) 'A behaviourist perspective on purchase and consumption', *European Journal of Marketing*, 27(8): 7–16.

Foxall, G. R. (2001) 'Foundations of consumer behaviour analysis', *Marketing Theory*, 1(2): 165–199.

Foxall, G. R., Oliveira-Castro, J. M., James, V. K. and Schrezenmaier, T. C. (2011) 'Consumer behaviour analysis and the behavioural perspective model', *Management Online Review (MORE)*. Online. Available HTTP: morexpertise.com/view.php?id=70 (accessed 10 October 2013).

Foxton, J. (2005) 'Live buzz marketing', in J. Kirby and P. Marsden (Eds) *Connected Marketing: The Viral, Buzz and Word of Mouth Revolution*. Burlington, MA: Butterworth-Heinemann.

Frances, J., Levačić, R., Mitchell, J. and Thompson, G. (1991) 'Introduction', in G. Thompson, J. Frances, R. Levačić and J. Mitchell (eds) *Markets, Hierarchies and Networks: The Coordination of Social Life*. London: Sage.

French, J. (2008) *Procurement Guide for Social Marketing Services*. London: National Centre for Social Marketing.

Friend, K. B. and Ladd, G. T. (2009) 'Youth gambling advertising: A review of the lessons learned from tobacco control', *Drugs: Education, Prevention, and Policy*, 16(4): 283–297.

Frith, K. T. and Mueller, B. (2010) *Advertising and Societies: Global Issues*, second edition. New York: Peter Land Publishing.

Frost, W. and Hall, C. M. (eds) (2009) *Tourism and National Parks*. London: Routledge.

Fujii, S. (2010) 'Can state regulation of car use activate a moral obligation to use sustainable modes of transport?' *International Journal of Sustainable Transportation*, 4(5): 313–320.

Fullagar, S., Markwell, K. and Wilson, E. (eds) (2012) *Slow Tourism*. Bristol: Channelview.

Gabriel, Y. (2000) *Storytelling in Organizations, Facts, Fictions, and Fantasies*. Oxford: Oxford University Press.

Gadenne, D., Sharma, B., Kerr, D. and Smith, T. (2011) 'The influence of consumers' environmental beliefs and attitudes on energy saving behaviours', *Energy Policy*, 39: 7684–7694.

Galer-Unti, R. A. (2009) 'Guerilla advocacy: Using aggressive marketing techniques for health policy change', *Health Promotion Practice*, 10(3): 325–327.

Gallopel-Morvan, K., Gabriel, P., Le Gall-Ely, M., Rieunier, S. and Urien, B. (2011) 'The use of visual warnings in social marketing: The case of tobacco', *Journal of Business Research*, 64(1): 7–11.

Gallup (2006) 'World Poll questions'. Online. Available HTTP: http://media.gallup.com/dataviz/www/WP_Questions_WHITE.pdf (accessed 10 October 2013).

Garside, R., Pearson, M. and Moxham, T. (2010) 'What influences the uptake of information to prevent skin cancer? A systematic review and synthesis of qualitative research', *Health Education Research*, 25(1): 162–182.

Gebhardt, W. A. and Maes, S. (2001) 'Integrating social-psychological frameworks for health behaviour research', *American Journal of Health Behavior*, 25: 528–536.

Geller, E. S. (1989) 'Applied behavior analysis and social marketing: An integration for environmental preservation', *Journal of Social Issues*, 45(1): 17–36.

George, A. and Bennett, A. (2005) *Case Studies and Theory Development in the Social Sciences*. Cambridge, MA: MIT Press.

George, R. and Frey, N. (2010) 'Creating change in responsible tourism management through social marketing', *South African Journal of Business Management*, 41(1), 11–23.

Geva-May, I. and Wildavsky, A. (1997) *An Operational Approach to Policy Analysis: The Craft. Prescriptions for Better Analysis*. Boston, MA: Kluwer Academic Publishers.

Giddens, A. (1984) *The Constitution of Society: Outline of the Theory of Structuration*. Cambridge: Polity Press.

Gilbert, D. (1989) 'Rural tourism and marketing: Synthesis and new ways of working', *Tourism Management*, 10(1): 39–50.

Glanz, K., Rimer, B. K. and Viswanath, K. (eds) (2008) *Health Behavior and Health Education: Theory, Research, and Practice*, fourth edition. San Francisco, CA: Jossey-Bass.

Glenane-Antoniadis, A., Whitwell. G., Bell, J. and Menguc, B. (2003) 'Extending the vision of social marketing through social capital theory: Marketing in the context of intricate exchange and market failure', *Marketing Theory*, 3: 323–343.

Glider, P., Midyett, S. J., Mills-Novoa, B., Johannessen, K. and Collins, C. (2001) 'Challenging the collegiate rite of passage: A campus-wide social marketing media campaign to reduce binge drinking', *Journal of Drug Education*, 31: 207–220.

Glover, K. (2006) 'Human trafficking and the sex tourism industry', *Crime and Justice International*, 22(2): 4–16.

Godin, G. and Kok, G. (1996) 'The theory of planned behavior: A review of its applications to health-related behaviors', *American Journal of Health Promotion*, 11(2): 87–98.

Godin, G., Conner, M. and Sheeran, P. (2005) 'Bridging the intention–behaviour gap: The role of moral norm', *British Journal of Social Psychology*, 44: 497–512.

Goldenberg, S. (2012) 'Extreme weather more persuasive on climate change than scientists', *The Guardian*, 14 December.

Goldstein, A., Cialdini, R. B. and Griskevicius, V. (2008) 'A room with a viewpoint: Using social norms to motivate environmental conservation in hotels', *Journal of Consumer Research*, 35: 472–482.

Goodall, B. (2006) 'Disabled access and heritage attractions', *Tourism Culture and Communication*, 7(1): 57–78.

Goodland, R. and Daly, H. (1996) 'Environmental sustainability: Universal and non-negotiable', *Ecological Applications*, 6: 1002–1017.

Goodwin, H. and Francis, J. (2003) 'Ethical and responsible tourism: Consumer trends in the UK', *Journal of Vacation Marketing*, 9: 271–284.

Gooroochurn, N. and Sinclair, M. T. (2005) 'Economics of tourism taxation: Evidence from Mauritius', *Annals of Tourism Research*, 32: 478–498.

Gordon, R. (2012) 'Rethinking and re-tooling the social marketing mix', *Australasian Marketing Journal*, 20(2): 122–126.

Gordon, R., McDermott, L., Stead, M. and Angus, K. (2006) 'The effectiveness of social marketing interventions for health improvement: What's the evidence?' *Public Health*, 120: 1133–1139.

Gössling, S. (2002) 'Global environmental consequences of tourism', *Global Environmental Change*, 12: 283–302.

Gössling, S. (2009) 'Carbon neutral destinations: A conceptual analysis', *Journal of Sustainable Tourism*, 17: 17–37.

Gössling, S. (2010) *Carbon Management in Tourism: Mitigating the Impacts on Climate Change*. London: Routledge.

Gössling, S. (2013) 'Advancing a clinical transport psychology', *Transportation Research Part F*, 19: 11–21.

Gössling, S. and Hall, C. M. (eds) (2006a) *Tourism and Global Environmental Change*. London: Routledge.

Gössling, S. and Hall, C.M. (2006b) 'Uncertainties in predicting tourist flows under scenarios of climate change', *Climatic Change*, 79(3–4): 163–173.

Gössling, S. and Hall, C. M. (2013) 'Sustainable culinary systems: An introduction', in C. M. Hall and S. Gössling (eds) *Sustainable Culinary Systems: Local Foods, Innovation, and Tourism and Hospitality*. London: Routledge.

Gössling, S. and Peeters, P. (2007) '"It does not harm the environment!" An analysis of industry discourses on tourism, air travel and the environment', *Journal of Sustainable Tourism*, 15: 402–417.

Gössling, S. and Schumacher, K. P. (2010) 'Implementing carbon neutral destination policies: Issues from the Seychelles', *Journal of Sustainable Tourism*, 18: 377–391.

Gössling, S. and Upham, P. (eds) (2012) *Climate Change and Aviation: Issues, Challenges and Solutions*, New York: Routledge.

Gössling, S., Broderick, J., Upham, P., Ceron, J. P., Dubois, G., Peeters, P. and Strasdas, W. (2007) 'Voluntary carbon offsetting schemes for aviation: Efficiency, credibility and sustainable tourism', *Journal of Sustainable Tourism*, 15: 223–248.

Gössling, S., Hall, C. M., Ekström, F., Brudvik Engeset, A. and Aall, C. (2012b) 'Transition management: A tool for implementing sustainable tourism scenarios?' *Journal of Sustainable Tourism*, 20: 899–916.

Gössling, S., Hall, C. M., Lane, B. and Weaver, D. (2008) 'The Helsingborg Statement on Sustainable Tourism', *Journal of Sustainable Tourism*, 16: 122–124.

Gössling, S., Hall, C. M., Peeters, P. and Scott, D. (2010) 'The future of tourism: Can tourism growth and climate policy be reconciled? A climate change mitigation perspective', *Tourism Recreation Research*, 35(2): 119–130.

Gössling, S., Hall, C. M. and Scott, D. (2009) 'The challenges of tourism as a development strategy in an era of global climate change', in E. Palosou (ed.) *Rethinking Development in a Carbon-Constrained World. Development Cooperation and Climate Change*. Helsinki: Ministry of Foreign Affairs.

Gössling, S., Hall, C. M. and Weaver, D. (eds) (2009) *Sustainable Tourism Futures: Perspectives on Systems, Restructuring and Innovations*. London: Routledge.

Gössling, S., Haglund, L., Kallgren, H., Revahl, M. and Hultman, J. (2009) 'Swedish air travellers and voluntary carbon offsets: Towards the co-creation of environmental value?', *Current Issues in Tourism*, 12(1): 1–19.

Gössling, S., Lindén, O., Helmersson, J., Liljenberg, J. and Quarm, S. (2007) 'Diving and global environmental change: a Mauritius case study', in B. Garrod and S. Gössling (eds) *New Frontiers in Marine Tourism: Diving Experiences, Management and Sustainability*. Oxford: Elsevier.

Gössling, S., Peeters, P. and Scott, D. (2008) 'Consequences of climate policy for international tourist arrivals in developing countries', *Third World Quarterly*, 29(5): 873–901.

Gössling, S., Scott, D., Hall, C. M., Ceron, J. and Dubois, G. (2012a) 'Consumer behaviour and demand response of tourists to climate change', *Annals of Tourism Research*, 39: 36–58.

Göymen, K. (2000) 'Tourism and governance in Turkey', *Annals of Tourism Research*, 27: 1025–1048.

Graham, C. (2005) 'The economics of happiness', *World Economics,* 6(3): 41–55.

Graham, C. (2011) 'Does more money make you happier? Why so much debate?' *Applied Research in Quality of Life*, 6(3): 219–239.

Graham-Dixon, A. (2008) *Michelangelo and the Sistine Chapel*. London: Weidenfeld & Nicolson.

Graham-Rowe, E., Skippon, S., Gardner, B. and Abraham, C. (2011) 'Can we reduce car use and, if so, how? A review of available evidence', *Transportation Research Part A: Policy and Practice*, 45(5): 401–418.

Greenberg, J. and Knight, G. (2004) 'Framing sweatshops: Nike, global production, and the American news media', *Communication and Critical/Cultural Studies*, 1(2): 151–175.

Greener, I. (2001) 'Social learning and macroeconomic policy in Britain', *Journal of Public Policy*, 21: 133–152.

Greenwood, J. (1993) 'Business interest groups in tourism governance', *Tourism Management*, 14: 335–348.

Gregson, J., Foerster, S. B., Orr, R., Jones, L., Benedict, J., Clarke, B., Hersey, J., Lewis, J. and Zotz, K. (2001) 'System, environmental, and policy changes: Using the social-ecological model as a framework for evaluating nutrition education and social marketing programs with low-income audiences', *Journal of Nutrition Education*, 33(Supplement 1): S4–S15.

Grier, S. and Bryant, C. A. (2005) 'Social marketing in public health', *Annual Review of Public Health*, 26: 319–339.

Grier, S. A. and Kumanyika, S. (2010) 'Targeted marketing and public health', *Annual Review of Public Health*, 31: 349–369.

Grier, S. A., Mensinger, J., Huang, S. H., Kumanyika, S. K. and Stettler, N. (2007) 'Fast-food marketing and children's fast-food consumption: Exploring parents' influences in an ethnically diverse sample', *Journal of Public Policy and Marketing*, 26: 221–235.

Griffin, E. (2011) *A First Look at Communication Theory*, eighth edition. New York: McGraw-Hill.

Griffin, T. (2004) 'A discourse analysis of UK sourced gap year overseas projects'. Unpublished Master's thesis, University of the West of England.

Groff, C. (1998) 'Demarketing in park and recreation management', *Managing Leisure*, 3(3): 128–135.

Groot, M., Hellberg, J. and Pickanen, L. (2011) 'New marketing tools and reputational risks – A study about managing the reputational risks that guerrilla marketing brings along'. Unpublished Masters Theses, Linnaeus University, Vaxjo, Sweden.

Gualini, E. (ed.) (2004) *Multilevel Governance and Institutional Change: The Europeanization of Regional Policy in Italy*. Aldershot: Ashgate.

Guion, D. T., Scammon, D. L. and Borders, A. L. (2007) 'Weathering the storm: A social marketing perspective on disaster preparedness and response with lessons from Hurricane Katrina', *Journal of Public Policy and Marketing*, 26(1): 20–32.

Gupta, R. and Derevensky, J. L. (2000) 'Adolescents with gambling problems: From research to treatment', *Journal of Gambling Studies*, 16(2–3), 315–342.

Haas, P. M. (2004) 'When does power listen to truth? A constructivist approach to the policy process', *Journal of European Public Policy*, 11(4): 569–592.

Haase, D., Lamers, M. and Amelung, B. (2009) 'Heading into uncharted territory? Exploring the institutional robustness of self-regulation in the Antarctic tourism sector', *Journal of Sustainable Tourism*, 17: 411–430.

Hager, M. A. and Brudney, J. L. (2011) 'Problems recruiting volunteers: Nature versus nurture', *Nonprofit Management and Leadership*, 22(2): 137–157.

Haldeman, T. and Turner, J. W. (2009) 'Implementing a community-based social marketing program to increase recycling', *Social Marketing Quarterly*, 15(3): 114–127.

Hale, E. D., Treharne, G. J. and Kitas, G. D. (2007) 'The Common-Sense Model of self-regulation of health and illness: how can we use it to understand and respond to our patients' needs?' *Rheumatology*, 46: 904–906.

Hall, C. M. (1992) 'Sex tourism in South-east Asia', in D. Harrison (ed.) *Tourism and the Less Developed Countries*. London: Belhaven.

Hall, C. M. (1994a) *Tourism and Politics: Policy, Power and Place*. Chichester: John Wiley.

Hall, C. M. (1994b) 'Ecotourism in Australia, New Zealand and the South Pacific: appropriate tourism or a new form of ecological imperialism?' in E. Cater and G. Lowman (eds) *Ecotourism: Sustainable Option*. Chichester: John Wiley & Sons.

Hall, C. M. (1997) 'Geography, marketing and the selling of places', *Journal of Travel and Tourism Marketing*, 6(3–4): 61–84.

Hall, C. M. (1998) 'The institutional setting: Tourism and the state', in D. Ioannides and K. Debbage (eds) *The Economic Geography of the Tourist Industry: A Supply-Side Analysis*. London: Routledge.

Hall, C. M. (1999) 'Rethinking collaboration and partnership: A public policy perspective', *Journal of Sustainable Tourism*, 7, 274–289.

Hall, C. M. (2002) 'Travel safety, terrorism and the media: The significance of the issue-attention cycle', *Current Issues in Tourism*, 5(5): 458–466.

Hall, C. M. (2005a) 'Reconsidering the geography of tourism and contemporary mobility', *Geographical Research*, 43: 125–139.

Hall, C. M. (2005b) *Tourism: Rethinking the Social Science of Mobility*. Harlow: Prentice Hall.

Hall, C. M. (2006a) 'Tourism, disease and global environmental change: the fourth transition', in S. Gössling and C. M. Hall (eds) *Tourism and Global Environmental Change: Ecological, Economic, Social and Political Interrelationships*. London: Routledge.

Hall, C. M. (2006b) 'New Zealand tourism entrepreneur attitudes and behaviours with respect to climate change adaptation and mitigation', *International Journal of Innovation and Sustainable Development*, 1(3): 229–237.

Hall, C. M. (2006c) Tourism, biodiversity and global environmental change', in S. Gössling and C. M. Hall (eds) *Tourism and Global Environmental Change: Ecological, Social, Economic and Political Interrelationships*. London: Routledge.

Hall, C. M. (2006d) 'Tourism, urbanisation and global environmental change', in S. Gössling and C. M. Hall (eds) *Tourism and Global Environmental Change: Ecological, Social, Economic and Political Interrelationships*. London: Routledge.

Hall, C. M. (2007a) 'Tourism, governance and the (mis-)location of power', in A. Church and T. Coles (eds) *Tourism, Power and Space*. London: Routledge.

Hall, C. M. (2007b) 'Pro-poor tourism: Do "tourism exchanges benefit primarily the countries of the South"?' *Current Issues in Tourism*, 10: 111–118.

Hall, C. M. (2007c) 'The possibilities of slow tourism: Can the slow movement help develop sustainable forms of tourism consumption?' Paper presented at Achieving Sustainable Tourism, Helsingborg, Sweden, 11–14 September.

Hall, C. M. (2008a) *Tourism Planning: Policies, Processes and Relationships*, second edition. London: Prentice Hall.

Hall, C. M. (2008b) 'Regulating the international trade in tourism services', in T. Coles and C. M. Hall (eds) *International Business and Tourism: Global Issues, Contemporary Interactions*. London: Routledge.

Hall, C. M. (2009a) 'Degrowing tourism: Décroissance, sustainable consumption and steady-state tourism', *Anatolia: An International Journal of Tourism and Hospitality Research*, 20: 46–61.

Hall, C. M. (2009b) 'Archetypal approaches to implementation and their implications for tourism policy', *Tourism Recreation Research*, 34: 235–245.

Hall, C. M. (2010a) 'Changing paradigms and global change: From sustainable to steady-state tourism', *Tourism Recreation Research*, 35: 131–145.

Hall, C. M. (2010b) 'Implementation of the Convention on Biological Diversity guidelines on biodiversity and tourism development', *Journal of Heritage Tourism*, 5(4): 267–284.

Hall, C. M. (2010c) 'Tourism and biodiversity: More significant than climate change?' *Journal of Heritage Tourism*, 5(4): 253–266.

Hall, C. M. (2010d) 'Crisis events in tourism: Subjects of crisis in tourism', *Current Issues in Tourism*, 13(5): 401–417.

Hall, C. M. (2011a) 'Policy learning and policy failure in sustainable tourism governance: From first and second to third order change?' *Journal of Sustainable Tourism*, 19: 649–671.

Hall, C. M. (2011b) 'A typology of governance and its implications for tourism policy analysis', *Journal of Sustainable Tourism*, 19: 437–457.

Hall, C. M. (2011c) 'Consumerism, tourism and voluntary simplicity: We all have to consume, but do we really have to travel so much to be happy?' *Tourism Recreation Research*, 36: 298–303.

Hall, C.M. (2013) 'Framing behavioural approaches to understanding and governing sustainable tourism consumption: Beyond neoliberalism, "nudging" and "green growth"?' *Journal of Sustainable Tourism*, 21(7): 1091–1109.

Hall, C. M. and Baird, T. (2013) 'Ecotourism, biological invasions and biosecurity', in R. Ballantyne and J. Packer (eds) *The International Handbook of Ecotourism*. Aldershot: Ashgate Publishing.

Hall, C. M. and Coles, T. E. (2008) 'Introduction: tourism and international business – tourism as international business', in T. E. Coles and C. M. Hall (eds) *International Business and Tourism: Global Issues, Contemporary Interactions*. London: Routledge.

Hall, C. M. and James, M. (2011) 'Medical tourism: Emerging biosecurity and nosocomial issues', *Tourism Review*, 66(1/2): 118–126.

Hall, C. M. and Jenkins, J. M. (1995) *Tourism and Public Policy*. London: Routledge.

Hall, C. M. and Lew, A. (eds) (1998) *Sustainable Tourism: A Geographical Perspective*. London: Prentice Hall.

Hall, C. M. and Lew, A. (2009) *Understanding and Managing Tourism Impacts: An Integrated Approach*. London: Routledge.

Hall, C. M. and McArthur, S. (1998) *Integrated Heritage Management*. Norwich: The Stationery Office.

Hall, C. M. and O'Sullivan, V. (1996) 'Tourism, political instability and social unrest', in A. Pizam and Y. Mansfield (eds) *Tourism, Crime and International Security Issues*. Chichester: John Wiley.

Hall, C. M. and Page, S. J. (2006) *The Geography of Tourism and Recreation: Environment, Place and Space*, third edition. London: Routledge.

Hall, C. M. and Sharples, L. (2008) 'Food events and the local food system', in C. M. Hall and L. Sharples (eds) *Food and Wine Festivals and Events Around the World: Development, Management and Markets*. Oxford: Butterworth-Heinemann.

Hall, C. M. and Williams, A. M. (2008) *Tourism and Innovation*. London: Routledge.

Hall, D. R. (ed.) (2004) *Tourism and Transition: Governance, Transformation and Development*. Wallingford: CABI.

Hall, D. R. and Brown, F. (2006) *Tourism and Welfare: Ethics, Responsibility and Sustained Well-Being*. Wallingford: CABI.

Hall, P. A. (1993) 'Policy paradigms, social learning, and the state: The case of economic policymaking in Britain', *Comparative Politics*, 25: 275–296.

Ham, C. and Hill, M. J. (1994) *The Policy Process in the Modern Capitalist State*, second edition. New York: Prentice Hall.

Hanson, J. A. and Benedict, J. A. (2002) 'Use of the health belief model to examine older adults' food-handling behaviors', *Journal of Nutrition Education and Behavior*, 34: S25–S30.

Haq, G., Whitelegg, J., Cinderby, S. and Owen, A. (2008) 'The use of personalised social marketing to foster voluntary behavioural change for sustainable travel and lifestyles', *Local Environment*, 13(7): 549–569.

Hardin, G. (1968) 'The tragedy of the commons: The population problem has no technical solution; it requires a fundamental extension in morality', *Science*, 162(3859): 1243–1248.

Hardoon, K. K. and Derevensky, J. L. (2002) 'Child and adolescent gambling behavior: Current knowledge', *Clinical Child Psychology and Psychiatry*, 7(2): 263–281.

Hares, A., Dickinson, J. and Wilkes, K. (2010) 'Climate change and the air travel decisions of UK tourists', *Journal of Transport Geography*, 18: 466–473.

Harland, P., Staats, H. and Wilke, H. A. (2007) 'Situational and personality factors as direct or personal norm mediated predictors of pro-environmental behavior: Questions derived from norm-activation theory', *Basic and Applied Social Psychology*, 29(4): 323–334.

Harrison, D. (2008) 'Pro-poor tourism: A critique', *Third World Quarterly*, 29(5): 851–868.

Harvey, D. (1990) *The Condition of Postmodernity: An Enquiry into the Origins of Cultural Change*. Oxford. Blackwell.

Hastings, G. (2003) 'Relational paradigms in social marketing', *Journal of Macromarketing*, 23(1): 6–15.

Hastings, G. (2007) *Social Marketing: Why Should the Devil Have All the Best Tunes?* Oxford: Butterworth-Heinemann.

Hastings, G. and Saren, M. (2003) 'The critical contribution of social marketing theory and application', *Marketing Theory*, 3(3): 305–322.

Hastings, G., Stead, M. and Webb, J. (2004) 'Fear appeals in social marketing: Strategic and ethical reasons for concern', *Psychology and Marketing*, 21(11): 961–986.

Hawkins, D. E. and Mann, S. (2007) 'The World Bank's role in tourism development', *Annals of Tourism Research,* 34: 348–363.

Hayabuchi, Y., Enomoto, Y., Yamasue, E., Okumura H., Ishihara, K. and Year, N. (2005) 'The role of environmental education and social system on the plastic bag problem', in Proceedings of 3rd Conference on the Public Sector, Ljubljana, Slovenia, 30 June–2 July.

Head, K. J. and Noar, S. M. (2013) 'Facilitating progress in health behaviour theory development and modification: the reasoned action approach as a case study', *Health Psychology Review*, in press, doi: 10.1080/17437199.2013.778165.

Health Canada (2000) *The Health Canada Policy Toolkit for Public Involvement in Decision Making.* Ottawa: Corporate Consultation Secretariat, Health Policy and Communications Branch, Health Canada.

Health Sponsorship Council (2006) 'Sunsmart'. Online. Available HTTP: www.sunsmart.org.nz (accessed 29 April 2009)

Heitzler, C. D., Ashbury, L. D. and Kusner, S. L. (2008) 'Bringing "play" to life. The use of experimental marketing in the VERB campaign', *American Journal of Preventative Medicine,* 34: 188–193.

Hellsten, S. and Mallin, C. (2006) 'Are "ethical" or "socially responsible" investments socially responsible?' *Journal of Business Ethics*, 66(4): 393–406.

Henley, N. and Donovan, R. J. (1999) 'Threat appeals in social marketing: Death as a "special case"', *International Journal of Nonprofit and Voluntary Sector Marketing*, 4(4): 300–319.

Henley, N., Raffin, S. and Caemmerer, B. (2011) 'The application of marketing principles to a social marketing campaign', *Marketing Intelligence and Planning*, 29: 697–706.

Henneberg, S. C. and O'Shaughnessy, N. J. (2007) 'Theory and concept development in political marketing: issues and an agenda', *Journal of Political Marketing*, 6(2–3): 5–31.

Henry, G. T. and Gordon, C. S. (2001) 'Tracking issue attention: Specifying the dynamics of the public agenda', *Public Opinion Quarterly*, 65(2): 157–177.

Heritier, A. (2002) 'New modes of governance in Europe: Policy-making without legislating?' in A. Heritier (eds) *Common Goods: Reinventing European and International Governance*. Oxford: Rowman & Littlefield Publishers.

Higgins-Desbiolles, F. (2003) 'Reconciliation tourism: Tourism healing divided societies', *Tourism Recreation Research*, 28: 35–44.

Hill, C. (1990) 'The paradox of tourism in Costa Rica', *Cultural Survival Quarterly*, 14(1): 14–22.

Hodson, D. and Maher I. (2001) 'The open method as a new mode of governance', *Journal of Common Market Studies*, 39: 719–746.

Holden, A. (2010) 'Exploring stakeholders' perceptions of sustainable tourism development in the Annapurna conservation area: issues and challenge', *Tourism and Hospitality Planning and Development*, 7: 337–351.

Hood, C. (1991) 'A public management for all seasons?' *Public Administration*, 69(1): 3–19.

Hoog, N., Stroebe, W. and de Wit, J. B. F. (2005) 'The impact of Fear Appeals on processing and acceptance of action recommendations', *Personality and Social Psychology Bulletin*, 31: 24–33.

Hooghe, L. (ed.) (1996) *Cohesion Policy and European Integration: Building Multi-level Governance*. Oxford: Oxford University Press.

Hooghe, L. and Marks, G. (2001) *Multi-level Governance and European Integration*. Oxford: Rowman & Littlefield Publishers.

Hooghe, L. and Marks, G. (2003) 'Unraveling the central state, but how? Types of multi-level governance', *The American Political Science Review*, 97: 233–243.

Hopper, J. R. and Nielsen, J. M. (1991) 'Recycling as altruistic behavior: Normative and behavioral strategies to expand participation in a community recycling program', *Environment and Behavior*, 23: 195–220.

Hornik, R. C. (2002) *Public Health Communication: Evidence for Behavior Change*. New York: Taylor & Francis.

Hovil, S. and Stokke, K. B. (2007) 'Network governance and policy integration – the case of regional coastal zone planning in Norway', *European Planning Studies*, 15: 927–944.

Hrubes, D., Ajzen, I. and Daigle, J. (2001) 'Predicting hunting intentions and behavior: An application of the theory of planned behavior', *Leisure Sciences*, 23(3): 165–178.

Hubbell, A. P. and Dearing, J. W. (2003) 'Local newspapers, community partnerships, and health improvement projects: Their roles in a comprehensive community initiative', *Journal of Community Health*, 28(5): 363–376.

Hughes, M., Weiler, B. and Curtis, J. (2012) 'What's the problem? River management, education, and public beliefs', *Ambio*, 41: 709–719.

Humphreys, A. and Grayson, K. (2008) 'The intersecting roles of consumer and producer: a critical perspective on co-production, co-creation and prosumption', *Sociology Compass*, 2(3): 963–980.

Hunecke, M., Blöbaum, A., Matthies, E. and Höger, R. (2001) 'Responsibility and environment: Ecological norm orientation and external factors in the domain of travel mode choice behavior', *Environment and Behavior*, 33: 830–852.

Huneke, M. E. (2005) 'The face of the un-consumer: An empirical examination of the practice of voluntary simplicity in the United States', *Psychology and Marketing*, 22(7), 527–550.

Hunt, S. D. (2012) 'Toward the institutionalization of macromarketing: Sustainable enterprise, sustainable marketing, sustainable development, and the sustainable society', *Journal of Macromarketing*, 32(4): 404–411.

Hurd, H., Mason, C. and Pinch, S. (1998) 'The geography of corporate philanthropy in the United Kingdom', *Environment and Planning C*, 16: 3–24.

Hutter, K. and Hoffmann, S. (2011) 'Guerrilla marketing: The nature of the concept and propositions for further research', *Asian Journal of Marketing,* 5: 39–54.

Hvenegaard, G. (1994) 'Ecotourism: A status report and conceptual framework', *Journal of Tourism Studies,* 5(2): 24–35.

IATA (2008) 'Aviation carbon offset programme: IATA guidelines and toolkit'. Online. Available HTTP: www.iata.org/whatwedo/environment/Documents/carbon-offset-guidelines-may2008.pdf (accessed 10 October 2013).

ICEBeRG and Francis, J. (2006) 'Designing theoretically-informed implementation interventions', *Implementation Science*, 1: 4, doi: 10.1186/1748-5908-1-4.

Information Daily (2010) '79% of Britons support charities using shock strategy to highlight awareness of their issue', *Information Daily*, 16 April. Online. Available HTTP: www.theinformationdaily.com/2010/04/16/79-of-britons-support-charities-using-shock-strategy-to-highlight-awareness-of-their-issue (accessed 1 April 2013).

Iyengar, S. and Kinder, D. K. (1987) *News That Matters: Television and American Opinion*. Chicago, IL: University of Chicago Press.

Izquierdo, C. C. and Samaniego, M. J. G. (2007) 'How alternative marketing strategies impact the performance of Spanish museums', *Journal of Management Development*, 26: 809–831.

Jackson, R. and Wangchuk, R. (2004) 'A community-based approach to mitigating livestock depredation by snow leopards', *Human Dimensions of Wildlife*, 9(4): 307–315.

Jackson, T. (2005) 'Live better by consuming less? Is there a "double dividend" in sustainable consumption', *Journal of Industrial Ecology*, 9(1–2): 19–36.

Jäger, T. and Eisend, M. (2013) 'Effects of fear-arousing and humorous appeals in social marketing advertising: the moderating role of prior attitude toward the advertised behavior', *Journal of Current Issues and Research in Advertising*, 34(1): 125–134.

Jahdi, K. S. and Acikdilli, G. (2009) 'Marketing communications and corporate social responsibility (CSR): Marriage of convenience or shotgun wedding?' *Journal of Business Ethics*, 88(1): 103–113.

Jalleh, G., Donovan, R. J., Giles-Corti, B. and Holman, C. A. J. (2002) 'Sponsorship: Impact on brand awareness and brand attitudes', *Social Marketing Quarterly*, 8(1): 35–45.

Jamal, T. and Watt, E. M. (2011) 'Climate change pedagogy and performative action: Toward community-based destination governance', *Journal of Sustainable Tourism*, 19: 571–588.

Jamrozy, U. (2007) 'Marketing of tourism: A paradigm shift toward sustainability', *International Journal of Culture, Tourism and Hospitality Research*, 1(2): 117–130.

Jansson, J., Marell, A. and Nordlund, A. (2010) 'Green consumer behavior: Determinants of curtailment and eco-innovation adoption', *Journal of Consumer Marketing*, 27(4): 358–370.

Jansson, J., Marell, A. and Nordlund, A. (2011) Exploring consumer adoption of a high involvement eco-innovation using value-belief-norm theory', *Journal of Consumer Behaviour*, 10(1): 51–60.

Jenkins, C. J. (1980) 'Tourism policies in developing countries: a critique', *International Journal of Tourism Management*, 1: 22–29.

Jenkins, C. J. (1982) 'The use of investment incentives for tourism projects in developing countries', *Tourism Management*, 3(2): 91–97.

Jenkins, C. J. and Henry, B. M. (1982) 'Government involvement in tourism in developing countries', *Annals of Tourism Research*, 9: 499–521.

Jenkins, H. and Yakovleva, N. (2006) 'Corporate social responsibility in the mining industry: Exploring trends in social and environmental disclosure', *Journal of Cleaner Production*, 14(3): 271–284.

Jenkins, J. M. (2000) 'The dynamics of regional tourism organisations in New South Wales, Australia: History, structures and operations', *Current Issues in Tourism*, 3: 175–203.

Jentoft, S. (2007) 'Limits of governability: Institutional implications for fisheries and coastal governance', *Marine Policy*, 31: 360–370.

Jessop, B. (1998) 'The rise of governance and the risks of failure: The case of economic development', *International Social Science Journal*, 50(155): 29–45.

Johnston, M. and Dixon, D. (2008) 'What happened to behaviour in the decade of behaviour?' *Psychology and Health*, 23: 509–513.

Joireman, J., Lasane, T. P., Bennet, J., Richards, D. and Solaimani, S. (2001) 'Integrating social value orientation and the consideration of future consequences within the extended norm activation model of proenvironmental behavior', *British Journal of Social Psychology*, 40: 133–155.

Jones, J. L. and Leary, M. R. (1994) 'Effects of appearance-based admonitions against sun exposure on tanning intentions in young adults', *Health Psychology*, 13(1): 86–90.

Jones, P. (2011) 'Conceptualising car "dependence"', in K. Lucas, E. Blumenberg and R. Weinberger (eds) *Auto Motives: Understanding Car Use Behaviours*. Bingley: Emerald Publishing.

Jones, R., Pykett, J. and Whitehead, M. (2011) 'Governing temptation: Changing behaviour in an age of libertarian paternalism', *Progress in Human Geography*, 35(4): 483–501.

Jones, S. (1982) 'Social marketing-dimensions of power and politics', *European Journal of Marketing*, 16(6): 46–53.

Jones, S. (2005) 'Community-based ecotourism: The significance of social capital', *Annals of Tourism Research,* 23(2): 303–325.

Jones, S. C. and Donovan, R. J. (2004) 'Does theory inform practice in health promotion in Australia?' *Health Education Research*, 19(1): 1–14.

Jordan, A. (2001) 'The European Union: an evolving system of multi-level governance ... or government?' *Policy and Politics*, 29(2): 193–208.

Jordan, A., Wurzel, R. K. W. and Zito, A. (2005) 'The rise of "new" policy instruments in comparative perspective: has governance eclipsed government?' *Political Studies*, 53: 477–496.

Judge, D., Stoker, G. and Wolman, H. (1995) 'Urban politics and theory: An introduction', in D. Judge, G. Stoker and H. Wolman (eds) *Theories of Urban Politics*. London: Sage.

Kaczynski, A. T. (2008) 'A more tenable marketing for leisure services and studies', *Leisure Sciences: An Interdisciplinary Journal*, 30: 253–272.

Kahneman, D., Krueger, A. B., Schkade, D., Schwarz, N. and Stone, A. A. (2006) 'Would you be happier if you were richer? A focusing illusion', *Science,* 312(5782): 1908–1910.

Kant, I. [1785] (1996) *The Metaphysics of Morals*, translated and edited by M. Gregor. Cambridge: Cambridge University Press.

Kaplan, A. and Haenlein, M. (2009) 'The increasing importance of public marketing: Explanations, applications and limits of marketing within public administration', *European Management Journal*, 27(3): 197–212.

Kaplan, A. and Haenlein, M. (2010) 'Users of the world, unite! The challenges and opportunities of social media', *Business Horizons,* 53: 59–68.

Kassirer, J. and McKenzie-Mohr, D. (1998) *Tools of Change: Proven Methods for Promoting Environmental Citizenship*. Ottawa: National Round Table on the Environment and the Economy.

Katyal, S. (2010) 'Stealth marketing and anti-branding: The love that dare not speak its name', *Buffalo Law Review*, 58: 795–849.

Kavaratzis, M. and Ashworth, G. (2008) 'Place marketing: How did we get here and where are we going?' *Journal of Place Management and Development*, 1(2): 150–165.

Kazbare, L., van Trijp, H. C. and Eskildsen, J. K. (2010) 'A-priori and post-hoc segmentation in the design of healthy eating campaigns', *Journal of Marketing Communications*, 16(1–2): 21–45.

Keen, S. (2011) *Debunking Economics – Revised and Expanded Edition: The Naked Emperor Dethroned?* London: Zed Books.

Keller, C., Fleury, J., Gregor-Holt, N. and Thompson, T. (1999) 'Predictive ability of social cognitive theory in exercise research: An integrated literature review', *Online Journal of Knowledge Synthesis for Nursing*, 6: 2.

Keller, C., Vega-López, S., Ainsworth, B., Nagle-Williams, A., Records, K., Permana, P. and Coonrod, D. (2012) 'Social marketing: Approach to cultural and contextual relevance in a community-based physical activity intervention', *Health Promotion International*, in press, doi: 10.1186/1748-5908-1-4.

Keller, E. W., Datoon, M. C. and Shaw, D. (2010) 'NPO branding: Preliminary lessons from major players', *International Journal of Nonprofit and Voluntary Sector Marketing*, 15(2): 105–121.

Keller, P. A. and Lehmann, D. R. (2008) 'Designing effective health communications: A meta-analysis', *Journal of Public Policy and Marketing*, 27(2): 117–130.

Kelly, K. J., Edwards, R. W., Comello, M. L. G., Plested, B. A., Thurman, P. J. and Slater, M. D. (2003) 'The Community Readiness Model: A complementary approach to social marketing', *Marketing Theory*, 3(4): 411–426.

Kennedy, A. L. (2010) 'Using community-based social marketing techniques to enhance environmental regulation', *Sustainability*, 2(4): 1138–1160.

Kern, C. L. (2006) 'Demarketing as a tool for managing visitor demand in national parks: An Australian case study'. Masters dissertation, University of Canberra.

Kern, K. and Bulkeley, H. (2009) 'Cities, Europeanization and multi-level governance: Governing climate change through transnational municipal networks', *Journal of Common Market Studies*, 47: 309–332.

Kersbergen, K. V. and Waarden, F. V. (2004) '"Governance" as a bridge between disciplines: Cross-disciplinary inspiration regarding shifts in governance and problems of governability, accountability and legitimacy', *European Journal of Political Research*, 43: 143–171.

Khanna, M. and Anton, W. (2002) 'What is driving corporate environmentalism: Opportunity or threat?', *Corporate Environmental Strategy*, 9(4): 409–417.

Kim, K., Uysal, M. and Sirgy, M. J. (2013) 'How does tourism in a community impact the quality of life of community residents?', *Tourism Management*, 36: 527–540.

Kim, M., Gibson, H. and Ko, Y. J. (2011) 'Understanding donors to university performing arts programs: Who are they and why do they contribute?' *Managing Leisure*, 16(1): 17–35.

Kim, Y. and Han, H. (2010) 'Intention to pay conventional-hotel prices at a green hotel: A modification of the theory of planned behavior', *Journal of Sustainable Tourism*, 18(8): 997–1014.

Kindra, G. S. and Taylor, D. W. (1995) 'Demarketing inappropriate health care consumption', *Journal of Health Care Marketing*, 15(2): 11–14.

King, J. (2002) 'Destination marketing organisations: Connecting the experience rather than promoting the place', *Journal of Vacation Marketing*, 8(2): 105–108.

Kingston, T. (2012) 'Vatican in row over "drunken tourist herds" destroying Sistine Chapel's majesty: Author Pietro Citati calls for limit on crowd numbers to preserve Michelangelo's art in Vatican City, Rome', *The Observer*, 29 September. Online. Available HTTP: www.guardian.co.uk/world/2012/sep/29/sistine-chapel-tourist-row (accessed 29 September 2012).

Kirby, J. and Marsden, P. (2005) *Connected Marketing: The Viral, Buzz and Word of Mouth Revolution*. Burlington, MA: Butterworth-Heinemann.

Kiss, A. (2004) 'Is community-based ecotourism a good use of biodiversity conservation funds?', *Trends in Ecology and Evolution*, 19(5): 232–237.

Kjaer, A. (2004) *Governance*. Cambridge: Polity Press.

Kleanhous, A. and Peck, J. (2006) *Let Them Eat Cake: Satisfying the New Consumer Appetite for Responsible Brands*. Godalming: World Wildlife Fund UK.

Kluvánková-Oravská, T., Chobotová, V., Banaszak, I., Slavikova, L. and Trifunovova, S. (2009) 'From government to governance for biodiversity: the perspective of central and Eastern European transition countries', *Environmental Policy and Governance*, 19: 186–196.

Knight, A. T., Cowling, R. M., Boshoff, A. F., Wilson, S. L. and Pierce, S. M. (2011) 'Walking in STEP: Lessons for linking spatial prioritisations to implementation strategies', *Biological Conservation*, 144(1): 202–211.

Knill, C. and Lenschow, A. (eds) (2000a) *Implementing EU Environmental Policy: New Directions and Old Problems*. Manchester: Manchester University Press.

Knill, C. and Lenschow, A. (2000b) 'Introduction: New approaches to reach effective implementation – political rhetoric or sound concepts?' in C. Knill and A. Lenschow (eds) *Implementing EU Environmental Policy: New Directions and Old Problems*. Manchester: Manchester University Press.

Knill, C. and Lenschow, A. (2003) 'Modes of regulation in the governance of the European Union: Towards a comprehensive evaluation', *European Integration Online Papers* (*EIOP*), 7(1). Online. Available HTTP: http://eiop.or.at/eiop/texte/2003-001a.htm (accessed 10 October 2013).

Kohl, J. (2005) 'Putting environmental interpretation to work for conservation in a park setting: Conceptualizing principal conservation strategies', *Applied Environmental Education and Communication*, 4(1): 43–54.

Kooiman, J. (2003) *Governing as Governance*. Los Angeles, CA: Sage.

Korda, R. C., Hills, J. M. and Gray, T. S. (2008) 'Fishery decline in Utila: Disentangling the web of governance', *Marine Policy*, 32: 968–979.

Korn, D. A. and Shaffer, H. J. (1999). 'Gambling and the health of the public: Adopting a public health perspective', *Journal of Gambling Studies*, 15(4): 289–365.

Kotler, P. (1973) 'The major tasks of marketing management', *The Journal of Marketing*, 37(4): 42–49.

Kotler, P. (1983) *Principles of Marketing*. Englewood Cliffs, NJ: Prentice Hall.

Kotler, P. (2005) 'The role played by the broadening of marketing movement in the history of marketing thought', *Journal of Public Policy and Marketing*, 24(1): 114–116.

Kotler, P. (2006) *Principles of Marketing*, third edition. Sydney: Pearson Education.

Kotler, P. and Armstrong, G. (2001) *Principals of Marketing*. Harlow: Prentice Hall.

Kotler, P. and Levy, S. J. (1971) 'Demarketing? Yes, demarketing!' *Harvard Business Review*, 49(6): 74–80.

Kotler, P. and Roberto, E. L. (1989) *Social Marketing: Strategies for Changing Public Behaviour*. New York: Free Press.

Kotler, P. and Zaltman, G. (1971) 'Social marketing: An approach to planned social change', *Journal of Marketing*, 35(3): 3–12.

Kotler, P., Armstrong, G., Saunders, J. and Wong, V. (2001) 'Marketing in a changing world', in D. W. Barnes (ed.) *Understanding Business Processes*. London: Routledge.

Kotler, P., Roberto, N. and Lee, N. (2002) *Social Marketing: Improving the Quality of Life*, second edition. Thousand Oaks, CA: Sage Publications.

Kraus, S., Harms, R. and Fink, M. (2009) 'Entrepreneurial marketing: Moving beyond marketing in new ventures', *International Entrepreneurship and Innovation Management,* 11(1): 19–34.

Krause, N. K. (2010) 'Air tax rise to mean fewer tourists – PM', *Dominion Post*, 3 November. Online. Available HTTP: www.stuff.co.nz/business/industries/4300903/Air-tax-rise-to-mean-fewer-tourists-PM (accessed 10 October 2013).

Krebs, P., Prochaska, J. O. and Rossi, J. S. (2010) 'A meta-analysis of computer-tailored interventions for health behavior change', *Preventative Medicine*, 51(3–4): 214–221.

Kreuter, M., Farrell, D., Olevitch, L. and Brennan, L. (2000) *Tailoring Health Messages: Customizing Communication With Computer Technology*. Mahwah, NJ: Lawrence Erlbaum.

Kreuter, M. W. and Wray, R. J. (2003) 'Tailored and targeted health communication: Strategies for enhancing information relevance', *American Journal of Health Behavior*, 27(Supplement 3), S227–S232.

Krippendorf, J. (1987) *The Holiday Makers*. Oxford: Butterworth-Heinemann.

Kroesen, M. (2013) 'Exploring people's viewpoints on air travel and climate change: understanding inconsistencies', *Journal of Sustainable Tourism*, 21(2): 271–290.

Kronenberg, J. and Lida, N. (2011) 'Simple living and sustainable consumption', *Problems of Sustainable Development*, 6(2): 67–74.

Kruger, O. (2005) 'The role of ecotourism in conservation: Panacea or Pandora's Box?', *Biodiversity and Conservation,* 14: 579–600.

Laczniak, G. R., Lusch, R. F. and Murphy, P. E. (1979) 'Social marketing: Its ethical dimensions', *Journal of Marketing*, 43(2): 29–36.

Lakatos, I. (1971) 'History of science and its rational reconstruction', in R. Buck and R. Cohen (eds) *Boston Studies in the Philosophy of Science Volume 8*. Dordrecht: Reidel.

Lam, T. and Hsu, C. H. (2006) 'Predicting behavioral intention of choosing a travel destination', *Tourism Management*, 27: 589–599.

Lane, B. (2009) 'Thirty years of sustainable tourism: Drivers, progress, problems—and the future', in S. Gössling, C. M. Hall and D. Weaver (eds) *Sustainable Tourism Futures: Perspectives on Systems, Restructuring and Innovations*. London: Routledge.

Lasn, K. (1999) *The Uncooling of America*. New York: Eagle Brook.

Latouche, S. (2004) 'Why less should be so much more: Degrowth economics', *Le Monde Diplomatique, English Edition LMD*, November. Online. Available HTTP: http://mondediplo.com/2004/11/14latouche (accessed 25 January 2009).

Latouche, S. (2006) 'How do we learn to want less? The globe downshifted', *Le Monde Diplomatique, English Edition LMD*, January. Online. Available HTTP: http://mondediplo.com/2006/01/13degrowth (accessed 25 January 2009).

Latour, B. and Woolgar, S. (1986) *Laboratory Life: The Construction of Scientific Facts*. Princeton, NJ: Princeton University Press.

Lazer, W. and Kelley, E. (1973) *Social Marketing: Perspectives and Viewpoints*. Homewood, IL: Richard D. Irwin.

Lebel, L. and Shamsub, H. (2012) 'Identifying tourists with sustainable behaviour: A study of international tourists to Thailand', *Journal of Environmental Management and Tourism*, 1(5): 26–40.

Lecocq, F. and Capoor, K. (2005) *State and Trends of the Carbon Market 2005*. Washington, DC: The World Bank Carbon Fund and the International Emissions Trading Association. Online. Available HTTP: www-wds.worldbank.org (accessed 19 November 2012).

Lee, J. E. and Lemyre, L. (2009) 'A social-cognitive perspective of terrorism risk perception and individual response in Canada', *Risk Analysis*, 29: 1265–1280.

Lee, J. S., Hsu, L. T., Han, H. and Kim, Y. (2010). 'Understanding how consumers view green hotels: How a hotel's green image can influence behavioural intentions', *Journal of Sustainable Tourism*, 18(7), 901–914.

Lee, M., Motion, J. and Conroy, D. (2009) 'Anti-consumption and brand avoidance', *Journal of Business Research*, 62(2): 169–180.

Lee, N. R., Rothschild, M. L. and Smith, W. (2011) *A Declaration of Social Marketing's Unique Principles and Distinctions*. Online. Available HTTP: www.i-socialmarketing.org/treasure/foundit.pdf (accessed 1 April 2013).

Lee, S. T. and Basnyat, I. (2013) 'From press release to news: Mapping the framing of the 2009 H1N1 A influenza pandemic', *Health Communication*, 28(2): 119–132.

Lefebvre, R. C. (2007) 'The new technology: The consumer as participant rather than target audience', *Social Marketing Quarterly*, 13: 31–42.

Lefebvre, R. C. (2011) 'An integrative model for social marketing', *Journal of Social Marketing*, 1(1): 54–72.

Lefebvre, R. C. (2012) 'Transformative social marketing: Co-creating the social marketing discipline and brand', *Journal of Social Marketing*, 2(2): 118–129.

Lefebvre, R. C. and Rochlin, L. (1997) 'Social marketing', in K. Glanz, F. M. Lewis and B. K. Rimer (eds) *Health Behavior and Health Education: Theory, Research and Practice*. San Francisco, CA: Jossey-Bass.

Leiper, N., Stear, L., Hing, N. and Firth, T. (2008) 'Partial industrialisation in tourism: A new model', *Current Issues in Tourism*, 11: 207–235.

Lemarié, L. and Chebat, J. C. (2013) 'Resist or comply: Promoting responsible gambling among youth', *Journal of Business Research*, 66: 137–140.

Lennon, J. J. (ed.) (2003) *Tourism Statistics: International Perspectives and Current Issues*. London: Continuum.

Leonard-Barton, D. (1981) 'Voluntary simplicity lifestyles and energy conservation', *Journal of Consumer Research*, 8: 243–252.

Leventhal, H. and Cameron, L. (1987) 'Behavioral theories and the problem of compliance', *Patient Education and Counseling*, 10(2): 117–138.

Leventhal, H., Leventhal, E. A. and Contrada, R. J. (1998) 'Self-regulation, health, and behavior: A perceptual–cognitive approach', *Psychology and Health*, 13(4): 717–733.

Leventhal, H., Safer, M. A. and Panagis, D. M. (1983) 'The impact of communications on the self-regulation of health beliefs, decisions, and behavior', *Health Education and Behavior*, 10(1): 3–29.

Levin, L. S. and Ziglio, E. (1996) 'Health promotion as an investment strategy: Considerations on theory and practice', *Health Promotion International*, 11(1): 33–40.

Levinson, J. C. (1987) 'Guerilla marketing: Winning without weapons', *Industrial Distribution*, 76(5): 87–90.

Levy, S. J. (1981) 'Interpreting consumer mythology: A structural approach to consumer behavior', *Journal of Marketing*, 45: 49–61.

Lewis, I. M., Watson, B. C. and Tay, R. S. (2007a) 'Examining the effectiveness of physical threats in road safety advertising: The role of the third-person effect, gender, and age', *Transportation Research Part F: Traffic Psychology and Behaviour*, 10(1): 48–60.

Lewis, I. M., Watson, B. C., Tay, R. S. and White, K. M. (2007b) 'The role of fear appeals in improving driver safety: A review of the effectiveness of fear-arousing (threat) appeals in road safety advertising', *International Journal of Behavioral and Consultation Therapy*, 3(2): 203–222.

Li, W. (2006) 'Community decision making, participation in development', *Annals of Tourism Research*, 33(1): 132–143.

Lill, D. C., Gross, C. W. and Peterson, R. T. (1986) 'The inclusion of social-responsibility themes by magazine advertisers: A longitudinal study', *Journal of Advertising*, 15(2): 35–41.

Lime, D. and Stankey, G. (1975) 'Carrying capacity: Maintaining outdoor recreation quality', in *Proceedings of the Forest Recreation Symposium*. Upper Darby, PA: Northeast Experiment Station.

Lindblom, C. E. (1977) *Politics and Markets*. New York: Basic Books.

Lombard, D., Neubauer, T. E., Canfield, D. and Winett, R. A. (1991) 'Behavioural community intervention to reduce the risk of skin cancer', *Journal of Applied Behaviour Analysis*, 24(4): 677–686.

Longo, J. (2007) *Communication in the Policy Process*. Victoria: Whitehall Policy Consulting.

Lorenzoni, I., Nicholson-Cole, S. and Whitmarsh, L. (2007) 'Barriers perceived to engaging with climate change among the UK public and their policy implications', *Global Environmental Change*, 17: 445–459.

Lorenzoni, I., Seyfang, G. and Nye, M. (2011) 'Carbon budgets and carbon capability: Lessons from personal carbon trading', in I. Whitmarsh, S. O'Neill and I. Lorenzoni (eds), *Engaging the Public with Climate Change: Behaviour Change and Communication*. London: Earthscan.

Luca, N. R. and Suggs, L. S. (2010) 'Strategies for the social marketing mix: A systematic review', *Social Marketing Quarterly*, 16(4): 122–149.

Luca, N. R. and Suggs, L. S. (2013) 'Theory and model use in social marketing health interventions', *Journal of Health Communication*, 18(1): 20–40.

Luck, D. J. (1974) 'Social marketing: Confusion compounded', *Journal of Marketing*, 38(4): 70–72.

Lund-Thomsen, P. (2004) 'Towards a critical framework on corporate social and environmental responsibility in the south: The case of Pakistan', *Development*, 47(3): 106–113.

Lynes, J. K. and Andrachuk, M. (2008) 'Motivations for corporate social and environmental responsibility: A case study of Scandinavian Airlines', *Journal of International Management*, 14: 377–390.

Lynes, J. K. and Dredge, D. (2006) 'Going green: Motivations for environmental commitment in the airline industry. A case study of Scandinavian Airlines', *Journal of Sustainable Tourism*, 14(2): 116–138.

Mackenzie, I. (2009) 'Safe sex campaign "wasted money"', BBC News, 29 May. Online. Available HTTP: http://news.bbc.co.uk/2/hi/uk_news/8074914.stm (accessed 1 April 2013).

MacKuen, M. B. and Coombs, S. L. (1981) *More Than News: Media Power in Public Affairs*. Beverly Hills, CA: Sage.

MacStravic, S. (1995) 'Remarketing, yes, remarketing health care', *Journal of Health Care Marketing*, 15(4): 57–58.

Madden, T. J., Ellen, P. S. and Ajzen, I. (1992) 'A comparison of the theory of planned behavior and the theory of reasoned action', *Personality and Social Psychology Bulletin*, 18(1): 3–9.

Madill, J. and O'Reilly, N. (2010) 'Investigating social marketing sponsorships: Terminology, stakeholders, and objectives', *Journal of Business Research*, 63(2): 133–139.

Maes, S. and Karoly, P. (2005) 'Self-regulation assessment and intervention in physical health and illness: A review', *Applied Psychology*, 54: 267–299.

Mah, M. W., Tam, Y. C. and Deshpande, S. (2008) 'Social marketing analysis of 2 years of hand hygiene promotion', *Infection Control and Hospital Epidemiology*, 29(3): 262–270.

Maibach, E. W. and Parrott, R. L. (eds) (1995) *Designing Health Messages: Approaches from Communication Theory and Public Health Practice*. Thousand Oaks, CA: Sage.

Mair, J. (2011) 'Exploring air travellers' voluntary carbon-offsetting behaviour', *Journal of Sustainable Tourism*, 19: 215–230.

Majone, G. (1980) 'The uses of policy analysis', in G. Raven (ed.) *Policy Studies Review Annual*, Vol. 4. Beverly Hills, CA: Sage.

Majone, G. (1981) 'Policies as theories', in I. L. Horowitz (ed.) *Policy Studies Review Annual*, Vol. 5. Beverly Hills, CA: Sage.

Majone, G. (1989) *Evidence, Argument, and Persuasion in the Policy Process*. New Haven, CT: Yale University Press.

Mannheimer, S. B., Morse, E., Matts, J. P., Andrews, L., Child, C., Schmetter B. and Friedland, G. H. (2006) 'Sustained benefit from a long-term antiretroviral adherence intervention: Results of a large randomized clinical trial', *Journal of Acquired Immune Deficiency Syndrome*, 43(Suppl 1): S41–S47.

Manning, M. (2009) 'The effects of subjective norms on behaviour in the theory of planned behaviour: A meta-analysis', *British Journal of Social Psychology*, 48: 649–705.

Manoochehri, J. (2001) *Consumption Opportunities: Strategies for Change*. Geneva: UNEP.

Marcell, K., Agyeman, J. and Rappaport, A. (2004) 'Cooling the campus: Experiences from a pilot study to reduce electricity use at Tufts University, USA, using social marketing methods', *International Journal of Sustainability in Higher Education*, 5(2): 169–189.

Marcus, B., Owen, N., Forsyth, L., Cavill, N. and Fridinger, F. (1998). 'Physical activity interventions using mass media, print media, and information technology'. *American Journal of Preventive Medicine*, 15(4), 362–378.

Maréchal, K. (2007) 'The economics of climate change and the change of climate in economics', *Energy Policy*, 35: 5181–5194.

Maréchal, K. (2010) 'Not irrational but habitual: The importance of "behavioural lock-in" in energy consumption', *Ecological Economics*, 69: 1104–1114.

Mark, A. and Elliott, R. (1997) 'Demarketing dysfunctional demand in the UK National Health Service', *International Journal of Health Planning and Management*, 12: 296–314.

Marks, G., Hooghe, L. and Blank, K. (1996) 'European integration from the 1980s: State-centric v. multi-level governance', *Journal of Common Market Studies*, 34: 341–378.

Markusen, A. (1999) 'Fuzzy concepts, scanty evidence, policy distance: The case for rigour and policy relevance in critical regional studies', *Regional Studies*, 33: 869–884.

Marnet, O. (2008) 'Behaviour and rationality in corporate governance', *International Journal of Behavioural Accounting and Finance*, 1(1): 4–22.

Martens, S. and Spaargaren, G. (2005) 'The politics of sustainable consumption: The case of the Netherlands', *Sustainability: Science, Practice, and Policy*, 1(1): 29–42.

Marx, K. [1867] (2001) *Capital: A Critique of Political Economy*. Harmondsworth: Penguin Books in association with New Left Review.

Matarrita-Cascante, D., Brennan, M. A. and Luloff, A. E. (2010) 'Community agency and sustainable tourism development: The case of La Fortuna, Costa Rica', *Journal of Sustainable Tourism*, 18(6): 735–756.

McDermott, L., Stead, M. and Hastings, G. (2005) 'What is and what is not social marketing: The challenge of reviewing the evidence', *Journal of Marketing Management*, 21: 545–553.

McDivitt, J. (2003) 'Is there a role for branding in social marketing?' *Social Marketing Quarterly*, 9(3): 11–17.

McDonald, S. (2009) 'Changing climate, changing minds: Applying the literature on media effects, public opinion, and the issue-attention cycle to increase public understanding of climate change', *International Journal of Sustainability Communication*, 4: 45–63.

McGehee, N. G. and Andereck, K. L. (2004). 'Factors predicting rural residents' support of tourism,' *Journal of Travel Research*, 43(2): 131–140.

McGehee, N. G. and Andereck, K. (2009) 'Volunteer tourism and the "voluntoured": the case of Tijuana, Mexico', *Journal of Sustainable Tourism*, 17(1): 39–51.

McGehee, N. G. and Santos, C. (2005) 'Social change, discourse and volunteer tourism', *Annals of Tourism Research,* 32(3): 760–779.

McGeoch, M. A., Chown, S. L. and Kalwij, J. M. (2006) 'A global indicator for biological invasion', *Conservation Biology*, 20: 1635–1646.

McGuigan, J. (2006) 'The politics of cultural studies and cool capitalism', *Cultural Politics*, 2: 137–158.

McKenzie-Mohr, D. (2000a) 'New ways to promote proenvironmental behavior: Promoting sustainable behavior: An introduction to community-based social marketing', *Journal of Social Issues*, 56(3): 543–554.

McKenzie-Mohr, D. (2000b) 'Fostering sustainable behaviour through community-based social marketing', *American Psychologist*, 55(5): 531–537.

McKenzie-Mohr, D. (2005) 'Community-based social marketing', *Water*, 32(2): 18–23.

McKenzie-Mohr, D. (2011) *Fostering Sustainable Behavior: An introduction to Community-Based Social Marketing*. Gabriola Island: New Society Publishers.

McKenzie-Mohr, D. and Smith, W. (1999) *Fostering Sustainable Behavior: An Introduction to Community-Based Social Marketing*. Gabriola Island: New Society Publishers.

McKercher, B. (1993) 'The unrecognized threat to tourism: Can tourism survive "sustainability"?', *Tourism Management*, 14(2): 131–136.

McKercher, B., Prideaux, B., Cheung, C. and Law, R. (2010) 'Achieving voluntary reductions in the carbon footprint of tourism and climate change', *Journal of Sustainable Tourism*, 18(3): 297–317.

McKercher, B., Weber, K. and du Cros, H. (2008) 'Rationalising inappropriate behaviour at contested sites', *Journal of Sustainable Tourism*, 16: 369–385.

McLeod, G., Insch, A. and Henry, J. (2011) 'Reducing barriers to sun protection – application of a holistic model for social marketing', *Australasian Marketing Journal*, 19(3): 212–222.

McMahon, L. (2002) 'The impact of social marketing on social engineering in economic restructuring', *Journal of Nonprofit and Public Sector Marketing*, 9(4): 75–84.

Meadowcroft, J. (2007) 'Who is in charge here? Governance for sustainable development in a complex world', *Journal of Environmental Policy and Planning*, 9: 299–314.

Meadows, D. H., Meadows, D. L., Randers, J. and Behrens III, W. W. (1972) *The Limits to Growth*. New York: Universe Books.

Medina, L. K. (2005) 'Ecotourism and certification: Confronting the principles and pragmatics of socially responsible tourism', *Journal of Sustainable Tourism*, 13: 281–295.

Meltsner, A. J. (1980) 'Don't slight communication: Some problems of analytical practice', in G. Majone and E. S. Quade (eds) *Pitfalls of Analysis*. Chichester: John Wiley & Sons.

Mendleson, N. and Polonsky, M. J. (1995) 'Using strategic alliances to develop credible green marketing', *Journal of Consumer Marketing*, 12(2): 4–18.

Mendoza, A. (1999) 'Feeling exploited by brand overkill', *Marketing*, 24. Online. Available HTTP: www.marketingmagazine.co.uk/news/52076/> (accessed 26 November 2012).

Menegaki, A. N. (2012) 'A social marketing mix for renewable energy in Europe based on consumer stated preference surveys', *Renewable Energy*, 39(1): 30–39.

Merritt, R. Truss, A. and Hopwood, T. (2011) 'Social marketing can help achieve sustainable behaviour change', Guardian Professional Network, guardian.co.uk, 17 March. Online. Available http: www. guardian.co.uk/sustainable-business/blog/social-marketing-behaviour-change? (accessed 1 April 2013).

Messerlian, C. and Derevensky, J. (2006) 'Social marketing campaigns for youth gambling prevention: Lessons learned from youth', *International Journal of Mental Health and Addiction*, 4(4): 294–306.

Messerlian, C., Byrne, A. M. and Derevensky, J. L. (2004) 'Gambling, youth and the Internet: Should we be concerned?', *The Canadian Child and Adolescent Psychiatry Review*, 13(1): 3–6.

Messerlian, C., Derevensky, J. and Gupta, R. (2005) 'Youth gambling problems: A public health perspective', *Health Promotion International*, 20(1): 69–80.

Michie, S. and Abraham, C. (2008) Advancing the science of behaviour change: A plea for scientific reporting', *Addiction*, 103(9): 1409–1410.

Michie, S. and West, R. (2013) 'Behaviour change theory and evidence: A presentation to government', *Health Psychology Review*, 7(1): 1–22.

Michie, S., Fixsen, D., Grimshaw, J. M. and Eccles, M. P. (2009) 'Specifying and reporting complex behaviour change interventions: The need for a scientific method', *Implement Science*, 4(40): 1–6.

Michie, S., Johnston, M., Abraham, C., Lawton, R., Parker, D. and Walker, A. (2005) 'Making psychological theory useful for implementing evidence based practice: A consensus approach', *Quality and Safety in Health Care*, 14: 26–33.

Michie, S., Johnston, M., Francis, J., Hardeman, W. and Eccles, M. (2008) 'From theory to intervention: Mapping theoretically derived behavioural determinants to behaviour change techniques', *Applied Psychology*, 57: 660–680.

Michielsen, K., Chersich, M., Temmerman, M., Dooms, T. and Van Rossem, R. (2012) 'Nothing as practical as a good theory? The theoretical basis of HIV prevention interventions for young people in sub-Saharan Africa: a systematic review', *AIDS Research and Treatment*, 2012, http://dx.doi.org/10.1155/2012/345327.

Michot, T. (2010) *Pro-Poor Tourism in Kumarakom, Kerala, South India: Policy Implementation and Impacts*, Guild of Independent Scholars and the Journal of Alternate Perspectives in the Social Sciences, Working Paper No.7. Online. Available HTTP: www.japss.org/upload/Working_Paper_no._7_March_2010_FINAL%5B1%5D.pdf (accessed 24 July 2013).

Miles, S. (1998) *Consumerism: As a Way of Life*. London: Sage.

Millar, C. and Aiken, D. (1995) 'Conflict resolution in aquaculture: A matter of trust', in A. Boghen (ed.) *Coldwater Aquaculture in Atlantic Canada*, second edition. Moncton, Canada: Canadian Institute for Research on Regional Development.

Miller, G. A. (2003) 'Consumerism in sustainable tourism: A survey of UK consumers', *Journal of Sustainable Tourism*, 11: 17–39.

Ministry for the Environment (2003) *Waste Campaign Pilot*. Wellington: Ministry for the Environment. Online. Available HTTP: www.mfe.govt.nz/issues/waste/waste-pilot/conference-paper.html (accessed 29 March 2008).

Ministry of Health (2009) 'Appointments to health dtatutory nodies. Information on a particular statutory body: Health sponsorship council'. Online. Available HTTP: www.moh.govt.nz/moh.nsf/wpg_Index/About-SBC+-+Crown+Entities+-+Health+Sponsorship+Council (accessed 12 May 2009).

Mobile Marketing Association (2007) 'Mobile research on event sponsorship and green efforts yields high response rate and rich data during live earth concerts'. Mobile Marketing Association Case Studies, 17 December. Online. Available HTTP: www.mmaglobal.com/studies/mobile-research-event-sponsorship-and-green-efforts-yields-high-response-rate-and-rich-datea (accessed 1 April 2013).

Modiano, M. (1988) 'Rowdy Brits not wanted in Greece', *Sunday Times*, 10 January.

Moor, L. (2012) 'Beyond cultural intermediaries? A socio-technical perspective on the market for social interventions', *European Journal of Cultural Studies*, 15: 563–580.

Moore, S. (2012) 'Some things are better left unsaid: How word of mouth influences the storyteller', *Journal of Consumer Research*, 38(6): 1140–1154.

Moore, S. R. (2005) 'The sociological impact of attitudes toward smoking: Secondary effects of the demarketing of smoking', *The Journal of Social Psychology*, 145: 703–718.

Morgan, G. (1986) *Images of Organization*. Newbury Park, CA: Sage.

Morgan, J. (2010) 'The rise of the casino resort', *Journal of Urban Regeneration and Renewal*, 3: 385–394.

Morgan, N., Pritchard, A. and Pride, R. (2002) *Destination Branding: Creating the Unique Destination Proposition*. Oxford: Butterworth-Heinemann.

Morse, S. S. (1993) 'AIDS and beyond: Defining the rules for viral traffic', in E. Fee and D. M. Fox (eds) *AIDS: The Making of a Chronic Disease*. Berkeley, CA: University of California Press.

Moser, S. C. (2010) 'Communicating climate change: History, challenges, process and future directions', *WIRES (Wiley Interdisciplinary Reviews): Climate Change*, 1(1): 31–53.

Mozumder, P., Berrens, R. P. and Bohara, A. K. (2006) 'Is there an environmental Kuznets curve for the risk of biodiversity loss?' *The Journal of Developing Areas*, 39(2): 175–190.

Mui, A. C., Glajchen, M., Chen, H. and Sun, J. (2013) 'Developing an older adult volunteer program in a New York Chinese community: An evidence-based approach', *Ageing International*, 38(2): 108–121.

Mulilis, J. P. and Lippa, R. (1990) 'Behavioral change in earthquake preparedness due to negative threat appeals: A test of protection motivation theory', *Journal of Applied Social Psychology*, 20(8): 619–638.

Munro, S., Lewin, S., Swart, T. and Volmink, J. (2007) 'A review of health behaviour theories: How useful are these for developing interventions to promote long-term medication adherence for TB and HIV/AIDS?' *BMC Public Health*, 7: 104.

Murphy, P. E. (1983) 'Tourism as a community industry – an ecological model of tourism development', *Tourism Management*, 4: 180–193.

Murphy, P. E. (1985) *Tourism: A Community Approach*. New York: Methuen.

Murray, J. B. (2002) 'The politics of consumption: A re-inquiry on Thompson and Haytko's (1997). Speaking of Fashion', *Journal of Consumer Research*, 29: 427–440.

Musgrove, F. (1974) *Ecstasy and Holiness: Counterculture and the Open Society*. Bloomington, IN: Indiana University Press.

Myers, D. G. (1993) *The Pursuit of Happiness: Who is Happy and Why?* New York: Avon.

Myers, D. G. (2003) 'Wealth and happiness: A limited relationship', in D. Doherty and A. Etzioni (eds) *Voluntary Simplicity: Responding to Consumer Culture*. Oxford: Rowman and Littlefield Publishers.

Myers, N., Mittermeier, R. A., Mittermeier, C. G., Da Fonseca, G. A. B. and Kent, J. (2000) 'Biodiversity hotspots for conservation priorities', *Nature*, 403: 853–858.

Nantongo, P., Byaruhanga, A. and Mugisha, A. (2007) 'Community-based conservation of critical sites: Uganda's experience', *Ostrich*, 78: 159–162.

National Research Council (1999) *Pathological Gambling: A Critical Review*. Washington, DC: National Academy Press.

National Safety Council (2013) 'About the National Safety Council'. Online. Available HTTP: www.nsc.org/about_us/Pages/Home.aspx (accessed 1 April 2013).

National Social Marketing Centre (NSMC) (2006) *Social Marketing Works: A Powerful and Adaptable Approach for Achieving and Sustaining Positive Behaviour*. London: National Consumer Council.

National Social Marketing Centre (2008) Online. Available HTTP: www.nsms.org.uk/public/default.aspx?PageID=10 (accessed 27 March 2008).

National Social Marketing Centre (2010a) *Social Marketing Benchmark Criteria*. London: NSMC. Online. Available HTTP: www.thensmc.com/sites/default/files/benchmark-criteria-090910.pdf (accessed 1 April 2013).

National Social Marketing Centre (2010b) 'What is social marketing?' Online. Available HTTP: www.nsmcentre.org.uk/node/794 (accessed 13 November 2013).

Nelson, F. (2007) *Emergent or Illusionary? Community Wildlife Management in Tanzania*. Drylands Issue Paper No. 146. London: International Institute for Environment and Development.

Nelson, M. R. and Paek, H. J. (2005) 'Cross-cultural differences in sexual advertising content in a transnational women's magazine', *Sex Roles*, 53(5–6): 371–383.

Newton-Ward, M. (2007) 'North Carolina's social marketing matrix team: Using social marketing concepts to institutionalize social Marketing capacity in a state health department', *Journal of Nonprofit & Public Sector Marketing*, 17(1–2): 55–82.

Nilsson, A., Borgstede, C. von and Biel, A. (2004) 'Willingness to accept climate change strategies: The effect of values and norms', *Journal of Environmental Psychology*, 24, 267–277.

Nilsson, J. H. and Gössling, S. (2013) 'Tourist responses to extreme environmental events: The case of Baltic Sea algal blooms', *Tourism Planning and Development*, 10(1): 32–44.

NMA Staff (2009) 'Thmbnls attracts over 220,000 visitors to its site', Ecoconsultancy, 26 March. Online. Available HTTP: http://econsultancy.com/nz/nma-archive/34193-thmbnls-attracts-over-220-000-visitors-to-its-site (accessed 1 April 2013).

Noar, S. M., Benac, C. N. and Harris, M. S. (2007) 'Does tailoring matter? Meta-analytic review of tailored print health behavior change interventions', *Psychological Bulletin*, 133(4): 673–693.

Nolan, J. M. (2010) '"An Inconvenient Truth" increases knowledge, concern, and willingness to reduce greenhouse gases', *Environment and Behavior*, 42: 643–658.

Nordlund, A. M. and Garvill, J. (2003) 'Effects of values, problem awareness, and personal norm on willingness to reduce personal car use', *Journal of Environmental Psychology*, 23: 339–347.

Northway, R., Davies, R., Mansell, I. and Jenkins, R. (2007) '"Policies don't protect people, it's how they are implemented": Policy and practice in protecting people with learning disabilities from abuse', *Social Policy and Administration*, 41(1): 86–104.

Norwegian Ministry of the Environment (1994) *Report of the Symposium on Sustainable Consumption*. Oslo.

Nunkoo, R. and Ramkissoon, H. (2010) 'Small island urban tourism: a residents' perspective', *Current Issues in Tourism*, 13: 37–60.

Nutbeam, D. (2000) 'Health literacy as a public health goal: A challenge for contemporary health education and communication strategies into the 21st century', *Health Promotion International*, 15(3): 259–267.

O'Brien, K., Sygna, L., Leichenko, R., Adger, W. N., Barnett, J., Mitchell, T., Schipper, L., Tanner, T., Vogel, C. and Mortreux, C. (2008) *Disaster Risk Reduction, Climate Change Adaptation and Human Security*. Report prepared for the Royal Norwegian Ministry of Foreign Affairs by the Global Environmental Change and Human Security (GECHS) Project, GECHS Report 2008: 3. Oslo: Ministry of Foreign Affairs.

Ockwell, D., O'Neill, S. and Whitmarsh, L. (2010) 'Behavioural insights: Motivating individual emissions cuts through communication', in C. Lever-Tracey (ed.) *Routledge Handbook of Climate Change and Society*. London: Routledge.

Okazaki, E. (2008) 'A community-based tourism model: Its conception and use', *Journal of Sustainable Tourism*, 16(5): 511–529.

Okun, M. A., Ruehlman, L., Karoly, P., Lutz, R., Fairholme, C. and Schaub, R. (2003) 'Social support and social norms: Do both contribute to predicting leisure-time exercise?' *American Journal of Health Behavior*, 27: 493–507.

Ong, T. F. and Musa, G. (2011) 'An examination of recreational divers' underwater behaviour by attitude–behaviour theories', *Current Issues in Tourism*, 14: 779–795.

Orlitzky, M., Siegel, D. S. and Waldman, D. A. (2011) 'Strategic corporate social responsibility and environmental sustainability', *Business and Society*, 50(1): 6–27.

O'Reilly, N. J. and Madill, J. J. (2007) 'Evaluating social marketing elements in sponsorship', *Social Marketing Quarterly*, 13(4): 1–25.

O'Sullivan, C. (2009) 'Mobile TV check-up: THMBNLS seriously underperforms', *GoMo News*, 4 March. Online. Available HTTP: www.gomonews.com/mobile-tv-check-up-thmbnls-seriously-underperforms/ (accessed 1 April 2013).

O'Toole, K. and Burdess, N. (2005) 'Governance at community level: Small towns in rural Victoria', *Australian Journal of Political Science*, 40: 239–254.

Owen, R. and Humphrey, P. (2009) 'The structure of online marketing communication channels', *Journal of Management and Marketing Research*, 2: 54–62.

Owens, B., Lee, D. S. and Lim, L. (2010) 'Flying into the future: Aviation emissions scenarios to 2050', *Environmental Science Technology*, 44: 2255–2260.

Oxman, A. D., Fretheim, A. and Flottorp, S. (2005) 'The OFF theory of research utilization', *Journal of Clinical Epidemiology*, 58(2): 113–116.

Paddison, R. (1993) 'City marketing, image reconstruction and urban regeneration', *Urban Studies*, 30: 339–349.

Padgett, S. M., Bekemeier, B. and Berkowitz, B. (2005) 'Building sustainable public health systems change at the state level', *Journal of Public Health Management and Practice*, 11(2): 109–115.

Palmer, A. and Koenig-Lewis, N. (2009) 'An experiential, social network-based approach to direct marketing', *Direct Marketing: An International Journal,* 3(3): 162–176.

Parry, S., Jones, R., Stern, P. and Robinson, M. (2013) '"Shockvertising": An exploratory investigation into attitudinal variations and emotional reactions to shock advertising', *Journal of Consumer Behaviour*, 12(2): 112–121.

PATA (2010) 'Pacific tourism leaders slam UK "tax on travel"', Pacific Asia Travel Association, press release 30 April. Online. Available HTTP: www.pata.org/press/pacifi c-tourism-leaders-slam-uk-tax-on-travel.

Patten, J. (1991) 'Government, business and the voluntary sector: A developing partnership', *Policy Studies*, 12(3): 4–10.

Pavlovich, K. (2001) 'The twin landscapes of Waitomo: Tourism network and sustainability through the Landcare Group', *Journal of Sustainable Tourism*, 9: 491–504.

Peattie, K. (1992) *Green Marketing*. London: Longman.

Peattie, S. and Peattie, K. (2003) 'Ready to fly solo? Reducing social marketing's dependence on commercial marketing theory', *Marketing Theory*, 3: 365–385.

Peattie, K. and Peattie, S. (2009) 'Social marketing: A pathway to consumption reduction?', *Journal of Business Research*, 62: 260–268.

Peattie, S., Clarke, P. and Peattie, K. (2005) 'Risk and responsibility in tourism: Promoting sun-safety', *Tourism Management*, 26: 399–408.

Peattie, K., Peattie, S. and Ponting, C. (2009) 'Climate change: A social and commercial marketing communications challenge', *EuroMed Journal of Business*, 4: 270–286.

Peattie, S., Peattie, K. and Thomas, R. (2012) 'Social marketing as transformational marketing in public services: The case of Project Bernie', *Public Management Review*, 14(7): 987–1010.

Pechlaner, H. and Tschurtschenthaler, P. (2003) 'Tourism policy, tourism organisations and change management in alpine regions and destinations: A European perspective', *Current Issues in Tourism*, 6: 508–539.

Pechmann, C., Zhao, G., Goldberg, M. E. and Reibling, E. T. (2003) 'What to convey in antismoking advertisements for adolescents: The use of protection motivation theory to identify effective message themes', *Journal of Marketing*, 67(2): 1–18.

Peeters, P., Gössling, S. and Lane, B. (2009) 'Moving towards low-carbon tourism: New opportunities for destinations and tour operators', in S. Gössling, C. M. Hall and D. Weaver (eds) *Sustainable Tourism Futures: Perspectives on Systems, Restructuring and Innovations*. London: Routledge.

Peeters, P., Szimba, E. and Duijnisveld, M. (2007) 'Major environmental impacts of European tourist transport', *Journal of Transport Geography*, 15: 83–93.

Pelling, E. and White, K. (2009) 'The theory of planned behaviour to young people's use of social networking websites', *Cyberpsychology and Behaviour,* 12: 755–759.

Penn, G. (2010) 'Simplicity and the city: Understanding the voluntary simplicity movement in Melbourne', *ISP Collection*. Paper 867. Brattleboro: SIT Graduate Institute.

Peters, B. G. (2000) 'Governance and comparative politics', in J. Pierre (ed.) *Debating Governance: Authenticity, Steering and Democracy*. Oxford: Oxford University Press.

Peters, B. G. and Hogwood B. W. (1985) 'In search of the issue-attention cycle', *Journal of Politics*, 47(1): 238–253.

Pettibone, K. G., Friend, K. B., Nargiso, J. E. and Florin, P. (2013) 'Evaluating environmental change strategies: Challenges and solutions', *American Journal of Community Psychology*, 51(1–2): 217–221.

Pforr, C. (2002) 'The makers and the shakers of tourism policy in the Northern Territory of Australia: A policy network analysis of actors and their relational constellations', *Journal of Hospitality and Tourism Management*, 9: 134–151.

Pforr, C. (2005) 'Three lenses of analysis for the study of tourism public policy: A case from Northern Australia', *Current Issues in Tourism*, 9: 323–343.

Pforr, C. (2006) 'Tourism policy in the making: An Australian network study', *Annals of Tourism Research*, 33: 87–108.

Phelps, J., Lewis, R., Mobilio, L., Perry, D. and Raman, N. (2004) 'Viral marketing or electronic word-of-mouth advertising: Examining consumer responses and motivations to pass along email', *Journal of Advertising Research*, 44(4): 333–348.

Pieniak, Z., Verbeke, W., Olsen, S. O., Hansen, K. B. and Brunsø, K. (2010) 'Health-related attitudes as a basis for segmenting European fish consumers', *Food Policy*, 35(5): 448–455.

Pierre, J. (ed.) (2000a) *Debating Governance: Authenticity, Steering and Democracy.* Oxford: Oxford University Press.

Pierre. J. (2000b) 'Introduction: Understanding governance', in J. Pierre (ed.) *Debating Governance: Authenticity, Steering and Democracy.* Oxford: Oxford University Press.

Pierre, J. (2009) 'Reinventing governance, reinventing democracy?' *Policy and Politics*, 37: 591–609.

Pierre, J. and Peters, B. G. (2000) *Governance, Politics and the State.* New York: St. Martin's Press.

Pierre, J. and Peters, B. G. (2005) *Governing Complex Societies: Trajectories and Scenarios.* Basingstoke: Palgrave.

Piga, C. A. G. (2003) 'Territorial planning and tourism development tax', *Annals of Tourism Research*, 30: 886–905.

Pimentel, D., McNair, S., Janecka, J., Wightman, J., Simmonds, C., O'Connell, C., Wong, E., Russel, L., Zern, J., Aquino, T. and Tsomondo, T. (2001) 'Economic and environmental threats of alien plant, animal, and microbe invasions', *Agriculture, Ecosystems and Environment*, 84(1): 1–20.

Pinkerton, E. (1999) 'Factors in overcoming barriers to implementing co-management in British Columbia salmon fisheries', *Conservation Ecology*, 3(2): 2. Online. Available HTTP: www.ecologyandsociety.org/vol3/iss2/art2/index.html.

Pirani, S. and Reizes, T. (2005) 'The Turning Point Social Marketing National Excellence Collaborative: integrating social marketing into routine public health practice', *Journal of Public Health Management and Practice,* 11(2): 131–138.

Pleuramom, A. (1999) 'Tourism, globalisation and sustainable development', *Third World Resurgence,* 103: 4–7.

Plotkin, B. J. and Hardiman, M. C. (2009) 'The International Health Tegulations (2005): Tuberculosis and air travel', *Travel Medicine and Infectious Disease*, 8: 90–95.

Polegato, R. and Bjerke, R. (2009) 'Cross-cultural differences in ad likeability and ad element likeability: The case of Benetton', *Journal of Promotion Management*, 15(3): 382–399.

Polonsky, M. J. and Speed, R. (2001) 'Linking sponsorship and cause related marketing: Complementarities and conflicts', *European Journal of Marketing*, 35(11–12): 1361–1389.

Polonsky, M., Hall, J., Vieceli, J., Atay, L., Akdemir, A. and Marangoz, M. (2013) 'Using strategic philanthropy to improve heritage tourist sites on the Gallipoli Peninsula, Turkey: Community perceptions of changing quality of life and of the sponsoring organization', *Journal of Sustainable Tourism*, 21: 376–395.

Pomering, A., Noble, G. and Johnson, L. W. (2011) 'Conceptualising a contemporary marketing mix for sustainable tourism', *Journal of Sustainable Tourism*, 19: 953–969.

Popper, K. (1978) *Three Worlds, the Tanner Lecture on Human Values.* Delivered at The University of Michigan, 7 April. Online. Available HTTP: www.tannerlectures.utah.edu/lectures/documents/popper80.pdf (accessed 1 April 2010).

Prakash, A. (2002) 'Green marketing, public policy and managerial strategies', *Business Strategy and the Environment*, 11(5): 285–297.

Pressman, J. L. and Wildavsky, A. B. (1973) *Implementation: How Great Expectations in Washington are Dashed in Oakland; Or, Why it's Amazing that Federal Programs Work at All, this Being a Saga of the Economic Development Administration as Told by Two Sympathetic Observers who Seek to Build Morals on a Foundation of Ruined Hopes.* San Francisco, CA: University of California Press.

Pressman, J. L. and Wildavsky, A. B. (1979) *Implementation*, second edition. Berkeley, CA: University of California Press.

Prochaska, J. O. and Velicer, W. F. (1997) 'The transtheoretical model of health behavior change', *American Journal of Health Promotion*, 12(1): 38–48.

Prochaska, J. O., Redding, C. A. and Evers, K. E. (2008) 'The transtheoretical model and stages of change', in K. Glanz, B. K. Rimer and K. Viswanath (eds) *Health Behavior and Health Education: Theory, Research, and Practice*, fourth edition. San Francisco, CA: Jossey-Bass.

Quinn, T. (2002) *Public Lands and Private Recreation Enterprise: Policy Issues from a Historical Perspective*. Bulletin General Technical Report – Pacific Northwest Research Station, No. PNW-GTR-556. Portland, OR: US Department of Agriculture, Forest Service, Pacific Northwest Research Station.

Raftopoulou, E. and Hogg, M. K. (2010) 'The political role of government-sponsored social marketing campaigns', *European Journal of Marketing*, 44(7–8): 1206–1227.

Raggio, R. D. and Folse, J. A. G. (2011) 'Expressions of gratitude in disaster management: An economic, social marketing, and public policy perspective on post-Katrina campaigns', *Journal of Public Policy and Marketing*, 30(2): 168–174.

Raymond, E. and Hall, C. M. (2008) 'The development of cross-cultural (mis)understanding through volunteer tourism', *Journal of Sustainable Tourism*, 16: 530–543.

Reeder, T. (2009) 'Helping workers avoid "sultry" sun', *New Zealand Doctor*, 3 November: 26.

Rhodes, M. (2005) 'The scientific objectives of the NEWGOV Project: A revised framework', Paper, NEWGOV Consortium Conference 30 May–31 May, European University Institute, Florence. Online. Available HTTP: www.eu-newgov.org/public/Consortium_Conference_2005.asp (accessed 1 April 2010).

Rhodes, R. A. W. (1997) *Understanding Governance: Policy Networks, Governance, Reflexivity and Accountability*. Buckingham: Open University Press.

Rhodes, C. and Brown, A. D. (2005) 'Narrative, organizations and research', *International Journal of Management Reviews*, 7(3): 167–188.

Ricciardi, A. (2007) 'Are modern biological invasions an unprecedented form of global change?' *Conservation Biology*, 21: 329–336.

Richards, G. (2006) 'The impact of travel experiences on the cultural, personal and social development of young people'. Online. Available HTTP: www.aboutwysetc.org/Docs/Summary%20Cultural%20 Survey%20Report.pdf (accessed 20 February 2007).

Richins, M. and Root-Shaffer, T. (1988) 'The role of evolvement and opinion leadership in consumer word-of-mouth: An implicit model made explicit', *Advances in Consumer Research*, 15: 32–36.

Ridder, D. T. D. and de Wit, J. B. F. (eds) (2006) *Self-regulation in Health Behavior*. Chichester: John Wiley & Sons.

Riecken, G., Babakus, E. and Yavas, U. (1995) 'Facing resource attraction challenges in the nonprofit sector: A behavioristic approach to fund raising and volunteer recruitment', *Journal of Professional Services Marketing*, 11(1): 45–70.

Ritzer, G. (1999) *Enchanting a Disenchanted World: Revolutionizing the Means of Consumption*. Thousand Oaks, CA: Pine Forge Press.

Ritzer, G. and Jurgenson, N. (2010) 'Production, consumption, prosumption: The nature of capitalism in the age of the digital "prosumer"', *Journal of Consumer Culture*, 10(1): 13–36.

Roberts, S. and Tribe, J. (2008) 'Sustainability indicators for small tourism enterprises – an exploratory perspective', *Journal of Sustainable Tourism*, 16(5): 575–594.

Roberts, T. (2004) 'Are western volunteers reproducing and reconstructing the legacy of colonialism in Ghana? An analysis of the experiences of returned volunteers'. Unpublished Master's thesis, Institute for Development Policy and Management Manchester.

Rogers, R. W. (1975) 'A protection motivation theory of fear appeals and attitude change', *The Journal of Psychology*, 91(1): 93–114.

Rogers, R. W. (1983) 'Cognitive and physiological processes in fear appeals and attitude change: A revised theory of protection motivation', in J. T. Cacioppo and R. E. Petty (eds) *Social Psychophysiology: A Source Book*. New York: Guilford Press.

Roper, W. (1993) 'Health communication takes on new dimensions at CDC', *Public Health Reports*, 108(2): 179–183.

Rosenstock, I. M., Strecher, V. J. and Becker, M. H. (1988) 'Social learning theory and the health belief model', *Health Education and Behavior*, 15(2): 175–183.

Rossiter, J. R. and Thornton, J. (2004) 'Fear-pattern analysis supports the fear-drive model for antispeeding road-safety TV ads', *Psychology and Marketing*, 21(11): 945–960.

Rotfeld, H. (2008) 'The stealth influence of covert marketing and much ado about what may be nothing', *Journal of Public Policy and Marketing*, 27(1): 63–68.

Rothschild, M. L. (1999) 'Carrots, sticks, and promises: A conceptual framework for the management of public health and social issue behaviors', *Journal of Marketing*, 63: 24–27.

Rowley, J. and Williams, C. (2008) 'The impact of brand sponsorship of music festivals', *Marketing Intelligence and Planning*, 26: 781–792.

Rumbo, J. D. (2002) 'Consumer resistance in a world of advertising clutter: The case of Adbusters', *Psychology and Marketing*, 19(2): 127–148.

Russell, S. V., Lafferty, G. and Loudon, R. (2008) 'Examining tourism operators' responses to environmental regulation: The role of regulatory perceptions and relationships', *Current Issues in Tourism*, 11: 126–143.

Russell, D., Mort, G. S. and Hume, M. (2009) 'Analysis of management narrative to understand social marketing strategy: The case of "Branding Logan City"', *Australasian Marketing Journal*, 17(4): 232–237.

Ryan, C. and Hall, C. M. (2001) *Sex Tourism: Marginal People and Liminalities*. London: Routledge.

Sabaté, E. (ed.) (2003) *Adherence to Long-term Therapies: Evidence for Action*. Geneva: World Health Organization.

Sacks, D. W., Stevenson, B. and Wolfers, J. (2010) *Subjective Well-being, Income, Economic Development and Growth*. Cambridge: National Bureau of Economic Research.

Sadler, G. R., Lee, H. C., Lim, R. S. H. and Fullerton, J. (2010) 'Recruitment of hard-to-reach population subgroups via adaptations of the snowball sampling strategy', *Nursing and Health Sciences*, 12(3): 369–374.

Saraiya, M., Glanz, K., Briss, P. A., Nichols, P., White, C., Das, D., Smith, J., Tannor, B., Hutchinson, A. B., Coates, R. C., Kerner, J. F., Hiatt, R. A., Buffler, P. and Rochester, P. (2004) 'Interventions to prevent skin cancer by reducing exposure to ultraviolet radiation: A systematic review', *American Journal of Preventive Medicine*, 27(5): 422–466.

Saveriades, A. (2000) 'Establishing the social tourism carrying capacity for the tourist resorts of the east coast of the Republic of Cyprus', *Tourism Management*, 21: 147–156.

Schellhorn, M. (2010) 'Development for whom? Social justice and the business of ecotourism', *Journal of Sustainable Tourism*, 18(1): 115–135.

Scheyvens, R. (2002) *Tourism for Development: Empowering Communities*. Harlow: Prentice Hall.

Scheyvens, R. and Momsen, J. (2008) 'Tourism and poverty reduction: Issues for small island states', *Tourism Geographies*, 10: 22–41.

Schilcher, D. (2007) 'Growth versus equity: The continuum of pro-poor tourism and neoliberal governance', *Current Issues in Tourism*, 10: 166–193.

Schneider, F., de Vries, H., Candel, M., van de Kar, A. and van Osch, L. (2013) 'Periodic email prompts to re-use an internet-delivered computer-tailored lifestyle program: Influence of prompt content and timing', *Journal of Medical Internet Research*, 15(1): e23.

Schor, J. (2003) 'The problem of over-consumption – why economists don't get it', in S. Doherty and A. Etzioni (eds) *Voluntary Simplicity: Responding to Consumer Culture*. Oxford: Rowman and Littlefield Publishers.

Schouten, H. (2013) 'Make Wellington a priority too – Cassels', *The Dominion Post*, Business, 11 May. Online. Available HTTP: www.stuff.co.nz/dominion-post/business/commercial-property/8661380/Make-Wellington-a-priority-too-Cassels (accessed 11 May 2013).

Schuitema, G., Steg, L. and Van Kruining, M. (2011) 'When are transport pricing policies fair and acceptable?' *Social Justice Research*, 24(1): 66–84.

Schwartz, S. H. (1970) 'Moral decision making and behavior', in J. Macaulay and L. Berkowitz (eds) *Altruism and Helping Behavior*. New York: Academic Press.

Schwartz, S. H. (1973) 'Normative explanations of helping behavior: A critique, proposal, and empirical test', *Journal of Experimental Social Psychology*, 9: 349–364.

Schwartz, S. H. (1974) 'Awareness of interpersonal consequences, responsibility denial, and volunteering', *Journal of Personality and Social Psychology*, 30: 57–56

Schwartz, S. H. (1975) 'The justice of need and the activation of humanitarian norms', *Journal of Social Issues*, 31: 111–136.

Schwartz, S. H. (1977) 'Normative influences on altruism', in L. Berkowitz (ed.) *Advances in Experimental Social Psychology*, Vol. 10. New York: Academic Press.

Schwartz, S. H. and Howard, J. A. (1981) 'A normative decision-making model of altruism', in J. P. Ruston and R. M. Sorrentino (eds) *Altruism and Helping Behavior: Social, Personality, and Developmental Perspectives*. Hillsdale, NJ: Lawrence Erlbaum.

Schweitzer, S. (2005) 'Peer-to-peer marketing: Building a buzz on campus. Companies enlist students to pitch products to their peers', *The Boston Globe*, 24 October: A1.

Scott, D. (2006) 'Climate change and sustainable tourism in the 21st century', in J. Cukier (ed.) *Tourism Research: Policy, Planning, and Prospects*. Waterloo: Department of Geography, University of Waterloo.

Scott, D. (2011) 'Why sustainable tourism must address climate change', *Journal of Sustainable Tourism*, 19: 17–34.

Scott, D. and Becken, S. (2010) 'Adapting to climate change and climate policy: Progress, problems and potentials', *Journal of Sustainable Tourism*, 18: 283–295.

Scott, D. and Lemieux, C. (2009) *Weather and Climate Information for Tourism*. White Paper commissioned for World Climate Conference 3. Geneva and Madrid: World Meteorological Organization and United Nations World Tourism Organization.

Scott, D., Amelung, B., Becken, S., Ceron, J-P., Dubois, G., Gössling, S., Peeters, P. and Simpson, M. (2008) 'Technical report', in *Climate Change and Tourism: Responding to Global Challenges*. Madrid: UNWTO, UNEP, WMO.

Scott, D., Gössling, S. and Hall, C. M. (2012a) 'International tourism and climate change'. *WIRES Climate Change*, 3(3).

Scott, D., Gössling, S. and Hall, C. M. (2012b) *Tourism and Climate Change: Impacts, Adaptation and Mitigation*. Abingdon: Routledge.

Scott, D., Peeters, P. and Gössling, S. (2010) 'Can tourism deliver its "aspirational" emission reduction targets?' *Journal of Sustainable Tourism,* 18: 393–408.

Scott, J. and Trubek, D. M. (2002) 'Mind the gap: Law and new approaches to governance in the European Union', *European Law Journal*, 8: 1–18.

Scott, N., Baggio, R. and Cooper, C. (eds) (2008) *Network Analysis and Tourism*. Clevedon: Channel View.

Scott, N., Cooper, C. and Baggio, R. (2008) 'Destination networks: Four Australian cases', *Annals of Tourism Research*, 35: 169–188.

Scott, S. V. (2001) 'How cautious is precautious? Antarctic tourism and the precautionary principle', *International and Comparative Law Quarterly*, 50: 963–971.

Seitanidi, M. M. and Ryan, A. (2007) 'A critical review of forms of corporate community involvement: From philanthropy to partnerships', *International Journal of Nonprofit and Voluntary Sector Marketing*, 12(3): 247–266.

Seligman, M. E. P. and Csikszentmihalyi, M. (2000) 'Positive psychology: An introduction', *American Psychologist*, 55(1): 5–14.

Selinger, E. and Powys White, K. (2012) 'Nudging cannot solve complex policy problems', *European Journal of Risk Regulation*, 2012(1): 26–31.

Seyfang, G. (2009) *Low-Carbon Currencies: The Potential of Time Banking and Local Money Systems for Community Carbon-Reduction*, CSERGE Working Paper EDM 09-04, CSERGE, School of Environmental Sciences, University of East Anglia.

Seyfang, G. (2011) *The New Economics of Sustainable Consumption: Seeds of Change*. Basingstoke: Palgrave Macmillan.

Shaffer, H. J. and Kidman, R. (2003). 'Shifting perspectives on gambling and addiction', *Journal of Gambling Studies*, 19(1): 1–6.

Shama, A. (1978) 'Management and consumers in an era of stagflation', *Journal of Marketing*, 42(3): 43–52.

Shanahan, K. J. and Hopkins, C. D. (2007) 'Truths, half-truths, and deception: Perceived social responsibility and intent to donate for a nonprofit using implicature, truth, and duplicity in print advertising', *Journal of Advertising*, 36(2): 33–48.

Shang, J., Basil, D. Z. and Wymer, W. (2010) 'Using social marketing to enhance hotel reuse programs', *Journal of Business Research*, 63: 166–172.

Sharif, B. (2011) 'Impact of Social Marketing on Consumption Reduction', *Journal of Applied Business and Economics*, 12(5): 111–125.

Sharp, A., Høj, S. and Wheeler, M. (2010) 'Proscription and its impact on anti-consumption behaviour and attitudes: The case of plastic bags', *Journal of Consumer Behaviour*, 9: 470–484.

Shaw, B. R., Radler, B. T. and Haack, J. (2011) 'Exploring the utility of the stages of change model to promote natural shorelines', *Lake and Reservoir Management*, 27(4): 310–320.

Shaw, B. R., Radler, B. and Haack, J. (2012) 'Comparing two direct mail strategies to sell native plants in a campaign to promote natural lake shorelines', *Social Marketing Quarterly*, 18(4): 274–280.

Shaw, D. and Newholm, T. (2002) 'Voluntary simplicity and the ethics of consumption', *Psychology and Marketing*, 19: 167–185.

Shead, N. W., Walsh, K., Taylor, A., Derevensky, J. L. and Gupta, R. (2011) 'Youth gambling prevention: Can public service announcements featuring celebrity spokespersons be effective?', *International Journal of Mental Health and Addiction*, 9(2): 165–179.

Sheth, J. N. and Sisodia, R. S. (2005) 'A dangerous divergence: Marketing and society', *Journal of Public Policy and Marketing*, 24(1): 160–162.

Sheth, J. N. and Sisodia, R. S. (eds) (2006) *Does Marketing Need Reform? Fresh Perspectives on the Future.* New York: M. E. Sharpe.

Shi, D. E. (1986) *The Simple Life: Plain Living and High Thinking in American Culture.* New York: Oxford University Press.

Shih, T.-J., Wijaya, R. and Brossard, D. (2008) 'Media coverage of public health epidemics: Linking framing and issue attention cycle toward an integrated theory of print news coverage of epidemics', *Mass Communication and Society*, 11: 141–160.

Shone, M. C. and Memon, P. A. (2008) 'Tourism, public policy and regional development: A turn from neo-liberalism to the new regionalism', *Local Economy*, 23: 290–304.

Shove, E. (2010) 'Beyond the ABC: climate change policy and theories of social change', *Environment and Planning A*, 42: 1273–1285.

Shrum, L. J., Lowrey, T. M. and McCarty, J. A. (1994) 'Recycling as a marketing problem: A framework for strategy development', *Psychology and Marketing*, 11(4): 393–416.

Shuptrine, F. K. and Osmanski, F. A. (1975) 'Marketing's changing role: Expanding or contracting?' *The Journal of Marketing*, 39(2): 58–66.

Siano, A., Eagle, L., Confetto, M. G. and Siglioccolo, M. (2010) 'Destination competitiveness and museum marketing strategies: An emerging issue in the Italian context', *Museum Management and Curatorship*, 25(3): 259–276.

Simon, H. A. (1959) 'Theories of decision making in economics', *American Economic Review*, 49: 253–283.

Simon, H. A. (1965) *Administrative Behavior*, second edition. New York: Free Press.

Simondson, C. (1995) 'Tourism, primitivism and power: An analysis of some advertising literature of the Australian tourism industry', *Olive Pink Society Bulletin*, 7(1–2): 22–27.

Simoni, J. M., Pearson, C. R., Pantalone, D. W., Marks, G. and Crepaz, N. (2006) 'Efficacy of interventions in improving highly active antiretroviral therapy adherence and HIV-1 RNA viral load: A meta-analytic review of randomized controlled trials', *Journal of Acquired Immune Deficiency Syndrome*, 43(Suppl 1): S23–S35.

Simpson, K. (2004) '"Doing development": The gap year, volunteer-tourists and a popular practice of development', *Journal of International Development*, 16: 681–692.

Simpson, K. (2005a) 'Dropping out or signing up? The professionalisation of youth travel', *Antipode*, 37: 447–469.

Simpson, K. (2005b) 'Broad horizons? Geographies and pedagogies of the gap year'. Unpublished PhD thesis, University of Newcastle.

Sinclair, A. (2010) 'Tourism businesses hope for a "staycation" summer', BBC Hampshire & Isle of Wight, 16 March. Online. Available HTTP: http://news.bbc.co.uk/local/hampshire/hi/people_and_places/newsid_8569000/8569934.stm.

Singh, S., Timothy, D. and Dowling, R. (eds) (2003) *Tourism in Destination Communities*. Wallingford: CABI.

Sirakaya, E. and Somez, S. (2000) 'Gender images in state tourism brochures: An overlooked area in socially responsible tourism marketing', *Journal of Travel Research,* 38: 353–362.

Sirakaya, E. and Woodside, A. G. (2005) 'Building and testing theories of decision making by travellers', *Tourism Management,* 26: 815–832.

Sjöberg, L., Holm, L. E., Ullén, H. and Brandberg, Y. (2004) 'Tanning and risk perception in adolescents', *Health, Risk and Society,* 6(1): 81–94.

Skin Cancer Control Steering Committee (2008) 'Strategic framework of the skin cancer control steering committee for the period 2008–2001'. Online. Available HTTP: www.sunsmart.org.nz/media/12179/scc%20strategy%202008-11%20final.pdf (accessed 10 May 2009).

Skinner, B. F. (1953) *Science and Human Behavior.* New York: Simon & Schuster.

Skinner, B. F. (1989) *Recent Issues in the Analysis of Behavior.* New York: Free Press

Slater, M. D., Kelly, K. and Edwards, R. W. (2000) 'Integrating social marketing, community readiness and media advocacy in community-based prevention efforts', *Social Marketing Quarterly,* 6(3): 125–137.

Slaughter, S. and Rhoades, G. (2004) *Academic Capitalism and the New Economy: Markets, State and Higher Education.* Baltimore, MD: Johns Hopkins University Press.

Smith, I. J. and Rodger, C. J. (2009) 'Carbon emission offsets for aviation-generated emissions due to international travel to and from New Zealand', *Energy Policy,* 37: 3438–3447.

Smith, L., Broad, S. and Weiler, B. (2008) 'A closer examination of the impact of zoo visits on visitor behaviour', *Journal of Sustainable Tourism,* 16(5): 544–562.

Smith, M. M. and Reynolds, L. J. (2007) 'The Street Team: An unconventional peer program for undergraduates', *Library Management,* 29(3): 145–158.

Smith, W. A. (2000) 'Social marketing: an evolving definition', *American Journal of Health Behavior,* 24(1): 11–17.

Social Marketing National Excellence Collaborative (SMNEC) (2002) *Social Marketing: A Resource Guide.* Seattle, WA: Turning Point.

Southerton, D., Chappells, H. and Van Vliet, B. (eds) (2004a) *Sustainable Consumption: The Implications of Changing Infrastructures of Provision.* Cheltenham: Edward Elgar Publishing.

Southerton, D., Van Vliet, B. and Chappells, H. (2004b) 'Introduction: Consumption, infrastructures and environmental sustainability', in D. Southerton, H. Chappells and B. Van Vliet (eds) *Sustainable consumption: The Implications of Changing Infrastructures of Provision.* Cheltenham: Edward Elgar Publishing.

Sowman, M. R. (1987) 'A procedure for assessing recreational carrying capacity of coastal resort areas', *Landscape and Urban Planning,* 14: 331–344.

Spence, A. and Pidgeon, N. F. (2009) 'Psychology, climate change and sustainable behaviour', *Environment: Science and Policy for Sustainable Development,* 51(6): 8–18.

Stead, M., Arnott, L. and Dempsey, E. (2013) 'Healthy heroes, magic meals, and a visiting alien community-led assets-based social marketing', *Social Marketing Quarterly,* 19(1): 26–39.

Stead, M., Gordon, R., Angus, K. and McDermott, L. (2007) 'A systematic review of social marketing effectiveness', *Health Education,* 107: 126–191.

Stebbins, R. A. (1992) *Amateurs, Professionals and Serious Leisure.* Montreal: McGill-Queens University Press.

Stebbins, R. A. and Graham, M. (eds) (2004) *Volunteering as Leisure – Leisure as Volunteering: An International Assessment.* Wallingford: CABI.

Steg, L. (2008) 'Promoting household energy conservation', *Energy Policy,* 36: 4449–4453.

Steg, L. and Abrahamse, W. (2010) 'How to promote energy savings among households: Theoretical and practical approaches', in V. Corral-Verdugo, C. H. Garcia-Cadena and M. Frias-Armenta (eds)

Psychology Approaches to Sustainability: Current Trends in Theory, Research and Applications. New York: Nova Science.

Steg, L. and Vlek, C. (2009) 'Encouraging pro-environmental behaviour: An integrative review and research agenda', *Journal of Environmental Psychology*, 29: 309–317.

Stem, C., Lassoie, J., Lee, D., Deshler, D. and Schelhas, J. (2003) 'Community participation in ecotourism benefits: The links to conservation practices', *Society and Natural Resources*, 16: 387–413.

Sterk, W. and Bunse, M. (2004) 'Voluntary compensation of greenhouse gas emissions'. Policy paper no. 3/2004. Online. Available HTTP: www.wupperinst.org/download/1078-compensation.pdf (accessed 19 November 2012).

Stern, N. (2006) *The Economics of Climate Change: The Stern Review.* London: HM Treasury.

Stern, P. C. (2000) 'New environmental theories: Toward a coherent theory of environmentally significant behavior', *Journal of Social Issues*, 56(3): 407–424.

Stern, P. C., Dietz, T. and Black, J. S. (1986) 'Support for environmental protection: The role of personal norms', *Population and Environment*, 8: 204–222.

Stoker, G. (1998) 'Governance as theory', *International Social Science Journal*, 50(155): 17–28.

Stroebe, W. (2000) *Social Psychology and Health*, second edition. Buckingham: Open University Press.

Stronza, A. and Gordillo, J. (2008) 'Community views of ecotourism', *Annals of Tourism Research*, 35(2): 448–468.

Stryker, J. E., Solky, B. A. and Emmons, K. M. (2005) 'A content analysis of news coverage of skin cancer prevention and detection, 1979 to 2003', *Archives of Dermatology*, 141(4): 491–496.

Stryker, S. and Burke, P. J. (2000) 'The past, present, and future of an identity theory', *Social Psychology Quarterly*, 284–297.

Stubbs, B., Warnaby, G. and Medway, D. (2002) 'Marketing at the public/private sector interface: Town centre management schemes in the south of England', *Cities*, 19(5): 317–326.

Sullivan, A. M. (2006) 'I am not a gambler, you are a gambler: Distinguishing between tolerable and intolerable gambling', *Leisure/Loisir*, 30: 171–192.

Sustainable Consumption Roundtable (SCR) (2006a) *I Will If you Will.* London: National Consumer Council and Sustainable Development Commission.

Sustainable Consumption Roundtable (2006b) *Shifting Opinions and Changing Behaviours.* A Consumer Forum report by Opinion Leader Research, May 2006. London: Sustainable Development Roundtable.

Sutcliffe, J. B. (1999) 'The 1999 reform of the structural fund regulations: Multi-level governance or renationalization?' *Journal of European Public Policy*, 7: 290–309.

Sutton, S. (1998) 'Predicting and explaining intentions and behavior: How well are we doing?' *Journal of Applied Social Psychology*, 28: 1317–1338.

Sutton, S. R. (1997) 'Theory of planned behaviour', in A. Baum, S. Newman, J. Weinman, R. West and C. McManus (eds) *Cambridge Handbook of Psychology, Health and Medicine.* Cambridge: Cambridge University Press.

Swim, J., Clayton, S., Doherty, T., Gifford, R., Howard, G., Reser, J., Stern, P. and Weber, E. (2010) *Psychology and Global Climate Change: Addressing a Multi-faceted Phenomenon and Set of Challenges.* Report of the American Psychological Association's task force on the interface between psychology and global climate change. American Psychological Association. Online. Available HTTP: www.apa.org/science/about/publications/climate-change.aspx (accessed 1 April 2013).

Swinburn, B., Gill, T. and Kumanyika, S. (2005) 'Obesity prevention: A proposed framework for translating evidence into action', *Obesity Reviews*, 6(1): 23–33.

Szmigin, I., Bengry-Howell, A., Griffin, C., Hackley, C. and Mistral, W. (2011) 'Social marketing, individual responsibility and the "culture of intoxication"', *European Journal of Marketing*, 45(5): 759–779.

Tajfel, H. and Turner, J. C. (1986) 'The social identity theory of intergroup behaviour', in S. Worchel and W. G. Austin (eds) *Psychology of Intergroup Relations*, second edition. Chicago, IL: Nelson-Hall.

Tan, E. J., Tanner, E. K., Seeman, T. E., Xue, Q. L., Rebok, G. W., Frick, K. D., McGill, S., Carlson, M. C., Wang, T., Pifiri, R. L., Whitfield, K. and Fried, L. P. (2010) 'Marketing public health through older adult volunteering: Experience Corps as a social marketing intervention', *American Journal of Public Health*, 100(4): 727–734.

Tan, S., Sinclair, C. and Foley, P. (2012) 'Running behind a tourist: Leisure-related skin cancer prophylaxis', *British Journal of Dermatology*, 167(S2): 70–75.

Tanner Jr, J. F., Day, E. and Crask, M. R. (1989) 'Protection motivation theory: An extension of fear appeals theory in communication', *Journal of Business Research*, 19(4): 267–276.

Tanner Jr, J. F., Hunt, J. B. and Eppright, D. R. (1991) 'The protection motivation model: A normative model of fear appeals', *The Journal of Marketing*, 55(3): 36–45.

Tao, T. and Wall, G. (2009) 'Tourism as a sustainable livelihood strategy', *Tourism Management*, 30(1): 90–98.

Taylor, G. (1995) 'The community approach: Does it really work?' *Tourism Management*, 16: 487–489.

Tearfund (2000a) *A Tearfund Guide to Tourism: Don't Forget Your Ethics*. London: Tearfund.

Tearfund (2000b) *Tourism: An Ethical Issue*. Market research report. London: Tearfund.

Tella, R. D. and MacCulloch, R. (2008) *Happiness Adaptation to Income Beyond 'Basic Needs'*. Cambridge: National Bureau of Economic Research.

Tervo-Kankare, K., Hall, C. M. and Saarinen, J. (2012) 'Christmas tourists' perceptions of climate change in Rovaniemi, Finnish Lapland', *Tourism Geographies*, 15(2): 292–317.

Thackeray, R. and Neiger, B. L. (2000) 'Establishing a relationship between behavior change theory and social marketing: Implications for health education', *Journal of Health Education*, 31(6): 331–335.

Thaler, R. H. and Sunstein, C. R. (2008) *Nudge: Improving Decisions about Health, Wealth and Happiness*. London: Yale University Press.

Theobald, W. F. (1979) *Evaluation of Recreation and Park Programs*. New York: John Wiley & Sons.

Thøgersen, J. (2006) 'Media attention and the market for "green" consumer products', *Business Strategy and the Environment*, 15(3): 145–156.

Thoits, P. A. and Hewitt, L. N. (2001) 'Volunteer work and well-being', *Journal of Health and Social Behavior*, 42: 115–131.

Thompson, C. J. and Haytko, D. L. (1997) 'Speaking of Fashion: Consumers' Uses of Fashion Discourses and the appropriation of countervailing cultural meanings', *Journal of Consumer Research*, 24: 15–42.

Thompson, F. (2008) 'The three faces of public management', *International Public Management Review*, 9(1): 1–17.

Thynne, I. (2008) 'Symposium introduction – climate change, governance and environmental services: Institutional perspectives, issues and challenges', *Public Administration and Development*, 28: 327–339.

Tikir, A. and Lehmann, B. (2011) 'Climate change, theory of planned behavior and values: A structural equation model with mediation analysis', *Climatic Change*, 104: 389–402.

Tinnish, S. M. and Mangal, S. M. (2012) 'Sustainable event marketing in the MICE industry: A theoretical framework', *Journal of Convention and Event Tourism*, 13(4): 227–249.

Todd, H. (2004) 'Future of guerilla marketing: Guerilla marketing has become a high tech, big money business', *Beverage World*, 123(8): 1–3.

Tosun, C. and Timothy, D. (2003) 'Arguments for community participation in tourism development', *Journal of Tourism Studies*, 14(2): 2–11.

TravelMole (2008) 'New UK departure taxes slammed', TravelMole, 25 November. Online. Available HTTP: www.travelmole.com/stories/1133123.php (accessed 10 October 2013).

Treib, O., Bähr, H. and Falkner, G. (2007) 'Modes of governance: towards a conceptual clarification', *Journal of European Public Policy*, 14(1): 1–20.

Treuren, G. and Lane, D. (2003) 'The tourism planning process in the context of organized interests, industry structure, state capacity, accumulation and sustainability', *Current Issues in Tourism*, 6(1): 1–22.

Trifiletti, L. B., Gielen, A. C., Sleet, D. A. and Hopkins, K. (2005) 'Behavioral and social sciences theories and models: Are they used in unintentional injury prevention research?' *Health Education Research*, 20: 298–307.

Triggle, N. (2006) 'From nanny state to a helping hand', BBC News', 25 July. Online. Available HTTP: http://news.bbc.co.uk/2/hi/health/5214276.stm (accessed 10 October 2013).

Triggle, N. (2013) 'Healthy lifestyles: Is a hug, shove, nudge or smack best?' BBC News Health, 17 February. Online. Available HTTP: www.bbc.co.uk/news/health-21593335 (accessed 1 April 2013).

Trousdale, W. J. (1999) 'Governance in context: Boracay Island, Philippines', *Annals of Tourism Research*, 26: 840–867.

Truong, V. D. (2013) 'Tourism policy development in Vietnam: A pro-poor perspective', *Journal of Policy Research in Tourism, Leisure and Events*, 5(1): 28–45.

Truong, V. D. and Hall, C. M. (2013) 'Social marketing and tourism: What is the evidence?' *Social Marketing Quarterly*, 19(2): 110–135.

Trusov, M., Bucklin, R. and Pauwels, K. (2009) 'Effects of word-of-mouth versus traditional marketing: Findings from an Internet social networking site', *Journal of Marketing*, 73(5): 90–102.

Tullberg, J. (2005) 'Reflections upon the responsive approach to corporate social responsibility', *Business Ethics: A European Review*, 14(3): 261–276.

Tunbridge, J. E. and Ashworth, G. J. (1996) *Dissonant Heritage: The Management of the Past as a Resource in Conflict*. Chichester: John Wiley & Sons.

Turning Point (Turning Point Social Marketing National Excellence Collaborative) (2002) *Social Marketing: A Resource Guide*. Seattle, WA: Turning Point.

Turning Point (2007) *The Basics of Social Marketing: How to Use Marketing to Change Behavior*. Seattle, WA: Turning Point.

TVNZ (2010) 'UK departure tax hike could hit NZ tourism', TVNZ News, 2 November. Online. Available HTTP: tvnz.co.nz/travel-news/uk-departure-tax-hike-could-hit-nz-tourism-3875281 (accessed 10 October 2013).

Tyler, D. and Dinan, C. (2001) 'The role of interested groups in England's emerging tourism policy network', *Current Issues in Tourism*, 4: 210–252.

Tzanopoulos, J. and Vogiatzakis, I. N. (2011) 'Processes and patterns of landscape change on a small Aegean island: The case of Sifnos, Greece', *Landscape and Urban Planning*, 99(1): 58–64.

UN and UNWTO (United Nations and United Nations World Tourism Organization) (2007) *International Recommendations on Tourism Statistics (IRTS) Provisional Draft*, New York/Madrid: UN and UNWTO.

UNCTAD (United Nations Conference on Trade and Development) (2010) *The Contribution of Tourism to Trade and Development*. Note by the UNCTAD Secretariat, TD/B/C.I/8. Geneva: UNCTAD.

Unruh, G. C. (2000) 'Understanding carbon lock-in', *Energy Policy*, 28: 817–830.

UNWTO (United Nations World Tourism Organization) (2006a) *International Tourist Arrivals, Tourism Market Trends, 2006 Edition – Annex*. Madrid: UNWTO.

UNWTO (2006b) *Report of the World Tourism Organization to the United Nations Secretary-General in preparation for the High Level Meeting on the Mid-Term Comprehensive Global Review of the Programme of Action for the Least Developed Countries for the Decade 2001–2010*. Madrid: UNWTO.

UNWTO (2007) 'Tourism will contribute to solutions for global climate change and poverty challenges', press release, UNWTO Press and Communications Department, 8 March. Berlin/Madrid: UNWTO.

UNWTO (2011) *Tourism Towards 2030: Global Overview*. UNWTO General Assembly, 19th Session, Gyeongju, Republic of Korea, 10 October. Madrid: UNWTO.

UNWTO (2012) *UNWTO Tourism Highlights. 2012 Edition*. Madrid: UNWTO.

UNWTO and United Nations Environment Programme (UNEP) (2008) *Climate Change and Tourism: Responding to Global Challenges*. Madrid/Paris: UNWTO/UNEP.

UNWTO and UNEP (2011) 'Tourism: Investing in the green economy', in *Towards a Green Economy*. Geneva: UNEP.

UNWTO, UNEP and WMO (World Meteorological Organization) (2008) *Climate Change and Tourism: Responding to Global Challenges*. Madrid: UNWTO, UNEP and WMO.

Van Dam, Y. K. and Apeldoorn, P. A. (1996) 'Sustainable marketing', *Journal of Macromarketing*, 16(2): 45–56.

van den Bergh, J. and Kemp, R. (2008) 'Transition lessons from economics', in J. van den Bergh and F. Bruinsma (eds) *Managing the Transition to Renewable Energy: Theory and Practice From Local, Regional and Macro Perspectives*. Cheltenham: Edward Elgar.

Van den Broucke, S. (2012) 'Theory-informed health promotion: Seeing the bigger picture by looking at the details', *Health Promotion International*, 27(2): 143–147.

Van Liere, K. D. and Dunlap, R. E. (1978) 'Moral norms and environmental behavior: An application of Schwartz's norm-activation model to yard burning', *Journal of Applied Social Psychology*, 8: 174–188.

Varey, R. J. (2011) 'A sustainable society logic for marketing', *Social Business*, 1(1): 69–83.

Vargo, S. L., Maglio, P. P. and Akaka, M. A. (2008) 'On value and value co-creation: A service systems and service logic perspective', *European Management Journal*, 26(3): 145–152.

Veer, E. (2011) 'How Facebook facilitates the breaking of social norms', *Research in Consumer Behaviour*, 13: 185–198.

Verbeek, D. and Mommaas, H. (2008) 'Transitions to sustainable tourism mobility: The social practices approach', *Journal of Sustainable Tourism*, 16: 629–644.

Vezina, R. and Paul, O. (1997) 'Provocation in advertising: A conceptualization and an empirical assessment', *International Journal of Research in Marketing*, 14(2): 177–192.

Viken, A. (2006) 'Svalbard, Norway', in G. Baldacchino (ed.) *Extreme Tourism: Lessons from the World's Cold Water Islands*. Oxford: Elsevier.

Waikayi, L., Fearon, C., Morris, L. and McLaughlin, H. (2012) 'Volunteer management: An exploratory case study within the British Red Cross', *Management Decision*, 50(3): 349–367.

Waitt, G., Caputi, P., Gibson, C., Farbotko, C., Head, L., Gill, N. and Stanes, E. (2012) 'Sustainable household capability: Which households are doing the work of environmental sustainability?' *Australian Geographer*, 43: 51–74.

Walker, J. L. (1977) 'Setting the agenda in the U.S. Senate', *British Journal of Political Science*, 7: 423–445.

Wall, A. P. (2005) 'Government demarketing: Different approaches and mixed messages', *European Journal of Marketing*, 39: 421–427.

Walle, A. H. (1997) 'Quantitative versus qualitative tourism research', *Annals of Tourism Research*, 24: 524–536.

Waller, D. S. (1999) 'Attitudes towards offensive advertising: An Australian study', *The Journal of Consumer Marketing*, 16(3): 288–294.

Waller, D. S. (2005) 'Advertising of controversial products: A cross-cultural study', *The Journal of Consumer Marketing*, 22(1): 6–13.

Walsh, D. C., Rudd, R. E., Moeykens, B. A. and Moloney, T. W. (1993) 'Social marketing for public health', *Health Affairs*, 12(2): 104–119.

Walsh, G., Hassan, L. M., Shiu, E., Andrews, J. C. and Hastings, G. (2010) 'Segmentation in social marketing: Insights from the European Union's multi-country, antismoking campaign', *European Journal of Marketing*, 44(7–8): 1140–1164.

Wanhill, S. R. C. (1986) 'Which investment incentives for tourism?' *Tourism Management*, 7(1): 2–7.

Wanta, W. and Hu, Y. W. (1993) 'The agenda-setting effects of international news coverage: An examination of differing news frames', *International Journal of Public Opinion Research*, 5: 250–264.

Warnaby, G. (2009) 'Towards a service-dominant place marketing logic', *Marketing Theory*, 9: 403–423.

Waters, R. D., Canfield, R. R., Foster, J. M. and Hardy, E. E. (2011) 'Applying the dialogic theory to social networking sites: Examining how university health centers convey health messages on Facebook', *Journal of Social Marketing*, 1(3): 211–227.

Watson, D., Clark, L. A. and Tellegen, A. (1988) 'Development and validation of brief measures of positive and negative affect: The PANAS scales', *Journal of Personality and Social Psychology*, 54: 1063–1070.

Wearing, S. (1998) 'The nature of ecotourism: The place of self, identity and communities as interacting elements of alternative tourism experiences'. Unpublished PhD thesis, Charles Sturt University, Albury, Australia.

Wearing, S. (2001) *Volunteer Tourism: Seeking Experiences That Make a Difference*. Wallingford: CABI.

Wearing, S. W. and Archer, D. (2001) 'Towards a framework for sustainable marketing of protected areas', *Australian Parks and Leisure*, 4(1): 33–40.

Wearing, S. W. and Archer, D. (2005) 'Developing an approach to marketing and demarketing of tourism for protected area management', in J. Senior (ed.) *Parks and Leisure Australia 2005 National Conference, Current Issues: Future Challenges*, 9–13 October, Hobart, Tasmania.

Wearing, S. W. and Nelson, H. (2004) *A Natural Partnership: Making National Parks a Tourism Priority.* Project Paper 3, Marketing and Promotion. Sydney: Tourism and Transport Forum Australia.

Wearing, S. W, Archer, D. and Beeton, S. (2007) *The Sustainable Marketing of Tourism in Protected Areas.* Gold Coast: Sustainable Tourism Cooperative Research Centre.

Weaver, A. C. and Morrison, B. B. (2008) 'Social networking', *Computer*, 41(2): 97–100.

Weaver, D. (2012) 'Alternative tourism as a contestable quality-of-life facilitator', in M. Uysal, R. Perdue and M. J. Sirgy (eds) *Handbook of Tourism and Quality-of-Life Research: Enhancing the Lives of Tourists and Residents of Host Communities.* Dordrecht: Springer.

Webb, T. L., Joseph, J., Yardley, L. and Michie, S. (2010) 'Using the internet to promote health behavior change: A systematic review and meta-analysis of the impact of theoretical basis, use of behavior change techniques, and mode of delivery on efficacy', *Journal of Medical Internet Research*, 12(1): e4. Online. Available HTTP: www.ncbi.nlm.nih.gov/pmc/articles/PMC2836773/ (accessed 1 April 2013).

Weber, E. U. (2006) 'Experience-based and description-based perceptions of long-term risk: Why global warming does not scare us (yet)', *Climatic Change*, 77: 103–120.

Webster, F. E. (1975) 'Social marketing: What makes it different?' *Management Decision*, 13(1): 70–77.

Weeden, C. (2002) 'Ethical tourism: An opportunity for competitive advantage?' *Journal of Vacation Marketing*, 8: 141–153.

Weiler, B., Brown, T. J. and Curtis, J. (2009) 'How to influence tourists visiting protected areas to make choices that make a difference for climate change', in I. Garvan (ed.) *Australian Protected Areas Congress 2008: Protected Areas in the Century of Change.* Brisbane: Queensland Government, Environmental Protection Agency. Online. Available HTTP: www.derm.qld.gov.au/services_resources/item_details.php?item_id=201767.

Weimer, D. L. (1998) 'Policy analysis and evidence: A craft perspective', *Policy Studies Journal*, 26(1): 114–128.

Westberg, K. and Pope, N. (2012) 'Building brand equity with cause-related marketing: A comparison with sponsorship and sales promotion', *Journal of Marketing Communications*, doi: 10.1080/13527266.2012.723025.

Westley, F., Holmgren, M. and Scheffer, M. (2010) 'From scientific speculation to effective adaptive management: A case study of the role of social marketing in promoting novel restoration strategies for degraded dry lands', *Ecology and Society*, 15(3): 6–22.

Wettstein, D., Suggs, L. S. and Lellig, C. (2012) 'Social marketing and alcohol misuse prevention in German-speaking countries', *Journal of Social Marketing*, 2(3): 187–206.

Wheeler, B. (1991) 'Tourism's troubled times: Responsible tourism is not the answer', *Tourism Management*, 12(2): 91–96.

White, M. (2008) 'Relocalize community. The call for a general consumption strike has prompted readers to ask: Can the world function without consumption?' *Journal of the Mental Environment*, Adbusters, 22 October. Online. Available HTTP: www.adbusters.org/category/tags/degrowth (accessed 25 January 2009).

Whitmarsh, L. (2009) 'Behavioural responses to climate change: Asymmetry of intentions and impacts', *Journal of Environmental Psychology*, 29: 13–23.

Whitmarsh, L. and O'Neill, S. (2010) 'Green identity, green living? The role of pro-environmental self-identity in determining consistency across diverse pro-environmental behaviours', *Journal of Environmental Psychology*, 30(3): 305–314.

Whitmarsh, L., O'Neill, S., Seyfang, G. and Lorenzoni, I. (2009) *Carbon Capability: What Does it Mean, How Prevalent is it, and How can We Promote it?* Tyndall Working Paper 132. Norwich: Tyndall Centre for Climate Change Research, University of East Anglia.

Whitmarsh, L., Seyfang, G. and O'Neill, S. (2011) 'Public engagement with carbon and climate change: To what extent is the public "carbon capable"?' *Global Environmental Change*, 21: 56–65.

Wiebe, G. D. (1952) 'Merchandising commodities and citizenship on television', *Public Opinion Quarterly*, 15: 679–691.

Wiener, C. S., Needham, M. D. and Wilkinson, P. F. (2009) 'Hawaii's real life marine park: Interpretation and impacts of commercial marine tourism in the Hawaiian Islands', *Current Issues in Tourism*, 12: 489–504.

Wildavsky, A. B. (1987) *Speaking Truth to Power: The Art and Craft of Policy Analysis*. New Brunswick, NJ: Transaction Books.

Williams, A. M. and Montanari, A. (1999) 'Sustainability and self-regulation: Critical perspectives', *Tourism Geographies*, 1(1): 26–40.

Wilson, B. (2010) 'World Cup 2018 bidders put economic case to Fifa'. BBC News Business, 14 May. Online. Available HTTP: www.bbc.co.uk/news/10110101 (accessed 10 October 2013).

Wincott, D. (2003) 'Slippery concepts, shifting context: (National) states and welfare in the Veit-Wilson/Atherton debate', *Social Policy and Administration*, 37: 305–315.

Wolf, J., Brown, K. and Conway, D. (2009) 'Ecological citizenship and climate change: Perceptions and practice', *Environmental Politics*, 18 (4): 503–521.

Wong, F. L., Greenwell, M., Gates, S. and Berkowitz, J. M. (2008) 'It's what you do! Reflections on the VERB™ campaign', *American Journal of Preventive Medicine*, 34(6): S175–S182.

Wood, B. D. and Peake, J. S. (1998) 'The dynamics of foreign policy agenda setting', *American Political Science Review*, 92: 173–184.

Wood, M. (2008) 'Applying commercial marketing theory to social marketing: A tale of 4Ps (and a B)', *Social Marketing Quarterly*, 14(1): 76–85.

Woodside, S. (2001) 'Every joke is a tiny revolution: Culture jamming and the role of humour'. Unpublished Masters thesis, University of Amsterdam, Media Studies.

WCED (World Commission on Environment and Development) (1987) *Our Common Future* (the Brundtland Report). London: Oxford University Press.

World Economic Forum (WEF) (2009a) *Towards a Low Carbon Travel and Tourism Sector*. Davos: WEF.

World Economic Forum (2009b) *The Travel and Tourism Competitiveness Report 2009: Managing in a Time of Turbulence*. Davos: WEF.

World Health Organization, World Meteorological Organization, United Nations Environment Programme and International Commission on Non-Ionizing Radiation Protection (2002) *Global Solar UV Index: A Practical Guide*. Geneva: World Health Organization. Online. Available HTTP: www.unep.org/pdf/Solar-Index_Guide.pdf (accessed 9 October 2013).

World Tourism Organization (WTO) (1991) *Guidelines for the Collection and Presentation of Domestic and International Tourism Statistics*. Madrid: WTO.

World Tourism Organization (1997). *Tourism 2020 Vision*. Madrid: WTO.

World Travel and Tourism Council (WTTC) (2004) *The Caribbean: The Impact of Travel and Tourism on Jobs and the Economy*. London: WTTC.

World Travel and Tourism Council (2012) *Progress and Priorities 2010–2011*. London: WTTC.

Wymer, W. (2010) 'Rethinking the boundaries of social marketing: Activism or advertising?' *Journal of Business Research*, 63(2): 99–103.

Wymer, W. (2011) 'Developing more effective social marketing strategies', *Journal of Social Marketing*, 1(1): 17–31.

Wymer, W. and Samu, S. (2003) 'Dimensions of business and nonprofit collaborative relationships', *Journal of Nonprofit and Public Sector Marketing*, 11(1): 3–22.

Yagade, A. and Dozier, D. M. (1990) 'The media agenda-setting effect of concrete versus abstract issues', *Journalism Quarterly*, 67: 3–10.

Yee, A. S. (2004) 'Cross-national concepts in supranational governance: state–society relations and EU-policy making', *Governance – An International Journal of Policy and Administration*, 17: 487–524.

Yu, P. and Waller, K. (2010) 'M matters: What's social marketing and media got to do with it?' *Alzheimer Disease and Associated Disorders*, 24: S7–S13.

Yu, X. (2008) 'Growth and degradation in the Orient's "Las Vegas": Issues of environment in Macau', *International Journal of Environmental Studies*, 65: 667–683.

Yüksel, F., Bramwell B. and Yüksel, A. (2005) 'Centralized and decentralized tourism governance in Turkey', *Annals of Tourism Research*, 32: 859–886.

Zampoukos, K. and Ioannides, D. (2011) 'The tourism labour conundrum: agenda for new research in the geography of hospitality workers', *Hospitality and Society*, 1: 25–45.

Zapata, M. J., Hall, C. M., Lindo, P. and Vanderschaeghen, M. (2011) 'Can community-based tourism contribute to development and poverty alleviation?' *Current Issues in Tourism*, 14: 725–749.

Zavestoski, S. (2002) 'The social–psychological bases of anticonsumption attitudes', *Psychology and Marketing*, 19: 149–165.

Zegre, S. J., Needham, M. D., Kruger, L. E. and Rosenberger, R. S. (2012) 'McDonaldization and commercial outdoor recreation and tourism in Alaska', *Managing Leisure*, 17(4): 333–348.

Zeithaml, C. P. and Zeithaml, V. A. (1984) 'Environmental management: Revising the marketing perspective', *The Journal of Marketing*, 48(2): 46–53.

Zepeda, L. and Deal, D. (2009) 'Organic and local food consumer behaviour: Alphabet theory', *International Journal of Consumer Studies*, 33: 697–705.

Zeppel, H. (2006) *Indigenous Ecotourism: Sustainable Development and Management*. Wallingford: CABI.

Zucker, H. G. (1978) 'The variable nature of news media influence', in B. D. Ruben (ed.) *Communication Yearbook*, Vol. 2. New Brunswick, NJ: Transaction Books.

Zuo, L. and Veil, S. (2006) 'Guerilla marketing and the Aqua Teen Hunger Force fiasco', *Public Relations Quarterly*, 51(4): 8–11.

INDEX